Public Budgeting Systems

PUBLIC BUDGETING SYSTEMS

Second Edition

Robert D. Lee, Jr.
Ronald W. Johnson
The Pennsylvania State University

University Park Press
Baltimore · London · Tokyo

UNIVERSITY PARK PRESS
International Publishers in Science, Medicine, and Education
300 North Charles Street
Baltimore, Maryland 21201

Copyright © 1977 by Robert D. Lee, Jr., and Ronald W. Johnson
Second Printing, March 1978
Third printing, October 1978
Fourth printing, February 1980
Fifth printing, April 1981

Typeset by The Composing Room of Michigan, Inc.
Manufactured in the United States of America
by the Maple Press Company

Library of Congress Cataloging in Publication Data

Lee, Robert D.
Public budgeting systems.

Bibliography: p. 357
Includes index.
1. Budget—United States. 2. Program budgeting—
United States. I. Johnson, Ronald Wayne, 1942—joint
author. II. Title.
HJ2051.L4 1977   353.007'22   77-1659
ISBN 0-8391-0988-1

CONTENTS

ILLUSTRATIONS

TABLES

PREFACE

This is a general book on public budgeting. Its purpose is to survey the current state of the art among all levels of government in the United States. We emphasize methods by which financial decisions are reached within a system context and ways in which different types of information are used in budgetary decision making. Of special concern is the use of program information or program budgeting, but at the same time, this book is not devoted exclusively to this subject. The emphasis upon program information seems warranted, because budget reforms since the early part of the century have sought to introduce greater program considerations into financial decisions.

Budgeting is considered within the context of a system containing numerous components and relationships. One problem of such an approach is that since all things within a system are related, it is difficult to find an appropriate place to begin. We have divided the text into chapters, but the reader should recognize that no single chapter can stand alone. In virtually every chapter, there are some issues relevant to the chapter that are treated elsewhere in the book.

A discussion of budgeting may be organized in various ways. Historical or chronological sequence would be one method of organization, although this approach would require discussing every topic of relevance for each period of time. Another method is by levels of government, with separate sections for local, state, and federal budgeting. Such an approach again would involve extensive rehashing of arguments at each level. Still another approach is by phases of the budget cycle, from the preparation of the budget through the auditing of past activities and expenditures. Rigid adherence to this approach would be inappropriate, because the budget cycle is not precisely defined and many issues cut across several phases of the cycle. Another approach would be to organize the discussion around the contrast between the technical and political problems of budgetary decision making.

The organization of this book is based upon a combination of these approaches. The first three chapters are an overall introduction to public budgeting. The first chapter, "Introduction," is a general discussion of the nature of budgetary decision making, including distinctions between private and public budgeting, the concept of responsibility in budgeting, the possibility of rationality in decision making, and the nature of budgeting and budget systems. Chapter 2, "The Public Sector in Perspective," reviews the scope of the public sector, the magnitude of government, the sources of revenues, and the purposes of government expenditures. Budget cycles are the topic of Chapter 3, which summarizes the basic steps in budgeting—preparation and submission, approval, execution, and audit. Together these chapters provide a basic framework for the remainder of the book.

The next two chapters focus upon program information in an historical context. The purpose of these chapters is to provide the reader with an understanding of how budget systems developed to their present states, to show both successes and failures in budget reform. Chapter 4, "Program Information and Budgetary Reform, 1900–1960," considers the literature of the budget reform movement. Here we see the extent to which program information has been emphasized since the beginning of this century. Chapter 5, "Planning-Programming-Budgeting in the 1960s," considers more recent experiments in budget reform.

The next four chapters, building upon the introductory materials in Chapters 1 through 3 and the historical focus upon program information in Chapters 4 and 5, discuss the current state of the art in budgeting, using the budget cycle as a framework. Chapter 6, "Budget Preparation," examines the various ways in which budget requests are prepared by agencies, the deliberations over these requests, decisions reached by the chief executive, and the various types of budget documents that flow from this process. The uses and limitations of analytic techniques are examined in Chapter 7, "Program Analysis." Chapter 8, "Budget Approval: The Role of the Legislature," discusses how legislative bodies act upon budget recommendations and includes a review of executive-legislative relations and efforts to strengthen legislative oversight of executive operations. Chapter 9, "Budget Execution, Accounting, and Information Systems," discusses the decision process following legislative action, the methods of accounting used, and the ways in which information is managed.

The following four chapters deal with selected aspects of budgeting. Chapter 10, "Capital Budgeting and Debt Management," examines the use of capital budgeting as a separate decision process and how governmental debt is managed; at the state and local levels, debt is largely the by-product of capital investments. Chapter 11, "Government Personnel," reviews how personnel expenditures impact on budgets, the relative roles of budgeting and personnel administration, and personnel aspects of ongoing budget systems. Intergovernmental relations are discussed in Chapter 12; the use of different levels of government with differing powers to raise revenues and provide services greatly complicate budgetary decision making. Chapter 13, "Government and the Economy," surveys the federal government's role in managing the economy and how economic conditions affect state and local governments.

The last chapter discusses the changing functions of budgeting. With the previous chapters having summarized the current state of the art of public budgeting, this chapter turns to the future and considers some of the potential effects of contemporary trends on budgeting.

This new edition retains much of the material from the first edition but also includes substantial new material. The new organization should improve readability and understanding. Coverage of both political and technical problems of budgeting has been retained along with such special topics as personnel and intergovernmental relations, topics which often receive little attention in other budgetary works. This edition gives more extensive treatment to budget preparation, budget documents, accounting, capital budgeting, and debt management than the first. Discussions of state and local budget systems have been greatly expanded throughout the book, so that major emphasis no longer is with the federal government; at the same time, important changes in federal budgeting have been included.

Since the publication of this book's first edition in 1973, the authors' careers have taken different directions. Professor Lee has continued to work on the development of budget systems, mainly in conjunction with projects of the Institute of Public Administration of The Pennsylvania State University. The new material on budget preparation, program budgeting, budget execution and accounting, capital budgeting, personnel, and intergovernmental relations, particularly in reference to state and local governments, is largely the product of that work. Also, the discussion of the role of the legislature is mainly the work of Professor Lee. Professor Johnson, now a member of the Political Science Department of The Pennsylvania State University, has focused his research on theories of policy making and implementation. His current work is reflected in this edition in updated discussions of decision making, the nature of the public sector, and economic policy. Co-authoring is not always an easy task, but we think our work is one of the more successful collaborations.

This new and expanded edition reviews the ever-changing systems of public budgeting in the United States, systems which inevitably affect every citizen in the nation. It is hoped that readers from a wide variety of backgrounds and with widely diverse purposes will find material in this book that makes public budgeting of interest to them.

ACKNOWLEDGMENTS

A book of this type cannot be the product of one or two individuals. Robert J. Mowitz, Director of the Institute of Public Administration of The Pennsylvania State University, is a co-author in a sense; he has suggested many ideas to us over the years. We also greatly appreciate the support he gave us through the resources of the Institute. Jesse Burkhead, though he had no contact with the actual manuscript, contributed indirectly through his insightful *Government Budgeting* (New York, Wiley, 1956) and more directly by having taught the senior author at Syracuse University. Wilfred E. Lewis, while Research Director for the President's Commission on Budget Concepts, introduced the junior author to public budgeting, and L. Vaughn Blankenship of the National Science Foundation refused to let the initial interest languish. To these people we are greatly indebted for many of their ideas.

Many others contributed through comments on the manuscript and through more general suggestions about the status and future of budgeting. First edition commentators and their affiliations at that time included: Frederick C. Mosher of the University of Virginia; Allen Schick of The Brookings Institution; Carl W. Tiller of the Office of Management and Budget; Robert LaPorte, Jr., of the Institute of Public Administration of The Pennsylvania State University; John M. Pierce of the Milton S. Hershey Medical Center of The Pennsylvania State University; Seymour S. Berlin, Sally Greenberg, and Edward A. Schroer of the U.S. Civil Service Commission; and Christ J. Zervanos and Charles J. Crawford of the Commonwealth of Pennsylvania. Stephen F. Jablonsky of the Accounting Department and the Institute of Public Administration of the Pennsylvania State University reviewed a portion of the current manuscript. Harry P. Hatry of the Urban Institute, although not reviewing the manuscript, did provide important ideas to the senior author. Administrators, academicians, and students have offered valued suggestions which we have tried to heed in this edition.

We could not have asked for more faithful, tireless, and accurate typists than particularly Gail Dillon and also Margaret Dieringer, Nancy Noll, and Barbara Summers.

The final product, is, of course, our own responsibility.

Now we know why authors dedicate books
to their spouses and children

Barbara	Bonnie
Robert	Neil
Craig	Jennifer
Cameron	

Public
Budgeting
Systems

INTRODUCTION

Public budgeting involves the selection of ends and the selection of means to reach those ends. Public budgeting systems are systems for making choices about ends and means. Complex channels for information exchange exist, channels which process information about what is desired and assessments about what is or is not being achieved. Series of intricate processes that link both political and economic values are integral to budgetary systems. Making budget choices about ends and means specifically involves making political decisions that allocate scarce resources between the private and public sectors of society and decisions that allocate these resources within the public sector among alternative uses. This book is an analysis of procedures and methods—past, present, and prospective—used in this resource allocation process.

This chapter examines the basic features of decision making and budgeting systems. First, some major characteristics of public budgeting that distinguish it from private forms of budgeting are discussed. Second, the development of budgeting as a means for holding government accountable for its actions is reviewed. Next, an account of what budgets and budgeting systems are is given. Finally, the role of information in budgetary decision making is reviewed.

SOME DISTINCTIONS ABOUT PUBLIC BUDGETING

Budgeting is a common phenomenon. To some extent, everybody does it. People budget time, dollars, food—almost everything. The corner grocer budgets, General Electric budgets, and so do governments. Moreover, important similarities in budgeting exist between large public and private bureaucracies. Budgeting is intended as a mechanism for setting goals and

1

objectives, for identifying weaknesses or inadequacies in organizations, and for controlling and integrating the diverse activities that are carried out by numerous subunits within large bureaucracies—both public and private. Budgeting is a means by which complex organizations can be guided so as to produce intended consequences.

Important differences also exist between the private and public spheres. In the first place, the amount of resources available for allocation vary greatly. Both family and corporate budgeting are constrained by a relatively fixed set of available resources. Income is comparatively fixed, and therefore outgo must be equal to or less than income. Of course, income can be expanded by increasing the level of production and work or by borrowing, but the opportunities for increasing income are limited.

Government, on the other hand, is bound only by the sum of all resources in the society, and in the United States at least, government does not use all of the possible resources available to it. Only in times of major crises, such as World War II, does government begin to approach the limits of its resources. During other times, much is left to the private sector, with government consuming only a fraction of society's work force and goods.

Another major distinction between private and public budgeting is that the former is characterized by the profit motive. In the private sector, profit serves as a ready standard for evaluating previous decisions— successful decisions are those that produce profits as measured in dollars. The concept of profit, however, can lead to gross oversimplifications about corporate decision making. Sometimes corporations forgo profits in the short run; in the case of "price wars" they attempt to increase their share of a given market. Sometimes they curtail profits intentionally in fear that a higher level of economic gain will result in governmental regulation. Sometimes their major objectives are to produce a good product and to build public confidence in the firm.

Regardless of the various influences of the profit motive in the private sector of society, governmental decision making, in general, lacks even this standard for measuring its activities. Possible exceptions are activities that are used to generate revenue, such as state control and sale of alcoholic beverages. In this example, the state government may seek a profit on the sale of beverages as a means of financing governmental programs. In other cases, there may be an expressed intention of making a given service self supporting. Postal service is an example of a governmental activity in which there is no attempt to earn a profit but only to limit or eliminate losses.

Some further distinctions between private and public sector budgeting provide the rationale for government undertaking certain functions instead of leaving them to private organizations. Public budgetary decisions, for example, frequently involve allocation of resources among competing programs that are not readily susceptible to measurement in terms of dollar costs and dollar returns. There is no ready means of comparing the net value of a life saved through cancer research and one enemy death on the battlefield; these units simply cannot be equated. The absence of clear-cut measures of profit and loss may be a partial explanation of why government, not business, provides these services.

In addition, many governmental services yield public or collective benefits, which are consumed by society as a whole, as distinct from corporate products, which are consumed by individuals and specific organizations.[1] When Ford Motor Company produces automobiles, they are utilized by persons buying the products. When the Department of Defense produces a network for detecting a possible launching of intercontinental missiles against the United States, that network is "consumed" by the public in general.[2] Once such a collective service is provided, it cannot be denied to anyone in the society, whether or not he or she contributes to its costs. Market mechanisms for setting prices often do not exist to evaluate returns on governmental expenditures. Without the pricing mechanism, consumer preferences, as expressed by the public's willingness to purchase goods and services, are not identifiable.

Whatever objectives other than profit private corporations may have, to stay in business they must seek economic efficiency and obtain the greatest possible dollar return on investments. In contrast, government may be intentionally inefficient, undertaking services the private sector would be reluctant to provide. For example, Social Security may be inefficient in the sense that while other governmental programs might provide greater economic returns to society, it has been agreed that at least some support should be provided to the elderly. Government is also charged with other unique responsibilities, such as the control of the

---

[1] See Peter O. Steiner, "The Public Sector and the Public Interest," in Robert Haveman and Julius Margolis, eds., *Public Expenditures and Policy Analysis* (Chicago: Markham, 1970), pp. 21–58. Also Bernard P. Herber, *Modern Public Finance: The Study of Public Sector Economics*, 3rd ed. (Homewood, Ill: Irwin, 1975), pp. 21–43. Both have good discussions of the concept of public goods.

[2] It should be noted that there are important exceptions to this set of ideas, and these exceptions are discussed under the heading, "The Relative Sizes of the Private and Public Sectors," in Chapter 2.

economy (see Chapter 13). Corporations, on the other hand, are dependent on economic conditions.

Another difference between private and public organizations lies in the clientele and the owners of the means of production. In theory, at least, both corporations and governments are answerable to their stockholders and clients, but in the private sector these individuals can disassociate themselves from firms, while their counterparts in the public sector are denied this choice. Private stockholders expect dollar returns on their investments, but because government costs and returns are not easily evaluated, the electorate has no simple measure for assessing returns on the taxes that are spent.

Finally, corporate budgetary decision making is usually more centralized than governmental decision making. Corporations can stop production of economically unprofitable goods such as Edsels and DeSotos; given the nature of the public decision-making process, however, government encounters more difficulty in making decisions both to inaugurate programs and to eliminate them. For example, it seems evident that welfare programs intended to aid the poor have not provided the kinds of results desired by either the electorate in general or welfare recipients in particular. Nevertheless, to change existing programs requires years of debate, negotiations, and political bargaining.

RESPONSIBLE GOVERNMENT AND BUDGETING

The emergence and reform of formal government budgeting can be traced to a concern for holding public officials responsible or accountable for their actions.[3] In a democracy budgeting is a device for limiting the powers of government. Two issues recur in the evolution of modern public budgeting as an instrument of accountability—responsibility *to whom* and *for what* purposes.

Responsible to Whom? Basically, responsibility in a democratic society entails holding elected officials answerable to their constituents. Elected executives and legislative representatives at all levels of government are, at least in theory, held accountable for their decisions on programs and budgets. In actuality, however, budget documents are not

---

[3] An extended discussion of an idea similar to this is found in Bertram M. Gross, "The New Systems Budgeting," *Public Administration Review*, 29 (1969): 113–37.

the main source of information for decisions by the electorate. Obviously, most voters do not diligently study the U.S. budget before casting their votes in presidential and congressional elections. Voters' decisions are based upon such a diversity of reasons that it is questionable whether elected officials ever receive a clear-cut mandate through the electoral process.

Because the public in a large society cannot be fully informed about the operations of government, this nation has used the concepts of separation of powers and checks and balances as means of providing for responsible government. Thus, the President is held responsible to Congress for preparation and submission of an executive budget. In most states and many localities, the chief executive has a similar responsibility to recommend a plan for taxes and expenditures. The legislative body passes upon these recommendations and subsequently holds the executive branch answerable for carrying out the decisions.

The development of an executive budget system for holding government accountable was a long process that can be traced as far back as the Magna Charta (1217). The main issue that resulted in this landmark document was the concern of the nobility over the Crown's taxing powers. Obviously, the Magna Charta did not produce a complete budget, but concentrated only upon holding the Crown accountable to the noblemen for its revenue actions.[4] At the time, the magnitude of public expenditures and the use of these funds for public services were of less concern than the power to levy and collect taxes. It was not until the English Consolidated Fund Act of 1787 that the rudiments of a complete system were established and it was 1822 before a complete account of revenues and expenditures was presented to Parliament.[5]

This concern with the power of the executive evidenced in the Magna Charta was carried over to the American experience. Fear of a strong executive was evidenced by the failure to include any executive under the Articles of Confederation (1781). Fear of "taxation without representation" probably explains why the Constitution (1789) is more explicit about taxing powers than the procedures to be followed in governmental spending.

The first decade under the Constitution saw important developments

---

[4] For a history of early budgeting, see Vincent J. Browne, *The Control of the Public Budget* (Washington: Public Affairs Press, 1949).

[5] Jesse Burkhead, *Government Budgeting* (New York: Wiley, 1956), pp. 2–4.

that could have resulted in an executive budget system, but subsequent years were to reverse the trend. The Treasury Act of 1789, establishing the Treasury Department, granted to the Secretary the power "to digest and prepare plans for the improvement of the revenue . . . [and] to prepare and report estimates of the public revenue and expenditures." Alexander Hamilton, the first Secretary of the Treasury, interpreted his mandate broadly and asserted strong leadership in financial affairs. Although that legislation did not grant the Secretary power to prepare a budget by recommending which programs should and should not be funded, such a development might have subsequently emerged.

Instead, Hamilton's apparent lack of deference to the Congress strengthened that body's support for greater legislative control over financial matters. To curtail the discretion of the executive, Congress resorted to the use of increasing numbers of line items, specifying in narrow detail for what purposes money could be spent.[6] The pattern emerged that each executive department would deal directly with the Congress, thereby curtailing the responsibilities of the Secretary of the Treasury. The budgetary function of the Treasury Department became primarily ministerial; the Book of Estimates, prepared by the Secretary and delivered to the Congress, which could have become the instrument for a coordinated set of budgetary recommendations, instead was simply a compilation of departmental requests for funds. A. E. Buck wrote, "Thus budget making became an exclusively legislative function in the national government and as such it continued for more than a century."[7]

By the beginning of the twentieth century, changing economic conditions were to stimulate the demand for more centralized and controlled forms of budgeting. E. E. Naylor has written that before this time there was little "enthusiasm for action . . ,since federal taxes were usually indirect and not severely felt by any particular individual or group."[8] By 1900, however, existing revenue sources no longer consistently produced sufficient sums to cover the costs of government. At the federal level, the tariff could not be expected to produce a surplus of funds as had been the case. Causes of this growing deficit were an expanded scope of governmental programs and, to a lesser extent, waste and corruption in government

[6] Arthur Smithies, *The Budgetary Process in the United States* (New York: McGraw-Hill, 1955), p. 50.

[7] A. E. Buck, *Public Budgeting* (New York: Harper and Brothers, 1929), p. 17.

[8] E. E. Naylor, *The Federal Budget System in Operation* (Washington: Printed privately, 1941), pp. 22–23.

finance. The latter is often credited as a major political factor that stimulated reform.

In terms of action taken to establish formal budget procedures, local government led the way. Municipal budget reform was closely associated with general reform of local government, especially for the establishment of the city-manager form of government. Two dates are critical. In 1899 a model municipal corporation act, released by the National Municipal League, featured a model charter that provided for a budget system whose preparation phase was under the control of the mayor. In 1906 the New York Bureau of Municipal Research was founded.[9] The following year the Bureau issued a study, "Making a Municipal Budget," which became the basis for establishing a budgetary system for New York City. By the mid-1920s most major U.S. cities had some form of a budget system.

Reform of state budgeting was particularly notable between 1910 and 1920. This reform was closely associated with the overall drive to hold the executive accountable by first giving him authority over the executive branch. The movement for the short ballot, aimed at eliminating many independently elected administrative officers, resulted in granting to governors greater control over their respective bureaucracies. Ohio, in 1910, was the first state to enact a law empowering the Governor to prepare and submit a budget. A. E. Buck, in assessing the effort at the state level, suggested that 1913 marked "the beginning of practical action in the states."[10] By 1920 some budget reform had occurred in 44 states, and by 1929 all states had a central budget office.[11]

Simultaneously, action occurred at the federal level, and much of what took place there contributed to the reforms at the local and state levels. Frederick A. Cleveland, who was director of the New York Bureau of Municipal Research and who played a key role in national reform, has written, "It was the uncontrolled and uncontrollable increase in the cost of government that finally jostled the public into an attitude of hostility."[12] In response to this public concern, President William Howard Taft requested and received from Congress in 1909 an appropriation of

---

[9] Burkhead, *Government Budgeting*, pp. 12–13.

[10] Buck, *Public Budgeting*, p. 14.

[11] Burkhead, *Government Budgeting*, p. 23. York Willbern, "Personnel and Money," in James W. Fesler, ed., *The 50 States and Their Local Governments* (New York: Knopf, 1967), p. 391.

[12] Frederick A. Cleveland, "Evolution of the Budget Idea in the United States," *Annals*, 62 (November 1915): 22.

$100,000 for a special Commission on Economy and Efficiency. Known as the Taft Commission, the group was headed by Cleveland and submitted its final report in 1912, recommending the establishment of a budgetary process under the direction of the President. This report was to spur great action at the state and local levels.

However, the Budget and Accounting Act, which established the new federal system, was not passed until 1921. In the interim, deficits were recorded every year between 1912 and 1919 except 1916. The largest deficit occurred in 1919 when expenditures were three times greater than revenues ($18.5 billion in expenditures as compared with $5.1 billion in revenues). During this period, vigorous debate centered around the issue of whether budget reform would in effect establish a superordinate executive over the legislative branch. President Woodrow Wilson in 1920 vetoed legislation that would have created a Bureau of the Budget and General Accounting Office on the grounds that the latter as an arm of Congress would violate the President's responsibilities over the executive branch. The following year virtually identical legislation was signed into law by President Warren G. Harding.

Thus, an executive budget system was established, despite a historical fear of a powerful chief executive. In 1939 the Bureau of the Budget was removed from the Treasury Department and placed in the newly formed Executive Office of the President. This shift reflected the growing importance of the Bureau in assisting the President in managing the government. Ten years later the budgetary task force of the First Hoover Commission on the Organization of the Executive Branch recommended that the Bureau of the Budget be reinstated in the Treasury Department, but the Commission as a whole opposed the recommendation.[13] The Budget and Accounting Procedures Act of 1950 reinforced the trend of Presidential control by explicitly granting him control over the "form and detail" of the budget document. The Second Hoover Commission in 1955 endorsed strengthening the President's power in budgeting as a means for "the restoration of the full control of the national purse to the Congress."[14] A President who had full control of the bureaucracy, then, could be held accountable by Congress for action taken by the bureaucracy.

---

[13] Commission on Organization of the Executive Branch of the Government, *General Management of the Executive Branch* (Washington: U.S. Government Printing Office, 1949).

[14] Commission on Organization of the Executive Branch of the Government, *Budget and Accounting* (Washington: U.S. Government Printing Office, 1955), p. ix.

Responsible for What? The earliest concern for financial responsibility was in terms of taxes. As indicated above, the Magna Charta imposed limitations not on the nature of the Crown's expenditures but on the procedures for raising revenue. This same concern for the revenue side of budgeting was characteristic of the early history of budgeting in this country. The Constitution is more explicit about the tax power of the government than about the nature or purposes of governmental expenditures.

The larger the public sector has become, however, the more has concern shifted to the purposes of expenditures. Increasing emphasis has been placed upon the accountability of government for what it spends. Expenditure accountability may be of several different forms. Allen Schick has suggested that this emphasis upon expenditure has gone through three stages in the twentieth century.[15] He identifies the first stage as one characterized by legislative concern for tight control over executive expenditures. The most prevalent means of exerting this type of expenditure control has been to appropriate by line item and by object of expenditure; financial audits, then, are used to ensure that money has in fact been spent for the items authorized for purchase. This focuses information for budgetary decision making upon the things government buys, such as personnel, travel, and supplies, rather than upon the accomplishments of governmental activities. In other words, responsibility is achieved by controlling the resources or input side.

The second stage is that of management orientation, which emphasizes the efficiency with which ongoing activities are conducted. Historically, this orientation is associated with the New Deal through the First Hoover Commission (1949). Emphasis was placed upon holding administrators accountable for the efficiency of their activities through methods such as work performance measurement.

Shick identifies the third stage of budget reform with post-Hoover Commission concerns for the planning function served by budgets. Traditional concerns for control of resource inputs may be accommodated in the short time frame of the coming budget year. Managerial concern for efficiency, although aided by a longer time perspective, also may be accommodated in a traditional budget year presentation. When the emphasis is shifted to accomplishing objectives, however, a longer time frame is

---

[15] Allen Schick, "The Road to PPB: The Stages of Budget Reform," *Public Administration Review*, 26 (1966): 243–58.

necessary. Many objectives of governmental programs cannot be accomplished in one budget year; a multi-year presentation of the budget is thus necessary to make the long-range implications of current budget decisions explicit.

Although Schick captured some of the history of budget reform in this three-stage typology, he perhaps overemphasized the recency of concern for planning for program results. We will argue in Chapter 4 that budget reform efforts for many decades have attempted to improve the capacity for decision-making systems to concentrate upon accomplishing desired ends. Perhaps Schick's typology is more appropriately considered in terms of where decision-making responsibility lies. The first stage would place the responsibility on the legislative branch as the principal authority for determining how values should be allocated. The administrator's job, then, is perfunctory. The second stage may be seen as the beginning of a shift toward broader executive duties but limited to a concern for efficient management rather than program accomplishment. The most recent stage, typified by program budgeting and management by objectives, reflects the development of executive responsibility for program formulation to achieve desired ends.

Most of the emphasis in this book is on the budget as an instrument for financial and program decision making at all levels of government—federal, state, and local. The one unique responsibility that most sharply differentiates federal budget decisions from state and local decisions is the federal responsibility for the overall state of the economy. The federal budget not only allocates resources among competitive programs, but it is also an instrument for achieving economic stability. This responsibility has been an accepted part of the federal budgetary process since the Full Employment Act (1946). The budget as an instrument of economic policy is discussed in Chapter 13.

Budgeting, then, is an important process by which accountability or responsibility can be provided in a political system. As has been discussed, responsibility varies in terms of to whom the system is accountable and for what purposes. Given these various forms of accountability and the types of choices that decision makers have available to them, different meanings can be attached to the terms budget and budgeting system. Varying with the purposes of a budget, decision makers will need different kinds and amounts of information to aid in their choices. The following sections and subsequent chapters, therefore, focus upon the kinds of information required for different budgetary choices and the kinds of procedures for generating that information.

BUDGETS AND BUDGETING SYSTEMS

What Is a Budget? In its simplest form a budget is a document or a collection of documents that refer to the financial condition of an organization (family, corporation, government), including information on revenues, expenditures, activities, and purposes or goals. In contrast with an accounting balance sheet which is retrospective in nature, referring to past conditions and current status, a budget is prospective, referring to expected future revenues, expenditures, and accomplishments. Historically, the word budget referred to a leather pouch, wallet, bag, or purse. Jesse Burkhead has observed, "In Britain the term was used to describe the leather bag in which the Chancellor of the Exchequer carried to Parliament the statement of the Government's needs and resources."[16] With the passage of time, the budget came to refer to the statement within the bag rather than the bag itself.

The status of the budget document is not consistent from one political jurisdiction to another. In the federal government, the budget is greatly limited in legal status. It is the official recommendation of the President to the Congress, but it is not the official document under which the government operates. As will be seen later, the official operating budget of the U.S. consists of several documents, namely appropriations acts (see Chapters 3, 6, and 8). In contrast, local budgets proposed by mayors may become the official working budgets as adopted in their entirety by the respective city councils.

In still other instances there may be a series of budget documents instead of one budget for any given government. These may include 1) an operating budget, which handles the bulk of ongoing operations, 2) a capital budget, which covers major new construction projects, and 3) a series of special fund budgets, which cover programs that are funded by specific revenue sources. Special fund budgets commonly include highway programs, which are financed through gasoline and tire sales taxes; in such cases, all revenue from these sources are earmarked for highway construction, improvement, and maintenance. Other special funds may be user fees

---

[16] Burkhead, *Government Budgeting*, p. 2.

for fishing and hunting licenses, with the proceeds used to stock streams and provide ample hunting opportunities.

The format of budget documents also varies. On the whole, budget documents tend to provide greater information on expenditures than on revenues. Usually, revenues are treated in a brief section, with the remainder of the document being devoted to expenditures. On the expenditure side, budgets are multipurpose in that no single document and no single definition can exhaust the functions budgets serve or the ways they are used. At the most general level three basic concepts are to be found in all budgets. Budgets may be understood as descriptions, explanations or causal assertions, and statements of preferences or values.

Budgets are first *descriptions* of the status of an organization—agency, ministry, entire government, any organizational unit. The budget document may describe what the organization purchases, what it does, and what it accomplishes. Descriptions of organizational activity are also common in budget documents; expenditures may be classified according to the activities they support. For example, a university budget may be subdivided into such major activities as instruction, research, and public service. Another type of description, organizational accomplishments, describes the consequences of resource consumption and work activities for those outside the organization. These require external verification of the impact of the organization on its environment.

As descriptions, budgets provide a discrete picture of an organization at a point or points in time in terms of resources consumed, work performed, and external impact. The dollar expenditures, according to these types of descriptions, may be the only qualitative information supplied. Or information may be supplied about the number and types of personnel; the quantity and kinds of equipment purchased; measures of performance such as numbers of buildings inspected, number of acres treated; and measures of impact such as numbers of accidents prevented, amount of increased crop yields, and so forth. Generally, the more descriptive material supplied, the more the organization can be held accountable for the funds spent, the activities supported by those expenditures, and the external accomplishments produced by those activities. Much of the history of budget reform is reflected in attempts to increase the quantity and quality of descriptive material available both to decision makers and to the public.

When budgets describe organizations in all three categories discussed in preceding paragraphs, they also at least implicitly serve a second major function—explanation of causal relationships. The expenditure of a specific amount for the purchase of labor and materials that will be combined in particular work activities alleges a causal sequence that will produce some given results. Regardless of how explicit the budget document may be or the statements of organizational officials may be, a causal process from resources through work activities to external results is always implied by budgetary decisions. Some organizations may have little accurate information about accomplishments, especially public organizations whose accomplishments are not measured as profit and loss. Governments may choose not to be very explicit about particular results either because they are difficult to measure, they are politically sensitive, or both. Regardless of the availability of information or the willingness of the organization to collect and use it, however, the budget is an expression of a set of causal relationships. These issues are discussed in detail in Chapter 6.

Finally, budgets are statements of preferences. Whether intended or not, the allocation of resources among different agencies, and/or among different activities, and/or among different accomplishments reveals preferences of those making the allocations. These may be the actual preferences of some decision makers, or more often they may be taken as the collective preferences of many decision makers produced by complex bargaining. This preference schedule reflects, if not any one individual's values, an aggregate of choices that become the collective value judgment for the local government, state, or nation.

What Is a Budgeting System?   Budgeting as a decision-making process can best be understood in terms of a system, which can be defined simply as a "set of units with relationships among them."[17] Budgetary decision making consists of the actions of executive officials (both in a central organization such as the governor's office or the mayor's staff and in executive line-agencies), legislative officials, organized interest groups, and perhaps even unorganized interests which may be manifested in a generally felt public concern about public needs and taxes. All these actions and interactions relate to each other, and understanding budgeting means understanding these relationships. Such understanding is best achieved by thinking in terms of complex systems.

A complex social system is composed of organizations, individuals, the

---

[17] James G. Miller, "Living Systems: Basic Concepts," *Behavioral Science*, 10 (1965): 200.

values held by these individuals, and the relationships among these units and values. A system may be thought of as a network typically consisting of many different parts with messages flowing among the parts.

In a budgetary system, the outputs flowing from this network of interactions are budget decisions that will vary greatly in their overall significance. Not every unit of the system will have equal decisional authority or power. A manager of a field office for a state health department is likely to have less power to make major budgetary decisions than the administrative head of the department, the governor, or the members of the legislative appropriations committee. Yet, each participant does contribute some input to the system. That field manager may alert others in the system to the rise of a new health problem and in doing so may have contributed greatly to the eventual establishment of a new health program to combat the problem. The regional health administrator may be concerned with $1,000 or $10,000 decisions, whereas others in the system will regularly consider issues involving millions or billions of dollars.

As with the outputs of any other system or network, budget decisions are seldom final and more commonly are sequential. Decisions are tentative in that each decision made is forwarded for action by another participant in the process. This does not mean that all decisions are reversible. Major breakthroughs, such as passage of the Elementary and Secondary Education Act of 1965, which provided sizable federal aid to education, are not readily abandoned. Subsequent budget decisions, therefore, are in large part bounded by previous decisions. These decisions tend to center on the question of changing the level of commitment—allocating more resources and different kinds of resources to achieve higher levels of impact or different types of impacts. Once a breakthrough is achieved, there will be little opportunity for deciding to eliminate the established program.

Another feature of a system is that a change in any part of it will alter other parts. Because all units are related, any change in the role or functioning of one unit necessarily will affect other units. In some instances, changes may be of such a modest nature that their ramifications are difficult to discern in other parts of the system. However, when major budgetary "reforms" are instituted, they assuredly will affect most participants. For example, if one unit in the system is granted greater authority, individuals and organizations having access to that unit will have their decisional involvement enhanced, whereas those groups associated with other units may have diminished roles.[18] Thus, budget reforms will be evaluated by each individual and institution in terms of how political strengths will be realigned under the reforms.

INFORMATION AND DECISION MAKING

To serve the multiple functions described in the preceding section, budgeting systems must produce and process a variety of information. Most of the major reforms, attempted or proposed, in public budgeting systems have been intended to provide participants with different types and greater quantities of information. Basically, there are two types—program and resource information. The latter form is traditional. People are accustomed to think of budgets in terms of monetary units and personnel. A budget would not be a budget if there were no dollar, ruble, or other monetary figures. Similarly, budgets commonly contain data on employees or personnel complement.

Conventional accounting systems have provided for most of the information used for budgetary decisions by most public organizations. This type of information, however, is limited to the internal aspects of organizations, to the location of organizational responsibility for expenditures and the resources purchased by those expenditures. When the decision-making system incorporates information about the results or impacts of programs, however, one must leave the boundaries of the organization to examine consequences for those outside. This step requires more extensive and more explicit clarification of governmental goals and objectives (discussed in Chapters 4 and 6) and increases the importance of analysis (see Chapter 7). This feature of contemporary budget reforms, such as program budgeting and management by objectives, with their emphasis on program information, has generated the most heat among critics of budget reform.

Much of this criticism has involved the argument that decision-making systems must take into account the limitations on human capabilities to use all the information that might be collected. Although there are sometimes subtle differences among theories of decision making, depending on their assumptions about the objectives of a decision system and the capacity of the system to utilize information, we may generally classify

---

[18] Aaron Wildavsky, *The Politics of the Budgetary Process*, 2nd ed. (Boston: Little, Brown, 1974), pp. 131–33.

the various theories into three basic approaches—pure rationality, muddling through or incrementalism, and limited rationality.

Decision making according to the pure rationality approach consists of a series of ordered, logical steps. First, a complete specification of an organization's or society's goals must be ranked by priority. Second, all possible alternatives are identified. The costs of each alternative are compared with anticipated benefits. Judgments are made as to which alternative comes closest to satisfying one's values. The alternative with the highest payoff and/or least cost is chosen. Pure rationality theories assume that complete and perfect information about all alternatives is both available and manageable. Decision making, therefore, is choosing among alternatives to maximize some objective function.

The applicability of the rationality model is limited. It is most consistent with notions of technical or economic rationality, where objectives can be stated with some precision and the range of feasible alternatives is not infinite.[19] Also, the model can be of use where it provides accurate predictions of behavior, such as assuming rational behavior in the private market and predicting future economic trends.[20] As a description of how government budgeting works, however, pure rationality obviously is inaccurate. The capability to meet the complete requirements of even one of the above steps is nonexistent. It has been argued that the costs of information are so high as to make it rational to be ignorant, to make decisions on the basis of limited search behavior and limited information.[21] As will be observed in following chapters, some attempts at budget reform have been criticized as attempts to impose an unworkable model, pure rationality, on government financial decision making. The use of program information has been a particular target for criticism.[22]

The second approach to decision making, muddling through (incre-

---

[19] The terms technical and economic rationality are two of five basic types of rationality identified by Paul Diesing, *Reason and Society* (Urbana: University of Illinois Press, 1962). The following discussion of the pure rationality model relies heavily upon Yehezkel Dror, *Public Policymaking Reexamined* (San Francisco: Chandler, 1967), pp. 132–41.

[20] See Milton Friedman, *Essays in Positive Economics* (Chicago: University of Chicago Press, 1953).

[21] Anthony Downs, *Inside Bureaucracy* (Boston: Little, Brown, 1967), pp. 247–52.

[22] See Aaron Wildavsky, "The Political Economy of Efficiency: Cost-Benefit Analysis, Systems Analysis, and Program Budgeting," *Public Administration Review*, 26 (1966): 292–310.

mentalism), has been advocated particularly by critics of pure rationality, such as Charles E. Lindblom, Aaron Wildavsky, and others.[23] According to this view, decision making involves a conflict of interests and a corresponding clash of information, resulting in the accommodation of diverse partisan interests through bargaining. "Real" decision making is presumed to begin as issues are raised by significant interest groups who request or demand changes from the existing state.[24] Decision making is not some conscious form of pure rationality, but is the process of incrementally adjusting existing practices in order to establish or reestablish consensus among participants. This process is known as "disjointed incrementalism."[25] Alternatives to the status quo are normally not considered unless brought to the attention of the decision-making process by partisan interests. There is only a marginal amount of planned search for alternatives to achieve desired ends. The decisional process is structured so that partisan interests have the opportunity to press their desires at some point in the deliberations. Decisions represent a consensus on policy reached through a political power-oriented bargaining process.

The most important characteristic of the muddling through or incrementalist approach as applied to budgeting is its emphasis upon the proposition that budgetary decisions are necessarily political.[26] Whereas a purely rational approach might suggest that budgetary decisions are attempts to allocate resources according to economic criteria, the incrementalist view stresses the extent to which political considerations outweigh calculations of optimality. The strongest criticisms of many budget reforms have tended to equate those reforms as seeking to establish the pure rationality model. As will be seen throughout the book, any "real" budget reform is forced to accommodate the political nature of decision making.

---

[23] Charles E. Lindblom, "The Science of 'Muddling Through,' " *Public Administration Review*, 19 (1959): 79–88. Charles E. Lindblom, "Decision Making in Taxation and Expenditures," in National Bureau of Economic Research, *Public Finances: Needs, Sources, and Utilization* (Princeton, N.J.: Princeton University Press, 1961), pp. 295–323.

[24] The incrementalist approach is most thoroughly applied to the budgetary process in Aaron Wildavsky, *The Politics of the Budgetary Process*, 2nd ed. (Boston: Little, Brown, 1974).

[25] David Braybrooke and Charles E. Lindblom, *A Strategy of Decision* (New York: Free Press, 1963).

[26] In addition to Wildavsky, *Politics of the Budgetary Process*, see Ira Sharkansky, *The Politics of Taxing and Spending* (New York: Bobbs-Merrill, 1969).

The third approach to decision making, a compromise between the other two theories, is what we call limited rationality. This model recognizes the inapplicability of pure rationality to complex problems.[27] While acknowledging the inherent constraints of human cognitive processes, limited rationality does not suggest that deliberate search for alternative approaches to goal achievement is of no avail. Search is used to find solutions that are satisfactory as distinguished from optimal or maximal.

This compromise between pure rationality and incrementalism can be understood in terms of Amitai Etzioni's model of mixed scanning.[28] Mixed scanning involves explicit concerns for both long-range action and action across a society-wide spectrum. The analogy of a camera with both a wide-angle and a close-up lens is employed to describe the concept. As wide-angle scanning is used to identify alternatives that appear to have some advantages, so limited rationality is able to avoid examining in detail all possible alternatives as prescribed under pure rationality. A more narrowly focused form of scanning, then, is used to analyze the alternatives selected by the first form of scanning. At this lower level of scanning, analysts may consider the immediate effects of incremental adjustments in present policies, but explicit attention is also directed at what these immediate effects portend for broader and more long-range concerns. Simultaneously, it is possible to be incremental and comprehensive with a short- and long-range perspective.

Limited rationality seems to occupy a nebulous middle ground between incrementalism and pure rationality. The reasons for this are that the middle ground is difficult to define with precision, and further, some of the theorists who support incrementalism and pure rationality may claim some share of this middle territory. The main point, however, is that decision theories are identifiably different in their emphasis upon both the values that decision making serves and the capacities of decision makers to serve those values. One model assumes virtually no limits on human capacities for processing information, another suggests that the only information that decision making should be sensitive to is partisan political interests, and the third attempts to strike a balance between the others.

---

[27] Herbert Simon, *Administrative Behavior*, 2nd ed. (New York: Macmillan, 1961). Richard M. Cyert and James G. March, *A Behavioral Theory of the Firm* (Englewood Cliffs, N.J.: Prentice-Hall, 1963).

[28] Amitai Etzioni, "Mixed Scanning: A 'Third' Approach to Decision Making," *Public Administration Review*, 27 (1967): 385–92.

The history of budgeting and budget reform, it is argued in this book, reflects the tensions among these approaches to decision making.

SUMMARY

While similarities between private and governmental budgeting can be drawn, important qualitative differences exist. These differences must be kept in mind when studying public budgeting systems. Public budgetary decisions arise most often because they relate to concerns beyond the scope or capabilities of the private market. Profit and loss measures provide the private sector with an index of the results of decisions and thus enable owners to hold managers accountable. The public sector measures of profit and loss are more ambiguous, thereby compounding the problem of accountability in government.

Budgeting is one means by which government may be held accountable for its actions, and accountability is essential to the concept of limited government. Through budgets, the electorate can obtain information to assess the quality of decisions made by political leaders. Accountability, perhaps more importantly in mass society, is also provided by the executive being held answerable to the legislature for the operations of government. Budgeting is a critical component in this exercise of legislative oversight of the executive. Within the executive branch, budgeting serves to hold administrators accountable to the President, a governor, or mayor.

The purposes of accountability are equally diverse. Accountability for taxes and expenditures are two purposes; responsibility for honesty, efficiency, and program results are other purposes. Still others include accountability for services, income distribution, and economic stability.

Major budgetary reforms have most often been proposed as a means of improving decision making and enhancing the accountability of government. These reforms usually involve expanding the amount of information available to decision makers. There are serious reservations, however, about the ability of the budget process to absorb and use new and better information. The concepts of pure rationality, incrementalism or muddling through, and limited rationality suggest divergent views of the feasibility of rational choice selection.

The complexity of budgeting is suggested by the notion of the process as a system of interrelated units and values. Information flow is the linkage among the units of such a system. The two basic types of information in a budgetary system are program and resource data. This information is interpreted by political actors from different political power positions. Budget reform efforts can be seen as an attempt to utilize information about resource costs and program results in combination with political values in order that budgeting be an instrument for the attainment of societal goals and objectives.

THE PUBLIC SECTOR
IN PERSPECTIVE

Generalizations about government are easy to make but are often misleading. All generalizations ignore some information, and sometimes information relevant to the conclusion is ignored. This is the danger when generalizing about the size of the public sector of society. While the generalization "government is vast" may be valid, it fails to recognize the difficulties in determining what is and is not government or that government is also small in some respects.

This chapter explores three main topics. The first relates to issues regarding the relative sizes of the private and public sectors of society and the reasons for the growth of government. The discussion extends beyond standard criteria for measuring the public sector in order to determine the extent to which the distinction between public and private is real or fictional. Second, the magnitude of government and the historical growth of local, state, and federal finances are considered. Third, the purposes of governmental expenditures are contrasted with the sources of revenue used by the three main levels of government in the United States.

RELATIVE SIZES OF THE PRIVATE AND PUBLIC SECTORS

Basic to all matters of public budgeting is the issue of what is the appropriate size of the public sector. This is inherently a political issue, not only in the partisan sense, but also in the sense that fundamental policy questions are raised as to what government should and should not do. At stake are congeries of competing public and private wants and needs.

The issue of size relates to values of freedom and societal needs. Keeping government small has been advocated to protect individuals from tyranny and to stimulate individual independence and initiative.[1] Faith in the value of the private sector, on the other hand, has been criticized as resulting in the underfinancing of public programs and the failure to confront major social problems.[2] Debates over the rise of the welfare and warfare states have been especially acrimonious, during this century.

The political system, of course, is not structured in such a way that an overriding decision is made as to the size of the public sector. The multiplicity of governments makes it virtually impossible to reach any single decision about the appropriate size of the public sector; some maintain that society "never makes any explicit decision about what the overall budget size should be, but determines that size merely by adding up all the items that more than pay for themselves in votes."[3] Decisions relevant to size are made in a political context within and between the executive and legislative branches and are made among the three major levels of government—local, state, and federal. Each set of decisions contributes toward an ultimate resolution of the question, but one must await the tally of all decisions before being able to perceive what has been deemed the appropriate size.

Government expands because decision makers have concluded that various societal conditions warrant intervention. There are four main types of reasons that have contributed to the expansion of the public sector: the sheer increase in population, technological change, both hot and cold war, and economic crises.[4]

---

[1] Frederich A. Hayek, *The Road to Serfdom* (Chicago: University of Chicago Press, 1954); Frazer B. Wilde, "A Proposal to Reduce Federal Expenditures," in Edmund S. Phelps, ed., *Private Wants and Public Needs* (New York: Norton, 1962), pp. 15–20; Peter Drucker and Herman Finer, *The Road to Reaction* (Boston: Little, Brown, 1945).

[2] John Kenneth Galbraith, *The Affluent Society* (Boston: Houghton Mifflin, 1958).

[3] Anthony Downs, "Why the Government Budget is too Small in a Democracy," *World Politics*, 12 (1960): 543–44. Also see Ryan C. Amacher, Robert D. Tollison, and Thomas D. Willett, "A Budget Size in a Democracy: A Review of the Arguments," *Public Finance Quarterly*, 3 (1975): 99–121.

[4] Herbert Kaufman, "The Growth of the Federal Personnel System," in Wallace S. Sayre, ed., *The Federal Government Service* (Englewood Cliffs, N.J.: Prentice-Hall, 1965), pp. 8–9. Also see James M. Buchanan and Marilyn R. Flowers, *The Public Finances: An Introductory Textbook*, 4th ed. (Homewood, Ill.: Irwin, 1975), pp. 54–63; Frederick D. Mosher and Orville F. Poland, *The Costs of American Governments* (New York: Dodd, Mead, 1964), pp. 19–21.

One may also reason that failures of the private market have stimulated governmental growth.[5] First, collective goods should be provided by government because these cannot be provided readily by the private sphere. In this category are defense, foreign aid, space exploration, and flood control. In programs such as these, all citizens benefit, and there is no easy means by which service can be limited only to those who are willing to pay.

Second, governmental involvement is warranted when important externalities are present. The air and water pollution produced by industrial firms, which are concerned mainly with making a profit, is a social cost and is a condition that government is expected to control. Similarly, education produces important externalities, in this case benefits, that affect society as a whole. If education were provided only to those willing to pay, persons not paying and not receiving education would become economic burdens upon society. Therefore in cases such as these, governmental intervention is justifiable.

Third, when conditions of great risk exist, governmental programs may become necessary. The private sector, being motivated by the search for profits, may be unwilling to risk heavy investments where future payoffs are dubious. One example is the development of atomic energy as a source of electrical power. Government assumes responsibilities in such instances when the private sector declines to engage in activities society has deemed to be desirable.

Fourth, where competition is of limited value, monopolies should be established. This standard applies to industries in which average unit costs decrease as outputs increase. Industries of this type include telephone service, electricity, natural gas, and mass transportation. The monopoly may be operated directly by government or by a regulated private corporation.

Finally, sometimes mere convenience is sufficient reason for government to undertake a service. Weather forecasting, for instance, could be provided by the private sector, but a centralized system of data collection and forecasting is more convenient.

While these reasons are helpful in understanding why government enters into the private sector, they do not suitably reflect the political considerations at stake when proposals are made for expanding or con-

---

[5] Otto Eckstein, *Public Finance*, 3rd ed. (Englewood Cliffs, N.J.: Prentice-Hall, 1973).

tracting the scope of the public sector. Any proposal for the expansion of services that results in an increase in taxes is likely to have some unfavorable political repercussions. Therefore, the size issue always relates both to governmental expenditures and revenues (taxes). Decision makers, no matter how crude or approximate their methods of calculating, attempt to weigh the merits of coping with the current situation with available resources against the merits of recommending new programs that may alleviate problems but at the same time raise the ire of taxpayers.

Major problems are encountered when attempts are made to gauge the size of the public and private sectors and to distinguish between one government and another. Government has become so deeply involved in the society that one may frequently have difficulty in discerning what is not at least quasi-public. Moreover, governments have extensive relationships with each other, to the point where a discussion of any single government becomes meaningless without a discussion of its relationships with other governments.

Statistical data on government revenues and expenditures fail to reflect adequately the size of government. For instance, the entire political campaign process is clearly governmental in that funds are expended to elect people to political offices, yet these monies are not recorded as governmental expenditures. It has been estimated that campaign spending for the 1974 congressional elections came to $88 million.[6] In other cases, the size of government is understated when some activities require relatively little money and manpower, yet the impact of these activities upon the private sector can be substantial. This is especially true with respect to regulatory activities, such as the control of interstate commerce by the federal government.

Complete reliance on revenue and expenditure data for measuring size is unwarranted for another reason. Sometimes the assumption is made that all government expenditures are a drain upon the private economy. In other words, zero-sum conditions are presumed in which government's gain is industry's loss. However, government expenditures can be nonexhaustive as well as exhaustive.[7] By the latter is meant that government consumes resources such as facilities and manpower that might otherwise have been used by the private sector. Nonexhaustive expenditures entail

---

[6] "CC Project Describes 1974 Political Money Tree," *In Common*, 7 (1976): 10.

[7] Francis M. Bator, *The Question of Government Spending* (New York: Harper and Brothers, 1960), pp. 9–39.

the redistribution of resources among components of the society rather than the consumption of resources. Interest payments on the national debt, unemployment compensation, aid to the indigent, and old-age and retirement benefits are some of the major examples of nonexhaustive expenditures. In this sense, then, the cost of government is actually less than the total dollar figures reported in budgets.

Government expenditures have specific effects upon industries, occupations, and geographic regions. These impacts are especially evident regarding defense.[8] Clusters of firms and their employees have become highly dependent upon defense outlays, resulting in what President Eisenhower in 1961 decried as the military-industrial complex. Many observers see a dangerous symbiotic relationship between the military, which has a penchant for new weaponry, and corporations that are eager to supply such weaponry.[9]

The impact of defense upon the private sector can be seen in terms of employment. In 1972 defense-oriented industries employed 3,486,000 persons. When this figure is combined with civilian and military personnel directly hired by the Department of Defense (DOD) and defense-related agencies, the combined staff of the defense system for 1972 was 7,040,000, or 8.4 percent of all employment, both public and private, in the United States for that year.[10] In other words, one out of every twelve workers in the nation was employed by military expenditures.

The impact of defense expenditures upon specific occupations has also been significant at different periods. Technical personnel in the aeronautical engineering field, physicists, and a variety of other scientific occupations are heavily engaged in defense-related work. The creation of demand for such manpower has the effect of attracting persons into educational programs that develop the requisite skills. The result is that people are

---

[8] Charles J. Hitch and Roland N. McKean, *The Economics of Defense in the Nuclear Age* (Cambridge, Mass.: Harvard University Press, 1967).

[9] Fred J. Cook, "Juggernaut: The Warfare State," *The Nation*, 193 (1961): 277–337; John Kenneth Galbraith, *The New Industrial State* (Boston: Houghton-Mifflin, 1967); Ralph P. Lapp, *The Weapons Culture* (New York: Norton, 1968); George McGovern, *A Time of War/A Time of Peace* (New York: Random House, 1968); Seymour Melman, *Pentagon Capitalism: The Political Economy of War* (New York: McGraw-Hill, 1970); William Proxmire, *Report from Wasteland: America's Military-Industrial Complex* (New York: Praeger, 1970); Herbert I. Schiller and Joseph D. Phillips, eds., *Super-State: Readings in the Military-Industrial Complex* (Urbana: University of Illinois Press, 1970).

[10] Bureau of the Census, *Statistical Abstract of the United States: 1975* (Washington: U.S. Government Printing Office, 1975), pp. 321–22.

attracted into technical career fields that are dependent upon continued defense spending and that suffer when cutbacks occur, as was evidenced in the 1970s.

Military research, development, and procurement are of such great magnitude that many specific industries and corporations become quasi-public institutions. For example, in 1968, 94 percent of Lockheed Aircraft's sales and 85 percent of General Dynamics' sales were to government.[11] Lockheed's commitment was so great that, in 1971, having suffered several setbacks with military hardware, the corporation was on the brink of bankruptcy. Also, military expenditures provide livelihoods for numerous consulting and research and development (R & D) firms, perhaps the best known "think tank" being the RAND Corporation of Santa Monica. Many of the employees of these firms are in effect career civil servants, judging from their length of service on government projects. The only difference is that their pay is higher working for "free enterprise" than it would be if they were directly employed by government.

The geographic impact of defense expenditures is equally important, because expenditures are not uniformly distributed throughout the nation.[12] The dependence upon defense is hardly a handicap for states when defense expenditures are rising, but declining expenditures can create severe problems. For instance, defense-generated jobs in California grew by 58,100 between 1965 and 1966 and by 86,600 between 1966 and 1967, but then dropped 7,600 the following year.[13] The effect is even more pronounced at the local level. An outstanding case is Vernon Parish, Louisiana, the site of Fort Polk. This county lost population in the 1950s but was the fastest-growing county in the nation in the 1960s, increasing by 194 percent. Military decisions to deactivate and then reactivate Polk's training center explain these major fluctuations in population.

Defense, the most striking example of private dependency upon public outlays, is not the sole example. Highway construction is another case involving large sums of public money. The employees of contracting firms specializing in highway construction are in effect governmental employees. The same is true for suppliers of road-building equipment such as Inter-

---

[11] The percent of government sales was obtained from corporation annual reports.

[12] Roger E. Bolton, *Defense Purchases and Regional Growth* (Washington: Brookings, 1966).

[13] Bureau of the Census, *Statistical Abstract of the United States: 1970* (Washington: U.S. Government Printing Office, 1970), p. 252.

national Harvester and Caterpillar Company. It also should be noted that companies of this type are major suppliers of equipment to the Defense Department.

In some cases, the impact of government on an industry is greater for what government does not do than for what it does. This condition exists in housing. The dollar value of public housing and redevelopment construction accounted for only 2 percent of all housing construction in 1975. FHA and VA mortgages covered 13 percent of all housing starts for that year.[14] Though these types of involvement are important, a more significant subsidy to housing is the federal government's allowance for a home buyer to deduct on his income tax return all interest paid on his home loan. In 1974 savings and loan associations, commercial banks, mutual savings banks, life insurance companies, and individuals held mortgage debts of $288.5 billion for nonfarm housing.[15] Had the income paid in interest on these debts been taxed, the revenue obtained would have far exceeded all federal outlays for public housing and redevelopment construction. The argument can be made that this provision in the tax law has a redistributional effect in favor of the middle class at the expense of the lower class.[16]

The lack of clear-cut distinctions between public and private and between one government and another is evident in education, particularly higher education. Elementary and secondary education is a function of local school districts, but in 1975, an estimated 37 percent of the funding came from state government and 8 percent from the federal government. Federal involvement is more pronounced at the higher education level. In 1975 public schools obtained an estimated 15 percent of their revenue from the federal government, and private schools obtained 19 percent.[17] In other words, private colleges and universities are somewhat more dependent upon federal support than are public ones. Both types can be regarded as quasi-federal institutions. The federal impact on research in higher education is even more pronounced. The fiscal 1977 budget included

---

[14] Bureau of the Census, *Statistical Abstract: 1975*, pp. 702 and 711.

[15] Bureau of the Census, *Statistical Abstract: 1975*, p. 462.

[16] For a more thorough analysis of this topic, see Alvin L. Schoor, "National Community and Housing Policy," in Bernard J. Frieden and Robert Morris, eds., *Urban Planning and Social Policy* (New York: Basic Books, 1968), pp. 107–18. Also see Arthur P. Solomon, *Housing the Urban Poor* (Cambridge, Mass.: M.I.T. Press, 1974).

[17] Bureau of the Census, *Statistical Abstract: 1975*, p. 112.

$2.6 billion in research and development funds to be committed to colleges and universities. This would fund over half of all college and university research and development.[18]

The above discussion indicates how the society is a scramble of private and public interests that cannot readily be isolated from each other. There is no simple means of determining what should be or what is the size of the public sector. Moreover, intergovernmental funding arrangements blur the distinctions among local governments, states, and the federal government (see Chapter 12). These considerations should be kept in mind in the following review of the magnitude and growth patterns of government.

THE MAGNITUDE AND GROWTH OF GOVERNMENT

There are many ways to measure the magnitude of government, but dollars and people are generally the easiest measures to apply.[19] By focusing upon revenues, expenditures, and numbers of employees, comparable standards can be used in contrasting governments with each other and with nongovernmental or private organizations. These measures, then, are the main ones utilized in this section.[20]

One approach to measuring organizations is to consider their revenues or receipts, thereby allowing for comparisons among both private and public organizations.[21] Using this measure, Figure 1 ranks the 25 largest

---

[18] Office of Management and Budget, *Special Analyses: Budget of the United States Government, Fiscal Year 1977* (Washington: U.S. Government Printing Office, 1976), p. 294.

[19] Statistical data used in this and the following section are drawn from several sources, some of which are not even in approximate agreement with each other. This problem is encountered especially when drawing comparisons among nations, as in Figure 1. Therefore, the data reported here must be considered of a "ball park" variety in which the park is very large. Because of these inherent limitations, discrepancies in the data can be found throughout the chapter and accompanying illustrations. When making international comparisons we have used the most recent year for which data for all countries are available, although more recent data are published for the U.S. state, local and national governments.

[20] For a comprehensive treatment of the magnitude and growth of American government, see Mosher and Poland, *The Costs of American Governments*. A more recent account with somewhat less data is Roger A. Freeman, *The Growth of American Government: A Morphology of the Welfare State* (Stanford, Cal.: Hoover Institution Press, Stanford University, 1975).

[21] The idea of comparing private and public organizations was suggested by Robert J. Mowitz, Director of the Institute of Public Administration, The Pennsylvania State University.

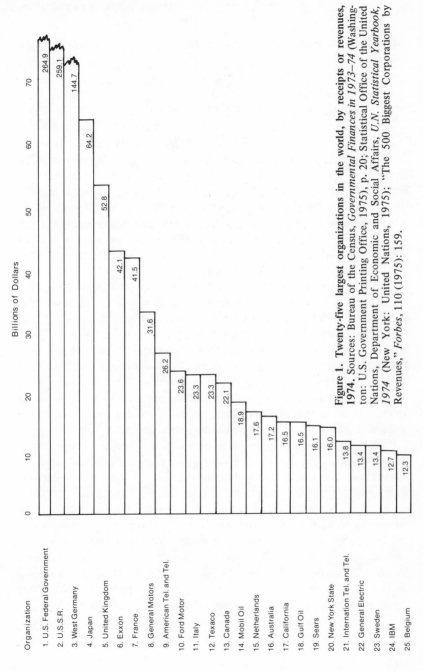

Billions of Dollars

Organization	
1. U.S. Federal Government	264.9
2. U.S.S.R.	259.1
3. West Germany	144.7
4. Japan	64.2
5. United Kingdom	52.8
6. Exxon	42.1
7. France	41.5
8. General Motors	31.6
9. American Tel. and Tel.	26.2
10. Ford Motor	23.6
11. Italy	23.3
12. Texaco	23.3
13. Canada	22.1
14. Mobil Oil	18.9
15. Netherlands	17.6
16. Australia	17.2
17. California	16.5
18. Gulf Oil	16.5
19. Sears	16.1
20. New York State	16.0
21. Internation Tel. and Tel.	13.8
22. General Electric	13.4
23. Sweden	13.4
24. IBM	12.7
25. Belgium	12.3

Figure 1. Twenty-five largest organizations in the world, by receipts or revenues, 1974. Sources: Bureau of the Census, *Governmental Finances in 1973–74* (Washington: U.S. Government Printing Office, 1975), p. 20; Statistical Office of the United Nations, Department of Economic and Social Affairs, *U.N. Statistical Yearbook, 1974* (New York: United Nations, 1975); "The 500 Biggest Corporations by Revenues," *Forbes*, 110 (1975): 159.

organizations in the world. Significantly, 14 of 25 are governments. Other governments might have appeared on this list if more reliable data were available; China is one such government. Three U.S. bureaucracies are included in the list—the U.S. federal government, California, and New York State. In a listing of the top 50 organizations in the United States, seven state governments are included (see Table 1). These states are California, Illinois, Michigan, New York, Ohio, Pennsylvania, and Texas.

An important aspect of these illustrations is that they dramatically underscore the need for caution in generalizing about governments or private corporations. Admittedly, one must recognize the important differences in the functions of government and industry and the methods by which these organizations make decisions. Differences also abound within each of these two types of organizations. Of course, the services provided and the methods of decision making are not identical in the Soviet Union, West Germany, the United Kingdom or any other nation.

On the other hand, the standard of size may provide useful insights into the operations of organizations. Size, for some research purposes, may be a better classification device than whether an organization is public or private, a national or a local government, and so forth. All industrial firms are not like General Motors, national governments are not of equal magnitude, all state governments are not like California's, and New York City is not simply a giant replica of Smalltown, U.S.A. The size of an organization may have substantial influence upon its methods of operations. It may be that all organizations of any given size, regardless of their private or public character, exhibit some common traits.

Although total expenditures or revenues are useful as approximate guides in measuring the size of government, these data need to be assessed in light of the varied capabilities of societies to support government. Unfortunately, reliable international data are often unavailable, and as a consequence, drawing useful comparisons among international organizations is impossible or of questionable value. To compare governments, one must have accurate reporting of revenues and expenditures of governments, something that is not always available, as in the case of China. Drawing comparisons requires having an accepted standard for converting currencies from marks, rubles, yens, pounds, and the like to dollars; and again, acceptable currency conversion tables are not available.

Given these limitations, it seems adequate to recognize that the American economy is one of the most prosperous in the world. In 1974, the per

TABLE 1

Fifty Largest U.S. Organizations by Revenues, 1974

1.	U.S. federal government	264.9	35.	Occidental Petroleum	5.5
2.	Exxon	42.1	36.	Bethlehem Steel	5.4
3.	General Motors	31.5	37.	Engelhard Mining and Chemical	5.4
4.	American Tel. & Tel.	26.2	38.	Union Carbide	5.3
5.	Ford	23.6	39.	Goodyear Tire and Rubber	5.3
6.	Texaco	23.3	40.	Aetna Life and Casualty	5.2
7.	Mobil Oil	18.9	41.	Tenneco	5.0
8.	Standard Oil (Cal.)	17.2	42.	Citicorp	5.0
9.	California	16.5	43.	Phillips Petroleum	5.0
10.	Gulf Oil	16.5	44.	International Harvester	5.0
11.	Sears	16.1	45.	Dow Chemical	5.0
12.	New York State	16.0	46.	Procter and Gamble	4.9
13.	International Tel. & Tel.	13.8	47.	Kroger	4.8
14.	General Electric	13.4	48.	LTV	4.8
15.	IBM	12.7	49.	Marcor	4.7
16.	New York City	11.3	50.	Esmark	4.6
17.	Chrysler	11.0			
18.	United States Steel	9.2			
19.	Standard Oil (Indiana)	9.1			
20.	Pennsylvania	8.3			
21.	Safeway	8.2			
22.	Shell Oil	7.6			
23.	Illinois	7.3			
24.	Continental Oil	7.0			
25.	E. I. DuPont	7.0			
26.	J. C. Penney	6.9			
27.	Great Atlantic and Pacific	6.9			
28.	Michigan	6.9			
29.	Atlantic Richfield	6.7			
30.	Ohio	6.1			
31.	Texas	5.9			
32.	Westinghouse Electric	5.8			
33.	General Tel. & Electric	5.7			
34.	S. S. Kresge	5.6			

Sources: Bureau of the Census, *Governmental Finances in 1973–74* (Washington, U.S. Government Printing Office, 1975), p. 20; "The 500 Biggest Corporations by Revenues," *Forbes*, 110(1975): 159–61.

TABLE 2
Federal Government Expenditures, Selected
Years, 1789–1975 (in Millions of Dollars)

1789–1791	$ 4	1855	$ 60	1915	$ 761
1800	11	1860	63	1920	6,403
1805	11	1865	1,298	1925	3,063
1810	8	1870	310	1930	3,440
1815	33	1875	275	1935	6,521
1820	18	1880	268	1940	9,062
1825	16	1885	260	1945	98,416
1830	15	1890	318	1950	39,617
1835	18	1895	356	1955	64,570
1840	24	1900	529	1960	97,284
1845	23	1905	567	1965	130,059
1850	40	1910	694	1970	208,190
				1975	324,601

Sources: 1789–1955 from Bureau of the Census, *Historical Statistics of the United States, Colonial Times–1957*
(Washington: U.S. Government Printing Office, 1960), p.
718; 1960–65 from Bureau of the Census, *Historical Statistics on Government Finances and Employment,* 1967 Census
of Governments, Vol. 6, No. 5 (Washington: U.S. Government Printing Office, 1969), pp. 36–37; 1970 from Bureau
of the Census, *Governmental Finances in 1969–70* (Washington: U.S. Government Printing Office, September, 1971), p.
21; 1975 from Office of Management and Budget, *Budget of
the United States, Fiscal 1977* (Washington: U.S. Government Printing Office, 1976), p. 368.

capita gross national product (GNP) in the United States was $5,979.[22]
This wealth has allowed for both big government and a large private sector.
The nation has been able to have large governmental expenditures ($2,271
per capita expenditures of all governments in the United States), while
these expenditures have been equal to slightly more than one-third of
GNP.[23] The contrasts that can be drawn regarding this great wealth and
large expenditures are striking. The government of New York City, for
example, normally spends more in one year than the entire GNP of
Thailand, a nation of 40 million people.

Because early records on state and local finance were not kept in any

---

[22] Bureau of the Census, *Statistical Abstract: 1975*, p. 845.

[23] Gross national product is discussed in Chapter 13.

uniform and complete manner, reliance must be placed upon federal expenditure data to obtain some overall perspective of the growth of government since the eighteenth century. Table 2 shows federal spending from 1789 through 1975. During this 186-year period, expenditures rose from $4.3 million in the first few years to approximately $325,000 million annually. The 1789 cost figure is a trivial sum measured by today's standards of big government, though obviously the economy and the population were much smaller then than now.

Focusing upon this century, there have been important differences between expenditure patterns of the federal government and those of state and local government (see Figure 2). Federal expenditures have fluctuated most, primarily because of war-related activities. The first year in which federal expenditures exceeded $1 billion was 1865, the peak year of the Civil War. For World War I, federal expenditures jumped in three years from $0.7 billion in 1916 to $18.5 billion in 1919, then dropped to $6.4 billion the following year. For World War II, expenditures increased from $13.3 billion in 1941 to $98.4 billion in 1945, then declined to $33.1 billion in 1948. For the Korean war, expenditures rose from $39.6 billion in 1950 to $74.3 billion in 1953, then dropped to $64.6 billion in 1955. In general, federal expenditures have risen during wartime and then declined, but not to the prewar level, thereby resulting in a cumulative increase over time. The Vietnam War era departed from this pattern; expenditures rose during and after the war. State and local expenditures, on the other hand, have fluctuated less and have increased annually, except for a period of slight decline during World War II.

A few words of caution regarding the interpretation of Figure 2 are warranted. The graph is based upon all expenditures for each governmental level, including intergovernmental transfers. The graph is useful from the standpoint of indicating expenditure levels for each type of government—revealing the magnitude of funds over which a type of government has some control—but it can be misinterpreted to exaggerate the total size of all public expenditures. Federal aid to state and local governments is included in the federal figure as well as in the state and local totals. The same duplication occurs with regard to state assistance to local government. Therefore, the total expenditures of the three levels of government would be greater than what actually was spent. (Later in this chapter we consider the extent of intergovernmental transactions.)

Important shifts have occurred in the extent to which the nation relies upon different levels of government. At the turn of the century, local

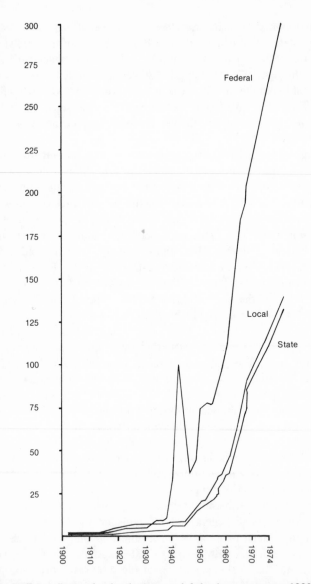

Figure 2. Expenditures for local, state, and federal governments, 1902–1974 (billions of dollars). Sources: Bureau of the Census, *Historical Statistics on Governmental Finances and Employment*, 1967 Census of Governments, Vol. 6, No. 5 (Washington: U.S. Government Printing Office, 1969), pp. 1 and 36–47; Bureau of the Census, *Governmental Finances in 1973–74* (Washington: U.S. Government Printing Office, November, 1975), p. 21.

governments were by far the biggest spenders, followed by the federal government, and then the states. During the Depression, federal spending spurted above local expenditures, and the gap has since been widening. Today, the federal government spends the most, followed by local governments, and then by the states. While state expenditures remain in third place, they have shown greater comparative growth and now almost match local funds. These changes reflect a shift in financing government away from the local level to the state and federal levels.

Just as total expenditures have increased, so have per capita expenditures. In 1902 the total of all governmental expenditures in the United States was only $20 per capita; in 1974 the comparable figure was $2,271 per capita, an increase of 11,000 percent. These data, however, overstate the rising cost of government by not deflating for general price increases or inflation that has occurred.

One means of controlling for price changes over time is to consider governmental expenditures as a percentage of GNP (see Figure 3). From 1902 to 1974 the cost of all government rose from 7.0 percent to 35 percent of GNP. Slight increases were recorded throughout the early 1900s, until a noteworthy increase to 21.4 percent occurred in 1932. The 20 percent level continued throughout the 1930s. World War II brought expenditures to an all-time high, in excess of half of GNP, but a sharp cutback followed in the postwar years. A much smaller increase occurred during the Korean War. Since the late 1950s governmental expenditures have been almost constant at 30–35 percent of GNP. Despite generally rising taxes and increased expenditures for the Southeast Asia war and social programs such as federal aid to education, the cost of government has not grown more rapidly than the economy as a whole.

Moreover, since the mid-1930s there was a remarkable consistency in federal nondefense expenditures as a percentage of GNP until the end of the Vietnam War (see Figure 4). Defense expenditures have risen during times of war and then have fallen, but not to the prewar level. Nondefense federal expenditures remained notably constant, between 4 and 9 percent of GNP, until the 1970s when social insurance (mostly old-age and survivors disability) programs pushed them to 13 percent of GNP.

The rise of big bureaucracy in the federal government can also be measured in terms of public employees. In 1816 there were less than 5,000 full- and part-time civilian employees in the federal service. Following the Civil War, however, greater growth was recorded. In 1871 there were over 50,000 federal employees, and by 1881 this number had doubled to 100,000. The fastest-growing period was from the Depression through

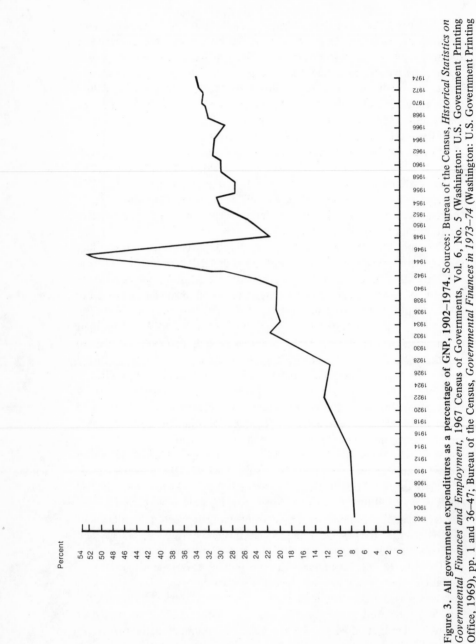

Figure 3. All government expenditures as a percentage of GNP, 1902–1974. Sources: Bureau of the Census, *Historical Statistics on Governmental Finances and Employment,* 1967 Census of Governments, Vol. 6, No. 5 (Washington: U.S. Government Printing Office, 1969), pp. 1 and 36–47; Bureau of the Census, *Governmental Finances in 1973–74* (Washington: U.S. Government Printing Office, November, 1975), p. 21.

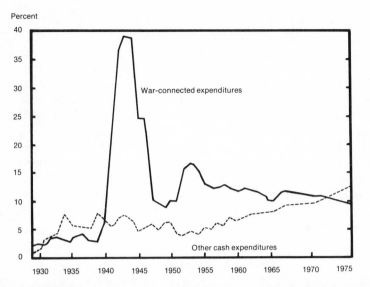

Figure 4. Federal "war-connected" and "other" cash expenditures as a percentage of GNP, 1929–1975. Sources: Modified from David J. Ott and Attiat F. Ott, *Federal Budget Policy*, rev. ed. (Washington: Brookings, 1969), p. 53. Copyright 1969 by The Brookings Institution. 1970 and 1975 figures from Office of Management and Budget, *Budget of the United States Government, Fiscal Year 1977* (Washington: U.S. Government Printing Office, 1976).

World War II. In 1931 there were still only 610,000 employees, but by 1945, the peak of the war-time economy, the federal civilian work force had climbed to nearly 4 million. Within a year, this was reduced to less than 3 million. Since then, only once, in 1950, has the federal work force dropped below 2 million. During the 1960s and early 1970s, federal civilian personnel remained at about 2.5 to 3 million.

While the size of the federal bureaucracy is extraordinarily large, government personnel are geographically dispersed. In 1974 California had 299,000 federal civilian employees, a figure equivalent to about half of the total population of Delaware. These employees alone, not counting their families, if located in the same area would constitute a metropolitan area of the size of Binghamton, New York; Colorado Springs, Colorado; or Corpus Christi, Texas. Comparable figures for federal employees in other states are Illinois with 108,000, New York with 178,000, and Texas with 152,000.[24]

---

[24] Bureau of the Census, *Statistical Abstract: 1975*, p. 246.

At the state and local levels the number of employees has also increased. State employment grew from less than 1 million in 1947 to 2.7 million in 1974. In the same period, local employment increased from 2.9 million to 7.2 million. Overall, there was an average of 30 employees per local government in 1952 and 92 in 1974. Significantly, the growth at the local level has been accompanied by a decline in the number of local governments. In 1972 there were 78,218 local governments, 24,000 fewer than a decade earlier. This decline is largely attributable to school district consolidation. While the number of school districts has dropped substantially, from 109,000 in 1942 to 17,000 in 1972, the number of municipalities and special districts has increased, townships have decreased, and counties have remained virtually constant.[25] Fewer and fewer governments are hiring more and more people who are spending more and more tax dollars.

SOURCES OF REVENUES AND
PURPOSES OF GOVERNMENTAL EXPENDITURES

Government does not simply get money and spend it in general. Revenue is obtained from specific sources and spent for specific public goods and services. The following discussion, then, considers the relationships between income and outgo, between the ways in which revenue is generated and the purpose of governmental expenditures.

Revenues Tax structure always has been and always will be a greatly debated topic. The core of the problem is to devise a tax system that is equitable, though equity can only be judged by values imposed by the beholder. Taxes are considered at best to be necessary evils, and commonly the citizen "prefers tax adjustments that will reduce his burden and increase that of other persons."[26] Perhaps the only way of pleasing everyone would be to eliminate taxes, though the resulting elimination of governmental programs would surely not be considered satisfactory.

There are basically two types of equity principles, the first being ability to pay.[27] Involved here are matters of horizontal and vertical

[25] Bureau of the Census, *Statistical Abstract: 1975*, pp. 251 and 273.

[26] John F. Due and Ann F. Friedlaender, *Government Finance: Economics of the Public Sector*, 5th ed. (Homewood, Ill.: Irwin, 1973), p. 228.

[27] The following discussion is based mainly upon Bernard P. Herber, *Modern Public Finance: The Study of Public Sector Economics*, 3rd ed. (Homewood, Ill.: Irwin, 1975), pp. 131–43.

equity. Horizontal equity refers to the equal treatment of equals, for example, that all persons of identical economic status would pay identical taxes. Vertical equity, on the other hand, refers to treating unequals unequally. The concept of sacrifice is used in which equity is said to exist when all persons sacrifice equally, though the dollar sacrifice may vary from person to person, depending upon his personal wealth.

The second principle is that of benefits, which attempts to relate revenues to expenditures. Citizens exchange purchasing power for government goods and services through the payment of taxes. Under an equitable system, the level of payments is equal to the benefits derived. Marginal utility considerations are required in that the unit value of a particular commodity decreases as each successive unit is provided. However, the benefit approach to taxation is limited in that the exclusion principle is inoperative in regard to many governmental programs. Using the example mentioned earlier, persons not willing to pay for military defense cannot be excluded from receiving benefits. The benefit theory, therefore, cannot be applied to this type of governmental program.

The issue of equity is frequently expressed in terms of the progressive, proportional, or regressive nature of a tax. A progressive tax is one in which the tax rate or percent increases as the tax base increases. A graduated income tax, for example, is progressive; an individual is taxed a higher percentage on additional income received. A regressive tax is of the converse nature, while a proportional tax lies between the two.

Equity cannot be assessed adequately without consideration of the difference between the immediate and final burden of a tax. The immediate effect of a corporate income tax, for instance, will be for firms to pay taxes, but the final effect will be for purchasers of these firms' products to pay the tax through higher prices. In this way, the incidence of a tax is shifted. The incidence of a tax can have a profound effect, intended or unintended, upon the distribution of income among groups in the society.[28]

Another complication in achieving equity is that of tax enforcement. Some taxes, such as wage taxes administered through payroll deductions, are easily enforced, whereas others are not. Taxes on illegal gambling are obviously difficult to enforce and are imposed for law enforcement purposes rather than as important means for raising revenue. The point is that

---

[28] Horst C. Recktenwald, *Tax Incidence and Income Redistribution* (Detroit: Wayne State University Press, 1971); Joseph A. Pechman and Benjamin A. Okner, *Who Bears the Tax Burden* (Washington: Brookings, 1974).

taxes vary according to their enforceability and that equity will not be achieved if some citizens pay disproportionately higher taxes than others.

Having recognized these important qualifications in judging tax structure, the revenue side of government budgeting can be considered. Table 3 displays the sources of revenue for the federal, state, and local governments in 1973–74. The first important item to understand from this table is that it covers the sources of revenue but not expenditures. Due to intergovernmental transfers of funds, governments may obtain revenue from many sources but not directly spend that money. This is true for all levels of government, including local governments which provide the states with some revenue (1.1 percent). As can be seen from the table, 24 percent of state government revenue and 38 percent of local government revenue come from other jurisdictions. Once again it is apparent that clear-cut distinctions among the three levels of government are nonexistent.

Regarding reliance upon different tax sources, important variations exist among the levels of government. There are five basic types of taxes: 1) income (personal, corporate, and payroll), 2) consumption spending (customs duties, excise, and sales taxes), 3) ownership and transfer of wealth (property tax, capital levies, death, and gift taxes), 4) business activity (gross receipts and capital stock), and 5) export taxes.[29] The last form, export taxes, is used particularly in developing nations, which have economies based upon the export of raw goods such as oil or lumber products.

Three tax sources provide 78 percent of the federal government's revenue. The largest single share (40 percent) is obtained through the individual income tax; 24 percent through social insurance, including old-age, survivors, disability, and health insurance and unemployment compensation; and 13 percent through the corporate income tax. Another 7 percent comes from sales and gross receipts taxes. Customs duties, which in 1792 provided 94 percent of all federal monies, provided only 1 percent in 1973–74.[30] In contrast, increasing reliance has been placed upon the individual income tax; the corporate income tax has declined from 30 percent in 1930 to less than 15 percent in the 1970s.[31]

---

[29] Due and Friedlaender, *Government Finance*, pp. 251–481.

[30] See David J. Ott and Attiat F. Ott, *Federal Budget Policy*, rev. ed. (Washington: Brookings, 1969), p. 56.

[31] For a thorough discussion of federal taxes, see Joseph A. Pechman, *Federal Tax Policy*, rev. ed. (New York: Norton, 1971). Also see Gerard M. Brennan, *The Federal Revenue System* (New York: General Learning, 1971).

TABLE 3

Governmental Revenue by Source and Level of Government, 1973–1974

Sources	All governments		Percentage distribution		
	Millions ($)	Percentage (%)	Federal	State	Local
Intergovernmental revenue	—	—	—	23.6	38.2
From federal government	—	—	—	22.5	7.1
From states	—	—	0.2	—	31.1
From local governments	—	—	—	1.1	—
Revenue from own sources	484,650	100.0	99.9	76.4	61.8
General revenue	383,831	79.2	75.4	63.3	53.6
Taxes	315,547	65.1	63.9	52.7	39.5
Property	47,754	9.9	—	0.9	32.4
Individual income	138,443	28.6	40.1	12.1	1.7
Corporation income (net)	44,635	9.2	13.4	4.3	—
Sales and gross receipts	66,632	13.7	7.1	28.8	3.9
Customs duties	3,450	0.7	1.2	—	—
General sales and gross receipts	26,314	5.4	—	18.9	2.6
Selective sales and gross receipts	36,868	7.6	5.9	12.3	1.3
Motor vehicle and operators licenses	3,755	0.8	—	2.5	0.2
Death and gift	6,465	1.3	1.7	1.0	—
All other	7,863	1.6	0.1	3.1	1.3
Charges and misc. general revenue	68,284	14.1	11.5	10.6	14.1
Utility revenue	9,392	1.9	—	—	6.6
Liquor stores revenue	2,355	0.5	—	1.5	0.2
Insurance trust revenue	89,072	18.4	24.4	11.7	1.4
Total revenue	484,650	100.0	100.0	100.0	100.0
			($289,059)	($140,815)	($143,193)

Source: Bureau of the Census, *Governmental Finances in 1973–74* (Washington: U.S. Government Printing Office, November, 1975), p. 20.

As already indicated, nearly one-fourth of state revenue comes from other governments, particularly the federal government. Of the remainder, sales and gross receipts taxes are the largest revenue source, providing 29 percent of all state funds. Another 12 percent is obtained from individual income taxes. Other state monies come from corporate income taxes, motor vehicle and operators' license fees, and social insurance deductions.

Local governments obtain more than one-third of their money from other governments and the rest mainly through property taxes. Of all local revenue, 32 percent comes from this source. Approximately 21 percent is obtained from charges, miscellaneous general revenue, and utility fees. Together, these local sources provide 53 percent of all funds for local government. Unlike the federal government, local governments rely very little upon individual income taxes (less than 2 percent), and unlike states, they rely little upon sales taxes (4 percent).[32]

A possible conclusion is that government in the United States depends upon a direct tax structure, as opposed to indirect taxes in which the burden can be shifted.[33] Seventy percent of federal revenue is obtained from direct taxes, particularly the personal income tax and Social Security deductions. The pattern is somewhat mitigated by the states' reliance upon sales and excise taxes and local reliance upon property taxes. "Nevertheless, even when all subordinate units are included, the American fiscal structure, relative to most other countries of the world, is more dependent on direct tax sources."[34]

Is the resulting tax structure a fair one? The question cannot be answered here, but some observations can be made. At the federal level, the personal income tax has been defended as a means of redistributing income in order to benefit the economically disadvantaged. However, issues abound regarding this. For example, the argument can be made that the exemptions and deductions allowed under the system have eroded the tax base. Mentioned earlier was the suggestion that the deduction for interest paid on home mortgages benefits the middle class far more than the poor. Similar issues can be found at the state and local levels. One major line of argument is that whatever "beneficial" redistributive effects there are within the federal tax structure, these are offset by state and

---

[32] For a discussion of the politics of local taxation, see Arnold J. Meltsner, *The Politics of City Revenue* (Berkeley: University of California Press, 1971).

[33] Buchanan and Flowers, *The Public Finances*, p. 224.

[34] Buchanan and Flowers, *The Public Finances*, p. 224.

local taxes. State sales taxes and local property taxes have been attacked as severely burdensome on low-income groups.[35]

During the early 1970s, the local property tax was challenged in some court cases on the grounds that the tax was inherently inequitable. Persons living in a community with high property values were able to enjoy better services, particularly better educational services, than those living in poorer areas. Lower federal courts and several state courts invalidated state systems for educational finance based on property taxation, but the Supreme Court in 1973 ruled that the issue is a matter for legislatures to determine rather than the courts (*San Antonio Independent School District vs. Rodriguez*, 411 US 1). The issues raised are not dead, however, as several state courts have ruled their own state systems in violation of state constitutions. New Jersey's summer program was closed by the State Supreme Court for a few days in 1976 when the state legislature failed to provide an alternative to property tax financing.

Another tax that has been the center of some controversy is the value added tax (VAT). The VAT is a levy on "the difference between receipts from sales and the amounts paid for materials, supplies, and services purchased from other firms."[36] In effect, the tax is charged on the additional value of a product or service created at each stage in the production process. This tax has been used widely in Europe and the Nixon Administration indicated some interest in it, although the proposal generated little enthusiasm. The VAT has been criticized as a thinly disguised sales tax, which would be essentially regressive. It has few current supporters.

Expenditures Expenditures are the product of a set of choices or decisions made as to what public goods and services should be produced. Total expenditures are the sum of decisions made at all levels of government. Each level of government, however, has discrete financial decision-making processes that are only partially dependent on the other levels. As the different levels depend on somewhat different sources for revenues, local, state, and the federal governments also spend their funds for somewhat different functions.

Because the federal government provides financial assistance to state

---

[35] For a summary of the issues regarding federal taxes, see Eckstein, *Public Finance*, pp. 51–69.

[36] Pechman, *Federal Tax Policy*, p. 162.

and local governments and the states to local governments and, in some cases, local governments to states, it is obvious that governments do not spend directly all the money that flows through them. In 1973–74, direct federal expenditures were $254 billion or 87 percent of all federal expenditures. State governments spent even a smaller percentage of their funds—$120 billion or 62 percent of all state expenditures. Local governments spent directly virtually all their funds—$126 billion or 92 percent.

Governmental expenditures by function and by level of government are displayed in Table 4; like the other illustrations used here, this one reports gross finances, including intergovernmental transfers. As can be seen from the percentage distributions, social insurance is the largest single function, occupying the place long held by defense and accounting for 20 percent of all expenditures by the federal, state, and local governments. For 1973–74, defense and international relations was still the largest federal expenditure, constituting 29 percent of the federal budget. This reflects a relative decline in defense expenditures in the 1970s along with rising federal expenditures for Social Security and state expenditures for unemployment compensation during the recession.

Some of the financial costs of defense are not reflected in these figures. Veterans' benefits and services, which are obvious by-products of defense and which constituted 4 percent of the fiscal 1977 budget, are not included. Much of the interest paid on the national debt can be ascribed to defense, given that major budgetary deficits have been incurred during wartime. Deficit spending in fiscal 1968, the height of the Southeast Asia war, amounted to $25 billion. Some aspects of the space program might also be charged to defense, because technological breakthroughs in space exploration are likely to have military applications.

Social insurance is the second largest program area in the federal government, constituting 26 percent of the budget; following that, all other program areas are comparatively small. The next largest "program" is interest paid on the national debt (8 percent). The remainder of the expenditures are divided into small segments among welfare, natural resources, education, postal service, highways, health, and other service functions.[37]

---

[37] For analysis of the functional pattern of federal expenditures and alternatives to the existing pattern, see Robert S. Benson and Harold Wolman, eds., *Counterbudget: A Blueprint for Changing National Priorities, 1971–1976* (New York: Praeger, 1971) and Barry M. Blechman, et al., *Setting National Priorities: The 1976 Budget* (Washington: Brookings, 1975).

TABLE 4

Expenditures by Function and Level of Government, 1973–1974

Function	All government expenditures (in millions of dollars)	Percent expenditures			
		All	Federal	State	Local
National defense and international relations	87,041	18.7	29.3	—	—
Postal service	11,235	2.4	3.4	—	—
Space research and technology	3,289	0.7	1.1	—	—
Education	81,653	17.5	4.5	35.9	44.0
Highways	20,189	4.3	1.7	12.1	5.8
Public welfare	31,031	6.7	6.4	17.3	7.7
Health and hospitals	21,668	4.7	2.3	6.5	6.8
Natural resources	15,757	3.4	4.3	2.3	0.6
Housing and urban renewal	7,629	1.6	2.2	0.4	2.4
Air transportation	2,922	0.6	0.6	0.2	0.8
Social insurance[a]	91,802	19.8	25.7	9.1	1.6
Interest on general debt	30,116	6.5	7.6	2.2	3.8
Other and combined	63,665	13.7	10.6	13.9	26.5
Total	465,667	100.0	100.0	100.0	100.0
			($297,236)	($130,481)	($127,634)

[a]Figures for social insurance include trust fund expenditures for things such as old age, survivors, disability, and health insurance and unemployment compensation.

Note: Percentages are based upon all expenditures, both direct and intergovernmental. Source: Bureau of the Census, *Governmental Finances in 1973–74* (Washington: U.S. Government Printing Office, November 1975), pp. 22–27.

TABLE 5

Federal Expenditures as Percent of Contributions to Functional Areas, 1973–1974

Functional area	All government expenditures	Direct and intergovernmental federal expenditures		Direct federal expenditures	
		Millions ($)	Percentage of all government expenditures	Millions ($)	Percentage of all government expenditures
National defense and international relations	87,041	87,041	100.0	87,041	100.0
Postal service	11,235	11,235	100.0	11,235	100.0
Space research and technology	3,289	3,289	100.0	3,289	100.0
Education	116,294	13,316	11.5	5,820	5.0
Highways	27,995	4,798	17.1	243	0.9
Public welfare	51,521	19,123	37.1	6,286	12.2
Health and hospitals	23,952	6,861	28.6	5,723	23.9
Natural resources	16,655	12,846	77.1	12,096	72.6
Housing and urban renewal	10,184	6,559	64.4	4,168	40.9
Air transportation	3,231	1,875	58.0	1,622	50.2
Social insurance	90,294	76,319	84.5	75,497	83.6
Interest on general debt	30,116	22,450	74.5	22,450	74.5
Other and combined	83,544	31,524	37.7	18,912	22.6
Total	555,351	297,236	53.5	254,382	45.8

Source: Bureau of the Census, *Governmental Finances in 1973–74* (Washington: U.S. Government Printing Office, November 1975), pp. 21–22.

State and local expenditures follow different patterns. In the first place, neither the states nor local governments are responsible for defense, postal service, or space exploration. Education is the largest expense for both types of government, 36 percent for states and 44 percent for local governments, particularly school districts. Welfare and highways are the next largest state functions (17 percent and 12 percent, respectively). Over one-fourth of all local expenditures are classified as "other" in the table and include activities such as police and fire protection, sewerage, parks and recreation, libraries, and parking facilities.

Expenditures as reported here cover intergovernmental transfers as well as direct outlays; double counting of funds results in that, for example, federal grants to states are reported under both federal and state expenditures. Though such an expenditure breakout has this weakness, the table is useful in indicating the purposes for which governments spend their resources. On the other hand, one should recognize that in many cases governments do not actually spend these funds but rather provide them to other governments. Also, these data do not reveal the relative contribution of different levels of government to a given program area.

These points can be clarified by examining Table 5, which displays federal expenditures as a percentage contribution to functional areas. For instance, in Table 4, highway expenditures constituted only 2 percent of the federal budget, but as shown in Table 5, these expenditures account for 17 percent of all outlays for highway construction. Also evident is that the federal government provides most of this money to other jurisdictions; only 1 percent of all highway money is actually spent by the federal government. Welfare, education, and housing are similar cases in which federal funds for these areas are spent by state and local governments. In contrast, the federal government directly spends most of its funds for social insurance and natural resources. Overall, federal expenditures were 54 percent of all government expenditures, and direct expenditures by the federal government were 46 percent of all outlays.[38]

---

[38] For discussions of governmental expenditures by functional areas, see the following: Buchanan and Flowers, *The Public Finances*, pp. 191–220; Mosher and Poland, *The Costs of American Governments*, pp. 102–33; Ott and Ott, *Federal Budget Policy*, pp. 125–44; Ira Sharkansky, *The Politics of Taxing and Spending* (Indianapolis: Bobbs-Merrill, 1969).

SUMMARY

The preceding discussion has shown that government is indeed very large, that the growth pattern of the public sector has been upward, and that today drawing a definitive line between the public and private sectors is virtually impossible. If present trends continue, government can be expected to become even larger, providing more service directly or ensuring the provision of services by regulating the private sector, or both.

At the same time, some popular myths about government do not necessarily withstand analysis. For example, despite common outcries against the rise of the welfare state, federal nondefense expenditures as a percentage of GNP has been nearly constant since the mid-1930s. Though government is growing, many governmental units remain small; in 1972, 80 percent of all local governments had fewer than 50 employees. Much of the growth of local governments has occurred not because of social welfare programs but because of increased resources devoted to education.

Governments in the United States specialize in both the types of revenue sources used and the functions for which revenues are expended. The federal government relies primarily upon personal and corporate income taxes and social insurance deductions; expenditures are concentrated in defense, international relations, and social insurance. States obtain nearly a quarter of their revenue from the federal government and the remainder largely from sales and individual income taxes. State expenditures are concentrated in education and to a lesser extent in highways and public welfare. Local governments receive one-third of their funds from other governments and another third from property taxes. The most expensive function of local government is education, followed by functions such as police, fire protection, sewerage, and recreation.

3

BUDGET CYCLES

Public budgeting systems, which are devices for selecting societal ends and means, consist of numerous participants and various processes that bring the participants into interaction. As was seen in the preceding chapters, the purpose of budgeting is to allocate scarce resources among competing public demands and wants in order to seek the attainment of societal goals and objectives. Those societal ends are expressed not by philosopher kings but by mortals who must operate within the context of some prescribed allocation process, namely the budgetary system.

This chapter provides an overview of the participants and processes involved in budgetary decision making; the purpose is to gain a perspective on the overall budgetary system. First, the phases of the budget cycle are reviewed. Any system has some structure or form, and budgetary systems are not exceptions. As will be seen, there are steps in the decision-making process; more elaborate discussions of these steps are presented in subsequent chapters. The second topic is the extent to which budget cycles are intermingled within government and among governments, the latter being discussed more fully in Chapter 12.

THE BUDGET CYCLE

In order to provide for responsible government, budgeting is geared to a cycle. The cycle allows for the system to absorb and respond to new information, and in doing so government is held accountable for its actions. While existing budget systems may be less than perfect in guaranteeing adherence to this principle of responsibility, the argument stands that periodicity contributes toward achieving and maintaining limited government. The budget cycle consists of four phases: preparation and submission, approval, execution, and audit.

Preparation and Submission The preparation and submission phase is the most difficult to describe because it has been subjected the most to reform efforts. Experiments in reformulating the preparation process abound. As a consequence, the pattern that was used last year is not necessarily the one used this year. Though the same institutional units may exist over time, both procedures and substantive content vary from year to year.

The responsibility for budget preparation varies greatly among jurisdictions. Budget reform efforts have pressed for executive budgeting in which the chief executive has exclusive responsibility for preparing a proposed budget and submitting it to the legislative body. At the federal level, the President has such exclusive control, though it should be recognized that many factors curtail the extent to which the President can make major changes in the budget. Preparation authority, however, is not always available to governors and local chief executives. While a majority of governors have responsibility for preparation and submission, some share budget-making authority with other elected administrative officers, civil service appointees, legislative leaders, or some combination of these. An extreme case is Mississippi, where the budget preparation phase is under the control of a legislative commission and not the governor.[1]

At the municipal level, the mayor may or may not have budget preparation powers. In cities where the mayor is strong—has administrative control over the executive branch—he normally does have budget-making power. This is not the case in weak-mayor systems and in cities operating under the commission plan, where each councilman or commissioner administers a given department. Usually, the city manager in a council-manager system has responsibility for preparation, though his ability to recommend may be tempered by his lack of independence. Managers may be reluctant to take bold stands because they are appointed by council rather than elected to office; managers commonly have no tenure and are subject to dismissal by the city council.[2]

---

[1] Great inconsistencies exist among available literature regarding budget preparation authority at the state level. Part of the problem is sorting out the official process from the real one. An executive-legislative board, for example, may have only the official power to provide budget advice to a governor but in actual practice that board may be largely responsible for preparing the budget. Some caution, therefore, is necessary in accepting each detail of general surveys of state budget practices.

[2] See John P. Crecine, *Governmental Problem Solving: A Computer Simulation of Municipal Budgeting* (Chicago: Rand McNally, 1969) and Lewis B. Friedman, *Budgeting Municipal Expenditures: A Study in Comparative Policy Making* (New York: Praeger, 1975).

Budget preparation at the federal level is primarily a function of a budget office that was established by the Budget and Accounting Act of 1921. That legislation established the Bureau of the Budget (BOB), which became a unit of the Treasury Department. With the passage of time, the role of the BOB increased in importance, and in 1939 the Bureau became part of the newly formed Executive Office of the President (EXOP). Given that the Bureau was thought to be the "right arm of the President"—a common referent in early budget literature—the move out of Treasury, a line department, into EXOP placed the Bureau under direct presidential supervision. In 1970 President Richard M. Nixon reorganized the Bureau, giving it a new title, the Office of Management and Budget (OMB). The intent of the reorganization was to bring "real business management into Government at the very highest level."[3]

In the federal government, preparation starts in the spring or for large agencies even earlier. Agencies begin by assessing their programs and considering which programs require revision and whether new programs should be recommended. At approximately the same time, estimates are made by the President's staff regarding anticipated economic trends in order to determine available revenue under existing tax legislation. The next step is for the President to issue general budget and fiscal policy guidelines, which are used by agencies in developing their respective budgets. These budget requests are submitted in late summer to the OMB. Throughout the fall and into the later months of the year, agency requests are reviewed by the OMB, and hearings are held between OMB and agency

---

[3] Richard M. Nixon as quoted in *The New York Times*, June 11, 1970. See Gary Bombardier, "The Managerial Function of OMB: Intergovernmental Relations as a Test Case," *Public Policy*, 13 (1975): 317–54; James W. Davis and Randall B. Ripley, "The Bureau of the Budget and Executive Branch Agencies: Notes on their Interaction," *Journal of Politics*, 29 (1969): 749–69; Charles G. Dawes, *The First Year of the Budget of the United States* (New York: Harper and Brothers, 1923); Rowland Egger, "The United States Bureau of the Budget," *Parliamentary Affairs*, 3 (1949): 39–54; Hugh Heclo, "OMB and the Presidency—the Problem of Neutral Competence," *The Public Interest*, No. 38 (Winter, 1975): 80–98; Fritz Morstein Marx, "The Bureau of the Budget: Its Evolution and Present Role," *American Political Science Review*, 39 (1945): 653–84 and 869–98; Robert E. Merriam, "The Bureau of the Budget as Part of the President's Staff," *Annals*, 30 (1956): 15–23; Don K. Price, "General Dawes and Executive Staff Work," *Public Administration Review*, 11 (1951): 167–72; Allen Schick, "The Budget Bureau That Was: Thoughts on the Rise, Decline, and Future of a Presidential Agency," in Harvey C. Mansfield, Allen Schick, and Thomas E. Cronin, *Papers on the Institutionalized Presidency* (Washington: Brookings, 1971), pp. 519–39; Henry P. Seidemann, "The Preparation of the National Budget," *Annals*, 13 (1924): 40–50; L. L. Wade, "The U.S. Bureau of the Budget as Agency Evaluator: Orientations to Action," *American Journal of Economics and Sociology*, 27 (1968): 55–62.

spokesmen. During this same period, agencies and OMB are involved in preparing the Current Services Budget, which shows the future budgetary effects of congressional decisions; according to the 1974 Congressional Budget and Impoundment Control Act, this budget must be submitted to Congress by November 10. Not until the last months of the year, particularly November and December, does the President become deeply involved in the process, which culminates in January with the submission of a proposed budget to the Congress.

At the state and local levels, a similar process is used where executive budgeting systems prevail. As will be seen in Chapter 6, the central budget office issues budget request instructions, reviews the submitted requests, and makes recommendations to the chief executive, who decides which items to recommend to the legislative body. The current services type of budget may or may not be used as well as a variety of other approaches. However, in jurisdictions not using executive budgeting, the chief executive and the budget office will play minor roles; in this type of system, the line agencies will direct their budget requests to the legislative body.

The preparation phase as well as the other three phases in the budget cycle is replete with political considerations, both bureaucratic and partisan. Each organizational unit is concerned with its own survival and advancement. Line agencies and their subunits strive for increased resources. Budget offices, on the other hand, often play negative roles, attempting to limit agency growth, but fear that their recommendations will be ignored by the chief executive. All members of the executive branch are concerned with their relationships with the legislative branch and the general citizenry. The chief executive is especially concerned with partisan calculations: Which alternatives will be advantageous to my political party? Of course there is concern with developing programs for the "common good," but this concern is played out in a complicated game of political maneuvering.[4]

One complaint of the preparation phase is that it tends to be highly fragmented. Organizational units within line agencies tend to be concerned

---

[4] For a discussion of political strategies used in the budgetary process, see Aaron Wildavsky, *The Politics of the Budgetary Process*, 2nd ed. (Boston: Little, Brown, 1974). The same material may also be found in sections of Wildavsky's *Budgeting: A Comparative Theory of Budgetary Processes* (Boston: Little, Brown, 1975) and with Naomi Caiden, *Planning and Budgeting in Poor Countries* (New York: Wiley, 1974). Also see Ira Sharkansky, *The Politics of Taxing and Spending* (Indianapolis: Bobbs-Merrill, 1969).

primarily with their own programs and frequently fail to take a broader perspective. Even the budget office may be myopic, although it will be forced into considering the budget as a whole. Only the chief executive is unquestionably committed to viewing the budget as a whole in the preparation phase.

Approval The budget is approved by a legislative body, whether it be the Congress, a state legislature, county board of supervisors, city council, or school board. The fragmented approach to budgeting in the preparation phase is not characteristic of the approval phase at the local level. A city council may have a separate finance committee, but normally the council as a whole participates actively in the approval process. Local legislative bodies may take several preliminary votes on pieces of the budget but then adopt the budget as a whole by a single vote.

States, however, separate tax and other revenue measures from appropriations or spending bills. About half of the states place most or all of their spending provisions in a single appropriation bill, but the others vary greatly, with some states having hundreds of appropriations bills.[5] Most state legislatures are free to augment or reduce the governor's budget, but some, such as those of Maryland and Nebraska, are restricted in their ability to increase the budget.

At the federal level, the revenue and appropriations processes have been fragmented greatly among committees and subcommittees. Not only have revenue raising and spending been treated as separate processes, but the expenditure side has been handled in a dozen or so major appropriations bills instead of being treated as a whole. The 1974 congressional budget reform has moved toward integration of these processes, although the same basic pieces of legislation are acted upon by the Congress. New Senate and House budget committees, consisting of representatives from several other standing committees, provide a structure for joint consideration of revenues and expenditures. The 1974 legislation also created the Congressional Budget Office, which provides staff support.

The final step of the approval stage is the signing of appropriations into law. The President, governors, and in some cases mayors have the power to veto. A veto sends the measure back to the legislative body for further consideration. Governors, unlike the President, often have item veto

[5] James H. Bowhay and Virginia D. Thrall, *State Legislative Appropriations Process* (Lexington, Ky.: Council of State Governments, 1975), p. 81.

power, which allows them to veto specific portions of the bill but still sign it. In no case can the executive augment parts of the budget beyond that provided by the legislature. Forty-two governors have some form of item veto power over appropriations bills.[6]

Execution Execution is the third phase, commencing with the fiscal year—October 1 in the federal government. Some form of centralized control during this phase is common at all levels of government, and such control is usually maintained by the budget office. Following congressional passage of an appropriations bill and its signing by the President, agencies must submit to the Office of Management and Budget a proposed plan for apportionment. This plan indicates the funds required for operations, typically on a quarterly basis. The apportionment process is used in part to ensure that agencies do not commit all their available funds in less than the 12-month fiscal year. The intent is to avoid the need for supplementary appropriations that involve additional legislation by the Congress.

The apportionment process is substantively important in that program adjustments must be made to bring planned spending into balance with available revenue. Since it is likely that an agency did not obtain the funds requested, either from the President in the preparation phase or from the Congress in the approval phase, plans for the coming fiscal year must be revised. To varying degrees, the apportionment process is also used by state and local governments.

The extent of this process is dependent upon the specificity of the appropriations bill and the powers of the executive. In cases where legislation is highly detailed, there is little discretionary power; for example, the California legislature in 1970 specifically appropriated $800 for the California Heritage Preservation Commission. If the entire appropriations bill had been spelled out in such detail, there would have been no need for agencies to readjust their budgets, because that would have been accomplished already by the legislature.

Additionally, the chief executive may assert control in the apportionment process through an informal item veto. This is accomplished by declining to release some funds to agencies. Thomas Jefferson was the first President known to impound funds. Richard Nixon used impoundment so

---

[6] *Book of the States, 1976–77* (Lexington, Ky.: Council of State Governments, 1976), pp. 124–27.

extensively that Congress attempted to reassert control by passing the 1974 reform legislation. According to this legislation, the President may propose deferrals, temporary postponements of spending, which become effective unless disapproved by a vote in either the House of Representatives or the Senate. Proposed presidential rescissions, proposals not to spend at all, must be approved by both chambers. Although these provisions are law, the constitutional issue remains as to whether the President has an inherent power to impound.

Once apportionments are made, allotments are made within agencies and departments. This process grants budgetary authority to subunits such as bureaus and divisions. Allotments are made on a monthly or quarterly basis and, like the apportionment process, the allotment process is used to control spending during the fiscal year. Control often may be extensive and detailed, requiring approval by the department budget office for any shift in available funds from one item to another, such as from travel to wages. Approval of such transfers may require clearance by the central budget office.[7]

Before an expenditure is made, some form of pre-audit is conducted. Basically, the pre-audit is used to ensure that funds are being committed for approved purposes and that an agency has in its budget sufficient resources to meet the proposed expenditure. The responsibility for this function varies widely, with some jurisdictions having the budget and/or accounting office responsible and others using independently elected controllers or comptrollers. Once approval is granted, the treasurer writes a check for the expenditure.

Audit Audit is the final phase of the budgetary process. The purpose of the audit is undergoing considerable change, but initially the purpose was largely to guarantee executive compliance with the provisions of appropriations bills—particularly, to ensure honesty in dispensing public monies and in preventing needless waste. In accord with these purposes, accounting procedures are prescribed and auditors check the books maintained by agency personnel. In recent years, the scope of auditing has been broadened to encompass studies of whether governmental programs achieve desired results.

In the federal government, considerable controversy was generated

---

[7] The terminology of apportionments and allotments is not consistent at the state level. In some cases, the terms are used interchangeably.

concerning the appropriate organizational location of the audit function. President Woodrow Wilson in 1920 vetoed legislation that would have established the federal budget system on the grounds that he opposed the creation of an auditing office answerable to the Congress rather than the President. Nevertheless, the General Accounting Office (GAO) was established in 1921 by the Budget and Accounting Act and was made an arm of the Congress, with the justification that an audit unit should be created outside of the executive branch so that it could provide objective assessments of expenditure practices. The GAO is headed by the Comptroller General, who is appointed by the President for only one term of 15 years, upon the advice and consent of the Senate. Within the GAO, there are approximately 3,800 professional accounting and auditing employees. During fiscal 1975, the GAO issued 1,043 audits, of which approximately 40 percent were related to defense.[8] Despite the GAO's title, the organization does not maintain accounts but rather audits the accounts of operating agencies. In recent years the GAO has been given responsibility for assessing the results of government programs in addition to the traditional responsibility for financial audits.

At the state and local levels, the issue over organizational responsibility for auditing has been resolved in different ways. The alternatives are to have the audit function performed by a unit answerable to the legislative body, the chief executive, directly to the citizenry, or some combination of these. The use of an elected auditor is defended on the grounds that objectivity can be achieved if the auditor is independent of the executive and legislative branches. The opposing arguments are that the electorate cannot suitably judge the qualifications of candidates for auditor and that the election process necessarily forces the auditor to become a biased rather than an objective analyst. About three-fourths of the states have legislative auditors and 19 have elected auditors; 11 states have two separate audit agencies.[9]

SCRAMBLED BUDGET CYCLES

Though it is easy to speak of a budget cycle, there is no single budget cycle in operation. Rather, a cycle exists for each budget period, and several

---

[8] Comptroller General of the United States, *Annual Report 75* (Washington: U.S. Government Printing Office, 1976), p. 221.

[9] *Book of the States, 1974–75* (Lexington, Ky.: Council of State Governments, 1974), p. 145.

cycles are in operation at any given time. The decision-making process is not one that simply moves from preparation and submission to approval, execution, and, finally, audit. Decision making is complicated by the existence of several budget cycles for which information is imperfect and incomplete. This pattern of overlapping cycles can be seen in Figure 5, which shows the sequencing of five budgets that might be typical of a large state. Only cycle 3 in the diagram displays the complete period covering 39 months. The preparation and submission phase requires at least 9 months, approval 6 months, execution 12 months, and audit 12 months. The same general pattern is found at the federal level, except that the execution phase begins on October 1, giving Congress approximately 9 months to consider the budget. As is indicated by the diagram, three or four budget periods are likely to be in progress at any point in time.

Budget preparation is particularly complicated by this scrambling or intermingling of cycles. In the first place, preparation begins perhaps 15 months or more before the budget is to go into effect. Moreover, much of the preparation phase is completed without knowledge of the legislature's actions in the preceding budget period. At the federal level this has been an especially difficult problem. Congress has been slow in passing appropriation bills and rarely was the approval phase completed by the start of the fiscal year when it began July 1. The usual procedure would be to pass a continuation bill permitting agencies to spend at the rate of the previous year's budget, while Congress continued to deliberate on the new year. Although the new budget calendar gives Congress an additional three months, which is expected to permit completion of the approval phase by

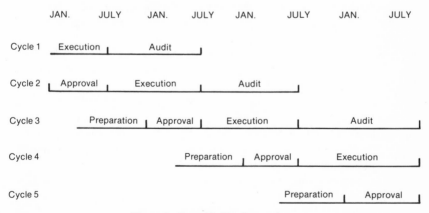

Figure 5. Scrambled budget cycles.

October 1, the problem of agency preparation of the following year's budget request remains. In any given year, an agency would be preparing a budget request during the spring and summer, yet during this same period Congress would be deliberating on the agency's upcoming budget.

At the same time that a budget is being prepared, another one is being executed; this may be the immediately preceding budget year, but it can be the one before. As can be seen in Figure 5, in the early stages of preparation for cycle 4 the execution phase is in operation for cycle 2. Under such conditions, the executive branch may not know the effects of ongoing programs and yet is required to begin a new budget, recommending changes upward or downward. Here, program analysis can be useful, but often such analysis is not completed at the time when decisions must be made. Completing the analysis, also, may be impossible in that there has not been sufficient experience under a given program. On occasion a new program may be created and an agency must recommend changes in the program for inclusion in the next budget without any time for assessing the merits of the program.

The cycle, particularly in the preparation phase, may be even longer than that which has been described so far; this is especially true when agencies must rely upon other agencies or subunits for information. For example, in preparing the education component of a state budget, a department of education will require budget information and requests from state universities and colleges early in order to meet deadlines imposed by the governor's budget office. The reliability and validity of data undoubtedly decrease as the lead time increases. Therefore, the earlier these schools submit their budget requests to the state capital, the less likely it is that such requests will be based upon accurate assessments of future requirements.

Another problem arises from intermingled budget cycles because the three main levels of government are interdependent. For the federal government, its main problem is assessing needs and finding resources to meet these needs. State government must assess its needs and those of local government, and then must search for funds by either raising state taxes, providing for new forms of taxation by local government, or obtaining federal revenues. When a governor prepares a budget, he must take into account whatever information is available concerning the likelihood of certain actions by the President and the Congress. For instance, the President may have recommended a major new medical health program that would significantly increase funds flowing to the states, but considerable doubt revolves around whether and at what level Congress will fund the program. In such a case, should a governor set aside resources for matching requirements in the event that the federal legislation is passed? The problem is worse at the local level, which is dependent for funds upon both the state and federal governments. In recognition of state and local needs for advance information about probable federal actions, the 1974 Congressional Budget and Impoundment Control Act requires that Congress adopt by May 15 of each year "a statement of any significant changes in the proposed levels of Federal assistance to State and local governments."[10]

In addition to these problems, budget cycles are complicated by a lack of uniformity in the budget period. While most state governments have budget years beginning July 1, three states do not—New York's begins April 1, Texas' September 1, and Alabama's corresponds to the federal fiscal year of October 1. Consistency does not even exist within each state. It is common for a state to be on a July 1 fiscal year, while local governments operate under different years, such as January 1, April 1, and September 1. Eleven different fiscal years are used by counties in Georgia.[11]

A case can be made for staggering the budget year for different levels of government; this practice might assist decision makers at one level by providing information about action taken at other levels. For example, the federal government would complete action on its budget by October 1; states could then begin a budget year the following April 1 and local governments July 1. Under such an arrangement, states could base their budgetary decisions upon knowledge regarding available financial support from Washington. Local governments would know the available aid from both Washington and the state capital.

Rearranging the dates for fiscal years is no panacea. Information about financial support from other governments is only one of many items of information used in decision making. Also, any slippage by the legislature in completing its appropriations work by the time a fiscal year begins would dissipate the advantages of staggered budget cycles. Before the federal fiscal year was changed to October 1, Congress almost always deliberated on appropriations beyond July 1, and that practice is not

---

[10] *Congressional Budget and Impoundment Control Act*, Title III, Sec. 301 (1974).

[11] Bureau of the Census, *Finances of County Governments*, 1972 Census of Governments, Vol. 4, No. 3 (Washington: U.S. Government Printing Office, 1974), pp. 88–93.

uncommon at the state level. In addition, there is no direct translation from appropriations to aid to other governments. Money does not automatically flow to states and communities as soon as an appropriations bill is passed by Congress. Instead, these governments must apply for assistance, a process that typically requires many months.[12]

Not only is there a lack of consistency on when budget years begin, but also there is no consistency on the length of the budget period. While the federal government and most local governments operate under annual budgets, 20 states have biennial (two-year) budgets. Under these systems, a governor typically submits his budget in January, and legislative action is supposed to be completed by June 30. The execution phase runs for 24 months beginning July 1. Such a system violates the once-standard principle of annuality.[13] The argument is that annual budgets allow for careful and frequent supervision of the executive by the legislature, and that this serves to guarantee responsibility in government. The problem with the annual budget, however, is that little "breathing time" is available; both the executive and legislative branches are continuously in the throes of budgeting. The biennial approach, on the other hand, relieves participants of many routine budget matters and may allow greater time for more thorough analysis of governmental activities.

One of the greatest dangers of a biennial system is that it may complicate, if not prohibit, prompt response to new conditions. The costs of not being able to adjust to changing conditions may far outweigh any benefits accruing from time saved with biennial budgeting. This consideration may explain why most of the more populous states, with the exceptions of Ohio and Texas, are on annual budget systems.

Still another consideration is whether under "normal" conditions sufficient amounts of new information become available to warrant annual systems. If program analysis were a well established part of the budgetary process, then conceivably new insights into the operations of programs would be a continuous input; in such instances, an annual process may be preferable. In other cases, where decision makers operate one year with

---

[12] See testimony of Robert J. Mowitz in U.S. Congress, Joint Committee on Congressional Operations, *The Federal Fiscal Year as it Relates to the Congressional Budget Process,* 92nd Cong., 1st sess. (Washington: U.S. Government Printing Office, 1971), pp. 179–85.

[13] See J. Wilner Sundelson, "Budgetary Principles," *Political Science Quarterly*, 50 (1935): 236–63. Also see *Annual or Biennial Budgets* (Lexington, Ky.: Council of State Governments, 1972).

virtually the same information as was available the preceding year, there would seem to be little need for annual budgets. Partially for this reason, there has been at least one proposal for abandoning the annual budget cycle for all programs.[14] New programs or proposed changes in existing programs would be submitted in any given year for legislative review, while continuing programs would be reviewed only periodically.

SUMMARY

The four phases of the budget cycle are preparation and submission, approval, execution, and audit. In general, the first and third phases are the responsibility of the executive branch, and the second is controlled by the legislative branch. The fourth phase in the federal system is directed by the General Accounting Office, which is answerable to Congress and not the President. Auditing at the state and local levels often is the responsibility of independently elected officials. A standard criticism of budgeting, especially at the federal level, is that the budget is seldom considered in its entirety. Within the executive branch, only the President and his immediate staff view the budget as a whole, while agencies are primarily concerned only with their own portions of the total. The same disjointed approach has been characteristic of the approval phase at the federal level, although important changes were adopted in 1974 to allow Congress to examine the budget in its entirety.

Budget cycles are intermingled. As many as four budget cycles may be in operation at any one time in a single government. This phenomenon complicates decision making; for example, budget preparation often is forced to proceed without knowledge as to what action the legislature will take on the previous year's budget. Moreover, the interdependent nature of the three levels of government contributes to a scrambling of cycles. One possible adjustment would be for a staggering of cycles. Another possibility would be for conversion to biennial budgets, a practice that is common at the state level.

---

[14] Aaron Wildavsky, "Toward a Radical Incrementalism: A Proposal to Aid Congress in Reform of the Budgetary Process," in Alfred de Grazia, ed., *Congress: The First Branch of Government* (Garden City, N.Y.: Doubleday, 1967), pp. 111–53.

PROGRAM INFORMATION AND BUDGETARY REFORM, 1900-1960

The two general types of information relevant for budgeting are program and resource information (see Chapter 1). The former refers to data about what government does and the accomplishments of those activities; the latter refers to the inputs necessary to perform those activities. The input side, which includes dollars, facilities, equipment, supplies, and manpower, has long been an established feature of budgetary systems. The use of program information, on the other hand, has been slow in developing as an integral part of budgeting.

The critical argument relating to these two types of information is that they must be considered in combination if budgeting is to be a rational process of allocating resources. Looking at what resources are utilized in conjunction with what products and services are provided is fundamental to the systems approach. Neither type of information alone provides sufficient knowledge to serve as a basis for decisions. Since the initial establishment of budgetary systems, therefore, the history of budgetary reform can be viewed as a struggle to develop program data and to link it with resource data.

This chapter examines proposals for reform and attempts at reform up to the early 1960s. Distinguishing between the literature and practice of budgeting is important because the two are not synonymous. In many instances, attempts to convert budget theory into practice have been

63

unsuccessful. The first section of this chapter reviews reform literature. The second section discusses nondefense experiments in budgetary reform. The third topic is the application of budgetary reform to defense, covering the period from World War II to the late 1950s.

SUMMARY OF BUDGETARY REFORM LITERATURE

In order to understand contemporary efforts relating to restructuring and redesigning budgetary systems, it is necessary to recognize the lengthy tradition behind that movement. As we noted in Chapter 1, budgeting can focus on expenditure control, management control, and planning control.[1] While there is some historical pattern to the development of these three emphases, they are not rigidly fixed to specific time periods, and both the management and planning phases have involved greater utilization of program information. Not only is there a blurring of distinctions among these stages in terms of the dates of their popularity, but the advocacy for the use of planning coupled with program information can be dated at least back to the early part of the century. Here we refer to planning as an effort to associate means with ends in order to attain goals and objectives in the future. Planning attempts to utilize knowledge of a system's characteristics to make adjustments in that system in order to produce the desired consequences or end products.

In the 1910s, before the establishment of the federal budgetary system, budgeting was often advocated as a means of allocating resources to obtain program results. Two of the most notable proponents were President William Howard Taft and the 1912 Taft Commission on Economy and Efficiency. In January 1912, Taft sent to Congress a special message in which he said:

> We want economy and efficiency; we want saving, and saving for a purpose. We want to save money to enable the Government to go into some of the beneficial projects which we are debarred from taking up now because we cannot increase our expenditures.[2]

The Taft Commission report reflected the same emphasis upon results:

> In order that he [the administrator] may think intelligently about the subject of his responsibility he must have before him regularly state-

---

[1] Allen Schick, "The Road to PPB: The Stages of Budget Reform," *Public Administration Review*, 26 (1966): 243–58.

[2] William Howard Taft, "Economy and Efficiency in the Government Service," House Doc. No. 458, January, 1912: 16.

ments which will reflect *results in terms of quality and quantity*; he must be able to measure quality and quantity of results by units of cost and units of efficiency [italics added].[3]

Although there was an obvious interest in economizing, in saving dollars, a parallel interest was that of being able to obtain the best return in program terms for resources spent.

There were other important spokesmen for program results in the 1910s. Frederick A. Cleveland suggested that budgeting was the process of deciding what needed to be accomplished and then determining "the financial resources which may be availed of to meet estimated financial needs."[4] Paul T. Beisser was one of the first to advocate unit cost measurement as a means of directly relating resource consumption with the provision of services.[5] Edward A. Fitzpatrick, while fearful of executive budgeting, reasoned that budgeting should be able to relate "how much protection of life and property the citizens are to receive, how much education . . . and other questions."[6] William F. Willoughby was critical of any budget system that was expressed only in terms of dollars. Such systems were considered to fall "far short of furnishing the information needed." According to Willoughby, the budget should show the "work accomplished or to be accomplished [and] the necessity or utility of such work."[7]

Examples of the interest in program information also can be found in the 1920s. One of the most noteworthy articles of the period was written by Lent D. Upson, who was critical of budget systems that concentrated mainly upon keeping government officials honest: "Scarcely a penny is spent for auditing operations, in checking the effectiveness of these honest expenditures."[8] He advocated budgeting as a device for comparing the effectiveness of alternative programs, for striving to produce desired improvements in social fields such as health. A. E. Buck's classic, *Public*

---

[3] Commission on Economy and Efficiency, *The Need for a National Budget*, House Doc. No. 854, 1912: 4–5.

[4] Frederick A. Cleveland, "Evolution of the Budget Idea in the United States," *Annals*, 62 (1915): 16.

[5] Paul T. Beisser, "Unit Costs in Recreational Facilities," *Annals*, 62 (1915): 140–47.

[6] Edward A. Fitzpatrick, *Budget Making in a Democracy: A New View of the Budget* (New York: Macmillan, 1918), p. 27.

[7] William F. Willoughby, *The Problems of a National Budget* (New York: Appleton, 1918), pp. 6 and 9.

[8] Lent D. Upson, "Half-time Budget Methods," *Annals*, 113 (1924): 74.

Budgeting, admittedly was not strongly committed to a program information orientation, but he did express interest in reforms which would
concentrate upon measuring the products of government activities. He
recommended budgeting within a multi-year time frame and criticized
annual or biennial systems as shortsighted.[9]

Writers in the 1930s exhibited the same kind of concern. Wylie
Kilpatrick, in a 1936 article that is strikingly in tune with contemporary
budget reforms, advocated budget systems that looked beyond immediate
governmental activities and instead focused upon the impacts of activities
upon society.[10] Morbidity and infant mortality rates, he suggested, could
be used for evaluating the effectiveness of governmental health programs.
In 1937 the President's Committee on Administrative Management, while
being largely concerned with the structural features of federal budgeting,
expressed an overall interest in reform to serve the purpose of planning.[11]

Although the use of program information and planning was advocated
throughout the first four decades of the century, these ideas received far
greater recognition beginning in the 1940s. V. O. Key, Jr., challenged
previous budgetary literature as largely mechanical and criticized it for
failing to focus upon the "basic budgeting problem" of comparing the
merits of alternative programs: "On what basis shall it be decided to
allocate X dollars to activity A instead of activity B?"[12] Robert A. Walker
and Harold D. Smith, in separate articles, suggested that budgeting should
be reformed to achieve program and financial planning on a multi-year
basis.[13] The 1949 Commission on Organization of the Executive Branch
of the Government, known as the First Hoover Commission, recommended that the federal budget be "based upon function, activities, and
projects: this we designate as a performance budget." Budgeting should be
in terms of "the work or the service to be accomplished."[14] In the same

---

[9] A. E. Buck, *Public Budgeting* (New York: Harper and Brothers, 1929), pp. 8
and 171–72.

[10] Wylie Kilpatrick, "Classification and Measurement of Public Expenditures,"
Annals, 183 (1936): 24.

[11] President's Committee on Administrative Management, *Report* (Washington:
U.S. Government Printing Office, 1937).

[12] V. O. Key, Jr., "The Lack of a Budgetary Theory," *American Political Science
Review*, 34 (1940): 1138.

[13] Robert A. Walker, "The Relation of Budgeting to Program Planning," *Public
Administration Review*, 4 (1944): 97–107; Harold D. Smith, "The Budget as an
Instrument of Legislative Control and Executive Management," *Public Administra-
tion Review*, 4 (1944): 181–88.

[14] Commission on Organization of the Executive Branch of the Government,

year Edward C. Banfield called for planning in terms of program results within a multi-year focus.[15]

More proponents of the same viewpoint emerged in the 1950s. Verne B. Lewis advanced the argument in behalf of marginal analysis to be employed in assessing the relative merits of augmenting one program rather than another.[16] Budgeting was described by Frederick C. Mosher as "the application of double-entry bookkeeping to planning. It compels the consideration of both sides of the ledger—what is to be done and what it is to cost."[17] Catheryn Seckler-Hudson wrote that performance budgeting "basically means a focus of attention on the *ends to be served by the government* rather than on the dollars to be spent."[18] The Second Hoover Commission supported the recommendations of its predecessor and advocated a budget system that evaluated the "relative size of programs."[19] The use of program information in budgeting was suggested by Arthur Smithies as a primary means of improving both executive and legislative decision making.[20] Jesse Burkhead's *Government Budgeting*, while basically descriptive rather than normative, devoted considerable discussion to performance and program budgeting.[21]

By the 1950s the use of program information in budgeting had become the mainstream of reform; at the same time two other schools of thought were emerging. One school, led by David Novick, Charles J. Hitch, Roland McKean, and others, was rooted in a series of technologies that were developed during and after World War II. As will be seen in the following chapter, these technologies were to be highly compatible with the budget

---

Budgeting and Accounting (Washington: U.S. Government Printing Office, 1949), p. 8.

[15] Edward C. Banfield, "Congress and the Budget: A Planner's Criticism," *American Political Science Review*, 43 (1949): 1217–28.

[16] Verne B. Lewis, "Toward a Theory of Budgeting," *Public Administration Review*, 12 (1952): 42–54.

[17] Frederick C. Mosher, *Program Budgeting: Theory and Practice with Particular Reference to the U.S. Department of Army* (Chicago: Public Administration Service, 1954), p. 48.

[18] Catheryn Seckler-Hudson, "Performance Budgeting in the Government of the United States," *Public Finance*, 7 (1954): 328.

[19] Commission on Organization of the Executive Branch of the Government, *Final Report to the Congress* (Washington: U.S. Government Printing Office, 1955); Commission on Organization of the Executive Branch of the Government, *Budget and Accounting* (Washington: U.S. Government Printing Office, 1955).

[20] Arthur Smithies, *The Budgetary Process in the United States* (New York: McGraw-Hill, 1955), pp. 198–225.

[21] Jesse Burkhead, *Government Budgeting* (New York: Wiley, 1956), pp. 133–82.

reform movement and were to serve as the theoretical foundation for planning-programming-budgetings (PPB) systems attempted in the 1960s. The other school, led by Charles E. Lindblom, Aaron Wildavsky, and others, challenged the budget reform movement on the grounds that political decision systems were not readily adaptable to program planning. Lindblom advanced the "muddling through" model of decision making (see Chapter 1), which ran counter to budgetary reform efforts. Wildavsky was to become the most outspoken skeptic of the feasibility of using program information in budgeting. In 1969 he concluded, *"No one knows how to do program budgeting."*[22]

The idea of using program information in budgeting, therefore, is not a recent discovery. Since at least the early 1900s, literature has advocated reforms in budgeting that would link resource and program data in order to plan for the attainment of desired ends in the future. Planning in budgeting is an old concept, but, as will be seen, the practice of budgeting often has fallen short of what reformists have advocated.

SOME NONDEFENSE EXPERIMENTS
IN BUDGETARY REFORM

While the literature on public budgeting has been evolving, so has the practice of budgeting. In this section we review some of the more important experiments that have been attempted in recasting budget systems to rely more extensively upon program information. These efforts range from the 1910s to the 1960s.

One of the earliest and most significant attempts to use budgeting as a vehicle for planning was begun in 1912 in the Borough of Richmond, New York City. A special program and budget system was devised for three functional areas—street cleaning, highways, and sewers. Unit cost data were gathered in great detail, such as the cost per cubic yard of refuse collected. A work plan was devised, indicating what services would be provided under the budget. This in effect was one of the first attempts at what would be called planning-programming-budgeting (PPB) in the 1960s and, more generally, program budgeting in the 1970s. The apparent purpose of the system was to provide accountability to the legislative branch by setting forth what accomplishments could be expected under

---

[22] Aaron Wildavsky, "Rescuing Policy Analysis from PPBS," *Public Administration Review*, 29 (1969): 193.

the budget. The work plan was itself included in the appropriation ordinance.

The major weakness of the system was its rigidity, and this contributed to its abandonment in 1915. Plans were developed well in advance of their implementation date, because considerable time was required for legislative action. By the time the plan had been incorporated into an appropriation ordinance, environmental conditions could have changed significantly, thereby rendering the data and plan obsolete.[23]

In retrospect it seems likely that the Richmond system faltered in part because of its reliance upon detailed information and perhaps excessive detail.[24] Attempting to keep data current was not satisfactorily accomplished. This matter is not a trivial one, for it is directly pertinent to later efforts to install PPB systems.

Turning to the 1930s, there were at least two noteworthy budget reform efforts. In the early 1930s, the U.S. Department of Agriculture established a Uniform Project System that later would be hailed as a forerunner to performance and program budgeting. According to Ralph S. Roberts, the system "convey[ed] an understanding of financial needs in terms of work to be done and ends to be achieved."[25] The other important development occurred in 1938 when the Tennessee Valley Authority converted to a new accounting structure intended to capture financial data in terms of programs (flood control, fertilizer, and the like) as well as the standard object of expenditure format (personal services, travel, and so forth).[26]

A flurry of budget reform activity aimed at bringing greater program data into the budget decision-making process occurred in response to the First Hoover Commission (1949). The proposal was for what was called "performance budgeting." In response to the Commission's recommendation, Congress specifically provided in the National Security Act Amendments of 1949 that performance budgeting be utilized in the military. The following year saw passage of the Budget and Accounting Procedures Act,

---

[23] Buck, *Public Budgeting*, pp. 170–71, 273–75, and 460–63.

[24] Burkhead, *Government Budgeting*, p. 134.

[25] Ralph S. Roberts, "USDA's Pioneering Performance Budget," *Public Administration Review*, 20 (1960): 75. Also see Don S. Burrows, "A Program Approach to Federal Budgeting," *Harvard Business Review*, 27 (1949): 277–78.

[26] Donald C. Kull, *Budget Administration in the Tennessee Valley Authority* (Knoxville: University of Tennessee, 1948), pp. 6–7. Also see Burkhead, *Government Budgeting*, pp. 158–62.

which in essence required performance budgeting for the entire federal government.

Among federal, state, and local agencies, performance budgeting seems to have been geared mainly toward developing work load and unit cost measures of activities. For the Post Office, the number of letters that could be processed by one employee was identified. With this knowledge and an estimate of the number of letters to be processed, the Post Office Department could calculate the manpower required for the coming budget year.[27] New York State, in its attempt at performance budgeting, separated fixed from variable costs to derive unit cost figures for such things as hospital x-ray departments, laundry facilities, and food service. "If, for example, the variable costs for the preceding year in the X-ray Department totalled $4,500, and there had been 3,000 x-ray examinations, the unit cost was $1.50 per x-ray examination."[28]

While it is difficult to reconstruct the past, it would seem that the efforts to install performance budgeting failed. There is little evidence that performance budgeting ever became the basis upon which decisions were made. The above-cited article on New York State's system had an editor's note that by the time the article was printed, the State had halted its experiment in performance budgeting. In other cases, performance budgeting apparently faded into the background without any formal action to abandon the approach. But some lasting effect was evident. Performance budgeting did introduce on a wide scale the use of program information in budget documents, and that type of information was to gain increasing attention in the coming years.

The demise of performance budgeting probably stems largely from the type of program information that was produced. Unit cost and work load data are of limited value to policy makers, such as legislators, chief executives, and department heads. Data of this type provide few insights into the effectiveness of organizational activities, namely whether objectives are being attained. However, unit cost and work load data are useful to managers in judging the efficiency of their organizational units. The efficiency of a school district, for instance, might be measured in terms of the cost per student, but the effectiveness might be measured by whether graduates can read and write, are accepted into universities, or obtain and retain well-paying jobs.

---

[27] See Schick, "The Road to PPB," pp. 252–53.

[28] Marion L. Henry and Willis Proctor, "New York State's Performance Budget Experiment," *Public Administration Review*, 20 (1960): 70.

Performance budgeting really did not disappear altogether. In the first place, many individuals did not make the distinction between performance budgeting as focusing upon work loads and program budgeting as focusing upon the results of governmental activities.[29] Therefore, performance budgeting continues, even though the popularity of the word "program" in the 1960s and 1970s all but buried "performance." Additionally, the use of work load information has not been abandoned. Today the federal budget contains such data as the number of applications processed and the number of loans granted.

One other major experiment worthy of note occurred in the Department of Agriculture in 1962, at a time when the Defense Department was developing and refining its planning-programming-budgeting system. The Department of Agriculture, an early leader in budgetary reform, engaged in an experiment with zero-base budgeting. Under this form of budgeting, each program is challenged for its very existence in every budget cycle (See Chapter 6). Each administrator must justify his unit's *raison d'être* each year. No base or minimum funding level is presumed for any activity. This approach is in direct contradiction with the line of reasoning that rationality defined as a comprehensive assessment of everything is impractical and impossible (see Chapter 1).

The Department of Agriculture experiment failed.[30] Zero-base budgeting, it was found, wasted valuable administrative time by requiring the rehashing of old issues that had already been resolved. The system was unrealistic; many programs were mandatory within the political arena and could not be dismantled no matter how compelling the available data and analysis. The excessive paperwork that was generated could not be reviewed by decision makers within the agency. Employees, dissatisfied with the zero-base method, expressed frustration over having worked strenuously to develop materials that were not read and that seemed to have no significant impact upon the process by which decisions were made.

BUDGETARY REFORMS IN DEFENSE

Budget reforms in defense deserve special treatment, if for no other reason than that defense is the largest single governmental "enterprise." Defense

---

[29] Smithies, *The Budgetary Process*, pp. 83–85.

[30] This discussion is based upon Aaron Wildavsky and Arthur Hammann, "Comprehensive Versus Incremental Budgeting in the Department of Agriculture," *Administrative Science Quarterly*, 10 (1965): 321–46.

is expensive and involves highly complex technology, which together pose some of the most difficult problems for decision making. This section summarizes the budgetary developments that occurred during the 1940s and 1950s; the development of a series of new management techniques that also emerged in defense during this period is reserved for the next chapter.

How performance and/or program budgeting began in defense is debatable. David Novick, perhaps rightfully known as the "father" of program budgeting, identified the beginning as the establishment of the Production Requirements Plan, a scheme he developed in 1941 to assign priorities and allocate resources among competing needs. The technique was refined and redesignated in 1942 as the Controlled Materials Plan and was used throughout World War II. This method, however, was not a budget system in the more familiar sense of dollars; instead, it allocated materials such as copper, steel, and aluminum. The technique, nevertheless, was intended to facilitate decision making along program lines.[31]

One of the most important factors that stimulated reform in defense budgeting was that the distinctions among the missions of the armed services had collapsed by the end of the war. Land, sea, and air combat were no longer sufficiently distinct missions that could be carried out solely by separate services; among other things, this meant that the practice of separate procurement for each service lost much of its rationale. This erosion of distinct missions for each service fostered the suggestion that complete unification of the services should be undertaken, an idea advocated by Secretary of State Stimson and Secretary of War (Army) Patterson. The argument lost, however, to the position of Secretary of the Navy Forrestal that something short of complete amalgamation would be appropriate. The National Security Act of 1947, consequently, created the post of Secretary of Defense to head the military but established the Air Force independent of the Army and allowed the three armed services executive department status.[32]

---

[31] David Novick, "The Origin and History of Program Budgeting," in David Novick, ed., *Program Budgeting*, 2nd ed. (New York: Holt, Rinehart and Winston, 1969), pp. xxi–xxiv.

[32] William A. Niskanen, "The Defense Resource Allocation Process," in Stephen Enke, ed., *Defense Management* (Englewood Cliffs, N.J.: Prentice-Hall, 1967), pp. 5–7; Novick, "The Department of Defense," in Novick, ed., *Program Budgeting*, pp. 81–86. A good organizational analysis of Defense from the 1950s to the early 1970s is Clark A. Murdock, *Defense Policy Formation: A Comparative Analysis of the McNamara Era* (Albany: State University of New York Press, 1974).

Since 1947 two major pieces of legislation have sought to bring the services closer together. Forrestal, who became the first Secretary of Defense, found the new system unsatisfactory; the services continued to operate as separate and competitive entities, with what was considered inadequate attention to a unified approach to defense. At Forrestal's suggestion, Truman submitted to Congress a proposal for a single executive department. The resulting 1949 National Security Act Amendments, while less than had been requested, did grant greater control to the Secretary of Defense and reduced the status of the three uniformed services. Another major step in the direction of unification was the passage of the Defense Reorganization Act of 1958. That legislation provided for unified commands on a mission and theater basis, integrating all services in terms of these commands. The legislation, though bringing the services together in terms of carrying out their missions, left them intact in planning for their respective units. During this period, more uniform procurement practices and standardization of clothing and equipment across the branches were adopted and continued into the 1970s.

In addition to reorganization as an approach for exerting greater control over the defense bureaucracy, fixed-ceiling budgeting was applied, particularly by President Truman in the postwar years. Under this method, the executive prescribes ceilings for departments, which then budget accordingly. Truman utilized an "arithmetic" approach, allowing the military a maximum of one-third of the budget after fixed charges.[33] The merit of such a method is that budget requests from departments are "realistic" in that departments do not request amounts far beyond the capability of the economy or the will of the political system to tax the economy.

The problem with the fixed ceiling method is that a false assumption is made; it is assumed that a rational distribution of funds can first be made before the need for programs is examined. As Lewis has stated the argument, "Prescribing a single fixed ceiling in advance for subordinate levels of the executive branch involves the danger of judging a case before the evidence is heard."[34] The decisions made at lower levels are admittedly within designated financial constraints but do not necessarily reflect actual needs for services. The prescribed ceiling can be either too high or too low. While the fixed ceiling method does keep agency budget requests

---

[33] Mosher, *Program Budgeting*, p. 45.
[34] Lewis, "Toward a Theory of Budgeting," p. 51.

within bounds, the approach tends to disregard environmental conditions to which governmental programs are supposed to respond.

If the military is a sufficient indicator of the strengths and weaknesses of fixed ceilings, the conclusion can be drawn that ceilings are only useful in periods of stability. When environmental conditions are changing rapidly, ceilings tend to be discarded. This was the case during the Korean War. Once committed to the war, the Truman Administration was forced to halt the use of arbitrary ceilings for the military. The practice, however, was reinstated during the Eisenhower Administration. General Maxwell Taylor complained that such guidelines were set without their military implications being determined:

> Economic and budgetary factors have come to play an overriding part in determining military posture. Each year the services receive rigid budget guidelines which control the growth, direction and evolution of the Armed Forces. These guidelines are often set with little knowledge of their strategic implications.[35]

Despite the long tradition among budget reformers that the budget should focus upon program results, ceilings were being set in advance of knowledge of program needs. A continuing problem, then, has been finding some means of planning simultaneously in terms of program needs and costs.[36]

Another important budgetary reform undertaken in defense was the conversion to what was called performance budgeting. This was mandated under Title IV of the 1949 National Security Act Amendments and was in direct response to the First Hoover Commission's recommendations. Much of what was done in the name of performance budgeting was the reduction in the number of appropriations under which a service operated. "The Navy reduced from 52 to 21 titles; the Army from 21 to 8. The new Air Force system provided a total of nine."[37] The intent was to regroup costs so that any one "program" would be funded only from a single appropriation; therefore, program costs would be more easily identifiable.

Another feature of the performance budgeting system was to move toward a single set of budget categories for all uniformed services. In 1950 the Department of Defense adopted a set of eight categories that were to

---

[35] Maxwell Taylor as quoted in William W. Kaufmann, *The McNamara Strategy* (New York: Harper and Row, 1964), p. 28.

[36] See Charles J. Hitch and Roland N. McKean, *The Economics of Defense in the Nuclear Age* (Cambridge, Mass.: Harvard University Press, 1967), pp. 46–48. The book was first published by RAND Corporation in 1960.

[37] Mosher, *Program Budgeting*, p. 84.

be largely adhered to for the next two and a half decades. The categories bore great resemblance to those devised by the Air Force. The new Defense Department categories were 1) military personnel costs, 2) maintenance and operation, 3) major procurement and production costs, 4) acquisition and construction of real property, 5) civilian components, 6) research and development, 7) industrial mobilization, and 8) establishment-wide activities.[38] This set of categories would presumably facilitate comparisons and analyses across organizational lines. Interestingly, the fiscal 1977 defense budget submitted by President Ford used many of these same categories originally adopted in 1950.

Inherent characteristics of defense complicate the use of performance and/or program budgeting; in particular, it is extraordinarily difficult to determine how much defense is enough. The problem is that defense is mainly of a deterrent and preparedness nature. The military is expected to have sufficient strength to deter an attack by a potential aggressor and to be sufficiently prepared for war if it does occur. The deterrent strategy is working when no attack has been launched. The absence of an attack, then, can be interpreted to mean that sufficient deterrence was provided, but this does not reveal whether excessive resources were committed to this end. As for the preparedness argument, that can only be tested in real combat situations. When the nation is not fighting a war, it is difficult to prove conclusively that the nation is or is not sufficiently prepared. These two factors, deterrence and preparedness, have been the main points of contention for decades as to whether defense is being funded adequately.

In light of this problem, performance budgeting, when based on work load and unit cost data, is of limited value; performance budgeting does not address the question of the adequacy of defense. As Mosher indicated, "Performance budgeting might require that funds for basic training be estimated on the basis of the total numbers to be trained and the over-all [per unit] cost of training each man."[39] Such data reveal the cost of training but not the amount of defense being purchased. Over time, the unit cost of training soldiers might be reduced, thereby making the training function increasingly efficient, but this type of data does not indicate whether soldiers are being taught the "right" things or whether the "right" number of soldiers is being trained.

If budgeting for defense is to consider the question of whether enough

---

[38] Mosher, *Program Budgeting*, p. 87.

[39] Mosher, *Program Budgeting*, p. 81.

or too many resources are being committed, then suitable budget categories need to be devised. This point has been stressed particularly by Charles J. Hitch and Roland McKean in their book, *The Economics of Defense in the Nuclear Age* (1960 and 1967). If budgets are to produce useful cost and program information, budget categories need to be established around clusters of activities that produce end products. The categories adopted in 1950 do not meet this criterion. Regarding the budget category of military personnel, Hitch and McKean suggested that the only non-dollar data of much value that has been reported has been the number of personnel in the services, but "since personnel are ingredients rather than end-products, even they are not very helpful."[40] Given that personnel are not one homogeneous mass but, instead, have different skills and perform different functions, data on the total number of personnel cannot produce meaningful insights into the end products of defense. The same argument can be applied to the other categories. The reform efforts in defense during the 1960s, therefore, attempted to resolve this problem through the use of PPB, and that topic is discussed in the next chapter.

SUMMARY

One of the main threads running through budgetary literature has been the need to utilize the budgetary process as a vehicle for planning. In particular, this has meant an attempt to incorporate program data into the system along with resource data, such as dollar and personnel costs. That line of argument dates from the turn of the century. A conflicting argument that emerged in the 1950s and was stressed by political scientists in the 1960s is that budgetary reform efforts have failed to recognize that any form of change will inevitably alter the political process. Some have questioned whether planning and budgeting can be linked, given the nature of the political decision-making process.

Budget reform efforts intended to utilize greater sums of program data have been numerous. Performance and program budgeting have been the main terms employed, though the distinctions between these are tenuous when applied to actual practices. If a distinction is to be made, performance budgeting focuses upon work load and unit cost data, while program budgeting focuses upon end products. One key problem with both of these approaches has been that of collecting usable data and not

---

[40] Hitch and McKean, *The Economics of Defense*, p. 60.

overburdening the powers of decision makers to absorb such data. This overburdening effect occurred in the 1912 experiment in New York City (Richmond) and the zero-base experiment in the U.S. Department of Agriculture in the early 1960s.

The Department of Defense has been an important center for budgetary reform. Since World War II, efforts have been made to bring together the services into a configuration that shows their interrelatedness in terms of missions. Fixed ceilings have been utilized, but this approach tended to disregard needs by first setting financial limits. A uniform set of budgetary categories has been imposed upon the services, allowing some comparisons across organizational lines. However, by the close of the 1950s, no method had been achieved by which the defense budget could be examined in terms of end products. The problem is conpounded by the fact that defense budgeting and planning is based upon deterrence and preparedness strategies.

The experience of budgetary reform has indicated that some things do not work. Exclusive reliance on work load and unit cost data cannot produce the kind of information needed in policy making. Zero-base budgeting is time-consuming and is ineffectual when applied each year to all governmental programs. Fixed-ceiling budgeting distributes resources before considering needs. These failures contributed to another approach to reform: planning-programming-budgeting (PPB) systems.

PLANNING-
PROGRAMMING-
BUDGETING
IN THE 1960s

The 1960s witnessed a flurry of budgetary reform activity. The slogan of the period was "planning-programming-budgeting systems," though many different types of things were done in the name of PPBS or PPB. At the beginning of the period, PPB was probably oversold as providing a solution to the decades-old problem of linking planning with budgeting. By the end of the decade, disenchantment had replaced the earlier enthusiasm. Though the term PPB had lost much of its luster by the early 1970s, the basic emphases and concepts associated with the system survived and are taken for granted in many governmental jurisdictions today. These ideas are part of the thrust to focus budgetary decision making upon the results of governmental activities.

This chapter traces the development of PPB systems in the 1960s. First we discuss a series of management techniques or technologies that had gained wide acceptance by the end of the 1950s. Second, we review the application of these new methods to defense and the operation of the Defense Department's PPB system. The third topic is the attempt to implement PPB in federal civilian agencies. Finally, the chapter considers state and local experiments with PPB.

NONBUDGETARY ANTECEDENTS TO PPB[1]

It is possible to state that PPB was simply part of the historical progression toward the inclusion of program information in government financial decision making, but such a statement is highly misleading. PPB, though compatible with historical trends in budgetary reform, grew out of a different set of conceptualizations. At least six closely related fields were important: operations research (OR), economic analysis, general systems theory, cybernetics, computer hardware, and systems analysis. Computers are included here, though they are machinery rather than a set of ideas, because this hardware was to perform an important function in the other five fields. The purpose of each of these technologies, or theories, developed from around the turn of the century but particularly during and after World War II, was to enhance the capabilities for managing organizations and their resources. Budgeting per se was of limited interest to the leading theorists in each of these fields. The more important focus was upon using systems' resources to achieve desired systems' goals. Such a concern, however, obviously had budgetary implications, and in a sense, one can say that these six fields backed into budgeting.

Because emergent disciplines have no fixed boundaries, these six areas cannot be treated as discrete entities. The exchange of ideas and information among them makes it impossible to draw clear-cut distinctions, and it should be stressed that today all six are sometimes treated as an integral whole, often under the heading of systems analysis. Yet, while each is related to the others, each also has its own original sources.

Not only has cross-fertilization been common among these fields but also it has been common with these vis-à-vis budgeting and planning. Neither budgeters nor planners suddenly learned of OR and the like on some given date in the early 1960s. Indeed, many of the ideas involved found their way into budgeting and planning before the advent of PPB. The previous chapter's discussion of budget reform efforts up to the 1960s, therefore, is not extraneous; reforms did lead to changes in the practice of budgeting. The point is not that PPB was a totally alien set of conceptions that was sprung upon public budgeting in the early 1960s. Rather, what is important is that the budget reform movement did get substantial stimulus from sources somewhat removed from budgeting.

OR, like the other fields to be discussed, defies precise definition, but

---

[1] The early thinking on this section was suggested by Robert J. Mowitz, Director of the Institute of Public Administration, The Pennsylvania State University.

an acceptable one is, ". . . the use of the scientific method to provide criteria for decisions concerning man-machine systems involving repeatable operations."[2] OR seeks to deal with problems resulting from the relationships among men and machines, the intent being to find optimal solutions to precisely posed problems. The focus is upon repetitive or recurrent operations.

The beginning of OR can be dated to 1872 when the British introduced the use of war games.[3] The problem was to find optimal means of using men and equipment in the conduct of war. The works of Frederick W. Taylor, an industrial engineer, also were precursors to the rise of OR. Beginning about 1880, Taylor dealt with such mundane but real industrial problems as the optimal dimensions of coal shovels used in stoking furnaces and the best means of loading and unloading railroad cars. More generally, Taylor sought means of producing the best results with minimum worker fatigue. His research gave rise to a new approach to management, "scientific management."[4] Other important antecedents to OR involved military applications during World War I: in England F. W. Lanchester dealt with problems of firepower; in the United States Thomas A. Edison studied antisubmarine warfare.[5]

Though these preliminary efforts were important to the rise of OR, most observers date its actual beginning to the resolution of military problems immediately before and during World War II. In England, Sir Henry Tizard and his associates, starting in 1935, began work that eventually led to the development of radar and, equally important, to methods of operation in the use of radar.[6] Following American entry into the war, the U.S. Army, Army Air Force, and Navy established OR teams. In the studies that were subsequently undertaken, the purpose was to improve the use of weaponry and manpower. Significantly, the persons who developed this field were primarily engineers, mathematicians, and physicists—not budgeters.

[2] David S. Stoller, *Operations Research: Process and Strategy* (Berkeley: University of California Press, 1964), p. 11.

[3] Maurice F. Ronayne, "Operations Research Can Help Public Administrators in Decision-Making," *International Review of Administrative Sciences,* 29 (1963): 227.

[4] Frederick W. Taylor, *The Principles of Scientific Management* (New York: Harper and Brothers, 1911).

[5] Stoller, *Operations Research,* p. 4.

[6] Alec M. Lee, *Systems Analysis Frameworks* (New York: Wiley, 1970), pp. 124–25; C. P. Snow, *Science and Government* (Cambridge, Mass.: Harvard University Press, 1961).

For many observers, OR came to be no more than the application of the scientific method to the operations of a system.[7] OR involves the specification of objectives, the design of a model representing the situation under investigation, and the collection and application of relevant data. The result is a set of highly quantitative techniques used in the analysis of data. These techniques include linear programming, queuing theory, game theory, and Monte Carlo techniques.[8]

Following the war, the scope of OR expanded as it was used to study civilian problems such as the routing of Post Office trucks to collect mail and the determination of the optimum number of check-out stands in stores. The term "management science" entered the vocabulary and came to be equated with OR. By 1959, Stafford Beer, a noted leader in the field, was able to state that OR was not the application of the scientific method or a science but was science itself.[9]

The second related field is cost benefit, cost effectiveness, cost utility, or, as used in this work, economic analysis.[10] The problems associated with analysis in general and economic analysis in particular are discussed in Chapter 7, but here it is important to note that such analysis is intended to determine whether the value of the benefits of a program or facility exceeds the costs. Such analysis can be used in evaluating possible alternatives. The purpose is to improve choice capability through the use of predictive instruments as to the likely consequences of possible alternatives.

Engineers must be given much credit for the early phases of economic analysis, but in recent decades economists have played more important roles. A. R. Prest and R. Turvey date economic analysis back to 1844 and J. Dupuit's paper on the utility of public works.[11] Arthur M. Wellington's *The Economic Theory of Railway Location,* published in 1887, can also

---

[7] C. West Churchman, Russel L. Ackoff, and E. Leonard Arnoff, *Introduction to Operations Research* (New York: Wiley, 1957), p. 18.

[8] For a discussion of these and other techniques, see Richard A. Johnson, Fremont E. Kast, and James E. Rosenzweig, *The Theory and Management of Systems,* 3rd ed. (New York: McGraw-Hill, 1973), pp. 205–21.

[9] Stafford Beer, "What Has Cybernetics to Do with Operational Research?," *Operational Research Quarterly,* 10 (March, 1959): 1–21.

[10] For a survey of economic analysis, see A. R. Prest and R. Turvey, "Cost-Benefit Analysis: A Survey," *Economic Journal,* 75 (1965): 683–735.

[11] J. Dupuit, "On the Measurement of Utility of Public Works," *International Economic Papers,* 2 (1844).

be cited as one of the first works in the field.[12] By the turn of the century, the Army Corps of Engineers had developed various techniques of tracing benefits derived from their programs, partly in order to assess localities for partial costs. Many of the contemporary economic theories of making choices in light of benefits and costs originated from the London School of Economics during the 1920s and 1930s.[13] A benchmark in the development of the field was the 1950 "Green Book" of the Subcommittee on Benefits and Costs of the Federal Inter-Agency River Basin Committee. This document attempted to codify and rank criteria for analysis.[14] Another major publication related to analysis and water resources was Roland N. McKean's 1958 book, *Efficiency in Government through Systems Analysis, with Emphasis on Water Resource Development.*[15] By the close of the 1950s, economic analysis had become a rather sophisticated and technical art.

The third field is that of general systems theory. As will be recalled from Chapter 1, a system is most simply defined as a set of units and the relationships among the units. Systems theory strives to find similarities in the structures and functioning of systems, regardless of the specific nature of the systems. The intent is to bridge two or more particular disciplines in order to avoid situations in which members of one discipline are unable to communicate with those of another. As Kenneth E. Boulding has written, "One wonders sometimes if science will not grind to a stop in an assemblage of walled-in hermits, each mumbling to himself words in a private language that only he can understand."[16]

Often operations research and systems theory are treated as if they were identical, but they originated from different sources. OR arose out of work by physical scientists and engineers, while systems theory was

---

[12] Arthur M. Wellington, *The Economic Theory of Railway Location* (New York: Wiley, 1887).

[13] James M. Buchanan, *Cost and Choice: An Inquiry in Economic Theory* (Chicago: Markham, 1969).

[14] Inter-Agency River Basin Committee, *Proposed Practices for Economic Analysis of River Basin Projects* (Washington: U.S. Government Printing Office, 1950). See Arthur Maass, "Benefit-Cost Analysis: Its Relevance to Public Investment Decisions," *Quarterly Journal of Economics*, 80 (1966): 208–26.

[15] This work overlaps greatly with other fields, especially operations research and systems analysis. Roland N. McKean, *Efficiency in Government through Systems Analysis, with Emphasis on Water Resource Development* (New York: Wiley, 1958).

[16] Kenneth E. Boulding, "General Systems Theory—The Skeleton of Science," *Management Science*, 2 (1956): 198.

primarily the product of biological scientists. Unlike OR, which was largely a by-product of war, systems theory was a product of the study of biological organisms. K. Ludwig von Bertalanffy, starting in the 1920s, broke from the popular biological emphasis upon the cell to concentrate upon organs in their relationships to one another. His 1951 article on general system theory is frequently cited as a benchmark in the field.[17] Other leaders in the field included bio-mathematician Anatol Rapoport, physiologist Ralph W. Gerard, and economist Kenneth E. Boulding.[18]

Cybernetics and information theory constitute the fourth important field. The term "cybernetics" was derived from a Greek word meaning "steersman" by Norbert Wiener, a mathematician. Cybernetics, then, is the science of control and communication.[19]

This field, like the others that have been discussed, can be traced to the turn of the century. Two physicists, Ludwig Bolzmann in Germany and Willard Gibbs in the United States, challenged the Newtonian approach in physics that sought universal laws; these men introduced the concept of probability to physics. Wiener wrote, "This revolution has had the effect that physics now no longer claims to deal with what will always happen, but rather with what will happen with an overwhelming probability."[20] Thus, determinism was replaced with "probabilism."

Cybernetics was not recognized as a discipline or subdiscipline until World War II.[21] Cybernetics was used in the development of servo-mechanisms, self-regulating systems that adjusted in accord with new inputs of information. Radar was joined with antiaircraft artillery in such a way that the velocity, direction, and altitude of a target were related to the properties of antiaircraft weaponry. Physicists, electrical engineers, and mathematicians were responsible for many of these developments. By the late 1940s cybernetics had become an established field of research.[22]

---

[17] Ludwig von Bertalanffy, "General System Theory: A New Approach to Unity of Science," *Human Biology,* 23 (1951): 303–61.

[18] See Ludwig von Bertalanffy, *General Systems Theory: Foundations, Development, Applications* (New York: Braziller, 1968), pp. 10–15 and 89–94; Anatol Rapoport, *Strategy and Conscience* (New York: Harper and Row, 1964).

[19] Norbert Wiener, *The Human Use of Human Beings* (Garden City, N.Y.: Doubleday, 1956), p. 16.

[20] Wiener, *Human Use of Human Beings,* p. 10.

[21] See Norbert Wiener, Arturo Rosenblueth, and Julian Bigelow, "Behavior, Purpose, and Teleology," *Philosophy of Science,* 10 (1943): 18–24.

[22] See Norbert Wiener, *Cybernetics* (New York: Wiley, 1948); Claude Shannon and Warren Weaver, *The Mathematical Theory of Communication* (Urbana: Uni-

The fifth field, the computer, is not a form of management technology but rather a machine or piece of hardware. Its importance is that it allows for complex data manipulations that previously were impossible or impractical. Charles Babbage, an English mathematician, is usually recognized as the main forerunner in the development of the computer. In 1823 he designed a "difference engine" and in 1833 an "analytical engine." Both were giant machines to be powered by steam and were intended to serve as calculating devices. Because of the technical limitations of the day, the engines were never built. One of Babbage's ideas, the use of punched cards, was adopted later by Herman Hollerith, a statistician working for the U.S. Census Bureau, and cards were used for the first time in the 1890 national census.

Computers began to take real form by the 1920s, though they were not to become reliable devices until the 1940s. In 1925 Vannevar Bush of the Massachusetts Institute of Technology constructed an analogue computer powered by electricity. Ten years later Bush and his associates built another computer that employed electrical switches in place of the gears that had previously served as counting devices. In 1944, the first fully automatic computer, the Mark I, was placed in operation. This was the product of Howard Aiken, a physicist, in conjunction with IBM engineers.[23]

Many of the initial applications of computers dealt with routine operations as distinguished from problem solving. Routine functions included storage of payroll data and the printing of checks. Researchers in operations research, economic analysis, and other fields, however, came to recognize the value of computers in testing models and in calculating the outcomes of possible alternatives. By the 1950s, computers had gained considerable acceptance in this regard, especially in terms of their military applications.

Systems analysis is the sixth and newest field. Its rise during the 1950s

versity of Illinois Press, 1949); J. von Neumann and O. Morgenstern, *Theory of Games and Economic Behavior* (Princeton, N.J.: Princeton University Press, 1947); Magorah Maruyama, "Cybernetics," in Fremont J. Lyden and Ernest G. Miller, eds., *Planning-Programming-Budgeting: A Systems Approach to Management* (Chicago: Markham, 1967), pp. 330–34.

[23] Much of the above discussion is based upon William G. Ouchi, "A Short History of the Development of Computer Hardware," in Thomas L. Whisler, *Information Technology and Organizational Change* (Belmont, Cal.: Wadsworth, 1970), pp. 129–34. Also see John A. Postley, *Computers and People* (New York: McGraw-Hill, 1960).

in many respects marks the breakdown in distinctions among the other fields that have been discussed. Systems analysis is eclectic in that it draws upon all of the above areas, and some observers today treat all of these as synonymous.[24] For some writers, systems analysis is the application of the scientific method, while for others it is "nothing more than quantitative or enlightened common sense aided by modern analytical methods." [25]

OR or at least its early versions can be distinguished from systems analysis. The latter considers alternative values in conducting analysis, whereas the former often operates within the limits of prescribed values. OR begins with the assumption that X is desired, and then attempts to design or revise a system in order to produce X. Systems analysis is not so delimited. Moreover, OR is commonly applied to repetitive problems having a narrow focus, but systems analysis deals with broader problems. Given that systems analysis works with varying value judgments and problems of greater scope, statistical techniques and computer applications may be more limited than in OR. The definition of systems analysis as the application of common sense is based upon the assumption that the scientific method does not allow for values to intervene in analysis, whereas common sense does not preclude such distortions.

Because systems analysis borrows extensively from many fields, citing a date for its beginning is difficult. Generally, one can say that it arose in connection with military problems faced following World War II and that persons associated with the RAND Corporation, a private consulting firm working mainly for the Air Force, were the major contributors to its development. Two of the most important early works in this field were McKean's *Efficiency in Government through Systems Analysis, with Emphasis on Water Resource Development* (1958) and Hitch and McKean's *The Economics of Defense in the Nuclear Age* (1960 and 1967).[26]

Although this series of events was outside the mainstream of budget reform, it served as the basis for major efforts in budgetary reform during the 1960s. As work developed in operations research, economic analysis, systems analysis, and the like, researchers almost backed into budgeting.

---

[24] Gene H. Fisher, *The Analytical Bases of Systems Analysis* (Santa Monica, Cal.: The RAND Corporation, May, 1966).

[25] Alain C. Enthoven, "The Systems Analysis Approach," in Harley H. Hinrichs and Graeme M. Taylor, eds., *Program Budgeting and Benefit-Cost Analysis* (Pacific Palisades, Cal.: Goodyear, 1969), p. 160.

[26] McKean, *Efficiency in Government;* Charles J. Hitch and Roland N. McKean, *The Economics of Defense in the Nuclear Age* (Cambridge, Mass.: Harvard University Press, 1967). The Hitch and McKean book was first published by the RAND Corporation in 1960.

As will be seen shortly, the introduction of the systems approach to government financial decision making was not an easy process. By the mid-1960s, however, the systems approach, at least in theory, had gained wide acceptance. A landmark in the literature was the volume edited by David Novick of RAND, *Program Budgeting* (1965 and 1969). This was the first major publication to treat public budgeting within a systems framework.[27]

MILITARY PPB

The techniques discussed in the preceding section were the foundation for the establishment of PPB in the Department of Defense in early 1961. Many of these techniques were not foreign to Defense but rather had been developed under the aegis of the Department. Considerable analytic capability was a part of Defense when Robert S. McNamara became Secretary in 1961. PPB was an extension of the developments that occurred in the 1940s and 1950s (see Chapter 4) and not a revolutionary break from the past.

There are several reasons why PPB started in Defense. Probably the most important one was that despite the authority to manage the military, the Secretary did not have the management support necessary. Secretary McNamara wrote:

> From the beginning in January, 1961, it seemed to me that the principal problem in efficient management of the Department's resources was not the lack of management authority. . . . The problem was rather the absence of the essential management tools needed to make sound decisions on the really crucial issues of national security.[28]

While McNamara surely was not the sole high official in the federal government having this sense of inability to manage, he must be recog-

---

[27] David Novick, ed., *Program Budgeting: Program Analysis and the Federal Budget* (Cambridge, Mass.: Harvard University Press, 1965), 2nd ed. (New York: Holt, Rinehart and Winston, 1969); E. S. Quade, *Systems Analysis Techniques for Planning-Programming-Budgeting* (Santa Monica, Cal.: The RAND Corporation, March, 1966).

[28] Robert S. McNamara, *The Essence of Security: Reflections in Office* (New York: Harper and Row, 1968), p. 88; Also see Henry L. Trewhitt, *McNamara: His Ordeal in the Pentagon* (New York: Harper and Row, 1971), and William A. Lucas and Raymond H. Dawson, *The Organizational Politics of Defense* (Pittsburgh: International Studies Association, University of Pittsburgh, 1974), pp. 81–100.

nized as having had the will to take steps to alter the status quo. "The role that McNamara chose was not an inevitable one."[29] He could have performed a traditional role, simply acting as referee among competing segments of the defense establishment.

The preceding chapter noted several of the reasons why new management techniques were considered necessary in Defense especially after World War II. Those reasons had not evaporated by 1961. The lack of clear-cut missions for the specific services intensified the need for a management approach that would consider the defense system as a whole. The increasing cost of weapons systems following the war also dramatized the need for improved planning and budgeting; errors became increasingly expensive. Time for contingency planning was contracted due to new weapons systems; minutes replaced weeks and months in terms of the time available to respond to situations. This shortening of response time required an extension of planning horizons. Finally, the fixed-ceiling approach to budgeting was deemed unsatisfactory. Under that method of budgeting, dollar limits upon military activities were prescribed before determination of program needs.[30] (Fixed-ceiling budgeting is discussed in Chapters 4 and 6.)

When McNamara took charge in 1961, he brought with him several people who had been associated with the RAND Corporation. RAND, a nonprofit "think tank," earlier had done extensive developmental work related to program budgeting. David Novick of RAND published reports in the 1950s recommending such a system for defense.[31] The McKean book on systems analysis (1958) and the Hitch and McKean book on defense (first published in 1960) were also RAND products.[32] The key person for PPB under McNamara was Charles J. Hitch, who became Assistant Secretary of Defense (Comptroller). Alain C. Enthoven was made head of the Office of Systems Analysis within the Comptroller's Office. In 1965, the analysis unit was separated, and Enthoven became Assistant Secretary for Systems Analysis. Hitch resigned in 1965 and was succeeded by Robert N. Anthony of the Harvard Business School.

---

[29] Alain C. Enthoven and K. Wayne Smith, *How Much is Enough? Shaping the Defense Program, 1961–1969* (New York: Harper and Row, 1971), p. 32.

[30] See David Novick, "The Department of Defense," in Novick, ed., *Program Budgeting*, 2nd ed., pp. 81–119.

[31] David Novick, *Efficiency and Economy in Government Through New Budgeting and Accounting Procedures* (Santa Monica, Cal.: RAND, June, 1956).

[32] McKean, *Efficiency in Government*; Hitch and McKean, *Economics of Defense*.

Simply stated, McNamara, Hitch, and the others sought to link planning with budgeting, which hitherto had operated independently. "These critically important functions were performed by two different groups of people—the planning by the military planners and the budgeting by the civilian Secretaries and the comptroller organizations."[33] Not only were these different operations, but the time horizons also varied. Budgeting looked ahead mainly to the next budget year, while military planning extended to intermediate and long-range time perspectives. The purpose of the Defense reforms of the 1960s, then, was what had been emphasized for decades in budgetary literature. The difference was that the Defense PPB was oriented in the systems approach to decision making.

The origin of the phrase "planning-programming-budgeting" is uncertain. Mosher used the term in his 1954 book on Army program budgeting.[34] During the early 1960s in Defense, PPB stood for program package budgeting, because a package was presented in terms of the resource inputs (personnel, equipment, and so forth) and outputs.[35] By 1965, when President Lyndon B. Johnson extended the system to civilian agencies, PPB had come to mean planning-programming-budgeting. It should be recognized that planning and programming are not distinctly different functions but rather differ only in degree. The terms have been defined as follows:

Planning is the production of the range of meaningful potentials for selection of courses of action through a systematic consideration of alternatives. *Programming* is the more specific determination of the manpower, material, and facilities necessary for accomplishing a program.[36]

At least in theory, the Defense PPB system was built upon the Joint Strategic Objectives Plan (JSOP), prepared annually by the Joint Chiefs of Staff since 1955–56. JSOP projects military forces on a multi-year basis, normally for 5 to 10 years. The problem with JSOP has always been that it tends to be simply an aggregation of "requirements" determined by the individual services without much guidance from the Office of the Secre-

---

[33] Charles J. Hitch, *Decision-Making for Defense* (Berkeley: University of California, 1965), p. 25.

[34] Frederick C. Mosher, *Program Budgeting: Theory and Practice with Particular Reference to the U.S. Department of the Army* (Chicago: Public Administration Service, 1954), pp. 47–77.

[35] Robert J. Massey, "Program Packages and the Program Budget in the Department of Defense," *Public Administration Review,* 23 (1963): 30–34.

[36] Novick, "Department of Defense": 91.

tary of Defense. The requirements set by JSOP, therefore, have been "blue sky," identifying needs far beyond the willingness of the decision system to commit resources to meet the plan's specifications; requirements regularly exceeded budget ceilings by 25 to 35 percent.[37] For some observers, JSOP indicated the greed of the uniformed services, while for others it unfairly forced the Joint Chiefs to "blue sky" defense so that the Secretary of Defense, the President, and Congress could take credit for cutbacks in military requests.[38] Whatever the case, JSOP was not part of the budget process before PPB. The plan was received by the Secretary of Defense and simply filed.[39] After the introduction of PPB, there was still great doubt whether JSOP played any major role in Defense decision making.[40]

The central component of the Defense system is the Five-Year Defense Program (FYDP); in the early years of the system the plan was called the Five-Year Force Structure and Financial Program. "The FYDP is an 8-year projection of forces and a 5-year projection of costs and manpower arranged in mission-oriented programs."[41] These mission-oriented programs form what is called the program structure, a classification system that begins with broad missions that are factored into subunits and activities. The structure groups like activities together, regardless of which branches of the services conduct them, thereby allowing for analyses across organizational lines. The major programs within the FYDP are strategic forces; general-purpose forces; intelligence and communications; airlift and sealift; guard and reserve forces; research and development; central supply and maintenance; training, medical, and other general personnel activities; administration and associated activities; and support of other nations. Once approved by the Secretary, the FYDP is binding on all military units.

During the 1960s, changes in the five-year program were made through the following procedures: If no major changes were to occur, all that

---

[37] Lucas and Dawson, *Organizational Politics of Defense,* p. 87.

[38] Grover Heiman, "Defense Reverses PPB Process," *Armed Forces Management,* 16 (1970): 43.

[39] Charles J. Hitch, "Program Budgeting," *Datamation,* 13 (1967): 37–40.

[40] Keith C. Clark and Laurence J. Leger, eds., *The President and the Management of National Security* (New York: Praeger, 1969), p. 186.

[41] Alain C. Enthoven and K. Wayne Smith, "The Planning, Programming, and Budgeting System in the Department of Defense: Current Status and Next Steps," in U.S. Congress, Joint Economic Committee, Subcommittee on Economy in Government, *The Analysis and Evaluation of Public Expenditures: The PPB System,* 91st Cong, 1st sess. (Washington: U.S. Government Printing Office, 1969), p. 956.

would be required would be an annual updating of the FYDP. Changes were introduced by the Draft Presidential Memorandum (DPM—now MPM, Major Program Memorandum) usually originating in Systems Analysis. While technically DPMs were the Secretary's response to the JSOP, in fact they were developed largely independent of this and reflected the Secretary's judgments on major issues, based upon analyses that had been conducted. The uniformed services, then, responded to these documents by submitting Program Change Requests (PCR) (variously called Program Change Proposals or Program Adjustment Requests). The Secretary's actions on these documents were transmitted via Program Change Decisions (PCD). The Program Change Decisions were used to update the Five-Year Defense Program.[42]

PPB in Defense, then, is based upon the limited rationality model of decision making (see Chapter 1). The FYDP organizes all Defense activities on a multi-year basis within a mission context. The FYDP, therefore, is a comprehensive plan and serves as a baseline from which incremental decisions are made. The increments are added to the plan through the DPM-PCR-PCD process.

Early controversy arose over the role of the Assistant Secretary for Systems Analysis in this change process. The contention was that Draft Presidential Memoranda tended to lock up the decision-making process before the services had an opportunity to respond. A continuing concern has been that the process has resulted in excessive centralization, though the opposing argument is that centralization was long overdue. There may well have been a tendency on the part of some participants to derogate the PPB system because decisions were made that to them seemed wrong.[43]

The basic structure of the PPB system developed in 1961 ". . . continues as the framework for the planning and execution of the defense program."[44] The press reported that the administrations after Presidents Kennedy and Johnson were more sympathetic to the military, but the overall decline in Defense budgets, including the budget requests made by Presidents Nixon and Ford, suggests the point is debatable. Nevertheless, changes were made to provide a greater role for the Joint Chiefs of Staff

---

[42] For a good summary of the process, see Steven Lazarus, "Defense PPBS—A 1969 Overview," *Defense Industry Bulletin,* 5 (June, 1969): 19–22.

[43] See William W. Kaufmann, *The McNamara Strategy* (New York: Harper and Row, 1964), pp. 168–203.

[44] *Annual Defense Department Report, FY1977* (Washington: U.S. Government Printing Office, 1976), p. 235.

and the services. In early 1970, "tentative fiscal guidance" was provided to these units through the issuance of a Strategic Guidance Memorandum by the Secretary. This marked a partial return to the use of budget ceilings that had been abandoned in 1961. Under the revised system the Joint Chiefs of Staff submit a Joint Strategic Objectives Plan but later issue to the military a Joint Force Memo, a projection of force requirements within the limits prescribed by "fiscal guidance." The military departments, in turn, respond by submitting Program Objective Memoranda (formerly the Program Change Requests), and the Secretary responds with Program Decision Memoranda (formerly Program Change Decisions). A weakened Office of Systems Analysis after McNamara also contributed to the military's regaining some policy initiative.[45]

Through the 1960s and into the 1970s, the format of the Defense budget submitted to Congress did not change appreciably. As was discussed in Chapter 4, the budget categories adopted in Defense in 1950 were much like those in use more than 25 years later. The fiscal 1977 budget had the categories of military personnel; operation and maintenance; procurement; research, development, test, and evaluation; military construction; family housing; civil defense; special foreign currency program; and revolving and management funds. Within each of these can be found a breakout according to the missions cited above. According to Hitch, one reason for not changing the budget was that congressmen are accustomed to the established procedure. He added that the old system was "easier for an appropriations committee." These budget categories were also defended on the grounds that they are useful for the operation of the Defense Department as distinguished from planning.[46]

In 1965 Hitch said, "The planning-programming-budgeting system is now well established and is working smoothly."[47] However, there is a difference between a smoothly functioning operation and an effective one. By the early 1970s, the effectiveness of the entire defense establishment, including PPB, was severely challenged.

Controversies over the military necessarily detracted from the acclaim that PPB had received in the early 1960s, no matter how removed PPB was

---

[45] Heiman, "Defense Reverses PPB Process," and *The New York Times*, September 29, 1969. See also Clark Murdock, *Defense Policy Formation: A Comparative Analysis of the McNamara Era* (Albany: State University of New York Press, 1974), pp. 44–137 and 167–79.

[46] Hitch, *Decision-Making for Defense*, pp. 29–30.

[47] Hitch, *Decision-Making for Defense*, p. 63.

from the specific controversy at hand. The Southeast Asia War had yielded dismal and tragic results. The Pentagon Papers, a multi-volume series of reports tracing the U.S. entry into Vietnam, raised serious questions as to whether analysis had been relied upon to any major extent in charting the nation's commitment in Southeast Asia.[48] Cost problems associated with the Air Force supercargo plane, the C-5A, and cost and technical problems related to the F-111 aircraft necessarily raised doubts about the competency of Defense management.[49]

None of these problems actually tested the value of PPB. Failures to conduct a war successfully, to keep costs down on weapons systems, or to produce an effective aircraft only prove that errors in judgment were made. PPB does not make decisions, either right or wrong, but merely supplies information to decision makers. As Enthoven has warned regarding the evaluation of PPB vis-à-vis the F-111, "Whether a good or a bad job of aeronautical engineering is done at some point, doesn't necessarily prove that the management system is good or bad."[50] Perhaps of equal importance is that PPB has played only a limited or nonexistent role in some of the most controversial military issues. For example, the F-111 decision was made outside of the PPB process; the Comptroller's Office was not consulted on the matter.[51] To allege that every failure in the Defense Department is because of PPB is clearly unjustified.

FEDERAL CIVILIAN PPB

Impressed with the changes in the Defense Department, President Lyndon B. Johnson announced on August 25, 1965 that the PPB system was to be applied to civilian agencies. Before cabinet members and agency heads, he stated:

> This program is aimed at finding new ways to do new jobs faster, better, less expensively; to insure sounder judgment through more accurate information; to pinpoint those things we ought to do more,

---

[48] See *The New York Times,* June–July, 1971.

[49] See Robert J. Art, *The TFX Decision: McNamara and the Military* (Boston: Little, Brown, 1968).

[50] Alain C. Enthoven in U.S. Senate, Committee on Government Operations, Subcommittee on National Security and International Operations, *Hearings: Planning-Programming-Budgeting,* 90th Cong., 1st sess. (Washington: U.S. Government Printing Office, 1967), p. 89.

[51] Enthoven in Subcommittee on National Security, *Hearings,* pp. 91–92.

and to spotlight those things we ought to do less; to make our decision-making process as up-to-date as our space-exploring equipment. In short, we want to trade in our surreys for automobiles, our old cannon for new missiles.[52]

This action was to spark massive reform efforts throughout all levels of government in the United States.[53]

The federal civilian PPB system was similar in structure to the Defense model. Corresponding to the Defense FYDP were the Program and Financial Plans (PFP).[54] These documents were to be based upon program structure having three levels—program categories, subcategories, and elements (see the following chapter for a general discussion of program structure). Comparable to the Draft Presidential Memoranda in Defense, the Bureau of the Budget (BOB) (later renamed the Office of Management and Budget (OMB)) was to identify major program issues to which departments were expected to respond. Departments in turn would propose changes by submitting Program Memoranda (PMs) to the Budget Bureau: the PMs corresponded to the Program Change Requests used in Defense. No provision was made for a document corresponding to the Defense Program Change Decision. Analyses used in PPB were to be called Special Studies or later Special Analytic Studies (SASs).[55]

The PPB experiment in the federal government would have completely altered the calendar from the pre-PPB era. Under PPB the process would begin with important guidance from BOB identifying major issues and suggesting specific analyses that would be needed. The first six to nine months of the preparation process was to focus on agency programs and plans with budgetary decisions flowing from these prior negotiations between agencies and BOB. Practice never reached these aspirations.

Coming into office in January 1969, the Nixon Administration initially did not abandon PPB but did retrench. The focus of the system was shifted from the development of program structures and Program and

---

[52] Lyndon B. Johnson, *Public Papers of the Presidents of the United States,* 2 (Washington: U.S. Government Printing Office, 1966), p. 916.

[53] See Leonard Merewitz and Stephen H. Sosnick, *The Budget's New Clothes* (Chicago: Markham, 1972); Harold A. Hovey, *The Planning-Programming-Budgeting Approach to Government Decision-Making* (New York: Praeger, 1968).

[54] Documentation of the structure and event schedules may be found in Budget Bureau Bulletin No. 66-3, issued October 12, 1965; revised in 1967 (No. 68-2) and in 1968 (No. 68-9).

[55] See Charles L. Schultze (former Director of the U.S. Bureau of the Budget), *The Politics and Economics of Public Spending* (Washington: Brookings, 1968).

Financial Plans to analysis.[56] Those PFPs that had been developed apparently had been of limited value. Analysis, however, was also curtailed. Major Policy Issues were reduced from 400 in 1968 to 75 in 1969. They were limited mainly to programs having "a budgetary impact of $50 million or more in fiscal year 1971 and/or $500 million during the next 5 years or an equivalent social impact."[57] In 1971 the Office of Management and Budget (OMB) (formerly BOB) further curtailed the extent of documentation required for agencies in submitting their budget requests. Agencies were relieved of the requirement for submitting PFPs, PMs, and SASs. For some observers, this action seemed to be an abandonment of PPB, but OMB reaffirmed support for "multi-year program planning, analysis, and evaluation."[58] While the emphasis on program results and analysis remained, PPB as a major structure and even as an acronym in the federal process was allowed a quiet death.[59]

One fact, perhaps not sufficiently recognized in 1965 when PPB was introduced in civilian agencies, was that important differences existed between the military and civilian sectors of government. In the first place, as discussed above, Defense had acquired an extensive background in analysis and planning before the inauguration of PPB. Many of the concepts and techniques employed by McNamara were not new, and consequently conversion to PPB was not thwarted for technical reasons. Civilian agencies, on the other hand, had limited analytic and planning staffs. Conversion to PPB in civilian agencies clearly would have been far more of a management "revolution" than had been the case in Defense.[60]

The translation from defense to civilian programs also was complicated by their essentially different natures. As was discussed in Chapter 1, the public sector does not have the simple criterion of profit for judging the adequacy or success of activities. However, Defense does have the concept of preparedness from which plans can be developed. It will be recalled that

---

[56] Office of Management and Budget, "Planning-Programming-Budgeting (PPB) System," Bulletin No. 68-9, Supplement No. 1, (July 17, 1969).

[57] Jack W. Carlson, "The Status and Next Step for Planning, Programming, and Budgeting," in Subcommittee on Economy in Government, *The Analysis and Evaluation of Public Expenditures*, p. 630.

[58] Office of Management and Budget, "Preparation and Submission of Budget Estimates," Circular A-11 (June, 1971).

[59] Allen Schick, "A Death in the Bureaucracy: The Demise of Federal PPB," *Public Administration Review*, 33 (1973): 146–56.

[60] See Aaron Wildavsky, "Rescuing Policy Analysis from PPBS," *Public Administration Review*, 29 (1969): 191.

the preparedness concept makes difficult the judgment of whether current defenses are inadequate, adequate, or excessive, but the idea does facilitate planning. By estimating the types of threats potential enemies could mount, strategies can be devised for meeting those situations. If analysis indicates that a potential aggressor could launch X number of missiles of Y characteristics in Z amount of time, weapons systems can be designed to respond to such an attack. Moreover, military decision making is keyed to man-machine tradeoffs. In responding to a given threat, which combination of soldiers, land-based missiles, aircraft, and submarines is optimal? Defense decision making also tends to be limited to calculating the military potential of only a few potential aggressors.

Civilian governmental programs, on the other hand, deal with attempting to alter social or asocial behavior. Such programs typically provide services whose effects are difficult to trace. Many intervening variables can alter the end results. For example, to reduce the number of burglaries and robberies, increased law enforcement may be instituted; despite the program, however, the number of crimes may rise. The increase in crime could be due to a greater number of drug addicts trying to support their habits or rising unemployment where poverty produces crime. Or another example would be the difficulty of quantifying ". . . the benefits to the individual, his family, and society generally of a program to rehabilitate alcoholics, particularly if one considers the impact of intervening causative factors."[61] In other words, civilian programs are said to be "soft."

The distinction between military and nonmilitary programs, however, should not be overextended. Both face serious measurement problems. As evidenced by the Southeast Asia War, body counts, bomb tonnage, and sorties flown reveal little about the waging of a war. Similarly, the number of people receiving welfare assistance, the number retrained for jobs, or the number of students being graduated from college fail to indicate whether people are better off because of governmental programs.

Another problem in translating PPB to civilian agencies was the question, "What is PPB?" The Defense system, it will be recalled, is based upon the limited-rationality model of decision making. Incremental decisions are used to adjust a multi-year plan based upon a mission-oriented program structure. Nonmilitary agencies, when they attempted to convert to PPB, took this approach at least in theory, but often settled for the use of more

---

[61] Stanley B. Botner, "Four Years of PPBS: An Appraisal," *Public Administration Review,* 30 (1970): 424.

analysis. In time, PPB almost came to mean the use of analysis rather than a reformulation of the entire decision-making process.

In mid-1968, the Bureau of the Budget conducted a study of the uses of the management system. As Harper, Kramer, and Rouse have summarized the study's findings, "The planning, programming, budgeting functions are not performed much differently in most agencies than they were before the introduction of PPBS."[62] Of the sixteen departments surveyed, the most successful were Agriculture, Health, Education, and Welfare (HEW), and the Office of Economic Opportunity. The six agencies making the least progress were Commerce, Housing and Urban Development (HUD), National Aeronautics and Space Administration (NASA), Post Office, and Transportation.

Six factors were said to characterize the most successful departments. 1) "A sufficient number of analysts were assigned to both bureau and agency level staffs." As of 1969, the agencies had 1,145 PPB positions of which 825 were professionals; however, considerably less than half were net additions, the others being reclassifications of previously existing positions.[63] 2) "The analysts were well qualified." 3) "The analytic effort had access through the formal organizational structure to the heads of the agencies and bureaus, to program managers, and to lateral, particularly budget, staffs." 4) "The informal relationships between analytic staffs and agency heads, program managers, and lateral staffs supported the analytic effort." 5) "Agency heads strongly supported the development and use of analytic outputs." 6) "The general attitude in the agency was that the analytic effort is primarily for the benefit of the agency rather than for the Bureau of the Budget." This last point was considered critical in that some agency personnel thought PPB an imposition of little value to them and believed that their duty was only to comply with Budget Office dictates.

One important characteristic of the federal experience was that the system was developed internally in each agency with only a modicum of coordination from the Bureau of the Budget (BOB) or OMB. Each department, using whatever capabilities it had or could acquire, was largely forced to "go-it-alone." HEW staked its effort on bringing in persons with Defense backgrounds. William Gorham, who had been Deputy Assistant

---

[62] Edwin L. Harper, Fred A. Kramer, and Andrew M. Rouse, "Implementation and Use of PPB in Sixteen Federal Agencies," *Public Administration Review,* 29 (1969): 624. All the following quotes are from the same reference and page.

[63] U.S. Congress, Joint Economic Committee, Subcommittees on Economy in Government, *The Analysis and Evaluation of Public Expenditures,* p. 636.

Secretary of Defense for Manpower, became HEW's Assistant Secretary for Planning and Evaluation. Robert N. Grosse, a former RAND economist who had worked with Hitch between 1961 and 1963, became head of the Economics and Costing Department of HEW in 1963 and Deputy Assistant Secretary for Program Coordination in 1966. By moving a few knowledgeable people into key positions, departments hoped to be able to do PPB.[64]

Without the continuous and extensive guidance from BOB-OMB, no coordinated version of the new PPB system was possible. It will be recalled that one of the reasons why McNamara introduced the system was to be able to make decisions across organization lines. This was accomplished through an integrated program structure based upon missions rather than services. In the civilian branch of the federal government, however, program structures were developed independently by the agencies, and this necessarily discouraged analyses of problems that involved two or more departments.

One of the most dismal experiments with PPB occurred in the State Department. Frederick C. Mosher, a long-time scholar of budgetary reform, evaluated the failure in that agency. Probably the most important conclusion to be drawn from Mosher's analysis is that conversion to PPB was a highly political process, not in terms of partisan efforts but in terms of which units in the bureaucracy would gain or lose status under the new system. The battles within State seemed to have been waged without much intervention on the part of Secretary Dean Rusk. Mosher concluded that for PPB to have become a reality, "continuing indication of support from the top—the President and the Secretary and Undersecretary of State"—would have been essential.[65] One should also add that not only is support

---

[64] For discussion of the HEW system, see Elizabeth B. Drew, "HEW Grapples with PPBS," *Public Interest*, No. 8 (Summer, 1967): 9–29; William Gorham, "Sharpening the Knife that Cuts the Public Pie," *Public Administration Review,* 28 (1968): 236–41; Arthur L. Levin, "Multisecting the Nation's Nondefense Programs," *Public Administration Review,* 31 (1971): 170–79; Alice M. Rivlin, *Systematic Thinking for Social Action* (Washington: Brookings, 1971); David R. Seidman, "PPB in HEW: Some Management Issues," in Fremont J. Lyden and Ernest G. Miller, eds., *Planning-Programming-Budgeting: A Systems Approach to Management,* 2nd ed. (Chicago: Markham, 1972), pp. 315–33.

[65] Frederick C. Mosher, "Program Budgeting in Foreign Affairs: Some Reflections," in U.S. Senate, Committee on Government Operations, Subcommittee on National Security and International Operations, *Planning-Programming-Budgeting,* 90th Cong., 2nd sess. (Washington: U.S. Government Printing Office, 1968), p. 24. Also see Frederick Mosher and John E. Harr, *Programming Systems and Foreign Policy Leadership* (New York: Oxford University Press, 1970).

essential but so is an understanding of the system and its uses. Defense Secretary McNamara had such an understanding. Also, one should be careful in generalizing about the need for executive commitment and involvement. Given the pressures of the day, no executive can be expected to devote most of his time to the installation and operations of PPB. What probably is required is a willingness on the part of the executive to act as referee when problems arise regarding the management system. The failure in the State Department also reflected the major problem of devising suitable measures for programs that are seemingly amorphous. It is difficult to measure whether the State Department is performing adequately.

It is still difficult to determine why some agencies were more successful than others in the use of PPB. An argument made in this work and in others has been that some organizations are more susceptible to the introduction of PPB than are others.[66] The State Department study reveals the problems of dealing with an inherently "soft" kind of program; it is not surprising that PPB did not succeed there. However, the argument is challenged by the Budget Office findings of 1968. The Department of Agriculture, one of the agencies identified as being more successful with the PPB experiment, has a long history of program budget reform (see Chapter 4). HEW, which has no such tradition and probably has some of the "softest" programs in government, also made noteworthy progress in establishing PPB. Although there were many problems and setbacks associated with the effort, HEW did receive recognition for having made important strides in the introduction of the system. In contrast, NASA is the closest analogue to Defense of the 16 agencies studied, yet it was among the group of least successful agencies. An explanation of NASA's lack of progress may be that the agency already had a decision system that was more sophisticated than the one being advocated by the budget office.

STATE AND LOCAL PPB

As the concepts of PPB were disseminated throughout the federal bureaucracy, state and local governments joined the movement. How much change actually occurred in the name of PPB and how much motion was mistaken for change is not obvious. But one is safe in concluding that efforts to install PPB systems did not revolutionize state and local governments.

---

[66] Harper, et al., "Implementation and Use of PPB," p. 632.

These governments had major handicaps. If the Defense Department had advantages over federal civilian agencies in installing PPB, surely the latter had advantages over state and local governments. The analytical talents available in these governments were undoubtedly far more limited. The use of performance criteria in managing programs also was probably more limited. Performance budgeting had been a failure at the state level. "When PPB arrived, one could not point to a single state that had reliable cost data for major segments of its budget or which had abandoned input controls in favor of performance controls."[67] This meant that a "great leap forward" would be required, broad jumping from object-of-expenditure control budgets to an end-product oriented planning and budgeting system.

Though preliminary work had begun in some states and localities in the early 1960s, the effort at this level gained major recognition with the formal establishment in 1967 of the State-Local Finances Project of The George Washington University. The project director was Selma J. Mushkin and deputy director was Harry P. Hatry. Conceived by members of the U.S. Bureau of the Budget, the project was intended to serve as a focal point for reform at the state and local levels. The project, supported with a Ford Foundation grant, was in cooperation with the Council of State Governments, the International City Managers (Management) Association, the National Association of Counties, the National Governors' Conference, the National League of Cities, and the United States Conference of Mayors. Known as 5-5-5, the project included five states—California, Michigan, New York, Vermont, and Wisconsin; five counties—Dade (Florida), Los Angeles (California), Nashville-Davidson (Tennessee), Nassau (New York), and Wayne (Michigan); and five cities—Dayton, Denver, Detroit, New Haven, and San Diego.

The project operated mainly on two fronts. First it attempted to provide direct advisory assistance to the 15 participating governments. Second, it served as a clearinghouse for information pertaining to PPB. On the first item, the project staff, given the number of governments involved, was incapable of providing continuous, direct, and extensive advice. Therefore, the governments were forced to develop their systems largely on their own. As for the second set of activities, the project produced many publications that were intended for use by any state or local government.

---

[67] Allen Schick, "The Status of PPB in the States: An Interim Report," Paper presented at the Joint National Meeting of the American Astronautical Society and the Operations Research Society, June 17–20, 1969. Also see Allen Schick, *Budget Innovation in the States* (Washington: Brookings, 1971).

Many of the reports were not much more than pamphlets, which could hardly be expected to bear the burden of explaining to government officials what PPB was and how to proceed in installing it.[68] Probably the most important function of the project was to serve as a rallying point. State and local officials in persuading their colleagues to move in the direction of PPB could point to the State-Local Finances Project as proof that the PPB system was a national movement.

Under the auspices of 5-5-5, questionnaires were sent in 1968 to state and local governments to assess how far PPB had progressed. The questionnaires were distributed by the Council of State Governments, the U.S. Conference of Mayors, the National League of Cities, and the National Association of Counties. Of the 40 states responding, 34 indicated they were considering introducing a PPB system and 28 reported having taken at least preliminary actions in this direction.[69] Questionnaires were sent to 1,134 counties and municipalities of which 356 responded and only 50 indicated having "taken steps to implement a PPB system."[70] If these results are valid indicators, then PPB affected at least a majority of the statehouses but a much smaller portion of city halls.[71]

Just as there was no uniformity regarding PPB among federal civilian agencies, uniformity was nonexistent at the state and local levels. Most of the states that experimented with PPB emphasized the development of program structure, multi-year plans and program memoranda, while only a few concentrated upon analysis as their main thrust.[72] By the mid-1970s, however, the emphasis had swung away from the structural features of PPB to the use of measurements of effectiveness and efficiency and program analysis.[73] Many of the states and municipalities in the 1960s took only cautious first steps with no timetable for completion of the

---

[68] PPB Notes 1 through 11, *Planning Programming Budgeting for City, State, County Objectives* (Washington: State-Local Finances Project, The George Washington University, 1967–69).

[69] Selma Mushkin, *Implementing PPB in State, City and County* (Washington: State-Local Finances Project, The George Washington University, 1969), p. 132.

[70] Mushkin, *Implementing PPB,* p. 139.

[71] See Harry P. Hatry, "Status of PPBS in Local and State Governments in the United States," *Policy Sciences,* 2 (1971): 177–89.

[72] Schick, "The Status of PPB," p. 19. Much of the discussion in this paragraph is based upon Schick's paper.

[73] According to a survey conducted by the National Association of State Budget Officers, by 1975 more than thirty states used effectiveness and productivity measures in their budget documents and approximately the same number of state budget offices were engaged in effectiveness and productivity analysis. The survey

installation process. Others began the effort on a pilot basis, attempting PPB in one department with expectations to expand the coverage. In some instances, analysis was begun as a first step with the assumption being that analysis could be used to prove the merits of PPB. Not always was the lead assumed by the budget office. Sometimes a planning unit or a particular department attempted to adopt the new system. In other cases, PPB was begun by developing a management information system, and millions of dollars were devoted to computerized information files. In the vast majority of cases, the efforts were moderate in attempting to alter existing decision-making systems. Crosswalking was used extensively for translating between programs and governmental units.[74]

By the close of the 1960s it was difficult to identify many ongoing PPB systems at the state and local levels. The final reports of the 5-5-5 project had some traces of optimism but no claims of success were in evidence. Of the governments participating, New Haven had done the least: "In short, New Haven has no progress to report simply because nothing beyond preliminary planning was ever achieved."[75] California's Programming and Budgeting System (PABS) had survived the change in administrations from Governor Edmund Brown to Governor Ronald Reagan, but by 1970 the system had collapsed. New York State, a forerunner in performance budgeting during the 1950s and an early leader in PPB, also abandoned its system. In 1970 the State initiated a new system, Program Analysis and Review (PAR), which emphasized analysis and greatly downgraded the use of multi-year programs and resource planning.[76]

---

was conducted with the support of the Institute of Public Administration of The Pennsylvania State University and the Pennsylvania Budget Office. See Robert D. Lee, Jr. and Raymond J. Staffeldt, "Executive and Legislative Use of Policy Analysis in the State Budgetary Process: Survey Results," *Policy Analysis,* 3 (Summer, 1977).

[74] See John G. Lauber, "PPBS in State Government—Maryland's Approach," *State Government,* 42 (1969): 31–37. U.S. Congress, Joint Economic Committee, Subcommittee on Economy in Government, *Innovations in Planning, Programming, and Budgeting in State and Local Governments,* 91st Cong., 1st sess. (Washington: U.S. Government Printing Office, 1969); William M. Capron, "PPB and State Budgeting"; Frederick C. Mosher, "Limitations and Problems of PPBS in the States"; and Selma J. Mushkin, "PPB in Cities," *Public Administration Review,* 29 (1969): 155–77.

[75] Dennis Rezendes, "New Haven, Connecticut," *PPB Pilot Project Reports* (Washington: State-Local Finances Project, The George Washington University, February, 1969), p. 141.

[76] Division of the Budget and Office of Planning Coordination, Executive Department, *Guidelines for Program Analysis and Review* (Albany: State of New York, June, 1970).

Nevertheless, there were some successes to report. Hawaii, not one of the original 5-5-5 states, had adopted a program budget system at the instigation of the legislature. New York City, also not of 5-5-5, made progress in the area of analysis, particularly with the assistance of the RAND Corporation and David Novick; later the RAND office in New York was closed, with apparently only modest improvements having been made in the New York City system. Pennsylvania, another non-5-5-5 government, developed one of the most complete systems surviving a change in governors in 1971 from Raymond P. Shafer to Milton J. Shapp. In Michigan, Governor William G. Milliken, after reviewing the limited success achieved earlier to install PPB, decided in favor of redesigning the state's managment information system and budget system. A Program Budget Evaluation System, modeled after the Pennsylvania PPB system, was installed in the early 1970s. Also, Massachusetts moved cautiously toward installing a Program Management System but later abandoned the effort.[77]

Efforts toward the installation of PPB were particularly noteworthy in the field of education. Major universities across the nation showed evidence of change.[78] The Western Interstate Commission on Higher Education (WICHE) had developed a budget and management information system based upon program structure. By the mid-1970s the WICHE taxonomy or variations of it had become standard for higher education institutions.[79] Moreover, school districts had made some efforts at installing PPB.[80]

---

[77] See Robert C. Casselman, "An Old State Takes a New Look at Public Management," *Public Administration Review,* 31 (1971): 427–34 and Robert C. Casselman, "Massachusetts Revisited: Chronology of a Failure," *Public Administration Review,* 33 (1973): 129–35. See Robert J. Mowitz, "State Planning, Programming, Budgeting Systems," mimeo (University Park: Institute of Public Administration, The Pennsylvania State University, 1971), for discussion and documents pertaining to the systems in Hawaii, Massachusetts, Michigan, New Mexico, Pennsylvania and Wisconsin.

[78] Marvin W. Peterson, "The Potential Impact of PPBS on Colleges and Universities," *Journal of Higher Education,* 42 (1971): 1–20.

[79] Western Interstate Commission on Higher Education, Planning and Management Division, *Program Classification Structure: Preliminary Edition for Review* (Boulder, Col.: WICHE, 1970). Also see Rodney T. Hartnett, *Accountability in Higher Education: A Consideration of Some of the Problems of Assessing College Impacts* (New York: College Entrance Examination Board, 1971); and Paul A. Montello, "Systems Planning for Higher Education," in Creta D. Sabine, ed., *Accountability: Systems Planning in Education* (Homewood, Ill.: ETC, 1973), pp. 119–42.

[80] Harry J. Hartley, *Educational Planning-Programming-Budgeting: A Systems Approach* (Englewood Cliffs, N.J.: Prentice-Hall, 1968); Robert D. Lee, Jr., "Plan-

Many causes can be cited for what went wrong with the installation of PPB at the state and local levels and at the federal level as well. One type involves political (partisan and nonpartisan) and administrative problems. The lack of a strong commitment on the part of the executive, as has already been cited, can be highly detrimental. In some cases, executives may have mistakenly believed PPB would require only modest changes rather than major revisions in the decision-making process. Hiring additional analysts and drafting PFPs and PMs are of little avail when most major decisions are made outside of the new procedures. If agencies are able to get whatever they want without complying with the requisites of the new system, then PPB exists in name only. Departments and agencies are perhaps inherently resistant to central direction from the President, governor, or mayor. The fear of opposition from the legislature is another possible reason for failure; if it is thought that the appropriations committee will not subscribe to the system, the executive may be reluctant to attempt a major overhaul of the decision process. Additionally, in many cases the executive may not be able to make major changes without prior approval of the legislature; and in many states, governors are incapable of commanding the executive branch in that some department heads are independently elected.

Where extensive changes were made in the executive budget process through PPB, resistance from legislatures often limited its effects to the budget preparation phase. The Michigan legislature refused to examine a program budget submission; Pennsylvania's legislature was not enthralled with the program format, although both the traditional and program budgets continued to be submitted until the 1976–77 budget which merged the two documents.[81]

Limited knowledge exists as to how change can be achieved.[82] It is safe to argue that large bureaucracies are more difficult to alter than small ones, and therefore one should expect problems in attempting to install PPB. Overselling the future benefits of a decision system that is not yet a

ning-Programming-Budgeting: A Revolutionary Approach to Management?," *Education and Urban Society*, 1 (1969): 469–75.

[81] Robert L. Harlow, "On the Decline and Fall of PPBS," *Public Finance Quarterly*, 1 (1973): 85–105.

[82] David A. Tansik and Michael Radnor, "An Organization Theory Perspective on the Development of New Organizational Functions," *Public Administration Review*, 31 (1971): 644–52; James E. Frank, "A Framework for Analysis of PPB Success and Causality," *Administrative Science Quarterly*, 18 (1973): 527–43.

reality is likely to breed skepticism. Administrative veterans have witnessed many fads and are unlikely to be enamored with the promised
fruits of any new management technique. This appears to have been what
happened with PPB. Also, attempting to convert to PPB within a few
months is likely to produce failure and more skepticism, yet many governments did exactly that. Converting to PPB at a very slow pace, however,
can be equally nonproductive, and the desired end may never be reached.

Even if these political and administrative problems did not exist, there
would be serious substantive and technical problems. In the first place, the
state-of-the-art in many fields is rudimentary at best. The development of
multi-year plans and the examination of alternatives can only be done
within the context of whatever problem is at hand. There is sufficient
doubt as to whether adequate knowledge exists as to how to design urban
transportation systems, how to rehabilitate convicted criminals, and how
to educate youth for an increasingly technological society. Moreover,
federalism produces overlapping programs such that it is difficult to trace
any particular set of benefits to the program of city X, state Y, or the
federal government. Not only are such causal relationships unknown but
there is also a paucity of data in many locales. Accounting systems are a
special problem unto themselves; they are highly complex systems that for
the most part are currently incapable of producing cost information by
program. Therefore, most PPB dollar figures cannot be believed because
they are based upon guesstimates. Even if there were usable data, governments often have few capable analysts to examine the data.[83]

The list of possible reasons for failure is limitless, but an alternative
approach might be to look briefly at one case of success, Pennsylvania.
The Pennsylvania PPB project was under the leadership of Robert J.
Mowitz, Director of the Institute of Public Administration of The Pennsylvania State University.[84] Unlike installation efforts elsewhere, the project
envisioned the development of a complete system within a 34-month
period. PPB was to be operational by January 1971. As Mowitz wrote: "A
piecemeal approach to the installation of a 'system' is a contradiction in

---

[83] Robert E. Millward, "PPBS: Problems of Implementation," *Journal of the
American Institute of Planners,* 34 (1968): 88–94.

[84] For a complete discussion of the system and its installation, see Robert J.
Mowitz, *The Design and Implementation of Pennsylvania's Planning, Programming,
Budgeting System* (Harrisburg: Commonwealth of Pennsylvania, 1970). William R.
Monat served on the project staff from March through December, 1968. Robert D.
Lee, Jr. was assistant project director from January, 1969 through December, 1970.

terms. Unless those necessarily related elements of the system are installed simultaneously, the system itself cannot be assembled."[85] This required a complete recasting of the decision process, including the development of program structures and multi-year plans (Commonwealth Program Plan and Agency Program Plans); a decision cycle including Program Policy Guidelines issued by the Governor, Program Revision Requests (somewhat analogous to Program Memoranda), and Program Revision Actions (comparable to the Defense Department's Program Change Decisions); the development of a management information system to support PPB; the institutionalization of analysis; and a revamping of the accounting system. All departments and agencies were included. The project had the complete support of the executive, something often cited in the literature as a critical factor in determining success or failure.

To control the installation process, the Program Evaluation and Review Technique (PERT) was used. PERT, which had been devised to control the development of the Polaris Fleet Ballistic Missile Program, is a complex form of charting used to identify the components of a system and their relationships. Two of the most important assumptions made in designing the PERT used in Pennsylvania were 1) installation should be rapid so as to allow the last calendar year of the project for debugging, and 2) the new planning and programming cycle was to be phased into the budget process because budgets would have to be transmitted to the legislature, regardless of the status of the installation project. While the installation was rushed, it was not in terms of a few months as had been tried elsewhere.[86]

Perhaps the most salient feature of the Pennsylvania project was that PPB was not simply added on. Rather, to the best of the planners' ability it became the new executive decision process. In other words, the system was institutionalized. No central PPB unit was established per se. While a PPB project office existed at the outset, it was phased out early as PPB became the new method of decision making and management. Old budget forms and procedures were replaced with new ones. Program Revision Requests in effect became the new way by which agencies submitted budget requests. The reformatting of the accounting system also was an

---

[85] Mowitz, *Design and Implementation*, p. 43.

[86] For a brief discussion of the Pennsylvania PERT, see Robert D. Lee, Jr., "Introducing Innovative Systems in Managing U.S. State Government," *International Review of Administrative Sciences*, 37 (1971): 378–86.

institutional change. Personnel position classifications involving PPB-type work were modified and new positions added. This is not to suggest that the system was ideal, but only to note that much more took place than the mere drafting of program structures, multi-year plans, and the like. Some people, displeased by what had been done, perceived the effort as a plot to force the new governor, who would take office in January 1971, to use PPB. However, as Mowitz has observed, "It seems reasonable to assume that a governor is better off knowing more about what has happened as a result of past decisions and what is likely to happen as a result of his decisions than he is if he knows less about these matters."[87]

SUMMARY

Planning-programming-budgeting (PPB) is compatible with the history of budget reforms intended to link program information to budgetary decision making. At the same time, much of PPB grew out of a series of concepts and techniques that were developed largely independent of budgeting. These are operations research, economic analysis, general systems theory, cybernetics, computers, and systems analysis.

The Department of Defense, despite whatever shortcomings one wishes to cite, was well grounded in these analytic techniques that had emerged mainly during and following World War II. The conversion to PPB, then, was a major change but not a revolutionary one. The system was based upon the limited rationality model of decision making in which multi-year plans are established and incremental decisions are used to adjust these plans.

Federal civilian agencies were required by 1965 to establish their own PPB systems with the guidance of the Bureau of the Budget. Much was lost in the translation from the military side to the civilian side of government. By the early 1970s analysis was the main surviving component of PPB.

State and local governments also tried PPB during the 1960s and met with only a modicum of success. The optimism of the early years of the decade was replaced with pessimism and skepticism in later years. Some governments admitted defeat in installing the system, while others retrenched and contemplated continued effort in the future. Though there were a few governments that exhibited the makings of viable PPB systems,

---

[87] Mowitz, *Design and Implementation,* p. 45.

the general tenor of the early 1970s was that PPB was an interesting but unsuccessful experiment. As will be seen in the next chapter, subsequent developments in budgeting, particularly at the local level, incorporate many of the concepts of PPB, but these changes were introduced with much less fanfare than was common in the 1960s.

BUDGET PREPARATION

Budget preparation entails preparing a plan for the coming year or years.[1] The plan may concentrate almost exclusively upon proposed resource use or may focus upon program results, both from a management and program planning perspective (see Chapter 1). The process in a given jurisdiction may require little program information, yet assumptions—explicitly or implicitly—are made about how resources will be used to provide services and to produce beneficial effects. Briefly, the preparation phase includes the issuing of budget instructions, the preparation of budget requests by line agencies, review by the central budget office, forecasting of revenues, executive decision making, and finally the preparation of a budget that is submitted to the legislative body.

Extensive variations exist among jurisdictions as to the means used in preparing a budget. This chapter is written mainly from the perspective of executive budgeting in which the chief executive has primary responsibility for preparation. It should be recognized, however, that many mayors and governors must share preparation authority with other executive officers and legislators. An extreme case is represented by cities having commission forms of government in which responsibility is divided among elected councilmen, each of whom has responsibility for preparing a budget for his or her department.

---

[1] Much of the material in this chapter was developed in conjunction with projects of the Institute of Public Administration of The Pennsylvania State University and particularly with the Institute's Director, Robert J. Mowitz. Also, Harry P. Hatry of the Urban Institute provided important information on the status of budgeting systems at the local level. We wish to thank the numerous municipalities which provided copies of their budgetary documents.

The three sections of this chapter focus upon budget requests, executive decision making, and budget documents. The first section examines the procedures used in requesting budgets, including the types of information assembled. Major attention is given to cities because in recent years municipalities have been important leaders in the field. The second section considers the factors involved in reaching budget decisions. The last section reviews various types of budget documents and their formats.

BUDGET REQUESTS

In this section we consider the ingredients that eventually result in budgets. The discussion begins with a review of information requested of agencies by budget officers. Next, attention is focused on various types of program data that are increasingly used in budget requests. This is followed by a discussion of approaches to bounding the size of agency requests and the total budget. A review of the time periods covered in the budget request is included. The section concludes with a discussion of problems entailed in using program structure as a part of program budgeting.

A budget cannot be prepared by the central budget office alone, but must be prepared in conjunction with agencies who provide various types of information. What information is requested by the budget office reflects in part the way decisions are to be made or are expected to be made. If the budget office only asks for dollar requests, obviously there will be no information to make judgments concerning program effectiveness. On the other hand, there is no need to assume that budget offices which require program information necessarily use it in deliberations. Another factor is the budget office's perception of how much information it can absorb. Sometimes budget offices ask for information that is far beyond their abilities to examine, simply in terms of not having sufficient time available for that purpose. Still another factor determining what information will be required is known demands from other budget participants, most notably the legislative body. The budget office may amass much data from the agencies, not because it or the chief executive has any intentions of using it for decision purposes but simply because each year the legislative body demands that information.

To facilitate preparation, the budget office issues instructions about how to assemble agency budget requests. At the federal level, these instructions are contained in the Office of Management and Budget (OMB) Circular A-11, "Preparation and Submission of Budget Estimates." Instructions such as these provide forms to be completed, reducing uncertainty among agencies as to what the budget office expects of them. Typically, a calendar will be provided explaining when requests are due for submission to the budget office and indicating a period when agencies may be called for hearings with the budget office. The instructions, then, tend to bound the amount of information that will be required of the agencies and available to the budget office, although the budget office may request additional information from given agencies.

No matter what the jurisdiction, there are standard items that can be found in virtually all budget instruction manuals. Where appropriate, agencies are asked to submit revenue data, such as an agency operating a loan program with a revolving fund. Most of the instructions, however, concentrate upon expenditures. The expenditures are keyed with the accounting system, using objects of expenditures such as personnel and travel (see Chapter 9). Also there may be detailed breakouts on personnel in terms of the number of persons in a given unit, their job titles, and current salaries. This type of information is presented in the budget document only in summary form (see Chapter 11). The instructions also allow for narrative statements to be provided by the agencies in order to justify the requests.

Separate sets of instructions may be provided for the operating and capital fund budgets. The latter, used extensively at the state and local levels, are primarily for requests on major fixed assets such as buildings and equipment. Chapter 10 discusses capital budgeting and the problems of linking capital and operating decision processes.

Program Measures As already noted, budget systems are making increased use of program information and therefore request instructions indicate what types of program data are to be supplied. The measures typically will have been negotiated between the budget office and the agencies before budget preparation time. In other words, when the agencies receive the request instructions, they already know what program information is to be supplied. Only by having such agreed upon measures can the agencies be in a position to provide the needed information; without that advance guidance, the agencies may not have established procedures for collecting the required data. One consideration in the selection of measures is what information the executive branch expects the legislative branch to request or demand (see Chapter 8).

There are numerous types of program information, with social indicators being the broadest or most general type.[2] These measures of the physical, social, and economic environments are intended to reflect what sometimes is called the quality of life. In the area of employment, social indicators could include job satisfaction broken out by age, sex, race, income, and occupation or median earnings by race and by sex.[3] Measures of this type are useful in assessing past and current trends and may provide decision makers with some insights into the need for programs. But often absent is any direct linkage between such indicators and a given governmental service. General social indicators derived from census sources and other statistical series in the absence of direct ties to governmental actions may be of little use for yearly budget decisions.[4] Comparatively low earnings for nonwhite males between the ages of 16 and 20 may be a function of discrimination, inadequate education and training, and generally unfavorable economic conditions.

A more narrowly focused measure and one of more direct relevance to budgeting is impacts, or sometimes called outcomes. Measures of this type concentrate upon effectiveness, whether desired effects or consequences are being achieved.[5] When a government service has affected "individuals, institutions [or] the environment," an impact has occurred.[6] Lent D.

---

[2] Raymond A. Bauer, ed., *Social Indicators* (Cambridge, Mass.: M.I.T. Press, 1966); Karl A. Fox, *Social Indicators and Social Theory* (New York: Wiley-Intrascience, 1974); Israel V. Sawhill, "The Role of Social Indicators and Social Reporting in Public Expenditure Decisions," in U.S. Congress, Joint Economic Comittee, Subcommittee on Economy in Government, *The Analysis and Evaluation of Public Expenditures: The PPB System*, 91st Cong., 1st sess. (Washington: U.S. Government Printing Office, 1969), pp. 473–85; Mark Schneider, "The 'Quality of Life' and Social Indicators Research," *Public Administration Review*, 36 (1976): 297–305; Nestor E. Terleckyj, "Measuring Possibilities of Social Change," *Looking Ahead* (National Planning Association), 18 (1970): 1–11; Leslie D. Wilcox, et al., *Social Indicators and Societal Monitoring: An Annotated Bibliography* (New York: Elsevier, 1972).

[3] Office of Management and Budget, *Social Indicators: 1973* (Washington: U.S. Government Printing Office, 1973), pp. 145–46. Also see current issues of Bureau of the Census, *Status: A Monthly Chartbook of Social and Economic Trends* (Washington: U.S. Government Printing Office, first issued July, 1976).

[4] Eugene J. Meehan, "Social Indicators and Policy Analysis," in Thomas J. Cook and Frank P. Scioli, Jr, eds., *Methodologies for Analyzing Public Policies* (Lexington, Mass.: Lexington Books, 1975), pp. 33–46.

[5] James Cutt, *Program Budgeting for Welfare: A Case Study of Canada* (New York: Praeger, 1973), pp. 261–79; Richard E. Winnie and Harry P. Hatry, *Measuring the Effectiveness of Local Government Services: Transportation* (Washington: Urban Institute, 1973); *Measuring the Effectiveness of Basic Municipal Services: Initial Report* (Washington: Urban Institute, 1974).

[6] Robert J. Mowitz, *The Design and Implementation of Pennsylvania's Planning,*

Upson, in the 1920s, was one of the first observers to advocate a budget system that focused upon program impacts.[7] In the employment case, an impact measure might be the average earnings of nonwhite males who completed a job training program or, even more focused, the average increase in hourly earnings after completion of the program compared with prior earnings. Such a measure needs to be assessed carefully, however, in that earnings may have increased in a given time period mainly because of an upturn in the economy or because of inflation and not because of training. A control group or other monitoring device may be necessary to determine earnings of those not trained in order to allow comparisons between the two groups.

Sometimes myth or doctrine leads to problems in the selection of impact measures.[8] In providing funds to police departments, the assumption is often made that crime will be controlled. This leads to the selection of impact measures dealing with crime rates. However, police actually have limited control over crime. It is possible that some persons will commit crimes on the assumption that civil liberty and other protections in the courts will lead to acquittal and that even if convicted, liberal probation and parole policies will greatly reduce the possible amount of time they will be incarcerated. Also, many crimes arise spontaneously. An argument between husband and wife might result in death for one of them. Two people in a tavern might argue, leading to one assaulting the other. In these situations, the police have no opportunity to prevent crime and thereby reduce the crime rate.[9] In other situations, police may be able to alter the measure, crime rate, by changing reporting and recording practices without affecting crime.

Because of the values or biases of the persons involved, some impacts may be selected and others ignored. The impact of highway construction programs can be gauged by reductions in travel time for commuters and the impact of urban renewal gauged by increased economic activity in the community. Still, there are several other possible impacts of these programs, many of which are negative. Anthony Downs has suggested 22 different types of losses that are imposed upon urban households by

Programming, Budgeting System (Harrisburg: Commonwealth of Pennsylvania, 1970), p. 17.

[7] Lent D. Upson, "Half-Time Budget Methods," *Annals*, 113 (1924): 73.

[8] Edmond H. Weiss, "The Fallacy of Appellation in Government Budgeting," *Public Administration Review*, 34 (1974): 377–79.

[9] Paul D. Staudohar, "An Experiment in Increasing Productivity of Police Service Employees," *Public Administration Review*, 35 (1975): 518–22.

highway construction and urban renewal. The losses include costs such as "reduction in employment opportunities and increased commuting costs" and "losses resulting from adverse environmental changes."[10] Impacts such as these can be quantified; yet, because of the value judgments of participants, these impacts may not be used.

In contrast with impacts, output measures reflect the immediate product of services being provided.[11] Returning to the employment example, the number of graduates of the training program would be the output. Comparisons can be made from year to year on whether the number of graduates is increasing or decreasing. The percent of persons enrolled who graduate—the completion rate or conversely the drop-out rate—can be calculated. Measures such as these are far easier to calculate than many impacts because data sources are within the organization. One only needs to keep accurate records of who enrolled and who graduated. Impacts, on the other hand, are external. In the case of earnings of graduates, a monitoring or follow-up system for the graduates would be necessary to obtain the appropriate data.

One drawback in using output measures without impacts is that an erroneous assumption may be made about causal relations. The employment example would suggest that training improves one's employability, but unless data are collected to verify such anticipated results, the system is operating strictly on faith or doctrine. It would certainly be possible that for a given group of people skill training was needed less than some other form of training, perhaps the development of a more positive outlook on work. Outputs, then, may encourage suboptimization, which is the improvement of operations for attaining subobjectives while risking the possibility of moving away from rather than toward larger values. An output measure stated as the number of applications processed for a grant-in-aid program may encourage administrators to process an increasing number at a lower unit cost. In doing so, the efficiency of the agency may be increased but the main intent of the grant program may be forgotten in the process. "The always present dangers of doing more efficiently the wrong things becomes a near certainty for suboptimizing

---

[10] Anthony Downs, *Urban Problems and Prospects* (Chicago: Markham, 1970), pp. 192–227.

[11] "Output Measures for a Multi-Year Program and Financial Plan," *PPB Note 7* (Washington: State-Local Finances Project, The George Washington University, June, 1967), pp. 10–11.

approaches."[12] Still, because of greater ease of data collection, output data and the following measures to be discussed are more commonly used than impacts.

Beyond outputs are activities. These constitute the work that is done to produce outputs. The number of total hours of instruction could be used for a job training program or the measure might be more focused, such as hours of instruction in lathe operations. Activities are sometimes measured as work load. The number of classroom disruptions requiring special consultations could be a reflection of work load; other work load measures could include the number of enrollees or the number of applicants to a program. Each application requires processing, perhaps including interviewing the applicant. If the number of applicants increases, though enrollments are kept constant because of space limitations, the work load will have increased even though output has not.

Work load is often the focus of management by objectives (MBO) efforts. Just as in the 1960s PPB meant many things to different people, so does MBO.[13] The approach taken in the federal government was intentionally unstructured and expected to serve as a means of furthering programmatic dialogues between the Office of Management and Budget and the line agencies. Other MBO systems, however, have been more structured and have tended to prescribe objectives in terms of work load. The objectives may be peculiar to a given year, such as redesigning the carpentry curriculum this year, or may be work load oriented with the same measures being used each year, such as train 100 persons as keypunch operators. Still another method of MBO is to identify targets or objectives for individual employees, such as to reorganize the filing system this year. MBO systems emphasize involvement of all strata of the bureaucracy in the development of objectives; participation by lower-level personnel in identifying the work to be done is considered important in motivating workers to be more productive.

---

[12] Yehezkel Dror, "Planning in the United States—Some Reactions by a Foreign Observer," *Public Administration Review*, 31 (1971): 399.

[13] Jong S. Jun, ed., "Management by Objectives in the Public Sector," *Public Administration Review*, 36 (1976): 1–45; Stephen J. Knezevich, *Program Budgeting: A Resource Allocation Decision System for Education* (Berkeley, Cal.: McCutchan, 1973), pp. 52–70; Bruce H. De Woolfson, Jr., "Public Sector MBO and PPB: Cross Fertilization in Management Systems," *Public Administration Review*, 35 (1975): 387–95.

Productivity is another term having many different meanings.[14] The National Center for Productivity and Quality of Working Life takes a broad approach to the term, subsuming virtually all forms of program measurement.[15] Others take a different approach, limiting productivity to comparisons of resource inputs and work. Ratios are typically used for productivity measurement such as the total cost of a job training program divided by the number of graduates, yielding an average cost per graduate. If average cost remains constant from one year to another, despite increases in salary rates and various supplies, then the assumption is made that the unit is more productive or efficient. Measures of this type can be developed for activities, such as average cost of processing one application for the job training program. An alternative to average cost is to use hours, months, or years of work.[16] Thus, a measure might be average hours to process an application or average number of person months or years of instruction per graduate.

One of the most involved forms of productivity measurement is that used in Sunnyvale, California.[17] Their Resource Allocation Plan tabulates activities, such as number of utility bills issued, business licenses issued,

---

[14] Steve Carter, "Trends in Local Government Productivity," *The Municipal Year Book, 1975* (Washington: International City Management Association, 1975), pp. 180–84; Raymond D. Horton, "Productivity and Productivity Bargaining in Government: A Critical Analysis," *Public Administration Review*, 36 (1976): 407–14; *Improving Productivity in State and Local Government* (New York: Committee for Economic Development, 1976); *Improving Program Performance* (Washington: District of Columbia Government, 1976); Robert J. Mowitz, "Some Problems in Dealing with Government Productivity," *Tax Review*, 37 (1976): 29–32; Chester A. Newland, ed., "Productivity in Government," *Public Administration Review*, 32 (1972): 739–850; *Performance Monitoring System Guidelines* (Washington: District of Columbia Government, 1976); "Productivity Management," *Public Management, 56* (June, 1974): 2–27; John P. Ross and Jesse Burkhead, *Productivity in the Local Government Sector* (Lexington, Mass.: Lexington Books, 1974).

[15] See Harry P. Hatry and Donald M. Fisk, *Improving Productivity and Productivity Measurement in Local Governments* (Washington: National Center for Productivity and Quality of Working Life, 1971); *Improving Municipal Productivity: Work Measurement for Better Management* (Washington: National Center for Productivity and Quality of Working Life, 1975); *Opportunities for Improving Productivity in Solid Waste Collection* (Washington: National Center for Productivity and Quality of Working Life, 1971).

[16] Robert S. Guy, "Program Budgeting for Smaller Governmental Units," *Governmental Finance*, 4 (August, 1975): 37–38.

[17] *Resource Allocation Plan Manual, 1976–77* and *Improving the Quality of Life; Resource Allocation Plan, 1976–77 to 1983–84* (Sunnyvale, Cal.: City of Sunnyvale, 1976).

and invoices issued; weights these according to all accounting transactions; tabulates work hours and costs related to revenue billing and collection; and then calculates ratios of work units to hours or average number of transactions per hour per person and dollar cost per transaction. Using one year as a base year, percentage increases and decreases in productivity for revenue billing and collection are derived.

Productivity measures, such as those used in Sunnyvale, require extensive record keeping. If a group of employees together perform several different activities, then a reporting system needs to account for the hours being committed to each activity by each employee. This is sometimes accomplished by daily report forms. State and local police often must submit daily reports on hours spent in patrolling, investigating, testifying in court, and report writing itself. Less complicated systems may use weekly, monthly, or quarterly report forms. On the cost side, accounting systems need to capture nonpersonnel expenditures related to activities. Problems abound here, such as whether paper and other supplies obtained by a given organizational unit should be charged to specific activities performed by the unit (see Chapter 9).

A final type of measure that is used gauges the need or demand for a program. Pennsylvania was perhaps the first state to use this type of measure, and Lakewood, Colorado, is one city that uses it. The need measure indicates the gap between the level of service and the need for it. Whereas the output measure may indicate the number of job training graduates, the need measure shows how many other persons are without adequate job skills and therefore in need of training. In Lakewood, the number of handicapped persons in the city is used as a need indicator for handicapped services.[18]

In discussing need, we have come full circle back to social indicators, prompting a few words of caution. We have relied here mainly upon the employment example in order to show differences among types of measures, but it should be understood that the differences may not be so obvious in other program areas. For example, dollar value of fire damage in a city might be considered a social indicator, an impact of the fire department, and an indicator of fire service need. Because a fire department responds to all reported residential fires, the number of these fires can be considered a measure of output, need, and work load.

---

[18] *Program Performance Budget, 1976* (Lakewood, Col.: City of Lakewood, 1975), p. 132.

Budget Request Guidance If the central budget office simply instructed agencies to request budgets for the coming year, probably several different types of responses would result, based upon different assumptions about the coming budget year. One agency might respond by requesting what it felt was needed. Another might respond in light of what resources it thought were available, resulting in a much lower request. Some agencies would respond in terms of what they thought was politically possible or likely. Others might use combinations of these approaches. The consequence would be budget requests based upon varied assumptions, and these requests would require different reactions by the budget office. To avoid such disparities in the assumptions made by requesting agencies, budget instructions often provide guidance to agencies.

One type of guidance is to assume basically no change in programs. A department's current budget is considered its base and any increases to be requested are only to cover additional operating costs, such as increased costs for personnel, supplies, and the like. An assumption is made that the government is committed or obligated to continue existing programs. In the past, this base approach has been used only implicitly, but more recent efforts have focused upon indicating explicitly the level of commitment. This is evidenced by the attempt to develop Program Financial Plans (PFPs) under the defunct PPB system at the federal level and the new Current Services Budget as required by the 1974 Congressional Budget and Impoundment Control Act. Pennsylvania has used this approach since the 1960s.

Explicitly determining what is current commitment is difficult, because programs often are created without any such explicit statement of commitment. The easiest cases are those programs in which there is an obligation to serve all claimants on the system. School districts, for example, are obligated to serve all eligible children, and therefore budget requests from units within the school district would be determined by the expected number of enrolled children. In other cases, the commitment may be in terms of the level of service, specifically outputs and work load. Using job training again, the unit could have a commitment to maintain the same number of graduates or alternatively the same number of students. If the former measure were used and the drop-out rate was increasing, then presumably additional resources would be required to increase enrollment in order to maintain a constant number of graduates. Consequently, the unit's budget request would increase more than what would be required to cover salary increases and inflation; the request would possibly include staff additions to handle the larger enrollment.

An alternative to the current commitment approach is fixed-ceiling budgeting, discussed in Chapter 4. Under this system, a dollar limit is set governmentwide, then factored into limits for departments, bureaus, and other subunits. The advantage is a set of budget requests that when totaled come to the desired ceiling. The disadvantage is that some organizational units may receive inadequate funding and others may be overfunded in terms of program priorities; this results from inadequate information about program requirements being available when limits are set.

A weakness of both the base and fixed-ceiling approaches is that by themselves they offer no suggestions for program changes. If the budget office and chief executive have only these types of budget requests, they lack information about alternative resource allocations. In response to this lack of information, a variety of "what-if" approaches to budget requests has been devised. These approaches ask agencies to develop alternatives. The "what-ifs" may be expressed in terms of: What if more or fewer dollars were available? What if program improvements were to be made in specific areas? and other ways.

One of the most common what-if approaches is open-ended or blue-sky budgeting, mentioned in Chapter 4. The question is asked: What if resources were available to meet all needs? Agencies are expected to ask for what they think they need to deal with problems assigned to them. This approach should not be confused with the absence of guidance in which some agencies might request "needed" funds and others might ask for lesser amounts. The advantage of the open-ended approach is that it surfaces perceived needs for service in comparison with existing service levels. The "needed" budget in contrast with the current budget can serve as the basis of discussions over preferred funding levels. The disadvantage is that open-ended requests may exceed the economic and political capabilities of the jurisdiction, so that the requests seem like fanciful wishlists. Agencies, realizing that their wishlists will not be filled, are likely to begrudge the effort required in preparing open-ended budgets and consequently may not prepare these documents with great thought and care.

Zero-base budgeting is another form of what-if budgeting, with the "what if" being the possible elimination of programs.[19] Rather than

---

[19] U.S. Senator Edmund S. Muskie (D, Maine), the first chairman of the new Senate Budget Committee, has been a proponent of zero-base budgeting. Also, see

assuming that a base exists, the approach asks what would happen if a program were discontinued. As discussed in Chapter 4, the U.S. Department of Agriculture experimented with this approach in the 1960s. More recently, the State of Georgia has used zero-base budgeting. For example, the state highway patrol program operating in rural areas was asked what if it were not to be refunded. The response was, "The State would not have a patrol force to patrol the rural areas."[20] A more thorough form of zero-base budgeting would attempt to provide quantitative measures of impact. The argument might be made that highway death rates would escalate because motorists would drive at excessive speeds knowing that the roads were unpatrolled.

The disadvantage of zero-base budgeting is analogous to that of open-ended budgeting. Both approaches make basically unrealistic assumptions. Whereas open-ended budgeting assumes unlimited resources, the zero-base approach makes the unrealistic assumption that decision makers have the capacity to eliminate programs. In reality, the political forces in any jurisdiction are such that few programs in any given year can be abandoned. For this reason, zero-base budgeting may be better applied to selective programs in any one year rather than governmentwide.[21] Proposals for zero-base budgeting for the federal government would have programs reviewed only once every four or five years, with all programs contributing to the same basic goal reviewed in the same year.[22]

Between the extremes of open-ended and zero-base budgeting are "what-if" approaches that produce more economically and politically acceptable budget requests. Percentages above and below the base or current commitment budget can be used. In other words, what if a 10 percent cut in resources were imposed or a 10 percent increase provided? Agencies can show where cuts would be made and what consequences would follow; alternatively, agencies can indicate how additional resources would be used (hiring additional staff, etc.) and what outputs and impacts would result.

Given the tight finances of municipalities in recent years, the percent-

Michael J. Scheiring, "Zero-Base Budgeting in New Jersey," *State Government*, 49 (1976): 174–79.

[20] Peter A. Pyhrr, *Zero-Base Budgeting: A Practical Management Tool for Evaluating Expenses* (New York: Wiley, 1973), p. 43.

[21] Mowitz, *Design and Implementation*, pp. 26–27.

[22] Joel Havemann, "Congress Tries to Break Ground Zero in Evaluating Federal Programs," *National Journal*, 8 (1976): 708.

age approach and variations of it have been used for budget trimming purposes more than for new or expanded programs. Denver, for example, uses a base budget plus a reduction budget that is 20 percent below the base.[23] Harrisburg and York, Pennsylvania, have used a no-growth method in which dollar requests for the coming year are to be no greater than the current budget.[24] The result is requests that in dollars show no growth and that indicate program cutbacks due to increased costs for personnel and the like. Fort Worth, Texas, has used a "base budget" request of 90 percent of the current year, with the additional 10 percent being negotiable.[25] The agencies in Forth Worth, then, may prepare an "activity change budget," showing requested program improvements.

Other what-if budget requests include variations on priority listings. San Diego County, California, has each department assign priorities to its programs.[26] The advantage is that decision makers are given the administrators' perceptions of what operations are thought to be critical. The disadvantage is that all programs may seem to be of equal importance; a city public works director would have difficulty deciding whether water or sewer services should have higher priority.

Because of this problem priorities are sometimes restricted to proposed program changes or improvements. The University of North Carolina submits a "continuation" or base budget plus a list of proposed program changes with each change having its own price tag One set of library improvements might be given second priority and another set sixteenth priority. In this way, the University conveys to decision makers that if X millions of dollars are available, priorities one through three should be funded; if more funds are available, then additional items may be selected. Such systems again are useful in conveying administrators' perceived priorities, although they should not become so rigid that, for example, the first twelve items in the list must be funded before the thirteenth may be funded. Should such a process develop, then administrators would place the most popular changes at the bottom of the list, and the least popular at the top.

All of the approaches discussed so far are basically nonsubstantive,

[23] *Budget Manual* (Denver, Col.: City and County of Denver, 1976).

[24] The Harrisburg and York systems have been developed by the Institute of Public Administration of The Pennsylvania State University.

[25] *1976–77 Budget Instructions Manual* (Fort Worth, Tex.: City of Fort Worth, 1976).

[26] *Budget Manual* (San Diego, Cal.: County of San Diego, 1976).

which suggests another approach, namely policy and program guidance. This method can entail budget offices issuing directives to departments indicating specific areas for which special justification and/or alternatives are requested. At the federal level, OMB has instructed agencies to prepare issue papers that explain the strengths and weaknesses of specified programs and that provide suggestions for program changes.

State governments are increasingly using policy/program guidance. Pennsylvania and Michigan issue Program Policy Guidelines that indicate to agencies the concerns of the governor, namely the issues that have high priority for the coming year.[27] A recent survey showed that 15 state budget offices in 1970 provided general written policy guidance, and the number had increased to 22 in 1975. In 1970, only one state said it provided written guidance by major programs but by 1975 the number had increased to 13.[28]

In response to such guidance, agencies prepare detailed program requests. There is likely to be a discussion of the range of available alternatives, possibly with detailed costing of each along with expected results of each. Where guidance is not directed at any one agency, two or more might submit competing requests, each attempting to show how its proposed alternative would deal with a problem. For example, both the city police and recreation departments might make budget proposals for dealing with juvenile delinquency.

The advantage of such guidance is that agencies are given "clues" as to what types of program requests are likely to receive favorable treatment. Agencies may be spared many hours of needless work in preparing requests that are fated for rejection. The policy/program guidance does not ensure executive approval of agency requests. The requests may be rejected simply because of inadequate funds or because the arguments for the proposed changes fail to be persuasive.

These forms of guidance that have been discussed are often used in combination. As we have seen, the University of North Carolina uses the base approach plus priority listing. The base approach can be combined

---

[27] The Program Policy Guidelines formats for these states were developed by Robert J. Mowitz, Director of the Institute of Public Administration of The Pennsylvania State University.

[28] Discussion is based upon previously unpublished data from a survey conducted by the National Association of State Budget Officers in conjunction with the Pennsylvania Budget Office and the Institute of Public Administration of The Pennsylvania State University.

with open-ended budgeting; Harrisburg and York, Pennsylvania, use these along with no-growth budgeting. Policy/program guidance can be coupled with priority listings, in which agencies indicate which changes should be given higher priority in relationship to the guidance that was provided.

Multi-year Requests All budget requests are multi-year in that they at least cover the current year plus the coming budget year and probably most cover the past year as well. States with biennial budgets obviously have multi-year requests. An issue, however, is whether budget requests should extend beyond the budget year, and if yes, how this is to be accomplished.

Two basic types of multi-year requests are used. One type uses current commitment, as explained above. The assumption is made that a program will continue over time with no appreciable changes in the way the service is provided. The other type deals with requests for program changes, possibly covering the elimination of a program but more likely covering requested program improvements or the creation of new programs.

The argument for multi-year requests is simple: without looking beyond the budget year, commitments of resources may be made that were never intended. This argument applies particularly for proposed expansions and new programs. For instance, the decision to fund the research, development, test and evaluation (RDT and E) of a new weapons system may appear relatively inexpensive. The first year or years will involve only starting the program whereas later years will involve large outlays for procurement. Indeed, agencies use such short time perspectives to their advantage; chief executives and legislative bodies are "sold" on programs that seem inexpensive and later are dismayed when told that unless funding continues and at a higher rate no benefits will have been gained from the expenditures to date.

In theory, the time horizon should be geared to the life cycle of each program. This is clearest in terms of specific projects or programs that have an obvious beginning and conclusion. A weapons system is one of the best examples. The system begins with research and concludes after it has become obsolete. The planning process involves estimating the response of potential aggressors and the ability of other nations to develop weapons that would neutralize the advantages of the system being contemplated. In other words, planned obsolescence is endemic to military programs.

On the other hand, many governmental programs have no forseeable conclusion. The need for education, roads, law enforcement, recreation, and the like will always exist. Each of these may have unique properties that suggest possible time horizons. Given the length of time required to design and construct schools, several year projections are needed; this type of projection can help a rapidly growing school district to be prepared to handle anticipated increased enrollments or to avoid overconstruction. Road requirements, on the other hand, are a function of user demand and the rate of deterioration of road surfaces. Multi-year requests can reveal when major increased expenditures will be required either to resurface existing roads or to expand the road network. In other words, roads and schools might well use different projection periods.

Given that an appropriate life cycle for multi-year requests is often not obvious, an arbitrary set of years may be imposed. The most common is the budget year plus the four succeeding years, known as a five-year projection. The federal government, according to the 1974 Congressional Budget and Impoundment Control Act, makes such projections as do some state governments. Although there is nothing magical about the number 5, it is thought that this allows a sufficient future perspective. To attempt to project beyond that point is difficult, because there are many unknowns. Using the road example, it may be largely unknown what the typical commuting pattern will be ten or more years from now. Will commuters be greater or lesser users of car pools? Will the average number of cars per family increase, thereby increasing the need for roads even though population may be relatively constant? Will rising fuel prices force radical changes in transportation habits?

In economically unstable periods, any type of projection—including the budget year as well as subsequent years—will be subject to possible error. The high inflation rates experienced in the mid-1970s could not have been easily foreseen earlier, yet such inflation caused severe problems for state and local governments in funding services at existing levels. Even when inflation rates decline, jurisdictions have difficulty deciding whether the current lower rates should be used for projections or the previously higher rates. Under these conditions, jurisdictions may be incapable of projecting requirements beyond the budget year.

Assuming projections can be made, however, these can be limited to finances or can include program data projections. The state-of-the-art tends to limit projections to finances, showing anticipated future financial requirements, but there is increasing use of program impact and output projections. The requests show what resources will be needed in future years along with the benefits that will be derived. Projections of this type are especially useful for proposed new or expanded programs, indicating to decision makers the linkage between meeting societal problems and expending resources.

Multi-year projections using cost and program data can be helpful in coping with severe economic conditions. Where program reductions are necessitated by inflation, agency requests can illustrate the consequences over a longer time period. Cuts in an agency's budget made this year may seem essential but may produce undesired future consequences. To live within available revenues, a city may reduce its road maintenance program with no noticeable reduction in road quality in the first year; however, by the second or third year following these cuts, the city may have a road network of substantially lower quality than before. Multi-year requests, then, can be used to inform decision makers that by living within available revenues and not increasing taxes, deteriorated roads will result.

Projecting program results is difficult at best, given that a governmental program is typically only part of a larger system. A fire department will have some influence upon the incidence and magnitude of fires, but other important factors include changes in the conditions of structures, their uses, changes in the density of structures, and also changes in weather conditions.

The multi-year request is a communication mechanism that can serve to develop understandings among the system participants as to what are current commitments. Agency officials indicate what their understanding is of the future of a program and what the resource requirements will be. Where program data are projected, agencies indicate what can be accomplished with resources. Holding agencies, chief executives, or legislative bodies to these multi-year projections, however, may be impossible. A fire department, as we have seen, may be unable to keep the incidence of fires to that which was projected. A new mayor may decide against the previously accepted "commitment" and reduce the size of fire personnel. The city council may change its views on fire needs, or a new council may be elected that has differing opinions from what was previously adopted. In other words, the multi-year request, once acted upon, is not cast in stone but instead can only offer some perspective on decisions that are being made.

Program Structure Some set of building blocks is essential in bringing together program and resource information based upon multi-year projections that are developed in accordance with request guidance issued from the budget office. Historically, requests have been prepared using the building blocks of organizational units—departments, bureaus, offices, and divisions. Requests of this type are necessary because on a day-to-day basis government operates by organizational unit; it is the organization that is held accountable for the use of resources.

Another set of building blocks used for budget requests is program structure.[29] This is a classification scheme that begins with broad societal aspirations, with these being factored into more narrowly focused purposes. Going down the structure, each succeeding level focuses less upon general values and more upon specific functions and operations of government. The broad value of protecting the citizenry and their property, for example, can include protection from crime which can be further refined to concentrate upon law enforcement and criminal rehabilitation.

Some standardization of terminology associated with program structure is developing, although issues remain to be resolved. At the highest level in the structure are programs that, in turn are factored into categories, subcategories, and elements. From a few to ten or more major programs are usually identified. Pennsylvania, for example, has used eight Commonwealth programs: direction and support services, protection of persons and property, health (physical and mental well-being), intellectual development and education, social development, economic development and income maintenance, transportation and communication, and recreation and cultural enrichment. A program structure suggested by Murray L. Weidenbaum for the federal government had only four programs—national security, public welfare, economic development, and general obligations.[30] In contrast, the federal budget has used three major functional

---

[29] Paul L. Brown, "Establishing a Program Structure," in Fremont J. Lyden and Ernest G. Miller, eds., *Planning-Programming-Budgeting: A Systems Approach to Management*, 2nd ed. (Chicago: Markham, 1972), pp. 183–95; A. E. Buck, *Public Budgeting* (New York: Harper & Brothers, 1929), p. 274; Werner Z. Hirsch, et al., *Local Government Program Budgeting: Theory and Practice* (New York: Praeger, 1974), pp. 190–214; Robert A. Huff and Marjorie O. Chandler, *A Taxonomy of Instructional Programs in Higher Education* (Washington: U.S. Government Printing Office, 1970); J. Michael Kavanagh, et al., *Program Budgeting for Urban Recreation: Current Status and Prospects in Los Angeles* (New York: Praeger, 1973), pp. 15–35; Creta D. Sabine, ed., *Accountability: Systems Planning in Education* (Homewood, Ill.: ETC, 1973); Donald C. Shoup and Stephen L. Mehay, *Program Budgeting for Urban Police Services* (New York: Praeger, 1972); Arthur Smithies, "Conceptual Framework for the Program Budget," in David Novick, ed., *Program Budgeting*, 2nd ed. (New York: Holt, Rinehart and Winston, 1969), p. 41; Tory N. Tjersland, "PDS is a Better Way," *Governmental Finance*, 4 (February, 1975): 10–19.

[30] Murray L. Weidenbaum, "A Government-Wide Program Budget" (St. Louis,

classes—national defense, human resources, and other nondefense—with the latter subdivided into physical resources, interest, and all other functions. The Congress has used fourteen and more functions to set spending levels since the 1974 budget reform. The point is that there is no obvious "ideal" number of programs to be used, but the use of few programs in a large, complex organization may necessitate a greater number of levels in the structure.

The choice of how many levels to use in a program structure is difficult. It may be viewed simply from an esthetic vantage point or more importantly in terms of program measurement theory.[31] Numerous levels in the structure are cumbersome, awkward, and esthetically cluttered; numerous levels are likely to produce confusion and excessive paperwork as forms are completed for each level. Many leveled program structures rather than simplifying the world in order to make it more intelligible may seem to make the world more complex.

More important than the esthetic argument is that a reasonable number of levels in the structure can provide a picture of how governmental activities produce (or fail to produce) desired results. Higher levels of the structure, then, may have program impacts associated with them, whereas lower levels have outputs and still lower levels have activities. The program structure in such cases becomes a series of if—then statements, asserting that if a given level of activities occurs, then a given set of outputs will be produced, which then will achieve a given set of impacts.

These purported causal linkages can be seen in Figure 6, which shows the breakout of Pennsylvania's program for protection of persons and property. Nine substantive categories are used, ranging from traffic and crime to water damage control and occupational health and safety. The

Mo.: Institute for Urban and Regional Studies, Washington University, February, 1967).

[31] See "Developing an Objective Oriented Governmental Program Structure," *PPB Note 5* (Washington: State-Local Finances Project, The George Washington University, April 1967); "Development of Initial Instructions to Inaugurate Planning-Programming-Budgeting System: Some Preliminary Considerations and Model Instruction to be Adapted for Local Use," *PPB Note 3* (Washington: State-Local Finances Project, The George Washington University, January 1967); Harry J. Hartley, *Educational Planning-Programming-Budgeting* (Englewood Cliffs, N.J.: Prentice-Hall, 1968); U.S. Department of Health, Education, and Welfare, Office of the Assistant Secretary for Planning and Evaluation, *Planning-Programming-Budgeting: Guidance for Program and Financial Plan*, rev. ed. (Washington: U.S. Government Printing Office, February 1968), pp. 15–53; U.S. Department of Health, Education, and Welfare, Office of the Secretary, *Operational Planning System Handbook* (Washington: U.S. Government Printing Office, 1974).

crime category is subdivided on the basis of process. First, the attempt is made to prevent crime. Second, when crimes occur, laws are enforced. Third, convicted criminals are reintegrated into society. These three subcategories, then, are subdivided into program elements. The figure shows those elements under the reintegration subcategory. The expressed assumption is that if government does the things identified at the element level, then offenders will be reintegrated and in turn crime will have been controlled and/or reduced.

While the breakout in Figure 6 on first glance may seem complete, one should recognize that other possible options have been excluded. For example, the structure fails to reveal the types of crime committed. Possible subcategories might have been crimes against persons (murder and rape), crimes against property (burglaries and embezzlements), and organized crime and vice (narcotics and prostitution). The structure also

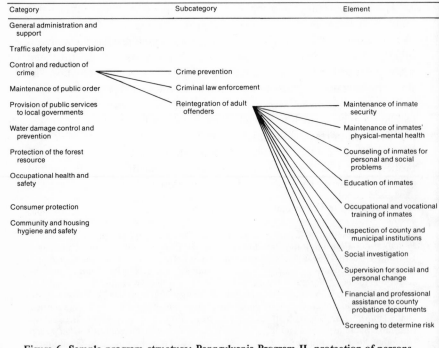

Figure 6. Sample program structure: Pennsylvania Program II, protection of persons and property. Source: Robert J. Mowitz, *The Design and Implementation of Pennsylvania's Planning, Programming, Budgeting System* (Harrisburg: Commonwealth of Pennsylvania, 1970), p. 52.

tribution of crime, whether based upon
in-rural breakout. Sometimes information
sidered desirable from the standpoint that
t is taking place within their respective
er, does not indicate the type of offenders,
economic background, level of educational
h. In other words, program structure by
y but in doing so must ignore some potentially useful forms oi ınıꞅ ion.[32]

Given the inability to be able to highlight many different items in a
program structure, as evidenced in the example of crime reduction, there is
a temptation to conclude that more than one structure should be employed. By using two, three, or more program structures, virtually all the
facets of any program could be identified. Such an approach, however,
seems ill-advised. First, it would necessitate the accumulation, storage, and
manipulation of more data, running the risk of overburdening existing
capabilities to comprehend such information. Second and more importantly, the use of several structures in effect avoids the need to make
any judgments on what is important and what should be the basis for
decision making. In actuality, the use of multi-structures says that decision
makers have little understanding of what they expect to be accomplished.
A mass of data would be provided with the expectation or hope that
someone would find some piece of information to be useful.

At the same time, this does not mean that any agency would be
restricted to collecting data only on those items identified in the program
structure. An agency presumably would gather considerably more data for
other purposes, particularly for internal management. However, that data
would not surface in conjunction with the program structure.

One of the main advantages of a program structure is that it concentrates upon program results and does not give the impression that governmental agencies exist for their own sake. The structure groups together
programs having similar purposes regardless of the organizational locations
of the programs. If two agencies are both concerned with increasing the
employability of minorities, then it is appropriate to have the relevant
portions of those organizational units reported in the same section of the
program structure. The federal government's experiment with PPB in

---

[32] For alternative approaches to health program structures, see Sidney Sonenblum, *Program Budgeting for Urban Health and Welfare Services with Special Reference to Los Angeles* (New York: Praeger, 1974), pp. 45–71.

civilian agencies in the 1960s and early 1970s failed to do this in that separate program structures were prepared for each department. State and local governments have tended to develop governmentwide structures.

The design of program structure, when the structure is intended to be a vehicle for program decision making, is not a trivial exercise. Arthur Smithies has observed:

> The way in which a program structure is set up for the government as a whole or for any major segment can have a profound effect on the decisions that are reached, so that the design of programs should be regarded as an important part of the decision-making process.[33]

Yet, despite the structure's significance, the design has often been delegated and redelegated down to junior-level analysts. The structure, however, should not be solely the product of low-level analysts or even the department secretary or chief executive. Because all decision makers will be affected, the structure needs to satisfy all participants, though only in terms of coverage and not in terms of satisfying each participant in assigning specific priorities.

One issue concerning the development of program structure is the relative roles of the executive and legislative branches. In an executive budgeting system, clearly the chief executive should have substantial control over the structure's design. Moreover, executive agencies should play key roles, because program expertise is concentrated there. On the other hand, a strong case for legislative involvement can be made. Because the legislature has responsibility for setting policy, that body should have the authority to specify legislative objectives or legislative intent and the means for measuring success or failure in achieving objectives. The federal 1974 reform legislation provides that the Comptroller General, if requested by a congressional committee, "shall assist, . . . in developing a statement of legislative objectives and goals and methods for assessing and reporting actual program performance in relation to such legislative objectives and goals."[34] Depending upon the extent to which this provision is used, much of the ambiguity surrounding the purposes of programs may be reduced; greater clarity of legislative intent will be provided as well as standards for program measurement.

To summarize, budget requests may be prepared by organizational unit and by program structure building blocks. The requests will include

---

[33] Smithies, "Conceptual Framework for the Program Budget," p. 41.

[34] Congressional Budget and Impoundment Control Act, Title VII (1974).

financial data, probably personnel data, and increasingly program data. Some form of guidance will be provided by the budget office; the guidance may be in terms of dollar availability or desired program changes. The requests will cover the past, current, and budget years and are likely to extend to other future years.

DECISIONS ON BUDGET REQUESTS

By the time a budget request has reached the budget office, an extensive series of discussions will have been completed within the line agency. In large agencies having several layers of organizational units, those at the bottom will have attempted to persuade their superiors for approval of requests for additional funding. The forces from the top downward tend to be negative in the sense that there is pressure to limit the growth of programs and the corresponding rise in expenditures. Yet, this does not mean that there are simply a set of no-men and yes-men who do battle within each agency or department. Middle managers up through departmental heads are required to take both positions, rejecting many of the proposals brought to them by subordinates and, in negotiating with their superiors, advocating those proposals that they accept.

Part of the negative influence within an agency is a function of superior levels attempting to determine what is likely to be "saleable" to the budget office and the chief executive. Agencies are aware that they are unlikely to get more than they request and are likely to get less. Therefore, they will avoid requesting too little but will not ask for exorbitant sums unless an open-ended budget system is in use. The requested sums will be "reasonable" or slightly above this level to allow for some cutbacks. Agencies tend to "pad" budget requests but not "overpad" them.

Once budget requests are submitted, the budget office begins the task of assessing these, leading eventually to recommendations to be made to the chief executive. The assessments will be based in part upon the budget office's experience with each agency. Six types of occasions bring the two into contact with each other. First, and most obvious, the office and agencies are brought together through the budget request process. Second, the office may act in a review capacity when agencies seek new legislation. In the federal government, the OMB performs a legislative clearance function for the President, thereby avoiding potentially embarrassing situations in which agency spokesmen and the President might endorse conflicting legislation. Third, the two come in contact during the execution phase of the budget cycle. Fourth, the resolution of management questions, the establishment of statistical standards, and the regulation of automatic data processing constitute other occasions that may bring the central budget office and agencies into contact with each other. At the federal level and frequently at the state level, the budget office is responsible for conducting management studies of the agencies. Fifth, the office often serves as an information collector for the chief executive. When the executive needs to know something, the budget bureau is frequently assigned the responsibility of contacting agencies. Sixth, "general learning and teaching contact" exists between the budget office and the agencies.[35]

Just as the interplay is extensive and vociferous within an agency in preparing a budget, so considerable tension exists between the central budget office and the agencies. The central office, as the agent of the chief executive, must assert a centralizing influence over the diverse interests of administrative units; these, on the other hand, can be expected to favor greater autonomy. Operating departments and agencies can be presumed to favor the advancement of their respective programs (seeking greater funds), while the budget office is forced to take the unpopular position of having to say no.[36]

Though the formal written request submitted by the agency is the beginning point for budget review, there is often need for more extensive communication between the two organizations. The budget examiner(s) assigned responsibility for reviewing the agency is the main link between the two; with the passage of time, examiners gain considerable knowledge about their agencies, providing a substantive expertise within the budget office. It is not uncommon for examiners eventually to become advocates for the agencies they review and frequently even to shift their employment to an operating agency. Still, the accusation is frequently made by agency officials that budget examiners, not being program oriented, are insensitive to the needs of operating units.

A budget examiner seeking further information has at least two main options regarding whom to contact in the agency. One is the agency's

---

[35] James W. Davis and Randall B. Ripley, "The Bureau of the Budget and Executive Branch Agencies: Notes on their Interaction," *Journal of Politics*, 29 (1967): 751–53; also see Rowland Egger, "The United States Bureau of the Budget," *Parliamentary Affairs*, 3 (1949): 39–54.

[36] For an analysis of staff-line conflicts in budgeting for private enterprises, see Chris Argyris, *The Impact of Budgets on People* (New York: Controllership Foundation, 1954).

budget office, because this unit prepared the budget request. However, a budget office may know comparatively little about its agency's substantive programs. The other is the operating bureau or office responsible for a given program. Some agencies insist upon a formal approach, requiring that requests for information flow through the agency budget office, which then obtains the needed data from operating units.[37]

The nature of the dialogue between the budget office and departments will hinge in large measure upon the extent to which the latter consider the former an important ally or an opponent. Only minimal information can be expected from the agency that is suspicious of the central budget office. A common concern is that the agency not release data that could be used to its own disadvantage. One important strategy that is sometimes employed is to attempt to win the confidence and support of the examiner; if this can be achieved, then the agency in effect has gained a spokesman for its program within the chief executive's staff.

At the same time, winning budget office approval is no guarantee of success for the agency. The resistant or recalcitrant agency, indeed, may be able to increase the caution with which the examiner makes recommendations reducing the agency's budget. At the federal level, the significance of OMB action may be mitigated, considering that the Congress has the power to pass appropriations. It has been suggested that opposition by the budget office to an agency's requests for funds may be helpful in winning legislative support. This dividend is partially a result of congressional distrust of the Office of Management and Budget; if the OMB opposes something, it must be good. Further, the agency and not the OMB must defend the budget request before Congress, and therefore, the office's utility to the agency is more important in the preparation phase than in the approval phase of the budget cycle. Some organizational units, such as the Federal Bureau of Investigation in the 1950s and 1960s, have been able to secure extensive support within the Congress, thereby providing the agencies with some autonomy vis-à-vis their respective departments and the OMB.[38]

After the budget office has completed its homework in reviewing an agency's request, hearings are held with agency representatives. The same

---

[37] Davis and Ripley, "The Bureau of the Budget," pp. 753–60.

[38] For a discussion of political strategies used in the budgetary process, see Aaron Wildavsky, *The Politics of the Budgetary Process*, 2nd ed. (Boston: Little, Brown, 1974); Ira Sharkansky, *The Politics of Taxing and Spending* (Indianapolis: Bobbs-Merrill, 1969).

tensions exist in this process as before, namely the agency takes a cautious approach in providing information to the budget office while the latter attempts to determine how much confidence to place in the agency's presentation. Whereas in the homework phase the budget office may have focused mainly on detail—how were certain figures reached on a given form?—now the assessment focuses upon broader concerns. The budget office must decide whether the recommended program submitted by the agency can accomplish what is promised and whether the anticipated accomplishments are worth seeking. The burden of proof rests with the agency. The operating agency that has a reputation for requesting excessive sums and for over-promising on results will be suspect, while the advantage lies with the agency that has a reputation for basing its requests upon careful analysis.[39]

The response of the budget office to agency requests will be in part a function of the office's assessment of its own powers and responsibilities in relation to the operating agencies and other central units. Few would deny to a budget office the ministerial or bookkeeping functions of assembling requests and carrying out the mechanical duties of designing, tabulating, and seeing to the printing of the budget. However, how many additional responsibilities the budget office has depends largely upon competition from other units and the management style of the chief executive.[40]

Because in an executive budgeting system the chief executive has the final say on what to recommend to the legislative body, the budget office will attempt to formulate recommendations thought to be in keeping with the executive's priorities. Examiners' recommendations that are known to be in conflict with the executive's position will not be strongly defended and may not even be presented. As part of the calculation of what to recommend, the budget office will assess the chances of agencies making direct appeals to the chief executive and thereby overturning the budget office's recommendations. If this strategy, sometimes known as making an end-run around the budget office, is successful, it can severely weaken the budget office's role. If an agency knows it can get what it wants by making

---

[39] L. L. Wade, "The U.S. Bureau of the Budget as Agency Evaluator: Orientations to Action," *American Journal of Economics and Sociology*, 27 (1968): 55–62.

[40] See Allen Schick, "The Budget Bureau That Was: Thoughts on the Rise, Decline, and Future of a Presidential Agency," in Harvey C. Mansfield, Allen Schick, and Thomas E. Cronin, *Papers on the Institutionalized Presidency* (Washington: Brookings, 1971), pp. 519–39.

direct appeals to the chief executive, the agency is likely to consider the budget office as only a bookkeeper that can be largely ignored.

The extent to which these end-runs are successful is a function of executive style. During the Nixon years, OMB was a strong force. Because President Nixon seemingly preferred not to deal directly with agency officials on their budgets, the agencies were forced to work directly with OMB. This style, however, is generally atypical. The more common approach at all levels of government is to maintain a relatively open system in which agency officials have access to the chief executive.

In addition to the competition between the central budget office and line agency, competition exists between the budget unit and other centrally located units. This is especially the case in the federal government. For example, the OMB shares the revenue-estimating function with the Council of Economic Advisers and Treasury Department. Other important competitors are the National Security Council, the Domestic Council, and members of the White House Office. At this level of the federal government, personalities become important. The roles of various participants are dependent upon the President's administrative style and his confidence in the abilities of key figures. Advice is accepted from those persons in whom the President has confidence.

In the international policy arena there are many participants, each of which can be expected to be sensitive to any major exercise of control by the central budget office. OMB control is likely to be resisted by the State Department, Defense Department, National Security Council, and the Central Intelligence Agency, all of which will argue that budgeters should not be responsible for decisions involving international security. Substantial controversy has always existed over who should be the dominant advisor to the President in such affairs. In the public's view, the very visible National Security Council has perhaps come to be considered the appropriate locus for advice. Created in 1947, the National Security Council is composed of the President, the Vice President, the Secretaries of State and Defense, and the Director of the Office of Emergency Preparedness. The OMB is not officially a part of the National Security Council, though it can be invited to meetings at the President's discretion.

The role of the National Security Council is dependent upon the President's inclinations. Until the outbreak of the Korean War, Truman used the Council little. Eisenhower relied upon it greatly, Kennedy largely ignored it until the Bay of Pigs, and Johnson used it substantially. In the early years of the Nixon Administration, the Council was used extensively, but as years passed, some observers thought that greater power was being assumed by Henry A. Kissinger when he was Assistant to the President in the White House Office. He apparently was able to retain this dominant role when he later became Secretary of State, and his power continued during the Ford Administration.

In the domestic arena the competition is not as fierce but is still challenging. In addition to line agencies, the Domestic Council is a potential competitor. Formed by President Nixon in 1970, the Council consists of the President, the Vice President, Department Secretaries (with the notable exceptions of the Secretaries of Defense and State), and other officials, including the Director of the Office of Management and Budget. The Domestic Council seems to have been created to perform a role in the civilian field similar to the National Security Council's role in the international field. By bringing key nondefense officials together, the Domestic Council is expected to provide a coordinated set of policy recommendations for the President.[41] At the same time, the President may rely upon trusted associates for advice. Eisenhower relied heavily upon Sherman Adams, Kennedy upon his brother Robert, and Nixon upon Attorney General John Mitchell, Secretary of the Treasury John Connally, and Counsellors to the President Arthur Burns and Daniel P. Moynihan. Ford appeared not to have a dominant personal advisor for domestic concerns.

This discussion has tended to emphasize the bureaucratic political calculations made by agencies and the budget office, but an unresolved issue is the extent to which the budget office should base its recommendations upon professional criteria and avoid partisan, and bureaucratic, politics. As an agency of the chief executive, the budget office is expected to develop recommendations that are compatible with executive priorities. On the other hand, budgeters as professionals are said to have a responsibility to report to the executive their views on the worthiness of programs. To report that a given program is operating well, simply because the executive wants to hear that, does a disservice. In making recommendations on the future of a program the budget office probably should not assume a fixed position, because then all objectivity may be lost. In other words, a role of "neutral competence" has been proposed in which the budget office retains its professional approach to budget recommendations

---

[41] Raymond J. Waldmann, "The Domestic Council:: Innovation in Presidential Government," *Public Administration Review*, 36 (1976): 260–68.

but simultaneously seeks to develop recommendations in tune with executive priorities.[42]

Only in the final stages of preparation does the chief executive become involved. Indeed, he or she will have intentionally avoided making many decisions, waiting as long as possible to be able to better assess the available options. At least four closely related factors will be considered: his or her own priorities, economic conditions, the position of the legislative body, and the preferences of the citizenry.

The executive has program preferences which he or she hopes to further through the budget process. Depending upon the type of budget requests that have been prepared, options may be presented not only in terms of dollars but also of program impacts and outputs. The executive will assess the recommendations made by both the budget office and the agencies. Judgments will be made either explicitly or only implicitly about the confidence to be placed in projected program accomplishments. A conclusion in many cases may be that the data presented are unreliable, thereby encouraging decisions to be made on some other basis, such as does a given department have a reputation for doing a good or mediocre job? In such cases, program information may eventually appear in the budget document, but the data may have played a negligible role in the decision process.

Economic conditions will be assessed from revenue estimating and economic policy standpoints. Revenue sources that fluctuate by economic conditions include personal income, corporate income, and sales taxes. The property tax is a more stable source, although during economic recessions there are more tax delinquencies. For small local jurisdictions relying primarily on the property tax, revenue estimating is often a simple and even casual process; changes in property assessments are reviewed in terms of tax rates and expected delinquencies. For federal, state, and large local governments, much more thorough analyses are conducted to develop revenue estimates, including computerized economic models.[43] If a state or local government forecasts reduced revenues, then either reducing expenditures or increasing taxes become the main available options. Increasing taxes during an economic slump, however, is not likely to be

---

[42] Hugh Heclo, "OMB and the Presidency—The Problem of 'Neutral Competence,' " *Public Interest*, No. 38 (1975): 80–98.

[43] Semoon Chang, "Forecasting Revenues to Municipal Government: The Case of Mobile, Alabama," *Governmental Finance*, 5 (February, 1976): 16–20.

politically acceptable, and therefore the executive may be forced into expenditure cuts to stay within projected revenues.

The federal government not only is concerned with revenue estimates but also with economic policy. The focus is the relative balance between projected revenues and possible expenditures, yielding budget surpluses or deficits. As will be seen in Chapter 13, expenditure and tax policies are used to stimulate economic growth, encourage price stability, further full employment, and strive for an equilibrium in the international balance of payments.[44] The chief executive, then, must compare these economic policy concerns with preferences for achieving program accomplishments. The decision may be reached that even though a given program improvement along with increased funding is needed, expenditure increases must be avoided for economic policy reasons.

A third set of considerations involves relationships with the legislative body. Stated simply, the executive assesses the chances of various recommendations receiving the approval of Congress, the state legislature, or the city council. This does not mean that the executive will recommend only that which is likely to be approved. The recommendation that is doomed to legislative rejection may be put forth by the executive as a means of preparing the legislature to approve the proposal in some future year, or the executive may be strongly committed to a proposal despite legislative opposition.

A fourth type of consideration and by no means the least important will be perceived citizen preferences in terms of both service and tax levels. Chief executives, being political animals, have a keen sense for what the general citizenry and interest groups desire. Results from national and state polls are watched for important trends. Some cities such as Nashville and particularly Dayton conduct surveys of citizens to identify attitudes about existing and desired services.

For the budget office, the final weeks of deliberation by the chief executive are often frustrating. Decisions are seemingly reached and then may be reversed. The executive may instruct the budget office that an agency's proposed change will be included in the budget, but after considering revenue estimates, the executive rejects the proposal. Materials prepared evenings and weekends by the budget office may find their way

---

[44] *Fiscal and Monetary Policies for Steady Economic Growth* (New York: Committee for Economic Development, 1969), pp. 23–35; Richard A. Musgrave and Peggy B. Musgrave, *Public Finance in Theory and Practice*, 2nd ed. (New York: McGraw-Hill, 1976).

to the paper shredder as decisions are changed. The approach may seem haphazard and probably is in many respects, but it is this way because of the numerous factors being evaluated simultaneously.

A common complaint made of the preparation phase is that the budget is only considered as a whole by the chief executive. An organizational unit within a department or agency is concerned primarily with its own piece of the budget, and the same is true of a department vis-à-vis other departments and the rest of the budget. Even within the central budget office, budget examiners will focus mainly on one or a few segments of the budget and not on the total package. The executive, however, must pull together the pieces of information and intelligence provided by various sources into a set of decisions that can be defended as a whole. The budget that is to be submitted to the legislative body is the chief executive's.

BUDGET DOCUMENTS

The final product of the preparation phase of budgeting is a budget document or documents that contain the decisions that have been reached in the months involving agency requests and executive review. The budget at this point is only a proposal, a set of recommended policies and programs set forth by the chief executive in an executive budgeting system. The budget will remain a proposal until the legislative body has acted on it.

The budget for any government may consist of one or several documents. Small jurisdictions often have only one budget, but large cities, counties, states, and the federal government have many budget documents. At the federal level, the following documents are used.

The *Current Services Budget*, which is released in November, was established by the 1974 reform legislation and was intended to show how continuing programs at existing levels would affect the following year's budget. This current-commitment type of budget was expected to show what resources would be required, assuming no congressional modifications in programs. The current services budget, however, can be used as a political tool by the President, because important judgments must be used in making projections; depending upon the strategy selected, this document can project little or major growth in expenditures.[45]

In January, the President releases *The Budget of the United States*,

---

[45] Joel Havemann, "Budget Reform/New Accounting Technique Could Become Political Tool," *National Journal*, 7 (1975): 1417.

which contains several hundred pages and provides substantial narrative discussions of programs along with supporting tables covering financial data but little program data.

The *Budget in Brief* is released at the same time and is a sypnosis of the budget intended for general public use. Similar summary documents are prepared by state governments and some local governments.

The U.S. *Budget Appendix*, the size of a major metropolitan telephone directory, is the main federal document providing extensive detail, including data on finances, personnel (see Chapter 11), pay increases, and other matters.

Special Analyses, another federal budget document released in January, contains selected discussions and tables on items such as borrowing and debt, aid to state and local governments, and capital expenditures (see Chapter 10). The content of this document varies from year to year. During the PPB era, program structure was presented, whereas in more recent years social and environmental programs have been highlighted.

Another document is the *Economic Report of the President*, prepared by the Council of Economic Advisers and not by OMB. The *Economic Report* discusses expected economic trends for the coming year and is the basis upon which the President's economic policy has been formulated.[46]

An issue concerning budget documents at all levels of government is the extent of their coverage. State and local governments are major users of special funds, which basically are financial accounts for special revenue sources and from which expenditures can be made only for specific purposes. A jurisdiction's general fund consists of revenue that can be used for all functions of the government. These different types of funds are discussed later in conjunction with accounting problems (Chapter 9), but here it should be noted that many jurisdictions have a general fund budget document and then one or more documents covering special funds. The result of these separate budgets is confusion over what is the size of the total budget and how much is being spent by any given agency, because the agency may be receiving support from several funds.

The coverage issue at the federal level is similar.[47] Until recent years,

---

[46] A budget document introduced by the Ford Administration in 1976 focused upon program issues and alternatives: Office of Management and Budget, *Seventy Issues: Fiscal Year 1977 Budget*, rev. ed. (Washington: U.S. Government Printing Office, April 1976).

[47] David J. Ott and Attiat F. Ott, *Federal Budget Policy*, rev. ed. (Washington: Brookings, 1969); "Budgetary Concepts: A Symposium," *Review of Economics and*

there were really three forms of federal budgets: the administrative budget, the consolidated cash statement, and the federal sector of the national income accounts. The main difference between the administrative budget and the consolidated cash statement was that the former did not include trust funds, particularly Social Security and highways, and the latter did. These funds were excluded on the grounds that they were earmarked for specific purposes and therefore were not subject to annual budget decision processes. The disadvantage of their exclusion was that the magnitude of federal revenues and expenditures was greatly understated. The third type of budget, national income accounts, shows the economic character of federal transactions such as the government's purchase of goods and services in the economy. This "budget," however, excludes governmental lending and borrowing.

These three types of budgets resulted in much confusion, which eventually led to the development of a new concept in budget coverage. Because each of the three approaches had different coverages, total revenues and expenditures varied from one to another, leading to different statements of budget surpluses and deficits. Persons could paint different pictures of federal finances—gloomy or bright—by choosing to discuss one budget statement and ignoring the other two. In response to this problem, Lyndon Johnson appointed in 1967 the President's Commission on Budget Concepts, whose eventual recommendation for a "unified budget" was incorporated in the 1969 budget.[48] In one summary table, four types of information were presented. First, the amount of appropriations requested was shown. Second, receipts, expenditures, and loans were tabulated along with the budget surplus or deficit. Trust funds were included in these figures. Third, the means of financing showed how the total deficit was to be financed or the surplus was to be spent. Fourth, the outstanding federal debt section showed total indebtedness and the total amount of federal credit programs, both direct loans and guaranteed or insured loans.

Although the unified budget did include trust funds, important items were excluded, and debate continues over what should be included and excluded. In accordance with the Commission on Budget Concepts, government-sponsored enterprises that are privately owned are excluded;

Statistics, 45 (1963): 113–47; Ronald W. Johnson, "Evolution of Budget Concepts in the President's Message: 1923–1968," in President's Commission on Budget Concepts, *Staff Papers and Other Materials Reviewed* (Washington: U.S. Government Printing Office, 1967), pp. 93–103.

[48] President's Commission on Budget Concepts, *Report* (Washington: U.S. Government Printing Office, 1967).

these enterprises include such organizations as the Federal Land Banks, the Federal Home Loan Banks, and the Federal National Mortgage Association. Information on these enterprises is presented in the *Budget Appendix* as "annexed budgets," but the finances of these enterprises are not part of the revenue/expenditure presentation of the unified budget.

Since adoption of the unified budget, important changes have been made. One change is that the summary table covering the four items discussed above is no longer presented. The same general types of information, however, are available through several tables. A far more important change has been the passage of legislation removing some federal agencies from the budget, creating what is called the "off-budget." The first to be removed was the Export-Import Bank in 1971.[49] Other off-budget agencies include the Postal Service, the Rural Telephone Bank, the Rural Electrification and Telephone revolving fund, and the Housing for the Elderly or Handicapped fund.

The off-budget, then, weakens the unified budget as a comprehensive picture of federal finances. If one examines only the unified budget, then the debt of the Postal Service will be overlooked. For example, the 1977 unified budget proposed by Gerald Ford contained a $43 billion deficit, but the off-budget contained an additional $11.1 billion debt. The Ford administration concluded, "In many cases there is little or no justification for off-budget treatment."[50]

Turning to other aspects of the budget document, both revenue and expenditure data are presented. The coverage of receipts or revenues is substantially less extensive than expenditures. At the federal level, seven types of receipts are reported: 1) individual income taxes, 2) corporation income taxes, 3) social insurance taxes and contributions, 4) excise taxes, 5) estate and gift taxes, 6) custom duties, and 7) miscellaneous receipts. State and local budgets include many of these sources, excluding customs duties, plus funds from other governments—state and federal aid to local governments and federal aid to states. The budget document on the revenue side may also discuss proposed changes in tax laws and particularly proposed tax rate changes.

The bulk of the budget document is devoted to the expenditure side of government finance, with the main classification usually being by organiza-

---

[49] The Export-Import Bank was to be returned to the unified budget as of October, 1976.

[50] Office of Management and Budget, *The Budget of the United States Government, 1977* (Washington: U.S. Government Printing Office, 1976), p. 12.

tional unit. Each department's budget is presented within which subunits are given separate treatment. A generally uniform format is used for each subunit. There is a heading for Bureau No. 1 in Department A, often followed by a brief narrative description of the bureau's responsibilities and functions. The legislation establishing the bureau and its programs may be cited in the narrative. Narratives contained in the federal *Budget Appendix* also contain proposed appropriation language that may be quite specific, as in the case of the Bureau of Indian Affairs: appropriations are "not to exceed $200,000 ... to assist the Pyramid Lake Paiute Tribe of Indians in the construction of facilities for the restoration of the Pyramid Lake fishery."[51]

In addition to the narrative are various tabular displays. Expenditures are reported by object classes, such as personnel, equipment, and travel (see Chapter 9). These financial tables may be primarily for information purposes or may later be incorporated in the legislative appropriation. When this practice is used, the legislative body is said to have adopted a line-item budget, a practice that reduces the President's, governor's, or mayor's flexibility in executing the budget. Tabular displays of personnel data, both in terms of number of employees and personnel costs, are common in budget documents (see Chapter 11).

Program data are increasingly common in budget documents of all types of governments. Much of the program data presented in the federal *Budget Appendix* is for outputs and activities. Table 6 illustrates some of the work load data to be found in the budget for the Department of Agriculture. These data show the number of acres treated for plant pest control. While the figures depict the level of effort maintained by the Department, they do not indicate the impact of these activities. The fact that a thousand acres have been treated to control gypsy moths does not necessarily mean that those acres are now under control. Moreover, the data do not indicate the extent of infestation in comparison with the level of treatment. Is the Department treating 5, 50, or 100 percent of the infested acres? Other breakouts do show impact and/or need types of information. Reported in Agriculture's program for animal diseases are the number of states free of brucellosis, cattle tuberculosis, and hog cholera. However, no evidence is presented to show the linkage between what the Department of Agriculture does and the incidence of disease. USDA

---

[51] Office of Management and Budget, *The Budget of the United States Government, 1977: Appendix* (Washington: U.S. Government Printing Office, 1976), p. 479.

TABLE 6
Work Load Data in U.S. Department of Agriculture Budget, Fiscal
1977, Plant Pest Control

	1975 act.	1976 est.	1977 est.
Acres treated (thousands):			
Boll weevil	598	750	750
Grasshopper	677	1,000	1,000
Gypsy moth	15		
Imported fire ant	12,679	18,000	18,000
Japanese beetle	16	5	
White fringed beetle	9		
Sterile insects released (millions):			
Mexican fruit fly	21	23	23
Pink bollworm (adult moth)	68	100	100
Parasites released: Cereal leaf beetle (sites)	820	450	450

Source: Office of Management and Budget, *Budget of the United States Government, 1977: Appendix* (Washington: U.S. Government Printing Office, 1976), p. 109.

reports that all states are free of hog cholera, but is that the result of the Department's efforts, state departments of agriculture, individual actions of farmers, or some combination of these?

An alternative to arranging the budget document by organizational unit is to use program structure.[52] The federal government does not have a program budget but, as mentioned earlier, does use broad functional classifications to summarize the budget.[53] The functional classifications are useful for highlighting the changing character of governmental expenditures over time, such as changes in the proportion of the budget committed to social services, but they are not linked explicitly to program descriptions or specific agency activities.

An example of a budget organized by program and not by organizational unit is that of Lakewood, Colorado. The major programs are safety, transportation, environment, leisure, development, and administration. Within each of these, portions of several department budgets may be

---

[52] Hirsch, *Local Government Program Budgeting*, pp. 62–109.

[53] For functional classes used in Britain and Canada, see James Cutt, *A Planning, Programming, and Budgeting Manual: Resource Allocation in Public Sector Economics* (New York: Praeger, 1974), pp. 111–36. Also see, David Novick, ed., *Current Practice in Program Budgeting (PPBS)* (New York: Crane, Russak, 1973).

reported; "safety" includes part or all of the departments of public safety, community services, and community development plus the municipal court, city attorney, and city clerk. Each of the major programs is subdivided so that "safety" includes traffic regulation, law enforcement, judicial system, (code and other) enforcement, and support services.

The types of program information displayed in Lakewood's budget are illustrated in Table 7; financial and personnel data are also included in the budget but are not shown here. The budget for traffic activities provides a program description, a set of performance objectives, and "analysis," which together may be considered the narrative. Tabular information is presented on demands, work loads, productivity, and effectiveness.

Dayton, Ohio, not only includes in its budget some of the various types of program data used by Lakewood but also contrasts these with results from citizen surveys. Figure 7 shows changes in citizen attitudes about the need for street repair, subdivided by neighborhoods, and the objectives and performance criteria used for streets. Overall, a slight increase in citizen-perceived need for street repair was recorded, even though the miles of street resurfaced had more than doubled; the narrative is used, then, to explain that the survey was conducted before completion of the resurfacing.

Program budgets such as Lakewood's and Dayton's typically require companion organizational budgets particularly because legislative bodies demand organizational budgets and are more likely to appropriate by organization than by program. Pennsylvania had these two types of budgets but changed to a single volume organized by department and within department by programs. The statewide program structure continues to exist even though the document is not organized on that basis. That state also is an example of a jurisdiction using multi-year projections for cost and program information. Table 8 shows program data for Pennsylvania's vocational secondary education subcategory. Data are presented for needs, work load (enrollments), outputs (graduates), and impacts (graduates employed).

Not all available program and resource information can be presented in budget documents, unless one is willing to have a totally unwieldy document.[54] The budget formats of some jurisdictions are rigid in prescribing

---

[54] S. Kenneth Howard has a perfect illustration of the point. A cartoon figure stands dwarfed by the size of the budget, and the caption reads, "Due to the enormous costs in preparing the State Budget this year there will only be one copy." S. Kenneth Howard, *Changing State Budgeting* (Lexington, Ky.: Council of State Governments, 1973), p. vi.

TABLE 7
Program Data for Traffic Activities in Lakewood, Colorado, 1976 Budget

Program: Traffic activities

Program description: Provides traffic patrol and control, traffic law enforcement, and traffic accident investigation to facilitate the safe flow of both vehicular and pedestrian traffic.

1. To prevent any increase in fatal traffic accidents
2. To prevent the increase in traffic injury accidents from exceeding 10 percent
3. To decrease non-injury accidents by 0.5 percent
4. To increase enforcement actions taken by at least 5 percent
5. That patrol agents, on the average, will devote no more than 15 percent of their available manhours to traffic activities
6. To assist the R-1 schools in establishing a junior patrol school crossing guard program as recommended in the Municipal Services and Operations Assessment

Measurement	Objective	1974 actual	1975 estimate	1976 projected
Demand				
Department objective: time budgeted for patrol agents	5	20.0%	20.0%	15.0%
Registered vehicles	–	84,761	86,100	87,260
Total traffic accidents	1–3	5,947	6,053	6,122
Work load				
Summons issued	4	16,781	17,950	18,848
Accident reports prepared	1–3	5,947	5,478	5,151
Percent patrol agent time on traffic activities	5	13.6%	14.0%	15.0%
Hours spent on traffic activities	5	21,235	22,631	25,723

Productivity				
Time spent per summons	4	15 min.	14 min.	13 min.
Time spent per accident report	1–3	45 min.	40 min.	35 min.
Cost per hour on traffic activities	—	$24.63	$26.55	$21.25
Effectiveness				
Percent change in traffic accidents/fatal	1	0.0%	–20.0%	0.0%
Percent change in traffic accident/injury	2	N/A	+11.0%	+10.0%
Percent change in traffic accidents/noninjury	3	N/A	–0.24%	–0.5%

Improved productivity in summons writing and accident reporting will allow increased hours for general traffic law enforcement with existing personnel and the new policy on private property accidents will require fewer accident reports to be prepared. The Department's objective for time spent on traffic activities is being reduced to more accurately reflect the availability of patrol division personnel for traffic activities. Cost savings will be experienced by converting the Crossing Guard Program to junior patrol status, with the Department continuing to provide a coordinator and clerical support.

Source: *Program Performance Budget, 1976* (Lakewood Col.: City of Lakewood, 1975), p. 6.

STREET REPAIR

Percentage of Residents Indicating Streets Needing Major
Repair: 1974
                                                   1975
                                                   change

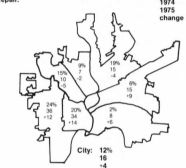

Sixteen percent of Dayton residents indicated that streets
in their neighborhoods needed major repair. Increases between 1974 and 1975 occurred in three of the six neighborhoods. The City's income tax program to resurface 9
miles of streets in 1975 had not been fully implemented at
the time this survey was taken, and its impact would therefore not have affected these results. Because the resurfacing program will be repeated again next year, this survey may indicate areas where resurfacing work is needed
most.

Key 231-3	Activity Street, alley, and bridge maintenance	Man-Year 144.6	Responsible Agency Public works	1976 Budget $2,807,920

Objectives	Performance Criteria	Units			
1. To provide for 285,000 square yards of seal treatment on alleys and secondary streets	1a. Number of square yards of seal treatment b. Date seal treatment completed	74 ACT. 	75 EST. 185,000 9/75	75 Y.T.D. 285,000 9/75	75 EST. 285,000 9/76
2. To maintain 120 lane miles of freeways at a cost not to exceed $3,000 per lane mile	2. Cost of maintenance per lane mile of freeway	$2,396	$2,450	$1,709	$3,000
3. To provide for at least 9 miles of street resurfacing per year	3a. Miles of street resurfaced b. Date street resurfacing completed	4.33	9 10/75	9.33 9/75	9 10/76
4. To repair or replace all guardrails and posts which are damaged in vehicular collisions; to replace those in hazardous areas within 2 days	4a. Number of posts replaced b. Sections of metal guardrail replaced c. Number of days required to make repairs in haz- ardous areas				600 400 2
5. To establish a visual rating system for cleanliness of streets and alleys and to implement same	5. Date for completion of street cleanliness rating system			10/76	10/76

**Figure 7. Citizen attitudes and program data for street repair in Dayton, Ohio, 1976
budget.** Source: *Program Strategies* (Dayton, Ohio: City of Dayton, 1976), pp. 64
and 67.

space limitations—perhaps one page set aside for each bureau or each
program subcategory or element. Such a format may increase the readability of the document, so that each subdivision, for example, begins a
new page. The disadvantage is that not all subunits are of equal importance, either in terms of budget size or political interest. Therefore, many
jurisdictions use more flexible formats, providing more information on
some agencies and programs and less information on others. Under these

TABLE 8

Program Data for Vocational Secondary Education in Pennsylvania, 1976–1977 Budget

	1974–75	1975–76	1976–77	1977–78	1978–79	1979–80	1980–81
Total enrollment in secondary vocational education	251,326	259,600	269,760	279,290	290,080	300,240	310,400
Secondary students who need secondary occupational programs	272,617	271,000	268,850	263,450	257,550	251,850	244,200
Enrollment in occupational programs	185,988	195,690	205,400	215,000	224,800	234,500	244,200
Graduates from occupational programs	63,780	66,926	70,250	73,560	76,900	80,200	83,500
Graduates available for employment	45,922	48,186	50,580	52,970	55,350	57,750	60,100
Graduates available for employment employed within three months	38,758	40,670	42,690	44,700	46,720	48,735	50,750

Source: *Governor's Executive Budget, 1976–77* (Harrisburg: Commonwealth of Pennsylvania, 1976), p. 240.

formats, larger agencies commonly receive more extensive coverage because they are more complex and have more varied activities. However,
agencies that are particularly popular or unpopular may receive more
extensive coverage regardless of their sizes. For example, the U.S. Forest
Service and the Federal Bureau of Investigation (FBI) each has approximately 20,000 employees, but the former has a substantially larger budget.
The Forest Service is typically covered in ten or more pages, while the FBI
is covered in two or three in the *Budget Appendix*.

The extent of detail in budget documents should not be interpreted as
a reflection of the amount of information transmitted to the legislature.
This section has only dealt with published documents and not the vast
materials prepared by agencies for legislative use. A recent survey has
shown that all but a few state legislatures receive the original agency
budget requests, and most receive these at the same time as the executive
budget agency.[55] Legislative hearings on the budget also lead to submission of supplemental data prepared by the agencies.

A final aspect of the budget document and the budget preparation/
submission phase is the executive budget message. Not all jurisdictions use
this device, but it is used more frequently today than when about all that
was said was "here is the budget." The budget message, sometimes presented orally to the legislature, gives the executive the opportunity to
highlight major recommendations and the rationale for them.

SUMMARY

Budget requests are prepared by agencies in accordance with instructions
provided by the central budget office. In addition to data on finances and
personnel, request instructions increasingly require program data. These
include social indicators, impacts, outputs, work loads and activities, and
data on the need for services. Productivity measures are used to relate
resource consumption, as measured in dollars and personnel, to the work
accomplished and the product of that work. Budget request manuals take
varied approaches to providing guidance on what to request. These approaches include current commitment, fixed-ceiling, zero-base, open-
ended, priority listings, and program guidance as well as several other
"what if" approaches. Request instructions also often require multi-year

---

[55] James H. Bowhay and Virgnia D. Thrall, *State Legislative Appropriations
Process* (Lexington, Ky.: Council of State Governments, 1975), p. 71.

projections; these are useful in assessing requests for new or expanded programs. Program structure can be used as the set of building blocks that brings together resource and program information in a multi-year framework.

The decision process in the preparation phase consists of numerous decision points. Lower level units within a department must determine the likelihood of winning approval for possible program changes; middle level managers and department heads must make similar calculations. The budget office judges whether it should take issue with departmental requests or recommend their approval to the chief executive. The President, governor, or mayor assesses his or her own priorities for tax, expenditure, and service levels. Program needs must be related to revenue estimates, and at the federal level, economic policy may take priority over program needs. Assessments are made as to the likelihood of getting approval of possible tax and expenditure increases by the legislative body. Possible citizen reactions to budget alternatives are considered. Tentative decisions are reached and then often reversed as these various factors are weighed.

The product of the preparation phase is a budget or set of budget documents that reflect executive decisions on policies and programs. The budget is a proposed plan which if approved will be executed during the budget year or biennium. One continuing issue concerning budget documents is their coverage. State and local governments often have a general fund budget that is separate from special funds. The federal government has what is called a "unified budget," but since its adoption during the Johnson Administration, important exclusions have been made, creating an "off-budget." Revenue and expenditure data are treated in all budgets, but the latter receive much more extensive treatment. A budget format is used, often structured by organizational unit with supporting narratives and tabular displays on costs, personnel, and program data. Some jurisdictions use two-budget formats, one for organizations and the other for programs. The various budget documents are published materials submitted to the legislature, but they do not begin to constitute all of the information made available.

7

PROGRAM
ANALYSIS

The use of program analysis is part of the longstanding trend toward developing linkages between financial and program decision making. As preceding chapters have indicated, reformists since the early 1900s have advocated decision systems that would focus upon the results of public expenditures. Analysis, though in no sense a new development, has gained in recognition as a means of relating information about what government does and costs to what is accomplished.[1] Today, there is little issue over whether analysis should be conducted. The issue is: How is analysis to be conducted and used in the decision-making system?

We discuss three main topics in this chapter. The first section considers the purposes or roles of analysis, what analysis is; the second section of the chapter reviews techniques of conducting analysis; the third discusses the limitations of analysis within a political framework.

FOCUS OF ANALYSIS

There are many types of analysis. One can study whether the detective division in a city police department should purchase or lease its photocopier; whether a central copier should be used for the entire police

---

[1] Prest and Turvey in their survey of cost benefit analysis date program analysis in the U.S. back to the River and Harbor Act of 1902 which required analysis of the costs of river and harbor projects undertaken by the Army Corps of Engineers in comparison with the amount of commerce benefited by these projects. A. R. Prest and R. Turvey, "Cost-Benefit Analysis: A Survey," *The Economic Journal,* 75 (1965): 683–735.

department or all of city hall; whether more police time should be assigned to crime control and less to traffic; or whether police services should be increased and fire services decreased.[2] The concern here is mainly with program analysis that concentrates upon effectiveness and efficiency analysis.

"Effectiveness" means the use of resources to obtain desired program results that impact upon persons or the environment. Such impacts might be a reduction in infant mortality produced by a prenatal health care program or a reduction in fire damage following an intensified fire inspection/prevention program. Efficiency análysis, on the other hand, focuses upon alternative uses of resources in reaching desired ends. Whereas effectiveness analysis might disregard the costs of a program and focus exclusively upon the results or impacts, efficiency analysis considers the costs of producing a given unit or set of results and whether alternative approaches might produce more results at the same cost or the same results at reduced costs. The term productivity analysis also has received much publicity in recent years. The National Center for Productivity and Quality of Working Life considers productivity analysis to include effectiveness and efficiency concerns. Others seem to restrict productivity to using resources efficiently in conducting work and without focusing upon results or impacts. The analytic techniques we discuss here would be the principal components of what is usually meant by productivity analysis.

Analytic efforts should first be directed to desired achievements. Is the program accomplishing what was intended? If this question is not answered and analysis focuses more upon outputs or the work being conducted, there is a danger that suboptimization will occur, that services will be provided efficiently but ineffectively (Chapter 6).

Sometimes the desired objectives are not explicit. A governmental program is created in response to a perceived problem, yet there may be no clear understanding as to how the new program will eliminate or alleviate the problem.[3] Program structure, as discussed in the preceding chapter, helps resolve this problem by positing sets of goals, objectives,

---

[2] For attempts to classify the various types of analysis, see Frank L. Lewis and Frank G. Zarb, "Federal Program Evaluation from the OMB Perspective," *Public Administration Review,* 34 (1974): 318–27. Richard Brown and Ray D. Pethtel, "A Matter of Facts: State Legislative Performance Auditing," *Public Administration Review,* 34 (1974): 318–27.

[3] Elmer B. Staats, "Evaluating the Effectiveness of Federal Social Programs," *The GAO Review,* 8 (1973): 1–7.

impacts, and outputs. Analysis makes a further contribution. Former Director of the Budget, Charles Schultze, has suggested:

> Systematic analysis does not simply accept objectives as immutably given and then proceed to seek the most effective or efficient means of achieving these objectives. One of its major contributions to the complex decision making process lies precisely in its consideration of both objectives and means, allowing analysis of each to influence the other.[4]

In making the argument, however, Schultze warns that he does not mean that analysts determine objectives for persons in decision-making positions. Analysis may suggest objectives previously not considered, and a good analyst may argue for their importance, but decision makers still have the final choice.

The point is that analysis may be able to inform decision makers about what might be accomplished with a given amount of resources but not what their choices should be. In providing explicit information about the linkages between costs and results, analysis enables decision makers to act on the basis of their political values with more explicit causal knowledge. For example, decision makers undoubtedly value a reduction in infant mortality. Competing alternative approaches to reducing infant mortality, however, cannot be evaluated directly in terms of that value, because the value of reducing infant deaths would be the same for each alternative. Analysis would be most useful, therefore, in assessing which alternative contributes the most to achieving the value.[5]

One critical problem for the analyst is defining the analytical problem, determining the boundaries of a system to be analyzed, and then assessing the extent to which a given government has the potential for affecting that system. The community development department of a central city, for example, in conducting an analysis of its housing rehabilitation program must isolate the components of the housing system. In doing so, the department will not only consider existing housing stock, but may well consider national trends in housing, construction methods, the availability of mortgage monies, the effects of freeways in allowing for dispersion of the population in metropolitan areas, and national economic trends. At some point, a boundary on the study must be imposed or else the

---

[4] Charles L. Schultze, *The Politics and Economics of Public Spending* (Washington: Brookings, 1968), p. 65.

[5] The example is from Schultze, *Politics and Economics,* pp. 55–56.

department will be analyzing the universe. Moreover, the department will quickly conclude that the city government has narrowly limited powers to affect the situation. The city may be able to do little to stem migration to the suburbs. Similarly, a city police department may have only limited capability to influence the crime rate. One effect of analysis, then, can be the shattering of myths and ideologies about what is possible given the state-of-the-art in managing systems.

Other basic constraints are imposed on the use of analysis. First is the scope of the study. Under program budgeting, analysis is designed to relate to program structure, and analysis can have a wide or a narrow focus in terms of the structure. Take as an example a program category of mental retardation having two subcategories of 1) prevention and detection and 2) treatment, care, and rehabilitation. Research can be geared to one or a few elements under one of these subcategories, such as inpatient versus outpatient care. This type of analysis tends to produce information regarding the alternative methods of serving retarded persons. At a wider level, analysis might be between the two subcategories. That form of research would raise questions such as, if more resources are committed to prevention and detection, can the costs of treatment and care be reduced? At a still higher level, analysis could focus upon all of mental retardation in contrast with mental health, or physical health problems such as cancer control, or even nonhealth problems dealing with defense, education, or transportation. This highest level of analysis is perhaps most appropriately termed policy analysis rather than program analysis because it examines questions of value of the magnitude of "guns or butter?" The scope of the analysis will determine the types of research techniques that can be applied.

The other set of parameters for analysis relates to the types of alternatives to be considered. Analysis may attempt to discover more efficient methods of performing a service without increasing costs. In other cases, analysis might be framed in terms of what alternatives are available if the commitment to a program were increased by X million dollars. Still, in other instances, research may be directed to find an alternative that would produce a given impact, for example, the elimination of cancer as a major disease within the next five years. In the last kind of research, the resource commitment is unconstrained and is only derived following an assessment of how to accomplish the desired results.

In addition to the analysis of alternatives, research is used for evaluating or auditing programs. Sometimes the term analysis is distinguished from evaluation in that the former is used to refer to the examination of "hypothetical alternative program solutions" and the latter concentrates upon existing programs. Joseph S. Wholey and others have written:

> Evaluation (1) assesses the *effectiveness* of an *ongoing* program in achieving its objectives, (2) relies on the principles of research design to distinguish a program's effects from those of other forces working in a situation and (3) aims at program improvement through a modification of current operations.[6]

Of course it is impossible in practice to audit existing programs without considering the alternatives that are available.

Evaluations or audits in program budgeting are used in part to keep agencies honest. Honesty, here, is measured in terms of whether agencies produced the results that were promised. Lent D. Upson in 1924 stressed the need for such evaluation: "The budget should be supplemented by an operation audit that will measure the effectiveness of expenditures as thoroughly as the financial audits measure the legality of expenditures."[7]

METHODS AND TECHNIQUES OF ANALYSIS

Program analysis techniques range from simple to complex.[8] Depending upon the preciseness of problem definition, the susceptibility of the

---

[6] Joseph S. Wholey, et al., *Federal Evaluation Policy: Analyzing the Effects of Public Programs* (Washington: Urban Institute, 1970), p. 23.

[7] Lent D. Upson, "Half-Time Budget Methods," *Annals,* 113 (1924): 74.

[8] For more thorough discussions of analytic techniques, see Francis G. Caro, ed., *Readings in Evaluation Research* (New York: Russell Sage Foundation, 1971); Kenneth M. Dolbeare, ed., *Public Policy Evaluation* (Beverly Hills, Cal.: Sage, 1975); Robert H. Haveman and Julius Margolis, eds., *Public Expenditures and Policy Analysis* (Chicago: Markam, 1970); Leonard Merewitz and Stephen H. Sosnick, *The Budget's New Clothes* (Chicago: Markham, 1971); E. J. Mishan, *Cost-Benefit Analysis: An Informal Introduction,* 2nd ed. (London: Allen and Unwin, 1975); E. J. Mishan, *Economics for Social Decisions: Elements of Cost-Benefit Analysis* (New York: Praeger, 1973); E. S. Quade, *Analysis for Public Decisions* (New York: American Elsevier, 1975); Henry W. Riecken and Robert F. Boruch, *Social Experimentation: A Method for Planning and Evaluating Social Intervention* (New York: Academic Press, 1974); Frank P. Scioli, Jr. and Thomas J. Cook, eds., *Methodologies for Analyzing Public Policies* (Lexington, Mass.: Lexington Books, 1975); Alan W. Steiss *Public Budgeting and Management* (Lexington, Mass.: Lexington Books, 1972), pp. 227–55; Elmer L. Struening and Marcia Guttentag, eds., *Handbook of Evaluation Research* (Beverly Hills, Cal.: Sage, 1975); R. E. Zeckhauser, et al., eds., *Benefit-Cost and Policy Analysis, 1974* (Chicago: Aldine, 1975). Relevant articles may be found in several relatively new journals such as *Evaluation, Policy Analysis,* and *Policy Studies Journal.*

problem to quantification, and the skills of the analyst, analysis ranges from primarily qualitative research to highly quantitative studies.

Harry Hatry and others have described the basic methodology of program analysis as consisting of eight steps:

1. Define problem
2. Identify relevant objectives
3. Select evaluation criteria
4. Specify client groups
5. Identify alternatives
6. Estimate costs of each alternative
7. Determine effectiveness of each alternative
8. Presentation of findings[9]

This description is useful in calling attention to the several phases of the research process that should not be overlooked.

Most techniques of program analysis predate formal program budgeting, being derived in large part from such antecedent fields as systems analysis, economic analysis, and operations research. As described in Chapter 5, systems analysis is the most general approach. Operations research and economic analysis provide more specific techniques for doing program analysis, as discussed below.

Although OR is sometimes considered synonymous with the application of the scientific method to problem solving,[10] in the narrower sense in which it was described in Chapter 5, OR refers to a set of algorithms for solving recurrent problems that can be expressed quantitatively. Several types of problems recur with such frequency in private business organizations that prototype solutions have been developed to handle them. These prototype models involve problems of allocation, inventory, replacement, queuing, sequencing and coordination, routing, gaming strategies, and search.[11] Specific techniques for solving these problems include linear programming, queuing theory, Monte Carlo or randomizing methods, and gaming theory.[12] Where government programs involve similar problems,

---

[9] Harry Hatry, et al., *Program Analysis for State and Local Governments* (Washington: Urban Institute, 1976), p. 4.

[10] Russell L. Ackoff and Maurice W. Sasieni, *Fundamentals of Operations Research* (New York: Wiley, 1968).

[11] Ackoff and Sasieni, *Fundamentals,* p. 13.

[12] See William Baumol, *Economic Theory and Operations Research,* 3rd ed. (Englewood Cliffs, N.J.: Prentice-Hall, 1972); Guy Black, *The Application of Sys-*

such as transportation scheduling, warehousing, inventory, or other routinized tasks, OR techniques are readily applicable. Problems associated with the postal service, for example, are susceptible to such analytic techniques. Allocation of personnel to fire houses, police patrol scheduling, street maintenance schedules, or even scheduling client interviews for large social service agencies may be analyzed with one or more OR models.

For those areas where OR techniques are applicable, the models provide efficient solutions. The basic requirement for the application of such techniques, however, is that a single objective be stated in a quantifiable form. The usual form is that some specific measure of production (output) is maximized or a measure of cost (input) is minimized. Because use of such techniques is restricted to narrow areas, usually not much attention is devoted to them in discussions of program analysis. It is simply noted here that some problems in the public sector are readily amenable to OR solutions.[13]

Economic analysis, as suggested by its name, is concerned with questions of economics, typically expressed in monetary terms. While OR is intended to determine the appropriate methods by which services can be provided or activities conducted, economic analysis is used to relate the costs of doing something with the expected consequences of the activity. Economic analysis is largely concerned with the question of economic efficiency, namely whether the economic consequences of an activity are equal to or greater in value than the costs.

Systems analysis uses both of these techniques, but it deals with broad issues of which only parts may be susceptible to OR and economic analysis methods. For example, OR may aid in deriving means for logistical support for combat troops, but systems analysis might go beyond this

tems Analysis to Government Operations (New York: Praeger, 1968); Richard A. Johnson, Theory and Management of Systems, 3rd ed. (New York: McGraw-Hill, 1973); Claude McMillan, ed., Systems Analysis: A Computer Approach to Decision Models (Homewood, Ill.: Irwin, 1973); Samuel B. Richmond, Operations Research for Management Decisions (New York: Ronald, 1968); J. K. Sengupta and K. A. Fox, Economic Analysis and Operations Research (New York: American Elsevier, 1975); Randall Schultz and Dennis P. Slevins, eds., Implementing Operations Research (New York: American Elsevier, 1975); Harvey M. Wagner, Principles of Operations Research, 2nd ed. (Englewood Cliffs, N.J.: Prentice Hall, 1975).

[13] Philip M. Morse and Laura W. Bacon, eds., Operations Research for Public Systems (Cambridge, Mass.: M.I.T. Press, 1967); Jack Byrd, Operations Research for Public Administrators and Social Scientists (Lexington, Mass.: Lexington Books, 1975); Alvin W. Drake, et al., eds., Analysis of Public Systems (Cambridge, Mass.: M.I.T. Press, 1972).

question to ask: Are there other means of handling a situation that would reduce the need for logistical support? Systems analysis is intended to minimize the danger of myopic vision in which techniques are emphasized over purpose. As Alain Enthoven has couched the argument, "It is better to be roughly right than exactly wrong."[14]

Within economic analysis, distinctions can be drawn between cost benefit and cost effectiveness. Both attempt to relate costs of programs to performance and to quantify costs in monetary terms, but they differ in the method of measuring the outcomes of programs. Cost effectiveness measures outcomes in a quantitative but nonmonetary form.[15] For example, program results might be in terms of the number of lives saved through a traffic program, the time saved for travelers due to a new supersonic passenger aircraft, or the number of families able to support themselves as a result of job training programs.

Cost benefit analysis, on the other hand, measures program outcomes in monetary form, thereby allowing for the development of ratios or other measures of the extent to which returns exceed costs or vice versa.[16] In the above examples of effectiveness analysis, the dollar value of the outcomes cited would be derived. In the case of travel time, the analysis would estimate the worth of time to travelers, assuming that travel time is wasted and that any savings in time would make people more productive.

The potential merit of cost benefit analysis over cost effectiveness analysis is that the former allows for analysis across subject areas. When the expressed ratio of benefits to costs of a program is 1.0, costs are equal to benefits. As the ratio increases, the benefits accruing have increased. In

---

[14] Alain Enthoven, "The Planning, Programing, and Budgeting System in the Department of Defense: Some Lessons from Experience," in U.S. Congress, Joint Economic Committee, Subcommittee on Economy in Government, *The Analysis and Evaluation of Public Expenditures: The PPB System,* 91st Cong., 1st sess. (Washington: U.S. Government Printing Office, 1969), p. 904. For more detailed discussions of systems analysis, see Frank E. Baker, ed., *Organizational Systems: General Systems Approaches to Complex Organizations* (Homewood, Ill.: Irwin, 1973); C. West Churchman, *Design of Inquiring Systems: Basic Concepts in Systems Analysis* (New York: Basic Books, 1972); F. Cortes, et al., *Systems Analysis for Social Scientists* (New York: Wiley, 1974); Grace J. Kelleher, ed., *Challenge to Systems Analysis: Public Policy and Social Change* (New York: Wiley, 1970).

[15] Robert H. Haveman, "Public Expenditures and Policy Analysis: An Overview," in Haveman and Margolis, *Public Expenditures and Policy Analysis,* pp. 6–7.

[16] Prest and Turvey, "Cost Benefit Analysis"; Robert Dorfman, ed., *Measuring Benefits of Government Investments* (Washington: Brookings, 1965), pp. 6–8; Samuel B. Chase, Jr., ed., *Problems in Public Expenditure Analysis* (Washington: Brookings, 1968), pp. 3–8; Haveman, "Public Expenditures," pp. 6–9.

theory, then, if a supersonic transport program would yield a ratio of 1.7 and a job training program would have a ratio of 2.5, then using the standard of economic efficiency and adjusting for differences in program magnitude, government would be advised to favor job training over transportation. Cost effectiveness analysis, in contrast, would not allow such direct comparisons because the effects would be expressed in time saved and families able to sustain themselves.

Aside from this major distinction, the two forms of economic analysis are basically identical.[17] Both approaches attempt to assess the desirability of alternatives. Both look at short- and long-run costs and benefits. And consequently both are troubled with the same kinds of methodological problems.

The first critical problem of either approach is that of estimating what are the causal relationships operative in the problem under analysis; this matter of causation has been noted several times in previous chapters. In examining alternative programs, the analysis will be required to make some assumptions about causation in order to proceed. Some reliance can be placed upon earlier experiences or evaluation of existing programs of similar character. For example, if one is analyzing a possible advertising program to persuade smokers to stop their habit, some reliance might be placed upon available research on advertising programs aimed at reducing drunk driving or encouraging annual physical examinations.

In some cases, there may be little available material from which to make an assessment of causal relationships. This is the case particularly when new technologies and materials must be developed as part of the project being analyzed. The analysis of a new fighter aircraft might require an assessment of what was required in developing new lightweight metals and in designing new instrumentation. Predictions, estimates, or guesstimates must be made regarding the relationships between resource inputs and technological breakthroughs.

Then there is the issue of what gets counted as a cost and a benefit.[18] Determining the financial costs of existing programs is often difficult, because accounting systems are designed to produce information by orga-

---

[17] Prest and Turvey, "Cost Benefit Analysis": 683.

[18] Robert H. Haveman and Burton A. Weisbrod, "Defining Benefits of Public Programs: Some Guidance for Policy Analysts," *Policy Analysis*, 1 (1975): 169–96; Werner Z. Hirsch, Sidney Sonenblum, and Ronald K. Teeples, *Local Government Program Budgeting: Theory and Practice* (New York: Praeger, 1974), pp. 11–61; Alice M. Rivlin, *Systematic Thinking for Social Action* (Washington: Brookings, 1971), pp. 46–63.

nizational unit and not by program. Even when this matter is resolved, all that is produced are the direct financial costs to government. Indeed a standard criticism of economic analysis is that it tends to consider only the costs to government and not the costs imposed upon others. Failure to consider all costs tends to weight the analysis in favor of the proposed project under review.

Indirect costs as well as benefits imposed or granted to others are referred to as externalities or spillover, secondary, and tertiary effects. These are costs and benefits that affect parties other than the ones directly involved. In the private sector, air and water pollution from industrial plants are externalities. The main concern of the private enterprise is making a profit, but part of the cost of production may be imposed upon persons living in the area. Residents of the area downstream and downwind of the plant pay a cost in terms of discomfort, poor health, and loss of water recreation opportunities. If a municipality downstream is required to treat water that has been polluted by the plant, the costs imposed are relatively easy to identify.

Most government expenditure decisions involve the same kinds of spillover effects. The costs of an urban renewal program may be assessed in terms of the outlays required for purchasing and clearing land to the exclusion of spillover costs upon families, businesses, and industries that must be relocated.[19] Haveman has observed that the secondary effects of government programs may be more complex than those of business and industry, involving effects upon population migration, regional interdependencies, state and local government budgets, and the international balance of payments.[20] The argument is made that there are no such things as secondary or spillover effects, that anyone or anything affected by a program should be part of the explicitly considered benefits and costs of that program.

Related to spillover costs and benefits are redistributive effects, a matter which analysis often ignores.[21] Involved here is the matter of whether some groups in the society will be benefited more than other groups. In the examples of travel time and job training mentioned above, the former presumably would benefit middle and upper income groups

---

[19] Anthony Downs, *Urban Problems and Prospects* (Chicago: Markham, 1970), pp. 192–227.

[20] Haveman, "Public Expenditures."

[21] Burton A. Weisbrod, "Concepts of Costs and Benefits," in Chase, ed., *Problems in Public Expenditure Analysis,* pp. 257–62.

while the latter would aid low income groups. Other criteria for judging redistribution include race, educational level, and occupational class.[22]

Even if an ideal model were designed displaying all of the relevant types of costs and benefits or effects, the problem of quantifying these remains. What are the monetary costs imposed upon families relocated by urban renewal? Part of the cost will be in moving expenses, perhaps higher rents, and greater costs for commuting to work. While these can be measured, it is much more difficult to set a dollar value on the mental anguish of having to move, of searching for new housing, and of leaving friends behind.

Much of the problem of setting dollar values in the analysis stems from the fact that governmental programs do not entail market prices. Despite various limitations, the private market does provide some standard for measuring the value of goods and services by the prices set for these. Much of economic analysis in the public sector, however, must impute the prices or values of programs. This practice is known as shadow pricing. The procedure is easiest in dealing with business-like operations of government such as in providing water and electrical power and most difficult in areas involving social values.[23]

The use of shadow pricing can be seen in terms of predicting the benefits of a proposed outdoor recreation project.[24] The average hourly value to a person attending the proposed new facility (the shadow price) can be assumed to be what an individual on the average spends per hour for other forms of outdoor recreation. This figure times the number attending will yield an approximate value of the recreational opportunities to be provided by the facility under study.

More detailed approaches can examine each form of outdoor recreation—hiking, swimming, tennis, skiing, golfing, picnicking, and so forth. In the case of swimming, one can derive the average spent per person for one hour of swimming at a private beach and impute that to be the value

[22] Ronald W. Johnson and John M. Pierce, "The Economic Evaluation of Policy Impacts: Cost-Benefit and Cost-Effectiveness Analysis," in Scioli and Cook, eds., *Methodologies for Analyzing Public Policies*, pp. 131–54.

[23] Julius Margolis, "Shadow Prices for Incorrect or Nonexistent Market Values," in Subcommittee on Economy in Government, *The Analysis and Evaluation of Public Expenditures*, pp. 533–46. Roland N. McKean, "The Use of Shadow Prices," in Chase, ed., *Problems in Public Expenditure Analysis*, pp. 33–65.

[24] This discussion is based upon Ruth P. Mack and Sumner Myers, "Outdoor Recreation," in Dorfman, ed., *Measuring Benefits of Government Investments*, pp. 71–101.

of swimming at a public beach. One of the obvious dangers of such an assumption, however, is that it ignores the possibility that part of the price for admission at a private beach may be a guarantee that fewer people or only the "right" kind of people will be admitted. Another danger is that free public services may keep the price of private services artificially low, thus understating the value of the public beach. A private beach adjacent to a public one may not be able to set a high admission rate, assuming that the beach owner wishes to attract customers.

Shadow pricing becomes increasingly difficult and the analysis more tenuous when the subject matter for study involves functions that are primarily governmental. There is no apparent method by which a dollar value can be set for a defense capability of killing via intercontinental missiles X million people of an aggressor nation within one hour. Similarly, it is difficult to calculate the dollar value of avoiding one traffic fatality. The calculations employed require assessing what kinds of people are killed in automobile accidents, how old they are, what income they would have earned in their lifetimes, and what contributions they would have made to society.[25]

Given the questionable assumptions that must be made in estimating the dollar value of saving a life, the argument can be made that cost effectiveness is preferable to cost benefit analysis. The former does not attempt to place a dollar value on life, but rather that calculation is left to decision makers. The disadvantage is that cost effectiveness, unlike cost benefit analysis, seldom will yield a single measure of effectiveness. A traffic safety program might be measured by the number of lives saved and by the dollar value of property damage caused by crashes. Because these are like apples and oranges, they cannot be added together. It also should be recognized, however, that while cost benefit analysis offers the potential for comparing dissimilar programs—education versus police protection—the validity of these comparisons is often dubious, considering the assumptions that must be made in assigning a dollar value to all program outcomes.

Imputing prices to governmental or nonmarket activities, however, is not the only major problem involved in economic analysis. Public expenditures represent a diversion of resources from the private to the public sector and a diversion of resources from current consumption to invest-

---

[25] See T. C. Schelling, "The Life You Save May Be Your Own," in Chase, ed., *Problems in Public Expenditure Analysis*, pp. 127–76.

ment in future returns. Investment in a project or program is warranted, therefore, only if the returns are greater than if the same funds were left to the private sector and if the future returns are worth the current sacrifice. Thus, the relevant concept of the cost of a public expenditure is the value of the benefits forgone by not leaving the money in the private sector where it would be consumed or invested.

However, a dollar diverted from the private to the public sector is not just an equivalent dollar cost or dollar benefit forgone. "Part of the money taken from the private sector decreases consumption immediately, while the rest decreases investment and therefore future consumption." Thus, the value of a dollar removed by government expenditure is worth the "discounted value of the future consumption that would have occurred if the investment [in the private economy] had been made."[26] Some charge must be made against that dollar removed from consumption in order to arrive at the current value of future consumption forgone. This charge is variously known as the discount or interest rate.[27]

The discount rate must in some way serve two purposes. First, it should be similar to an interest charge that reflects the cost of removing a dollar from private-sector uses and diverting it to the public sector. If a dollar could earn a 6 percent rate of return in the private sector, investment in the public sector would be warranted (in an economic sense) only if the rate of return from the public investment would be at least 6 percent. Second, the discount rate must take into consideration the time pattern of expenditures and returns. In general, people prefer present consumption to future consumption. A dollar that might be spent for current consumption is worth more than a dollar that might be consumed ten years from now. Normally people do not willingly save unless they receive interest in compensation for the temporary loss of consumption. A discount rate, then, must provide a means of showing what the present value is of dollars to be spent or returned in the future.

The relationships among costs, returns, and time are depicted graphi-

---

[26] M. S. Feldstein, quoted in Prest and Turvey, "Cost Benefit Analysis," pp. 686–87.

[27] Robert L. Banks and Arnold Kotz, "The Program Budget and the Interest Rate for Public Investment," *Public Administration Review,* 26 (1966): 283–92; John F. Due and Ann F. Friedlaender, *Government Finance: Economics of the Public Sector,* 5th ed. (Homewood, Ill.: Irwin, 1973), pp. 170–75; Richard A. Musgrave and Peggy B. Musgrave, *Public Finance in Theory and Practice* (New York: McGraw-Hill, 1973), pp. 146–60.

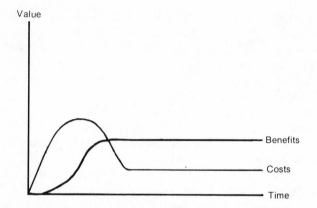

Figure 8. Relationship of costs and benefits to time. The value scale is expressed in common units, usually dollars. The time scale goes from one unit, such as one year, through the expected lifespan of the project.

cally in Figure 8. Most investment projects involve an early expenditure of heavy capital costs followed by a tapering off to operating costs. Returns are nonexistent or minimal for the first few years and then increase rapidly. The shape of the return curve after that point depends on the nature of the particular investment and is arbitrarily drawn for illustrative purposes in the figure. The comparison of costs to benefits over time makes the necessity for discounting obvious. Higher costs occur earlier in most projects. The higher benefits that occur later are valued less because of the time factor. Costs and benefits must therefore be compared within each time period (usually each year), and the differences summed over the lifespan of the project. This is in essence what a discount rate accomplishes. The longer it takes for returns to occur, the more their value is discounted. In effect, it is compound interest in reverse. Costs occurring earlier are subject to less discounting. Thus, for a project to be economically feasible, total benefits must not just exceed total costs, but the discounted values of benefits must exceed the discounted costs.[28]

It is obvious that the choice of a discount rate has an important influence on investment decisions. Too low a rate understates the value of current consumption or of leaving the money to the private sector. Too high a rate uneconomically favors current consumption over future bene-

---

[28] Jesse Burkhead and Jerry Miner, *Public Expenditure* (Chicago: Aldine-Atherton, 1971), pp. 223–24, 228–36; E. J. Mishan, *Cost-Benefit Analysis.*

fits and results in less investment than is worthwhile. The choice of a discount rate may thus determine the outcome of the analysis.[29]

As might be expected, then, considerable debate has centered around the issue of determining the discount rate to be applied. Private market rates are inappropriate because they include calculations of the risks of loss involved in making loans. Because loans to government are largely free of risk (at least until New York City's recent problems), because they are guaranteed against default, the private rate is considered to be too high. Another alternative is to use the rate charged to government for borrowing. This rate also has not been uniformly accepted, because it excludes any element of risk that would certainly not be the case if the decision were wholly within the private sector. Discount rates including at least some degree of risk seem to be the preferred choice of economists. The lack of agreement on deriving discount rates, nevertheless, has meant that varying rates are applied.

Fortunately the situation is not as hopeless as it might seem. The use of a theoretically correct discount rate is of most importance only when an attempt is made to reflect accurately the social opportunity cost of capital between the public and private sectors. Most government budgetary decisions, on the contrary, are usually only indirectly involved in the private versus public question. For the most part, the total public sector share of gross national product (GNP) is predetermined, from the standpoint that there will be no change or only a modest change in taxes. Therefore, the decision makers' choices to which analysis is normally addressed are not between the private and public sectors but between competing programs within the public sector.

Under these circumstances, where the decision is not geared to a theoretically optimal distribution of resources, it is important that the analyst provide a clear indication of the discount rates that are applied in the analysis. To that end analysis of program alternatives may employ several discount rates to determine the sensitivity of the analysis to discounting. A study of Navy tankers by the General Accounting Office, for example, found that when a 6 percent rate was used the Navy should purchase tankers but a 10 percent rate indicated leasing to be a more economical arrangement.[30] The point is that an arbitrary choice of a

---

[29] William J. Baumol, "On the Discount Rate for Public Projects," in Subcommittee on Economy in Government, *The Analysis and Evaluation of Public Expenditures*, pp. 489–503.

[30] Comptroller General of the United States, *Annual Report, 1974* (Washington: U.S. Government Printing Office, 1975), pp. 73–74.

discount rate without consideration of other ranges can produce misleading results.

ORGANIZATIONAL LOCUS AND USE OF ANALYSIS

With the increasing interest in analysis has come a proliferation of analytic units. Central budget offices, other central units such as planning departments, and line agencies have developed analytic capabilities. Legislative analytic units have also increased in number.[31] The 1974 Congressional Budget and Impoundment Control Act specifically empowers standing committees and the Comptroller General to "review and evaluate the results of Government programs and activities."[32] The New York Commission on Expenditure Review and the Virginia Legislative Audit and Review Commission are important examples of state legislative program evaluation units.[33]

Analysis has become widespread at the state level, as revealed by a recent survey conducted by the National Association of State Budget Officers (NASBO).[34] Whereas in 1970 only 8 state budget offices were conducting effectiveness analysis and 14 efficiency analysis, today more than 30 are performing these types of analysis. Major line agencies in approximately 20 states are conducting analysis. Also 16 state legislatures are reported to be engaged in effectiveness analysis and 14 in efficiency analysis. No pattern is discernible as to which types of states do and do not conduct analysis. Big-budget states are not necessarily more prone to analysis than smaller-budget states. The survey results seem to show that where analysis is prominent in the executive branch, it tends also to be more prominent in the legislature, although no cause-and-effect relationship should be assumed.

---

[31] S. Kenneth Howard, *Changing State Budgeting* (Lexington, Ky.: Council of State Governments, 1973), pp. 176–79; Susan Salasin and Laurence Kivens, "Fostering Federal Program Evaluation: A Current OMB Initiative," *Evaluation*, 2, No. 2 (1975): 37–41.

[32] Congressional Budget and Impoundment Control Act, Title VII, Sec. 701–2, 1974. See *Evaluating Governmental Performance: Changes and Challenges for GAO;* Keith E. Marvin and James L. Hedrick, "GAO Helps Congress Evaluate Programs," *Public Administration Review,* 34 (1974): 327–33.

[33] Brown and Pethtel, "A Matter of Facts"; Mark Lincoln Chadwin, "The Nature of Legislative Program Evaluation," *Evaluation,* 2, No. 2 (1975): 45–49.

[34] Robert D. Lee, Jr. and Raymond J. Staffeldt, "Executive and Legislative Use of Policy Analysis in the State Budgetary Process: Survey Results," *Policy Analysis,* 3 (Summer, 1977).

Local governments are also doing analysis, but there are no figures as to how many.[35] Fairfax County, Virginia, is an example of one government that has conducted numerous studies. Some have focused on effectiveness, such as the effect of fire and rescue response time on injuries and property loss, and some have focused on efficiency, such as considering the possibility of reducing the number of fueling stations for county vehicles.[36] A problem that many municipalities and other local governments face is that they are too small to be able to afford a large analytic staff, especially given currently restrictive budgets at the local level. Greater dissemination of analyses may be of help in allowing more than one community to benefit from the findings of a given study. One possible drawback is that communities may be reluctant to apply the findings of another city's study on the grounds that the two cities are dissimilar in important respects.

Whether the analytic unit be local, state, or federal, that unit has limited resources and must choose carefully the targets of analysis.[37] If the analysis unit commits all of its resources to one study each year, that means many programs will go unreviewed. At the opposite extreme, numerous "quick-and-dirty" studies can be conducted in a year, but at the risk of excessive superficiality. Central analytic units may take a mixed strategy of conducting both short and long analyses and diversifying these over a wide range of programs and departments. Criteria used in selecting targets for analysis would also include the dollar magnitude of a program and the political feasibility of changing it.

Producing reports and studies is not the same as using them in policy deliberations. The NASBO survey shows that only 11 states report that executive budget decisions are based substantially on effectiveness analyses and 13 states on efficiency analysis. In a mere 6 states the legislature is using analysis substantially in decision making. The complaint from analysts that their findings and recommendations are often unheeded is com-

---

[35] For a model of an urban analysis process, see David C. Caputo, "Evaluating Urban Public Policy: A Developmental Model and Some Reservations," *Public Administration Review,* 33 (1973): 113–19.

[36] "Reduction of Fueling Stations," (Fairfax County, Va.: Office of Research and Statistics, County of Fairfax, 1974); William B. Fetsch, "Emergency Response Time Analysis," (Fairfax County, Va.: Office of Research and Statistics, County of Fairfax, 1974).

[37] Edwin L. Harper, Fred A. Kramer, and Andrew M. Rouse, "Personnel Limitations of 'Instant Analysis,'" in David Novick, ed., *Current Practice in Program Budgeting* (New York: Crane, Russak, 1973), pp. 201–5.

mon, although some have cautioned against over-reliance on less than fully persuasive analyses.[38]

One reason for the limited use of analyses may be the analyses themselves. Any decision maker needs to analyze an analysis before using it.[39] Analysis is, of course, subjective from the standpoint of selecting out possible causal relationships to examine and determining which benefits and costs to count.[40] The decision maker needs to maintain a healthy skepticism and be aware of the technical difficulties, discussed in the preceding section, that might determine the outcome of a study.

Some analyses may serve the purpose of a "fund-raising prospectus."[41] A state department of transportation study which concludes that the department needs more funds may be the product of over-zealous analysts eager to serve the needs of their department. As Charles Hitch, former Assistant Secretary of Defense (Controller), has written:

> There is no question but that the systems analysis groups working within the defense establishment tend to take on the philosophical coloration of their sponsoring organizations, if for no other reason than that they are exposed to the same environment and the same influences.[42]

An analysis which concludes that the funding of a proposal would save thousands of lives but provides no method for verifying such results is bound to be criticized as a propaganda weapon.

There are many other factors that can make an analysis of limited use. The topic may be too politically hot or excessively trivial for decision makers to act upon. The data base may have been weak, resulting in highly

---

[38] Selma J. Mushkin, "Evaluations: Use with Caution," *Evaluation*, 1 (1973): 30–35.

[39] Heber D. Bouland, "Evaluating Results of Government Programs," *The GAO Review*, 8 (1973): 48–54; Stanley La Vallee, "What to Look for in Auditing Cost-Benefit Studies," *The GAO Review*, 9 (1974): 40–47.

[40] Fred A. Kramer, "Policy Analysis as Ideology," *Public Administration Review*, 35 (1975): 509–17.

[41] Robert N. Anthony, "Closing the Loop Between Planning and Performance," *Public Administration Review*, 31 (1971): 389.

[42] Charles J. Hitch, *Decision-Making for Defense* (Berkeley: University of California Press, 1965), p. 57. Also see Guy Benveniste, *The Politics of Expertise* (Berkeley, Cal.: Glendessary, 1972); Ida R. Hoos, *Systems Analysis in Public Policy: A Critique* (Berkeley: University of California Press, 1972); Arnold J. Meltsner, "Bureaucratic Policy Analysts," *Policy Analysis*, 1 (1975): 115–31; Aaron Wildavsky, *Budgeting: A Comparative Theory of Budgetary Processes* (Boston: Little, Brown, 1975), pp. 315–34.

qualified and tentative conclusions; in such a case the decision makers will probably rely on their hunches more than on those of the analysts. The report may be extremely technical. "Too many studies are becoming so complex that they are almost impossible for anyone except (and sometimes including) the authors to understand."[43] Confronted with a host of perplexing equations composed of seemingly unintelligible symbols, the decision maker may side with the analysts, assuming they know what they are doing, or reject the analysis on the grounds that the analysts have been intentionally confusing and probably have lied. Sometimes the analysis may be ambiguous as to how the recommendations are to be implemented and whether implementation is feasible.[44]

Beyond the analyses is the nature of the decision system.[45] It may be that a program budget system is more likely to use available analyses because the decision structure is specifically geared to that effect. More generally, however, decision systems are such that many immediate changes are impossible. An analysis which concluded that a bridge was unnecessary but was not released until after construction was underway probably would have little impact. This may in part be a timing problem of when studies are completed, but the problem remains that many decisions have been made that are largely irreversible in the near future. Official estimates are that only 24 percent of the 1977 federal budget was controllable due to commitments such as Social Security, unemployment assistance, Medicare/Medicaid, public assistance, interest payments on debt, and general revenue sharing.[46] State and local governments face

---

[43] Alain C. Enthoven and K. Wayne Smith, "The Planning, Programing, and Budgeting System in the Department of Defense: Current Status and Next Steps," in Subcommittee on Economy in Government, *The Analysis and Evaluation of Public Expenditures,* p. 968.

[44] Hatry, *Program Analysis for State and Local Governments,* pp. 97–102; Walter Williams, "Implementation Analysis and Assessment," *Policy Analysis,* 1 (1975): 531–66.

[45] Daniel A. Dreyfus, "The Limitations of Policy Research in Congressional Decision Making," *Policy Studies Journal,* 4 (1976): 269–74; Joseph L. Falkson, "Minor Skirmish in a Monumental Struggle: HEW's Analysis of Mental Health Services," *Policy Analysis,* 2 (1976): 93–119; Victor G. Nielsen, "Why Evaluation Does Not Improve Program Effectiveness," *Policy Studies Journal,* 3 (1975): 385–90.

[46] Office of Management and Budget, *The Budget of the United States Government, Fiscal Year 1977* (Washington: U.S. Government Printing Office, 1976), pp. 354–55. Also see Martha Derthick, *Uncontrollable Spending for Social Services Grants* (Washington: Brookings, 1975).

similar problems; where arbitration is used in collective bargaining with public employees, the jurisdiction is compelled to meet the wage settlement provided by the arbitration panel.

Because of political constraints the real portion of the budget that is controllable is much smaller than the 24 percent figure. There may be many programs that most observers would admit are ineffective, yet political pressures can successfully ensure their funding. In such a case, the most that analysis may be expected to accomplish would be redirecting the funds for the same purpose but in a more effective way.[47]

Implementation of analysis is further complicated by interagency and intergovernmental relations. The benefits of an improved municipal law enforcement program may not be gained if courts are unable to cope with increased numbers of arrests and prosecutions.[48] Moreover, societal problems do not respect political boundaries, and problems do not coincide with each other. One mix of governmental units may be appropriate for dealing with air pollution problems and another with physical health.[49] Intergovernmental decision mechanisms are weak, at best, in dealing with problems, yet analysis may indicate that a given problem essentially must be dealt with on an intergovernmental basis.

Finally, one must consider the increasing maturity in the conduct and use of analysis. In the 1960s, discussions tended to focus upon the need for analysis, but today, as has been seen, analysis is common. There is need now for a perspective on the ongoing use of analysis after the initial enthusiasm or even excitement of its introduction has dissipated. The agency that basically lied with analysis and was discovered may have difficulty in having its analyses accepted by the executive and legislature. How will decision makers respond to analyses that result in negative findings? The agency whose budget is cut because it found weaknesses in its programs may be less than enthusiastic about conducting further analyses. Has there been an excessive proliferation of analytic units? Should they be reduced in number and coordinated more carefully with each other?[50] Also, all analysts will confront the constant problem of

---

[47] Rivlin, *Systematic Thinking,* pp. 56–60; Carol H. Weiss, *Evaluation Research: Methods of Assessing Program Effectiveness* (Englewood Cliffs, N.J.: Prentice-Hall, 1972), pp. 110–28.

[48] This presupposes, for example purposes only, that increased arrests yield reductions in crime.

[49] Schultze, *Politics and Economics,* p. 218.

[50] Laurence E. Lynn, Jr., "A Federal Evaluation Office?," *Evaluation,* 1, No. 2 (1973): 56–59.

objectivity. No study can be purely objective, but in an ongoing analytic effort the problem is increased. When a city budget office examines the solid waste collection program, makes recommendations, and has those recommendations adopted, can the budget office two years later objectively evaluate the new approach to solid waste? It would seem that analysts must be cautious in assuming an advocacy role.

SUMMARY

In this chapter program analysis has been treated in a less restricted fashion than the theoretical concerns of economic analysis for optimum resource allocation. The budgetary process is a political process of reconciling conflicting social and political claims on society's resources. Because there is no exact correspondence between economic efficiency and social and political criteria, analysis must work with multiple objectives. Therefore, the principal purpose of program analysis is to provide information about the causal linkages between program inputs and program impacts.

Considering program analysis in an information support role meets one basic political objection to analysis—that it attempts to replace political criteria for decision making with a narrow economic conception of rationality. Program analysis, on the contrary, does not replace politics but rather is part of politics. Budgetary decisions are political decisions, and the purpose of analysis is to provide information that will influence those decisions. To argue otherwise would obviate the need for any analysis at all.

There are divergent forms of analysis, including operations research, economic analysis, and the more general approach of systems analysis. Much of the discussion in this chapter has pertained to economic analysis, which can be subdivided into cost benefit and cost effectiveness analysis. These two are similar, except that cost benefit quantifies program outcomes in monetary terms whereas cost effectiveness quantifies in program terms, such as the number of lives saved. Many of the problems associated with economic analysis relate to the assumptions that must be made in terms of deriving cost and benefit data, particularly through the use of shadow prices and discount rates.

Although the difficulties associated with conducting analysis are real, they should not be used as excuses for avoiding analysis. Choices will be made whether or not there is analysis. Too often these choices have been made with doctrine supplying the assumption that beneficial results will occur.[51] Analysis should supply information that at least confronts doctrinaire assumptions. Further, there is no necessity that all results be measured in terms of dollar values. Choices among programs can be made on the basis of political and social values that are not readily transformed into dollar values.

Finally, there are many political and institutional factors that limit or alter the use of analysis. Because analysis is part of the political process, one can expect analysis on occasion to be designed to produce the desired conclusions. Even when studies conclude that existing programs are not yielding the intended impacts, these studies can serve as justification for expanding rather than shrinking these programs. Beyond the politics of the situation are institutional constraints that deter the translation of analytic findings into program decisions for the coming budget year. The multiplicity of political jurisdictions coupled with the existence of problems that do not coincide geographically impede the implementation of any optimal solution that might be derived from analysis.

[51] Robert J. Mowitz, *The Design and Implementation of Pennsylvania's Planning, Programming, Budgeting System* (Harrisburg: Commonwealth of Pennsylvania, 1970), p. 42.

8

BUDGET APPROVAL: ROLE OF THE LEGISLATURE

The struggle over the budget has only begun when the budget document is presented to the legislative body. Budget preparation at the state and federal levels will have consumed months but the product of the process is only a proposal. The distinction between preparation and approval is sometimes phrased as "the executive proposes and the legislature disposes." The process is distinctly different from parliamentary governments such as the British one in which the executive and legislative functions are controlled by the same political party. In such systems, the proposed budget presented to the legislature is the one that is adopted; the approval phase is largely pro forma. In the United States, however, the legislative body typically may approve a budget that differs greatly from what has been proposed.

The legislative role in budgeting is examined in this chapter. Major emphasis is given to state and federal processes, because these are more complex than those of local governments. Many of the topics discussed, however, have relevance to local legislative bodies.[1] While few local governments have the equivalents of a house and a senate, these jurisdictions may have legislative units as large as some state legislatures and may have

---

[1] See James D. Barber, *Power in Committees: An Experiment in the Governmental Process* (Chicago: Rand McNally, 1966); John P. Crecine, *Governmental Problem Solving: A Computer Simulation of Municipal Budgeting* (Chicago: Rand McNally, 1969); Lewis B. Friedman, *Budgeting Municipal Expenditures: A Study in Comparative Policy Making* (New York: Praeger, 1975); Donald Gerwin, *Budgeting Public Funds: The Decision Process in an Urban School District* (Madison: University of Wisconsin Press, 1969).

elaborate committee systems somewhat like those of Congress and state legislatures. Moreover, all local legislative units must interact with the executive, resulting in conflicts and problems that are akin to those found at the state and federal levels. The first section of this chapter considers the structural parameters within which legislatures act upon budgets. The second section examines the relationships between the legislative and executive branches, and the final section focuses upon the changing role of the legislature as an overseer of the executive branch.

STRUCTURAL PARAMETERS

Structural features of the legislature greatly affect the ways in which it deals with budget matters. Some of the features are constitutionally mandated, whereas others are imposed by the legislature itself, and still others are part of the overall political system and less subject to possible alteration. In this section we first consider some of these basic characteristics and the problems that result from them. Then, the discussion focuses upon efforts to reform this process, especially at the federal level where problems have been particularly acute.

Fragmentation has been the overriding characteristic of state legislatures and the Congress with regard to budgeting.[2] As will be seen in this and the following sections, fragmentation is a by-product of numerous forces. Constitutionally imposed bicameralism divides the legislature into two chambers, a house and a senate.[3] The extensive use of committees makes a legislature not one unit but a series of little legislatures.[4] The fact

---

[2] For discussions of state legislatures, see Thomas J. Anton, *The Politics of State Expenditures in Illinois* (Urbana: University of Illinois Press, 1966); Donald G. Herzberg and Alan Rosenthal, eds., *Strenghtening the States: Essays on Legislative Reform* (Garden City, N.Y.: Doubleday, 1972); Malcolm E. Jewell, *The State Legislature: Politics and Practice*, 2nd ed. (New York: Random House, 1969); Wilder Crane and Meredith Watts, *State Legislative Systems* (Englewood Cliffs, N.J.: Prentice-Hall, 1968). For discussions of Congress, see Ernest S. Griffith and Francis R. Valeo, *Congress: Its Contemporary Role*, 5th ed. (New York: New York University Press, 1975); David R. Mayhew, *Congress: The Electoral Connection* (New Haven, Conn.: Yale University Press, 1974); Thomas P. Murphy, *The New Politics Congress* (Lexington, Mass.: Lexington Books, 1974); Gary Orfield, *Congressional Power: Congress and Social Change* (New York: Harcourt Brace Jovanovich, 1975); Norman J. Ornstein, ed., *Congress in Change: Evolution and Reform* (New York: Praeger, 1975).

[3] Nebraska is the only exception, with a unicameral or single-house legislature. The terms "house" and "senate" are used here to refer to the lower and upper chambers of state legislatures, although these terms are not used in every state.

[4] George Goodwin, Jr., *The Little Legislatures: Committees of Congress* (Amherst: University of Massachusetts Press, 1970).

that legislative members are elected makes each independent of the others, and the quest for re-election may contribute further to fragmentation.

Political parties might be expected to serve as a unifying force. The party having a majority in a state senate, for example, will have majority representation on each committee as well as having one of its members serving as chairman of each committee. However, political parties are weak and are unable to control their own party members. On any given issue there may be no guarantee that all or even a majority of the party's members will vote as a block. The problem is further complicated in that the two chambers can be controlled by different parties or both may be controlled by one party while the chief executive is of another party. Many members of the legislative body and especially persons in leadership positions have served long tenures and are not always amenable to changes proposed by the executive, regardless of party affiliations.

Committees are the instruments through which legislatures conduct their business, and these committees further contribute to fragmentation.[5] The committee system is probably unavoidable, given the complexity of governmental problems and the size of legislative bodies. The United States House of Representatives has 435 members and the Senate 100. Among the states, New Hampshire has the largest legislature with 424 members and Nebraska the smallest with 49 members. Most states have more than 100 legislators.[6] Given the number of legislators, operating as a committee-of-the-whole to deal with multi-million or multi-billion dollar budgets is not practical. Congress abandoned the committee-of-the-whole approach in 1796, not long after the adoption of the Constitution.

Under the committee system, legislation is handled by parallel committees in each chamber. These committees report out bills that are acted upon by the full membership of the house and senate. When differences exist in the two bills, a conference committee is usually appointed, which reports a revised bill that again is acted upon by both houses; the conference committee is composed of members from the two committees that prepared the legislation.[7] Once the chambers have passed identical bills, the legislation is ready for signing or vetoing by the governor or President.

---

[5] Richard F. Fenno, Jr., *Congressmen in Committees* (Boston: Little, Brown, 1973).

[6] *Book of the States, 1976–1977* (Lexington, Ky.: Council of State Governments, 1976), p. 44.

[7] David J. Vogler, *The Third House: Conference Committees in the United States Congress* (Evanston, Ill.: Northwestern University Press, 1971).

Fragmentation is increased by assigning the revenue and spending portions of the budget to different committees. This practice has existed at the federal level since 1865, when the House Appropriations Committee was formed to handle spending measures while the already existing Ways and Means Committee continued to handle revenue and especially tax measures.[8] The Senate followed the House's lead in 1867 by creating an Appropriations Committee in addition to the already existing Finance Committee. At the state level, this fragmentation is also common. Only 11 state houses and 18 state senates have combined revenue and appropriation committees.[9] If separate revenue and expenditure committees are free to act independently, then the situation is analogous to a couple with one earning income and the other spending with only occasional references to how much is earned. This situation can obviously lead to financial catastrophe. Despite the obvious, however, Congress until recent years had no mechanism for coordinating the two processes and many states still do not coordinate the two.[10]

At the federal level, the fragmentation has been extended further by the use of subcommittees in the House Ways and Means, Senate Finance, and two Appropriations Committees.[11] About a dozen subcommittees exist in each Appropriations Committee, each of which has been responsible for preparing legislation on one piece of the expenditure side of the budget. The Congress, then, has acted not on expenditures as a whole but has passed a dozen or so appropriation bills for any given budget. Because these subcommittees operated at varying speeds, the appropriations bills were not acted upon by the full House or Senate at one time, but rather individually over a period of several months. State governments make less use of subcommittees but like Congress often have several appropriations bills. About half of the states have a major appropriation bill covering most of the budget, but this major bill may be followed by numerous,

---

[8] See Richard F. Fenno, Jr., *The Power of the Purse: Appropriations Politics in Congress* (Boston: Little, Brown, 1966); John F. Manley, *The Politics of Finance: The House Committee on Ways and Means* (Boston: Little, Brown, 1970); Ralph Nader Congress Project, *The Revenue Committees: A Study of the House Ways and Means and Senate Finance Committees and the House and Senate Appropriations Committees*, Richard Spohn and Charles McCollum, project directors (New York: Grossman, 1975).

[9] James H. Bowhay and Virginia D. Thrall, *State Legislative Appropriations Process* (Lexington, Ky.: Council of State Governments, 1975), p. 59.

[10] Bowhay and Thrall, *State Legislative Appropriations Process*, p. 97.

[11] John W. Kingdon, "A House Appropriations Subcommittee: Influences on Budgetary Decisions," *Southwestern Social Science Quarterly*, 47 (1966): 68–78.

smaller ones. The other states vary greatly, with some having hundreds of appropriations bills, albeit many of which involve inconsequential sums.[12]

The method of appropriating has direct bearing upon the ability of the legislative body to control expenditures. State legislatures may pass appropriations bills which require that the contemplated spending occur within the budget year. If an agency has unspent funds at the end of the year, spending authority lapses and the money remains in the treasury. In contrast, Congress has acted less directly on expenditures. A regular appropriation bill grants what is called budget authority to commit the government to expenditures to pay for those commitments. The executive may be restricted to making financial commitments or obligations in the budget year, but in many instances outlays will not occur until after the close of that year and perhaps even subsequent years. The problem for Congress has been that by acting on budget authority there is no mechanism for controlling expenditures within a given year, yet expenditures are especially important for fiscal policy purposes. As will be seen in Chapter 13, policy makers attempt to affect the economy by adjusting total revenues collected and total outlays.[13]

Appropriations bills and the committees that produce this legislation are not the only means by which policies are set and money is spent. Contributing to fragmentation is the existence of standing substantive committees, as distinguished from the money committees dealing with revenues and expenditures. An artificial distinction is drawn between setting substantive policy such as in the areas of education and criminal justice and determining expenditure levels. Each chamber of a state legislature has numerous committees; the North Carolina legislature, for instance, has about 40 standing or permanent committees in the House and more than 20 in the Senate.[14] A substantive committee and the appropriations committee of the legislature may have differing perceptions of funding needs for a given program or agency. Some states have no mechanism for coordinating these committees, although in recent years there has been increasing emphasis given to finding appropriate coordinating mechanisms.

At the federal level, the substantive committees provide authorizations

---

[12] Bowhay and Thrall, *State Legislative Appropriations Process*, p. 81.

[13] For convenience purposes, the terms "expenditures" and "outlays" have been used interchangeably. However, outlays in a technical sense refer to expenditures plus loans that are subject to repayment.

[14] *Book of the States*, p. 63.

as distinguished from appropriations; legislation is passed allowing for the establishment or continuation of a program. This legislation may also set a maximum spending level, such as X billion dollars for five years. Under the "normal" process, an agency first receives an authorization through standing committees, such as Foreign Affairs in the House and Foreign Relations in the Senate, and then obtains appropriations through the Appropriations Committees.

The demarcation between the processes of authorizing and appropriating is weakened by what is called backdoor spending which provides spending authority without Appropriations Committee action for a given budget year.[15] One of the most important types of backdoor spending is contract authority provided by substantive committees. This type of authority allows agencies to enter into contracts that obligate the government to spend even though funds are not made available to cover these obligations. Later, an agency which has made such contracts will be required to obtain appropriations from the Appropriations Committees, but the Committees will have little choice other than honoring the contracts.

Borrowing authority or authority to spend debt receipts is a second form of backdoor spending. An agency is authorized to borrow from the Treasury, incur obligations, and spend debt receipts, all of which are beyond the control of the Appropriations Committees. In theory, the agency has some source of revenue that is expected to repay the loan, thus not affecting tax revenues. Farm price supports and public housing have been funded in this way. A problem emerges in that repayment may often allow further borrowing, again without action of the Appropriations Committees. Borrowing authority, therefore, can reduce Congress's ability to control outlays, and thereby can prevent Congress from developing its own economic policy.

A third type of backdoor spending is the permanent appropriation. The appropriation may be permanent for an indefinite period of time or permanent for a fixed period, for example five years. General revenue

---

[15] Sun Kil Kim, "The Politics of a Congressional Budgetary Process: 'Backdoor Spending,'" *Western Political Quarterly*, 21 (1968): 606–23; Allen Schick, "Backdoor Spending Authority," in U.S. Senate, Committee on Government Operations, *Improving Congressional Control Over the Budget: A Compendium of Materials*, 93rd Cong., 1st sess. (Washington: U.S. Government Printing Office, 1973), pp. 293–302. Also see Martha Derthick, *Uncontrollable Spending for Social Service Grants* (Washington: Brookings, 1975).

sharing (GRS) is an example of the latter. Other permanent appropriations cover interest to be paid on the national debt and trust funds for Social Security, highways, and federal employee retirements. The justification for permanent appropriations on trust funds is mainly that the expenditures must be guaranteed as part of good faith; government has collected monies for Social Security and has little choice but to make the appropriate payments to individuals. The permanent appropriation for GRS is supported as providing state and local governments with assurances of continued financial aid, thereby reducing some of the uncertainties in their budget processes. Permanent appropriations for interest on the debt provide guarantees to investors that their monies have been invested safely.

Mandatory spending is the fourth type of backdoor spending that provides an open-ended guarantee of benefits to all qualifying applicants. Persons with black lung disease are entitled to benefits, and therefore expenditures are a function of the number of persons qualifying for assistance. Veterans' benefits and Medicare are other important examples. Although these open-ended programs may require annual appropriations, the Appropriations Committees again have no choice but to provide the required funds.

The effect of backdoor spending has been that almost any committee within Congress may have an important role in financial decisions. When backdoor spending is coupled with appropriations that allow expenditures to occur after the close of a budget year, the problem of "totals" results. Until important changes were made in 1974, no mechanism was available for coordinating total revenues with total expenditures.[16]

This fragmentary approach to decision making has not been the only criticism of legislatures. One long-standing complaint has been that all legislative bodies—local, state, and federal—have inadequate information to deal with the budget. The increasing use of program information presented in budgets, as discussed in Chapter 6, is in part a response to this criticism. Also, proposals have been presented for more extensive information systems to support legislatures (see Chapter 9).[17] Computerized systems have been proposed to provide needed program and financial information, not

---

[16] William Proxmire, et al., *Can Congress Control Spending?* (Washington: American Enterprise Institute, 1973); *Uncontrollable Federal Budget Outlays* (New York: Tax Foundation, 1975).

[17] U.S. Congress, Joint Committee on Congressional Operations, *Fiscal and Budgetary Information for the Congress*, 92nd Cong., 2nd sess. (Washington: U.S. Government Printing Office, 1972).

merely to provide the more common information on the status of bills.[18] One response to the information problem has been the proposal for more staff to digest that information for legislators; greater staff presumably would facilitate more rational choices being made in budgeting.

Still another problem is time.[19] Legislatures often have six months or less to act upon the budget. Until the 1974 reform legislation, the President submitted his budget in January and Congress was expected to complete its work on the budget by June 30. With members of the House being elected for two-year terms and a third of the Senate seats up for election every two years, a good portion of the early months of alternate years is spent by Congress in reorganizing itself, thereby reducing the amount of time available for budget deliberations. The consequence has been that Congress almost never has completed its work on time in recent years. When the fiscal year began and an agency had not received its appropriation, Congress passed a continuing resolution allowing the agency to spend at the previous year's level until a regular appropriation was passed. In 1971, Congress never did finalize the appropriation for Transportation and the same was true in 1973 for the Labor-HEW appropriation.[20] The conclusion seemed to follow that greater time was needed for budget approval.

The various problems discussed here are probably more manageable at the state level, and some states have taken important steps in resolving them. About half of the states refer all bills with possible financial effects to the appropriations committees; fiscal impact notes are drafted, which indicate the expected costs of proposed legislation. Also, some states such as Florida and Missouri assign chairmen of the substantive committees to the appropriations committees, thereby linking the financial and non-financial decision processes. Hawaii uses a system in which lump-sum amounts for program areas are determined and then the substantive committees make allocations within their fields; the recommendations of these substantive committees are incorporated into a general appropriation

---

[18] Bill status systems provide immediate information on who introduced a bill, when it was introduced, and its current status, such as hearings have been scheduled for a given date by a specified committee.

[19] U.S. Congress, Joint Committee on Congressional Operations, *The Federal Fiscal Year as it Relates to the Congressional Budget Process*, 92nd Cong., 1st sess. (Washington: U.S. Government Printing Office, 1971).

[20] U.S. Senate, Committee on the Budget, *Congressional Budget Reform*, 93rd Cong., 2nd sess. (Washington: U.S. Government Printing Office, 1975), p. 4.

bill handled by the Appropriations Committees. The Hawaii system does have the potential disadvantages of fixed-ceiling budgeting, judging the case before hearing the evidence (Chapters 4 and 6).[21]

The fixed-ceiling or legislative budget has been tried by Congress. As required by the Legislative Reorganization Act of 1946, a maximum ceiling on the amount to be appropriated each year was to be prepared by a joint committee consisting of members from House Ways and Means, Senate Finance, and the two Appropriations Committees. A concurrent resolution was to be passed, agreeing not to appropriate above estimated revenue unless the public debt was increased in the same resolution. Therefore, as with the case of fixed-ceiling budgeting in the executive branch, Congress would determine in advance the resources to be allocated before considering program needs.

The failure of the legislative budget is summarized succinctly, almost satirically, in the following excerpt from *Congressional Quarterly*:

> In 1947, both houses adopted a concurrent resolution but the Senate added amendments. Congress could not agree on dividing an expected surplus between tax reduction and debt retirement. In 1948, both houses adopted the same legislative budget, but Congress appropriated $6 billion more than the ceiling in the resolution. In 1949, the process broke down entirely when the deadline for a budget was moved from February 15 to May 1. By that date, eleven appropriation bills had passed the House and nine had passed the Senate; the legislative budget was never produced.[22]

The problem with the legislative budget essentially was that its requirements contradicted established practices that were (and still are) a response to the political environment. The fixed-ceiling approach required consideration of the budget as a single entity without reference to local concerns and without examination of the interests affected, both of which the appropriations process brings to the forefront. Because Congress obviously could not rely on the executive branch for the total revenue and spending estimates, it assumed a sufficient ability on the part of legislative staffs to develop alternative and credible estimates. The approach failed to

---

[21] Bowhay and Thrall, *State Legislative Appropriations Process*, pp. 39–40 and 109.

[22] "Congress's Fiscal Role is Object of Growing Concern," *Congressional Quarterly Weekly Report*, 21 (1963): 889. Also see Louis Fisher, "Experience with a Legislative Budget (1947–1949)," in U.S. Senate, Committee on Government Operations, *Improving Congressional Control of the Budget: Hearings, Part 2*, 93rd Cong., 1st sess. (Washington: U.S. Government Printing Office, 1973), pp. 237–39.

take into account the realities of the political pressures on Congress and the lack of any real relationship between an overall revenue/expenditure estimate and legislative practice.

The failure of the legislative budget was followed with a one-time attempt to appropriate all funds in a single omnibus bill rather than in the numerous separate appropriations bills. One feature the omnibus appropriation shared with the legislative budget was the attempt to look at the budget as a whole. The profusion of appropriations bills makes it difficult to hold total spending in line, and thus a single appropriations bill presumably would focus more attention on the single question of total spending. The omnibus appropriations approved for fiscal year 1951 did leave Congress two months sooner than the last of the previous year's appropriations bills, and its total was $2.3 billion less than the President had requested.

Despite the praise the omnibus approach received from some reformers, the House Appropriations Committee voted the following year to return to the traditional method of separate bills. The Senate Appropriations Committee was equally opposed to the omnibus approach; all of the subcommittee chairmen issued statements condemning it.[23] The Budget Bureau was also critical of the approach, unless the President were given the ability to veto individual items without vetoing the whole measure. Critics of the approach charged that it was too general, that it led to casual consideration of important details, and that it was still not an overall budget because it ignored the possibility of supplemental and deficiency appropriations. A brief attempt by the Senate in 1953 to revive the omnibus bill died in the House.

With the legislative budget and omnibus appropriation reforms having failed, congressional reform was dormant until the 1970s. The problems discussed persisted throughout the 1950s and 1960s but were not brought to a head until President Nixon began using impoundments extensively, which is discussed in the following section. Here it only needs to be noted that impoundments are decisions not to spend monies appropriated by the legislature. Nixon's justification for his increased use of impoundments was based primarily on the argument that Congress was unable to overcome its own fragmentation, that the fragmentary approach to the budget was particularly damaging to economic policy.

---

[23] Robert Ash Wallace, "Congressional Control of the Budget," *Midwest Journal of Political Science*, 3 (1959): 161.

TABLE 9
Congressional Budget Process Timetable

On or before:	Action to be completed:
November 10	President submits current services budget
14th day after Congress meets	President submits his budget
March 15	Committees and joint committees submit reports to Budget Committees
April 1	Congressional Budget Office submits report to Budget Committees
April 15	Budget Committees report first concurrent resolution on the budget to their Houses
May 15	Committees report bills and resolutions authorizing new budget authority
May 15	Congress completes action on first concurrent resolution on the budget
7th day after Labor Day	Congress completes action on bills and resolutions providing new budget authority and new spending authority
September 15	Congress completes action on second required concurrent resolution on the budget
September 25	Congress completes action on reconciliation bill or resolution, or both, implementing second required concurrent resolution
October 1	Fiscal year begins

Source: Congressional Budget and Impoundment Control Act, Title III, section 300 (1974).

The resulting Congressional Budget and Impoundment Control Act of 1974 is a landmark effort in reformulating congressional budget action. [24] The timetable that has been created can be seen in Table 9. The process begins with submission of a Current Services Budget to Congress no later than November 10; this presidential document, as discussed in Chapter 6, is intended to show future financial requirements that will arise due to

---

[24] For discussions of the politics which led to the legislation and discussions of the legislation itself, see James J. Finley, "The 1974 Congressional Initiative in Budget Making," *Public Administration Review*, 35 (1975): 270–78; James A. Thurber, "Congressional Budget Reform and New Demands for Policy Analysis," *Policy Analysis*, 2 (1976): 197–214.

existing legislation. In January, the President submits a proposed budget that shows how he would diverge from the current services budget. Substantive committees review the proposed budget and make recommendations on their portions of the budget to the newly-created House Budget Committee (HBC) and Senate Budget Committee (SBC). These Committees include representatives from the four major money committees and the substantive committees. Hearings are held by the Budget Committees, which by April 15 are to report out the first concurrent resolution. This resolution recommends 1) total outlays and new budget authority, 2) outlays and authority by major function, 3) the surplus or deficit expected, 4) total revenues, indicating increases and decreases, 5) the appropriate level of debt, and 6) any other relevant matters. Any differences between the House and Senate versions are resolved, and action on the first resolution is to be completed by May 15. No revenue or spending bills may be adopted by the Congress until the first resolution has been adopted.

Following the passage of the first resolution, Congress to some extent reverts to its old procedures. Subcommittees of the Appropriations Committees consider specific appropriations bills and the revenue committees consider their portion of the budget. One important difference, however, is that appropriations subcommittees are expected to stay within the functional ceilings contained within the concurrent resolution. Another difference is that the Budget Committees may serve as watchdogs, seeing that legislation is not substantially at variance with the resolution. The Budget Committees' powers in this respect are mainly persuasive, perhaps showing the membership that expanding a given program in an appropriation bill will drastically affect the originally planned balance between revenues and expenditures. The HBC and SBC have no formal powers to require compliance with the functional ceiling in the concurrent resolution.

To allow for no changes in revenues, total outlays, and functional outlays after passage of the May resolution would be inadvisable; such an approach would have the disadvantages of fixed-ceiling budgeting. Therefore, a second resolution to be adopted by September 15 is used. The second resolution allows for taking into account possible economic changes that might indicate the need for adjusting revenues or expenditures either upward or downward. Testimony on various programs also might reveal the need for changes in the resource commitments contained in the first resolution. The second resolution contains information similar to that of the first plus directions to the relevant committees as to how spending and revenue measures are to be adjusted. The work is to be completed before October 1, the beginning of the new fiscal year. Significantly, Congress may not adjourn until completing its budgetary work, a factor that is expected to encourage timely action, considering that general elections are held in early November and the month of October is needed for political campaigning. By having the budget year begin on October 1, Congress has the better part of nine months to deliberate on the President's recommendations.

Insufficient experience with the new system prevents any firm forecast of the effects of the 1974 legislation.[25] The process that has been described was put through a dry run in 1975 but was not fully implemented until 1976. The legislative budget experience of the 1940s gives credence to predictions of failure. On the positive side, the controversies of recent years have made both executive and legislative participants fully aware of the need for reform; this awareness may encourage participants to make the reforms a success. The new legislation has answered the criticism of inadequate staff by providing not only staff for the two Budget Committees but also creating the Congressional Budget Office, directed initially by Alice M. Rivlin. As will be seen in Chapter 11, there have been some conflicts among these staff units, with their roles yet to be clarified. Also, in response to the criticism that Congress lacked needed information, the legislation requires that five-year budget projections be made, provides for the General Accounting Office to review the results of programs, and allows for the Congressional Budget Office to obtain computer facilities for information processing.

If the new process works, much of the old fragmentation will be replaced with a unified approach to budgeting. Such a change would affect the relative roles of committees and the political strategies employed. Rotation of memberships on the House Budget Committee is required by the legislation but this is not the case with the Senate Budget Committee. Rotation has the presumed advantages of encouraging democratic decision making and conversely discouraging the rise of a powerful chairman. A disadvantage is the HBC membership may be seen as less attractive than membership on other committees: with less prestige may come less power. Assuming that the process succeeds in reorienting congressional decision

---

[25] See relevant issues of *Congressional Quarterly Weekly Report* and *National Journal*. Also see *The New Congressional Budget Process and the Economy* (New York: Committee for Economic Development, 1975).

making, then lobbying efforts of federal agencies, state and local governments, and private organizations will necessarily change. Under the fragmentary process, lobbying might be successful when applied to a subcommittee of the Appropriations Committees, but under the new system,
Appropriations Committee actions might be undone through the second
concurrent resolution process.

LEGISLATIVE-EXECUTIVE INTERACTIONS

The previous discussion focused attention upon the internal workings of
legislative bodies in order to convey a picture of how these bodies handle
the budget. In this section, we turn to how the executive relates to the
legislative body. Having seen that legislatures are not integrated wholes but
rather consist of numerous subunits, this section considers how the executive relates to those subunits, especially to the two legislative chambers
and their subcommittees.

The executive and legislative branches in American government are
typically said to be co-equal, and therefore, the two branches tend to be
wary of possible diminution of their powers and may seek strategies for
demonstrating their independence. Confrontations between the two are
sometimes akin to tests of strength, with each branch showing it is not
subservient to the other.

Co-equal status in general is not the same as co-equal status in budgeting.[26] In a formal sense, the legislature is responsible for setting policy and
the executive for executing policy. Where conflicts arise are the extent to
which the executive becomes involved in policy making and the legislature
in policy execution. The movement toward executive budget systems has
placed the executive in the policy-making process, because the preparation
of budget proposals by the executive is the drafting of proposed policies.
Congress, state legislatures, and city councils have found themselves in the
position of reactors to executive recommendations and often not the
formulators of policy. To demonstrate their independence, then, legislatures may feel a compulsion to alter the proposed budget, no matter how
compatible its recommendations may be with their own preferences.
Legislative independence can be asserted by cutting or augmenting various
segments of the executive's budget.

---

[26] For a historical review of national legislative-executive differences in budget
control, see Thomas C. Stanton, "Conceptual Underpinnings of the Federal Budget
Process," *Federal Accountant*, 24 (1975): 44–51.

Constitutional and legal constraints greatly affect the extent of executive and legislative powers in budgeting. The Budget and Accounting Act of 1921 and comparable legislation at the state level have granted substantial budgetary powers to the President and governors. Yet, states such as Georgia, Texas, and New Mexico have strong legislatures that produce their own budgets in addition to the executive budgets. While the Arizona and Colorado legislatures initially do not prepare their own budgets, the governor's budget is almost ignored or is revised substantially.[27] In most states, the legislature is free to adjust the governor's budget either upward or downward, but in a few cases, as in Maryland, the legislature is limited to budget cutting. Courts have interpreted constitutions as to presidential and gubernatorial budget powers, but many constitutional questions remain, in part because both the executive and the legislature may prefer ambiguity to possible court decisions that might favor the opposing branch of government.[28]

The legislative and executive branches have different constituencies and as a result have different perspectives on the budget.[29] While the perspectives surely are different, specifying the differences has become increasingly difficult. One common interpretation has been that the chief executive, being elected by the jurisdiction's entire constituency, has a broader perspective on the budget; a governor will attempt to satisfy the diverse needs of citizens throughout the state. Legislative bodies, on the other hand, have been seen as consisting of parochial individuals, who may be less impressed with government-wide problems and therefore more likely to cut budgets. The legislature, then, is seen as a protector of the treasury and as a budget cutter.

This distinction between parochialism and cosmopolitanism also has been drawn between the two federal legislative chambers: Senators, serving larger constitutencies than Congressmen, are said to be more

---

[27] Bowhay and Thrall, *State Legislative Appropriations Process*, p. 31; Alan P. Balutis and Daron K. Butler, "Introduction," and Daron K. Butler, "The Legislative Budget in Texas," in Alan P. Balutis and Daron K. Butler, eds., *The Political Pursestrings: The Role of the Legislature in the Budgetary Process* (New York: Halstead, 1975), pp. 15–47 and 173–99.

[28] For a legal approach to executive-legislative relations, see Louis Fisher, *Presidential Spending Power* (Princeton, N.J.: Princeton University Press, 1975).

[29] Frederick J. Lawton, "Legislative-Executive Relationships in Budgeting as Viewed by the Executive," in Robert T. Golembiewski and Jack Rabin, eds., *Public Budgeting and Finance: Readings in Theory and Practice*, 2nd ed., (Itasca, Ill.: Peacock, 1975), pp. 54–65; Aaron Wildavsky, "The Political Implications of Budgetary Reform," *Public Administration Review*, 21 (1971): 183–90.

attuned to the varying needs of city dwellers, suburbanites, and farmers. At the state level, both houses of each legislature are established on the basis of population, so that all state senators in a given state will represent approximately the same number of constituents, unlike U.S. Senators, of which there are two for each state regardless of population size. Even with this relative equality within each state chamber, the two may have different perspectives because each senator typically represents two or three times as many people as a state representative.

This interpretation of the legislature as performing primarily the role of budget cutter may not be appropriate for contemporary times.[30] In recent years, for example, Congress has appropriated funds beyond what was requested by the President. This phenomenon may be a function of having a basically conservative President and a more liberal Congress or may be a function of different constituencies. Whether this has happened at the state and local levels is uncertain; given restrictions on state and local indebtedness, the legislative bodies of these governments may have difficulty exceeding executive recommendations without having to increase taxes.[31] Nevertheless, the case can be made that legislative bodies are likely to strive for restoring budget cuts proposed by the executive, as occurred during the Nixon and Ford Administrations, and may seek to augment programs. Legislative bodies conceivably are more susceptible to lobbying pressures to retain and increase spending levels than are chief executives. A chief executive may feel relatively immune from political setbacks stemming from proposed budget cuts in selected areas. Selective cuts may cost the executive few votes in a bid for re-election, whereas those same cuts could have dire effects on the political futures of many legislators.

Like the legislative branch, the executive branch is not an integrated whole. An executive budget system provides the chief executive with control over budget preparation, but there is no guarantee that all units within the executive branch will subscribe fully to the budget's recommendations. The chief executive will not be uniformly in support of all portions of the budget; some recommendations will have been approved because of perceived political considerations. The executive may have

---

[30] Orfield, *Congressional Power*, pp. 283–84.

[31] Ira Sharkansky, "Agency Requests, Gubernatorial Support and Budget Success in State Legislatures," *American Political Science Review*, 62 (1968): 1220–31; Ira Sharkansky, *The Politics of Taxing and Spending* (Indianapolis: Bobbs-Merrill, 1969), pp. 83–145.

accepted a proposal advocated by organized labor but may not actively push for the proposal's approval. Typically, the chief executive will single out a few major recommendations for which approval is sought, with other recommendations being considered of low priority. The budget office will be expected to make general presentations on the overall recommendations contained in the budget, although the budget office may be lukewarm to many of those recommendations. Detailed defense of specific recommendations is normally the responsibility of the operating agencies. Because the heads of the agencies in a strong executive system are the appointees of the chief executive, they have an obligation to defend the budget recommendations, even though higher funding levels may be preferred. As a result, agencies attempt to calculate the extent to which they can be "faithful" and yet reveal their preferences for greater resources.[32]

One set of calculations from both the executive and legislative branch perspectives involves the relative roles of the two chambers. At the federal level, the Constitution requires that revenue or tax bills begin in the House of Representatives, namely with the Ways and Means Committee (Article I, Section 7). Until the 1974 reform legislation, the normal procedure was for the Senate Finance Committee to wait until the House completed action, before taking up the tax bill. Appropriations were handled in a similar manner, although the practice was based on custom and not the Constitution; appropriations bills began in the House and later were referred to the Senate. Under that system, strategists were able to concentrate their attentions on first one committee and then another as the legislation found its way through Congress.

Before the 1974 reform legislation and its implementation in 1976, the two Appropriations Committees and their respective subcommittees assumed different roles vis-à-vis the executive and the proposed budget. The difference in the sizes of the two committees is important. Because the House Committee is about twice the size of the Senate Committee (approximately 50 and 25 members, respectively), House members can specialize in particular segments of the budget whereas Senators must attempt to become informed on a large number of areas within the budget, and consequently may be viewed as amateurs. Members of the Senate Committee, in contrast, might consider themselves to have a broader awareness of total budget needs while House members were excessively

---

[32] Aaron Wildavsky, *The Politics of the Budgetary Process*, 2nd ed. (Boston: Little, Brown, 1974), pp. 88–90.

parochial. Also, given the step-by-step approach of appropriations from one chamber to another, the House Committee tended to focus on the proposed budget whereas the Senate Committee focused on what the House did to the proposed budget. Studies have indicated that the House Committee, seeing itself as a guardian of the Treasury, tended to cut the President's recommendations and often cut below what seemed reasonable on the assumption that the Senate would restore much of what had been cut. Usually, the bill that came out of the conference committee tended to be closer to the higher funding level approved by the Senate than that of the House.[33]

From the vantage point of executive agencies, the strategy was often to avoid as many cuts as possible in the House Appropriations Committee and then seek restoration of cut funds plus perhaps additional funds from the Senate Appropriations Committee. Any increase in funding above the President's recommendations, of course, had to be sought with finesse, avoiding any overt opposition to the President's recommendations. This could be achieved by encouraging agency clientele to lobby in behalf of the agency's programs. Also, the agency might work to have individual committee members ask questions that might open the door for explanations of how additional resources could be used.

The two Appropriations Committees, their subcommittees, and the use of conference committees remain, but the relationships necessarily must change, provided Congress adheres to the new process. One important change is that the Appropriations Committees are involved simultaneously rather than serially. The House Appropriations Committee in 1976 reported out the 11 major executive agency bills within the same week— actually the same day, June 8—and Senate Appropriations reported out 10 of the 11 parallel bills within the following three weeks (see Table 10). Three bills—HUD, VA, NASA; Interior; and Transportation—were initially approved by both houses in the same week, and the two chambers approved six other measures within a week of each other.

The timing of these appropriations bills is important in two respects. First, because the Senate actions occur almost at the same time as those of the House, the former can no longer reach decisions that are basically reactions to the House appropriations bills. Second, the timing does not

[33] Fenno, *Power of the Purse*, p. 538. Also see Stephen Horn, *Unused Power: The Work of the Senate Committee on Appropriations* (Washington: Brookings, 1970); Jeffrey L. Pressman, *House vs. Senate: Conflict in the Appropriations Process* (New Haven, Conn.: Yale University Press, 1966).

TABLE 10

Sequence of Congressional Actions on Executive Agency Appropriations, Fiscal 1977

	Jun. 6–19	Jun. 20–Jul. 3	Jul. 4–17	Jul. 18–31	Aug. 1–14	Aug. 15–28	Aug. 29–Sept. 11	Sept. 12–25	Sept. 26–Oct. 9
Agriculture	A,B	C,D,E,F,G	J						
Defense	A,B			C	D		E,F	G,J	
Foreign aid	A	B,C					D	E	F,G,J
HUD, VA, NASA	A	B,C,D		E,F,G	J				
Interior	A	B,C,D,E		F,G,J					
Labor, HEW	A	B,C,D			E,F			G	H,I
Military construction	A,B	C,D,E,F,G	J						
Public works, ERDA	A,B,C	D,E,F,G	J						
State, Justice, Commerce, Judiciary	A,B	C,D,E,F,G	J						
Transportation	A	B,C,D			E,F,G,J				
Treasury, Postal Service	A,B,C	D,E,F,G	J						

A, House report; B, House vote; C, Senate report; D, Senate vote; E, Conference report; F, House vote on Conference report; G, Senate vote on Conference bill; G, Senate vote on Conference bill; H, veto; I, veto override; J, signed into law.

allow agencies to use the Senate as an appeals court and forces agencies into simultaneous relations with both chambers. An agency cannot concentrate its energies on getting a "good" bill out of the House and then focusing its energies on the Senate.

When Congress completed its work on appropriations is another item to note in Table 10. By the week ending July 3, 5 of the 11 bills were ready for presidential action and another 4 had been approved by both chambers and were in various stages of the conference committee final action process. This set a record for promptness. On the other hand, passage of these bills near what was once the beginning of the fiscal year may suggest that, when Congress so desires, it can act promptly, and the action conversely raises the question of whether Congress will be able to continue to act as promptly.

A point also in doubt is whether the process can be maintained substantively over time. Meeting the various deadlines of new legislation is not the same as keeping within the guidelines set by the first resolution. The initial experience under the legislation was generally positive. Appropriations bills were approximately in balance with what had been set forth in the first concurrent resolution. On the negative side, however, tax legislation in 1976 was not fully in harmony with the concurrent resolution.

Turning to state legislatures, less is known about how they interact with the executive branch on budgetary problems. Revenue bills start in the house in about 20 states; in another half dozen states, appropriations begin simultaneously in both houses, and in another 5 to 10 states, some bills begin in one house and some in the other. The remaining states use combinations of these approaches.[34]

Given the variations in the ways state legislatures reach decisions on the budget, executive-legislative relations can be expected to vary widely. As has been noted in previous discussions, state legislatures are often strong forces in the budget process and may largely disregard the governor's recommendations. Strong state legislatures may in some instances enhance the independence of executive agencies, so that they have less commitment to the governor's recommendations than do federal agencies to the President's recommendations.

---

[34] Bowhay and Thrall, *State Legislative Appropriations Process*, p. 83. In recent years, surveys such as that by Bowhay and Thrall have provided valuable information about state budgetary processes; however, there is still need for in-depth comparative analyses, particularly focusing upon budget processes in state legislatures.

Regardless of what level of government is considered, executive-legislative relationships inevitably can be characterized as cat-and-mouse games, although it is not always clear as to who is the cat and who is the mouse. Strategies are devised in each branch to deal with the other. On the executive side, a general posture that is almost ubiquitous is to cultivate clientele who will support requests for increased funding; such support can be garnered from the general citizenry, particular interest groups, and from within the legislature. Agencies are sensitive to where they locate various facilities; a new facility in a key legislator's district may gain the support of that legislator. These are strategies agencies pursue continuously as a matter of general posture.[35]

Contingent strategies, on the other hand, are limited to particular situations. No comprehensive cataloging of them is possible, because they vary from agency to agency and from circumstance to circumstance. However, they arise out of three basic perceptions of what is possible in a given budget period. "First, defending the agency's base by guarding against cuts in old programs. Second, increasing the size of the base by moving ahead with old programs. Third, expanding the base by adding new programs."[36]

The three basic attitudes appear to be in order of increasing optimism about the prospects for persuading the legislature that the agency is a deserving one. A pessimistic view leads an agency to devote most of its efforts to protecting what it already is doing. A somewhat more optimistic view leads to attempts to expand present programs. A real optimist tries to obtain new programs; on occasion it may be easier to obtain approval of a new program than expansion of an existing one. Manifestations of these attitudes might lead to such ploys as cutting the popular portion of a program in order to force the legislature to put it back into the budget in response to public pressure; thus the base has been protected, with possibly an additional increment being supplied. Another ploy has been to include a new project in the budget with an initial request for a very small beginning, thus getting the legislature accustomed to the program. This has been termed "the wedge or the camel's nose."[37] This tactic should make multi-year projections of spending especially appealing to members of legislatures (see Chapter 6).

---

[35] Wildavsky, *Politics of the Budgetary Process*, pp. 63–126.

[36] Wildavsky, *Politics of the Budgetary Process*, p. 65.

[37] Wildavsky, *Politics of the Budgetary Process*, p. 111.

While various strategies may be influential, there are limits to their effectiveness. Legislatures are influenced by personal values and committee role expectations as well as agency budget strategies and presentations. Agency strategies may influence the behavior of members of the appropriations committees, but perhaps the influence is limited in the sense of exploiting rather than creating favorable predispositions.[38]

In response, legislators also devise a number of strategies for dealing with their budgetary responsibilities and with agency strategies. The biggest problem seems to be the large capacity of agencies to produce reams of information in support of their requests relative to the more limited capacity of a legislature, no matter how large the staff, to process all that information. Legislative strategies, then, may be seen as methods by which complex choices are simplified.

An appropriations subcommittee finds it difficult, if not impossible, for example, to decide rationally if $593.3 million is the exact amount that should be granted to an agency.[39] Thus, Congressmen in appropriations hearings are looking for other ways to determine what should be granted an agency. They place all of the burden for calculation upon the executive and demand that an agency justify its need for certain funds in response to probing questions from the subcommittee. Detailed questions, which to outsiders may seem petty and trivial, are designed to determine how much confidence the subcommittee can place in the executive's testimony.

> If the director [of a program] can answer a detailed question about an object of expenditure, e.g. the cost of justification of a new fence or flagpole, without hesitation or assistance (a question we might not "expect" a director to know without staff assistance), the committee members are likely to feel he can probably answer the more general questions and justify the broader request.[40]

Out of this process of review by both legislative chambers come appropriations bills, but the approval phase is not necessarily completed. More than 40 governors have the item veto power which permits reductions in amounts that have been appropriated; state legislatures may seek to override these vetoes. At the federal level, the President can veto only the entire bill. When this power is exercised, the House and Senate may

---

[38] Kingdon, "A House Appropriations Subcommittee," pp. 68–78.

[39] James E. Jernberg, "Information Change and Congressional Behavior: A Caveat for PPB Reformers," *Journal of Politics*, 31 (1969): 736.

[40] Jernberg, "Information Change and Congressional Behavior," p. 736.

override the veto by a two-thirds vote, but should the veto be sustained, the legislation is referred back to committee for further review. The disadvantage of the veto power both for Congress and the President is that much time and energy may be consumed in redrafting the legislation and negotiating an agreement between the two branches. As a result, the impoundment procedure has been used.

Impoundments have constituted a highly controversial issue for a long time.[41] Impoundments are simply executive decisions not to spend appropriated funds. The procedure at the state level, when not restricted by various legislative provisions, may be considered an informal item veto. At the federal level, Thomas Jefferson was possibly the first President to impound funds, and since his administration probably most Presidents have impounded monies, often at the outrage of major segments of Congress.[42]

The issue came to a head during the early 1970s when Richard Nixon extended the use of impoundments over a wide range of appropriations. The argument was made that the President had a constitutionally implied power to impound, given the constitutional requirement that he faithfully execute the laws. Because the Employment Act of 1946 assigned to the President responsibility for economic policy and because Congress had no means of coordinating revenue and spending legislation, the President supposedly had the responsibility of limiting expenditures to achieve desired economic objectives. In previous decades, Presidents often had been confronted with Congresses that were unwilling to appropriate funds which were requested by the President; legislative power in budgeting was evidenced in budget cuts. During the Nixon Administration, however, congressional power was shown by increasing appropriations over what the executive requested, appropriations which to Nixon would yield excessive budget deficits. Were the government to spend at the level provided by Congress, so argued the Administration, extraordinary inflation would result. The impoundment power was also defended on the grounds that cutbacks were necessary to keep within the public debt ceiling set by

[41] Louis Fisher, "The Politics of Impounded Funds," *Administrative Science Quarterly*, 15 (1970): 361–77; Fisher, *Presidential Spending Power*, pp. 147–201; U.S. Senate, Committee on Government Operations and Committee on the Judiciary, *Impoundment of Appropriated Funds by the President*, 93rd Cong., 1st sess. (Washington: U.S. Government Printing Office, 1973).

[42] Joseph Cooper, "Analysis of Alleged 1803 Precedent for Impoundment Practice in Nixon Administration," in U.S. Senate, Committee on Government Operations, *Impoundment of Appropriated Funds by the President*, pp. 676–77.

Congress. Also, the Anti-Deficiency Act of 1950, allowing the executive to establish agency reserves in the apportionment process (see Chapters 3 and 9), was used as further support.

Not only were impoundments used for economic reasons but they were also used as political tools for what was hoped would force important policy changes. The Nixon Administration, having concluded that many grant-in-aid programs to state and local governments were ineffective, recommended that these be replaced with special revenue sharing or block grants (see Chapter 12). Impoundment, therefore, was used to halt spending on programs considered to be ineffective. The resulting drying up of funds was expected to bring pressures on Congress to enact block-grant legislation, particularly in the areas of education, criminal justice, manpower, and community development.

The strategy used by the Nixon Administration backfired. Several court suits developed, which generally were decided in favor of releasing funds. The one case that was decided by the Supreme Court dealt with grants for sewers and sewage treatment plants; *Train vs. New York City* (420 US 35) was decided in early 1975 during the Ford Administration, which had continued the impoundment of funds originally made by the Nixon Administration. The Court decided in favor of the funds being released on the grounds that the President could not overturn the congressionally determined policy that these funds were urgently needed; urgent problems prohibited delays in spending. The Court did not address the issue of whether the President has a constitutional power to impound monies.

The Nixon strategy also backfired in that Congress asserted itself in imposing new procedures for impoundments; the resulting Congressional Budget and Impoundment Control Act represents a compromise between the two branches, but a compromise that the Nixon Administration was forced to accept. Under this legislation two forms of impoundments are permissible—rescissions and deferrals. When in the judgment of the President part or all funds of a given appropriation are not needed, a rescission proposal may be made to Congress; the rescission does not take effect unless approved by Congress within 45 working days. The other type of impoundment, deferral, is a proposal to delay obligations or expenditures. As with rescissions, deferral proposals must be submitted to Congress, but these become effective unless either the House or Senate passes a resolution disapproving the proposal. Deferrals may be made only for the fiscal year in which they are submitted to Congress.

To set further limits on impoundments, the reform legislation empowers the Comptroller General to file civil suit where the executive branch has withheld budget authority contrary to the established procedures. The first suit under the act, *Staats vs. Lynn*, was filed in April 1975 and involved what the Ford Administration called a deferral of funds for a lower-income housing program (section 235 housing). The funds had been impounded originally during the Nixon Administration, and the Ford Administration proposed continuation, with the deferral to expire only 52 days short of the close of the fiscal year. Comptroller General Staats concluded this was a rescission and not a deferral, and the Senate strengthened the argument by passing a resolution to reject the deferral. Attorneys for the Administration argued that this was basically a conflict between Congress and the President and not properly the domain of the courts. The argument also was made that the Comptroller General was attempting to enforce the laws, a responsibility given to the President by the Constitution. Despite the important issues raised, they were not to be resolved. In late 1975 the funds were released by the Administration and the case was dropped.[43]

Neither branch of government has been fully satisfied with the rescission and deferral procedures. Both sides have complained about the time that is consumed in the process. From the executive perspective, exorbitant amounts of time are required in preparing the statements to be submitted to Congress; 250 impoundments were proposed in fiscal 1975 and 122 in 1976.[44] From the congressional perspective, proposed rescissions and deferrals have taken valuable time away from other important responsibilities, namely dealing with tax and appropriations legislation for the upcoming budget year. Also, the procedure opens the door to executive strategies to keep the Congress in continuous turmoil over finances. Before the new procedures, executive-legislative conflicts could be resolved by Congress rejecting or sustaining Presidential vetoes of appropriations. Now, the fact that Congress overrides a veto may mean little, because the issue can be reopened several times through the rescission/deferral process. If Congress fails to allow a rescission, the President can submit a proposed deferral; if the deferral is disapproved, a substitute deferral can be proposed. Another complaint about the procedures has been the 45 working-

---

[43] Thomas F. Williamson, "GAO Goes to Court: The Impoundment Case," *The GAO Review*, 11 (Spring, 1976): 55–64.

[44] Joel Havemann, "Congress, OMB Play Waiting Game Over Impoundments," *National Journal*, 8 (1976): 110–12.

day time limit on rescissions. At the earliest, rescissions cannot go into effect for about three months, but this time limit can be extended greatly due to congressional recesses; the result is an extended period of uncertainty, which may work to the disadvantage of all involved parties.

LEGISLATIVE OVERSIGHT

Not only are the executive and legislative branches typically separated in American governments, but each branch is provided with powers that can be used to limit the powers of the other. The basic structure of this checks-and-balance system is set forth in the U.S. Constitution, state constitutions, and city charters. However, constitutional and statutory provisions must be implemented on a daily basis, and the extent to which one branch limits the other may fluctuate over time. In this section, we consider the increasing interest being given to the legislative body's overseeing of executive operations.

One of the primary limitations on the potential for increased legislative oversight is the inherent nature of legislative bodies. Re-election is paramount in the minds of each legislator, and therefore, roles such as legislative oversight will be viewed as to how they might affect the chances of re-elections.[45] Because U.S. Congressmen and Senators and members of state legislatures represent different geographical areas, each member will perceive somewhat differently how any given topic before the legislature may influence voters in the coming election. Voters and consequently their legislative representatives are concerned with the distribution of benefits. Legislation that brings benefits to one's district, whether in direct services, payments to individuals, grants to lower-level governments, or employment through the location of governmental installations, are viewed positively. Whether these programs are effective or provided efficiently may be of less concern. On the other hand, legislation proposing tax increases is unpopular.

As long as spending decisions can be made independent of tax decisions, as was the case in Congress until the mid-1970s, there is no problem. When the two types of decisions must be balanced, however, then choices are more difficult. Legislators may be forced to tell their constituents that programs cannot be expanded unless taxes are increased. Alternatively, legislators look to the executive branch for finding procedures for increas-

---

[45] Mayhew, *Congress*, p. 5.

ing efficiency and effectiveness in order to improve programs with little or no increase in costs. This explains much of the reason for the increased interest in legislative oversight, just as similar problems led to the creation of the Taft Commission on Economy and Efficiency and ultimately to the establishment of executive budget systems (Chapter 4).

There are, of course, other reasons for the current legislative oversight movement. Watergate and related scandals plus crises in finance, such as in New York City, aroused concern for the danger of unchecked government. The abuses of the Nixon Administration revived interest in providing mechanisms to ensure integrity in administration. Moreover, legislators are not mere political animals exclusively concerned with their re-election chances but rather are sincerely interested in using government to alleviate societal problems. Frustrated by what is perceived as inept administration, legislators are attracted to expanding their roles in the hope of improving government operations. The once-common line of argument that legislators do not want to be bothered with information about programs was only partially true in the past and has even less application today.[46]

Numerous methods exist for exercising legislative oversight.[47] Providing authorization, revenue, and appropriations legislation constitute one set of methods. Other familiar devices are laws that prescribe the structure of executive agencies and personnel policies involving hiring, promotion, and dismissal procedures. A familiar type of informal oversight is the practice of individual legislators contacting agency personnel about specific day-to-day operations; although the legislator may have no official power to command any action of an agency, his or her wishes will not be treated casually by agency personnel.[48] Legislative investigations or the simple threat of investigations are other instruments of oversight. A legislative committee chairman may greatly influence an agency by suggesting that investigative hearings will be scheduled unless certain practices are changed within the agency.

An instrument that is being used increasingly is the requirement of legislative approval before an administrative decision can be implemented.

---

[46] See Aaron Wildavsky, *Budgeting: A Comparative Theory of Budgetary Processes* (Boston: Little, Brown, 1975), pp. 353–65.

[47] Sotirios A. Barber, *The Constitution and the Delegation of Congressional Power* (Chicago: University of Chicago Press, 1975), pp. 109–27. Joseph P. Harris, *Congressional Control of Administration* (Garden City, N.Y.: Doubleday, 1964).

[48] Michael W. Kirst, *Government without Passing Laws: Congress' Non-Statutory Techniques for Appropriations Control* (Chapel Hill: University of North Carolina Press, 1969).

For example, the regulations pending in 1975 on sex equality in public education, including sports, were subject to a provision that they could not go into effect until Congress had been given an opportunity to block them by concurrent resolution. Other provisions authorize Congress merely by committee action to block routine administrative decisions, such as the content of experimental education programs. Congressional vetoes also may affect certification for foreign oil shipments from the Alaska pipeline, and one bill pending in 1975 would require submission of the National Science Foundation's proposed grants.[49]

Depending upon one's perspective, these types of requirements help enforce honesty, efficiency, and effectiveness in government or are examples of legislative meddling in executive affairs.

Increasing effort is being made to specify lesiglative intent in order to reduce executive discretion. In the past, ambiguous language was used as a deliberate tool for delegating responsibilities to the executive and increasing executive flexibility in carrying out policies. The opposite is common today. A reading of *Train vs. New York City*, discussed above, will show how Congress has been careful in its choice of words in legislation and how the executive has attempted to find loopholes that would provide greater discretion. State legislatures use several methods for establishing legislative intent: by wording contained in line items, footnotes and concluding sections to appropriations bills, by committee reports, and by letters of intent delivered to the governor. "Executive agencies' fun-and-games with the enacted budget are the cause of much of this increased concern."[50] In reaction to this new thrust, governors have attempted to use their item veto power to eliminate some of the wording contained in appropriations bills, a tactic that is resulting in numerous legal confrontations.

A problem of legislatures is enforcing legislative intent. What if an agency stays within the legal prescriptions of legislative intent but violates its spirit? The main recourse is to penalize the agency in the following year. Punitive action, however, often is not possible in terms of cutting the agency's budget; citizens benefiting by agency programs would be harmed as well as the agency itself. Therefore, the main punitive alternative may be to impose more restrictions on the agency, such as making legislative

---

[49] Robert G. Dixon, Jr., "Congress, Shared Administration, and Executive Privilege," in Harvey C. Mansfield, Sr., ed., *Congress Against the President* (New York: Praeger, 1975), p. 127.

[50] Bowhay and Thrall, *State Legislative Appropriations Process*, pp. 36 and 91–92.

intent more explicit, specifically prohibiting various practices, and perhaps increasing the line items in the agency's budget in order to hamstring flexibility.

As part of legislative intent, there is increasing specificity of information that agencies are expected to collect and provide to the legislature. This practice denies agencies the tactic of confessing ignorance about their own programs; if legislation indicates an agency is to collect specific data, the agency will be expected to deliver it. The effect is to reduce ambiguity but also to raise potential for conflict over the release of information. Legislatures often request rather than demand information. Where efforts are made to demand information, the chief executive may wave the flag of executive privilege, that the executive has the privilege of withholding some information on the grounds that some degree of confidentiality is necessary in executive operations.

This position was tested in 1974 in regard to President Nixon's refusal to release taped conversations relating to Watergate. The Supreme Court in *United States vs. Nixon* (418 US 683) ruled that the tapes could not be withheld from the criminal investigation of the Special Prosecutor. The decision did not release the tapes to Congress and, indeed, a lower court decision specifically denied Congressional access to the tapes. The Court of Appeals for the District of Columbia ruled that presumption was in favor of executive privilege and that the Ervin Committee investigating Watergate had failed to prove a public need sufficient to make an exception to executive privilege (*Senate Select Committee on Presidential Campaign Activities vs. Nixon*, 498 F 2d 725). The House Judiciary Committee, on the other hand, subpoenaed the same tapes but did not seek court enforcement. Had the Committee pursued such a course, the door might have been opened to judicial involvement in impeachment proceedings, a constitutional responsibility of the Congress.[51]

Another type of oversight mechanism is zero-base legislative budgets and sunset legislation. Under these proposals, the sun would set on each program after a specified period of years, unless the program was reauthorized by the legislature.[52] Before the sunset date, an agency would be required to present a zero-base budget, indicating its programs' achievements and what would result if the programs were not renewed. Depending on how these proposals are implemented, they might provide greater

---

[51] Dixon, "Congress, Shared Administration, and Executive Privilege," pp. 125–40.

[52] Such a bill was reported out of committee in the U.S. Senate in 1976.

leverage for the legislature but also could result in massive and pointless paper work (see Chapters 4 and 6).

Program budgeting and analysis constitute another approach to legislative oversight. Legislatures are increasingly demanding impact and output data from agencies; such demands have reinforcing effects on chief executives' efforts to install program budgeting. Agencies "get the message" when both the chief executive and the legislative body are demanding program information. Not only are legislatures demanding information but they are demanding program analyses and are developing their own capabilities to do analysis.[53] New York State's Legislative Commission on Expenditure Review and Virginia's Joint Legislative Audit and Review Commission are examples of state legislative analysis units.[54] As of 1975 the Legislative Program Evaluation Section, affiliated with the National Conference of State Legislatures, had 45 legislative agencies and 200 individuals as members.[55] At the federal level, the Legislative Reorganization Act of 1970 and the 1974 budget reform legislation have strengthened support for the General Accounting Office to conduct program evaluations. Of the roughly $200 million a year the federal government spends on program evaluation, the GAO spends about a third or half of its own budget on analysis.[56] As analytic capabilities increase, the demand for analysis likely will increase.[57] There no longer is any issue as to whether legislative units will engage in analysis.

---

[53] See General Accounting Office, *Civil Agencies Make Limited Use of Cost-Benefit Analysis in Support of Budget Requests* (Washington: U.S. Government Printing Office, 1975); General Accounting Office, *Summaries of GAO Conclusions and Recommendations on Appropriation Matters for Civil Departments and Agencies* (Washington: U.S. Government Printing Office, 1975); Joseph F. Kyle, "The Florida Legislative Budget Review Process," in Balutis and Butler, eds., *Political Pursestrings*, pp. 69–79; Eli B. Silverman, "Legislative Budgetary Oversight in New York," *State Government*, 48 (1975): 128–30; Eli B. Silverman, "Public Budgeting and Public Administration: Enter the Legislature," *Public Finance Quarterly*, 2 (1974): 472–84; Symposium on "Clients and Analysts: Congress," *Policy Analysis*, 2 (1976): 197–323.

[54] Richard Brown and Ray D. Pethtel, "A Matter of Facts: State Legislative Performance Auditing," *Public Administrative Review*, 34 (1974): 318–27. Also see Donald L. Tucker, "Legislative Overview: Progress in Florida," *State Government*, 49 (1976): 115–20.

[55] Mark Lincoln Chadwin, "The Nature of Legislative Program Evaluation," *Evaluation*, 2, No. 2 (1975): 48.

[56] Joel Havemann, "Congress Tries to Break Ground Zero in Evaluating Federal Programs," *National Journal*, 8 (1976): 713.

[57] Elmer B. Staats, "The Challenge of Evaluating Federal Social Programs," *Evaluation*, 1, No. 3 (1975): 50–54; Thurber, "Congressional Budget Reform and New Demands for Policy Analysis," pp. 197–214.

While numerous methods of oversight are available, the organizational locus of oversight remains a problem along with a parallel problem of making oversight effective. The oversight function can be housed in any combination of legislative committees and staff units.[58] Oversight may be practiced by substantive committees, appropriations committees, and at the federal level by the Senate and House Budget Committees. The Government Operations Committees in the U.S. House and Senate could perform this function.[59] The Congress or a state legislature could create a new joint committee on oversight. There have been proposals for the creation of quasi-independent oversight organizations that would be controlled by neither the executive nor legislative bodies.

The effectiveness of the oversight function will be curtailed, however, as long as legislatures are fragmented. A coherent approach to oversight is not possible when committee powers overlap; every federal agency must deal with at least one substantive committee, the Appropriations Committee, and the Budget Committee in each chamber of Congress. That means there are at least six different committees that can proffer different advice and direction to the agency. Moreover, these committees may not have the backing of the full legislative body, so that what one committee might say an agency should do is not necessarily what the legislature as a whole would say.

An impediment to oversight is the prima donna roles of legislators vis-à-vis each other and their staff. The deference afforded legislators to each other tends to thwart a unified approach to oversight; legislators, especially those having seniority, are allowed considerable freedom in dealing with agencies, freedom that can result in conflicting legislative pressures on any one agency. Moreover, legislators are keenly sensitive to having their staffs act in subordinate and inferior capacities.[60] For a staff unit to evaluate a program enacted by the legislative body, to find the program inadequate, and to suggest means of improving it is likely to be viewed by many legislators as affronts to their responsibility for setting policy. The question would be raised: Who are these employees of ours who dare suggest what should be done? The legislative body already feels

---

[58] Barber, *Constitution and the Delegation of Congressional Power*, pp. 121–22; Griffith and Valeo, *Congress*, pp. 63–75.

[59] Thomas A. Henderson, *Congressional Oversight of Executive Agencies: A Study of the House Committee on Government Operations* (Gainesville: University Presses of Florida, 1970).

[60] Alton Frye, "Congressional Politics and Policy Analysis: Bridging the Gap," *Policy Analysis,* 2 (1976): 275–76.

threatened by executive agenda setting without giving rise to another group of in-house agenda setters. For this reason, legislative analytic units can be expected to be cautious in program analysis, to be tentative in reaching conclusions and recommendations, to test the waters with one toe before taking the deep plunge. Analyses by legislative units may concentrate less on the "big" issues and more on trivial programs or ones toward which there is legislative indifference.

Any change in a system necessarily affects all parts of it. To suggest that legislative oversight needs strengthening is to suggest that institutional arrangements in legislative bodies be altered. The roles of committees and especially their chairmen may require adjustments that can easily be perceived as threats to existing powers. Yet, despite these threats, change is taking place. At the federal level, the 1974 legislation seemingly diminishes the autonomy of the four money committees. Despite this apparent reduction in authority, the committee members basically supported the change, and at least during the initial years of experience under the law, the money committees seemed committed to making the new procedures work.

Whether legislative oversight will strengthen the legislature at the expense of the executive remains an open question in part because the future of oversight, itself, is an open question. There are numerous forces at work to encourage and discourage expansion of the oversight function. Early in this century, executive budgeting was perceived by some as a threat to legislative powers. To the extent that the executive has set the agenda for legislative action, legislatures have played diminished roles. In more recent times, program budgeting has been seen as an executive weapon to be used against the legislature; through the program budget the executive is said to gain greater control over agencies at the expense of the legislative body. Certainly, oversight in its various forms is intended to reassert the role of the legislature as a co-equal with the executive branch. An uncertainty is whether the scales might tip so that the legislature could be said to have usurped executive responsibilities.

SUMMARY

Legislative bodies are fragmented, often resulting in a fragmented approach to budgeting. Bicamerlism and the committee system contribute to the fragmentation. Revenue and expenditure legislation are often handled by separate committees. The use of numerous appropriations bills frequently blocks legislative bodies from reaching decisions on total spending. In recent years, efforts have been made to overcome some of this fragmentation at both the federal and state levels. The Congressional Budget and Impoundment Control Act superimposed new Budget Committees over the existing money and other standing committees; whether the system will resolve the apparent problems is yet to be determined.

The relative roles of the executive and legislative branches in budgeting are changing. Earlier budget reforms gave the chief executive the power of agenda setting through the preparation of a proposed budget. Recent efforts, such as the 1974 reforms in Congress, are directed at reasserting the co-equal status of the legislative branch. The burden of proof in justifying expenditures for programs, however, remains with the executive. Within the process, both executive agencies and legislative committees devise strategies to deal with each other. At the federal level, a new set of relationships has emerged with the establishment of rescission and deferral processes.

Legislative oversight is increasingly popular. Oversight can be accomplished by many means; in addition to legislation affecting agency budgets, legislatures may specify agency structures and personnel procedures. Prior legislative approval of some administrative decisions may be required. Legislative investigative hearings serve the oversight function along with detailed specification of legislative intent. Zero-base budgeting, sunset legislation, program budgeting, and analysis are other avenues for oversight. Working against an effective oversight role, however, are the structural features of legislative bodies as well as general political factors, such as the ever-present concern of legislators to be re-elected.

9

BUDGET EXECUTION, ACCOUNTING, AND INFORMATION SYSTEMS

Once the budget has been approved, the execution phase of the cycle begins.[1] Of course, one should recognize that at the federal level, at least before the introduction of the 1974 Congressional Budget and Impoundment Control Act, it has been common for many agencies to enter the execution phase only with a continuing resolution to spend at the previous year's rate rather than spend under a new appropriation. The same practice sometimes occurs at the state level, while local governments usually are required by state law to complete the budget approval phase by the beginning of the new fiscal year.

This chapter has three sections. The first deals with the overall patterns of execution; the second section discusses approaches to accounting; and the third discusses information systems. It should be understood that accounting and information systems are important not only in budget execution but in the other three parts of the cycle as well.

BUDGET EXECUTION

Execution is the action phase of budgeting in which the plans contained in the budget are put into operation. The term "plans" is used here not to

---

[1] Stephen F. Jablonsky, Assistant Professor of Accounting and Public Administration of The Pennsylvania State University, was especially helpful in reviewing a draft

refer exclusively to planning in program budgeting. Every budget either explicitly or implicitly contains plans concerning the work to be done and the achievements to be gained. Execution, then, involves converting those plans into operations. At stake is not merely the implementation of budget documents or appropriation bills that have been approved by the legislative body but also the entire administration of governmental programs. In this section, we consider first the steps taken immediately following the completion of the approval phase and then the ongoing day-to-day operations of budget execution.

In acting on the budget, the legislature will have provided some indication of what is called "legislative intent." Such intent may be expressed in terms of the dollars to be available for an organizational unit for specific object classes such as personnel, or even minor object classes such as overtime pay; approximately half of the state legislatures appropriate by object class.[2] These specifications, however, only indicate the resources to be used and not the purposes to be served. As a result, the appropriations bill may contain substantial narrative on what services the organizational unit may or may not provide.

Depending upon the specificity of the appropriation, the executive branch may have great or little flexibility in the execution phase. Some flexibility seems essential if for no other reason than that the legislative body could not readily specify all aspects of all operations of all agencies. Moreover, flexibility is needed to allow agencies to respond to changing situations.

Most legislative action, therefore, leaves the door open to further decision making; the process of decision making is not completed once the legislative body has acted on the budget. The adopted budget or appropriations are viewed by the various segments of the executive branch as containing legislative intent or mandates. However, because not all of the recommendations of the chief executive and line agencies will have been approved, the appropriations will also be examined to find ways in which specific legislative provisions can be interpreted to conform with the priorities of the various segments of the bureaucracy. A primary concern will be to avoid "bending" the law to the point of arousing legislative ire, which could result in excessively detailed appropriations in subsequent years.

---

of this chapter. Any remaining flaws in the discussion are, of course, the responsibility of the authors.

  [2] *Budgetary Processes in the States: A Tabular Display* (Lexington, Ky.: Council of State Governments, 1975), Table XII.

At the state and federal levels, the game is played in the context of an apportionment process.[3] Line agencies submit plans to the central budget office concerning how appropriated funds will be utilized, often including a proposed expenditure plan for each quarter of the fiscal year. The budget office, acting at the direction of the chief executive, may require modification of these proposals and eventually approves apportionments for each agency. Following the approval of apportionments by the budget office, allotments are made within departments. This process grants expenditure authority to subunits. At the local level this process may be relatively informal.

The chief executive has greater negative powers than positive ones in the apportionment process. The executive cannot approve apportionments for projects prohibited in the appropriation nor exceed dollar amounts for specified items.[4] On the negative side, the chief executive may be able to reduce or eliminate some appropriated items. As was seen in Chapter 8, until recently Presidents were relatively free to impound monies; the 1974 reform legislation through the rescission and deferral processes, however, has provided mechanisms for congressional overrides of presidential preferences not to spend. At the state level and sometimes the local level, the line-item veto serves the same negative role.

Agencies come to the apportionment process less than fully satisfied with their appropriations bills and preferring as little central control as possible. An operating agency typically will have been granted only part of the monies requested, but what is contained in its appropriation will be considered "ours" and preferably not subject to extensive budget office control. Because the agency probably will receive less than originally requested, the apportionment plan may propose how specific services will be affected. The budget office, again acting for the chief executive, may direct a different service configuration given available funds. The agency will rebut, explaining why its proposal should be approved. Eventually some form of compromise will be reached.

In addition to apportionments, another major concern at the outset of the executive phase and throughout the fiscal year is cash flow, because revenue collection and expenditures do not coincide with each other. State

---

[3] Instructions for this process at the federal level are contained in OMB Circular A-34, "Instructions on Budget Execution."

[4] Chief executives may have limited ability to exceed some items, such as flexibility to exceed by 5 percent the amount provided for salaries of a given organizational unit. "Creative" executives are adept at "finding" discretionary funds that can be used for projects for which the legislative body did not provide.

and local sales tax receipts may be relatively constant during the year, but this is not the case with local property taxes. As a result, the jurisdiction from month to month may be spending more or less than it is receiving in revenues during the same time period.

An overall cash flow plan will be devised balancing revenues by expected date of receipt with expected expenditures. Funds not needed immediately will be invested, such as in the case of a school district whose expenditures decline sharply during the summer months. The investments will be scheduled so that they are available when needed, as in the case of quarterly state aid payments made to local school districts. The funds typically will be handled by the treasurer and not the budget office, but close coordination between these two units on cash flow problems is obviously essential.

There are numerous kinds of instruments used for investments. State and local governments use bank demand deposits that permit immediate withdrawals; because these accounts yield no interest, the amount of revenue maintained in them is kept to a minimum to meet immediate cash requirements. These governments also invest funds in a variety of interest-yielding sources, including time deposits, U.S. Treasury Securities, and corporate stock. A recent problem has resulted from investing employee retirement funds in corporate stocks whose values have sometimes depreciated rather than appreciated. State constitutions and statutes may restrict the methods of investment available to both state and local governments.[5] Most of the federal government's funds are deposited with Federal Reserve banks and branches; other funds are in tax and loan accounts in more than 12,000 commercial banks.[6]

Turning to daily operations, a line agency seeks flexibility in running its programs but is continuously bombarded by external pressures. Not only will there be controls imposed on the agency in terms of budgeting,

---

[5] See Merlin M. Hackbart and Robert S. Johnson, *State Cash Balance Management Policy* (Lexington, Ky.: Council of State Governments, 1975); Lennox L. Moak and Albert M. Hillhouse, *Concepts and Practices in Local Government Finance* (Chicago: Municipal Finance Officers Association, 1975), pp. 197–206; Harold I. Steinberg, "Cash Management for Local Government," *Governmental Finance*, 4 (November, 1975): 5–10 as well as other articles in this issue of *Governmental Finance*; James C. Van Horne, "Cash Management," in J. Richard Aronson and Eli Schwartz, eds., *Management Policies in Local Government Finance* (Washington: International City Management Association, 1975), pp. 248–62.

[6] *Financial Management Functions in the Federal Government* (Washington: U.S. Government Printing Office, 1974), pp. 2-4–2-6.

but there will be other pressures such as complaints and demands from agency clientele. The agency in many instances will be forced to tell its clientele that services cannot be expanded because insufficient funds were provided in the budget. The chief executive or members of the executive's immediate staff may also apply pressures, sometimes largely for political reasons; the Nixon Administration is a prime example. Individual legislators will also apply pressures. A member of the city council may encourage the police department to expand patrols in a given neighborhood which can only be done by either reducing services elsewhere or adding staff with additional funds.

From the perspective of the central administration, the budget is of little value unless used as a controlling mechanism for agency operations; unless agencies are required to live within their budgets, the process becomes an empty exercise. Therefore, various controls are imposed upon agencies, with one control being the pre-audit. After having an approved apportionment plan and receiving an allotment, the agency is still not free to spend but rather must submit a request to obligate the government to spend resources. In a large government, the request may pass through a department or agency budget office for approval and then to the central budget office. The request is matched against the unit's budget to determine whether the proposed expenditure is authorized and whether sufficient funds are available in the agency's budget. If the request is approved, an encumbrance for the specified amount is entered to indicate that the previous total is no longer available to the agency. In this way, agencies are kept within the constraints of their budgets.

The pre-audit function may be carried out by several different units. Not only may the budget office be involved but also an accounting department. Often at the state and local levels, independent comptrollers, controllers, or auditor generals have pre-audit responsibilities. These elected officials have the duty of providing another, presumably independent, check upon financial transactions. Once the pre-audit requirements have been met, the treasurer typically is responsible for the issuance of a check.

The scope of the pre-audit control varies from jurisdiction to jurisdiction. Items for possible control are an organizational unit, objects of expenditure, and programs. A recent survey conducted by the National Association of State Budget Officers indicated that central budget offices in 29 states control by department and 18 of these by departmental subunits; the latter type of control reduces management flexibility within the departments. The same survey showed that 30 central budget offices control by major object and at least 5 control by minor object. There are more than 20 states that control by program.[7]

Object control is important to the agency because as the year progresses the needs for various types of resources may change. An agency may conclude it was overbudgeted on one item and that these surplus funds could be better utilized on other items. Where minor object controls are used, an agency might be required to have central budget office approval to shift funds from salaries to wages; major object control would involve shifting funds from salaries to nonpersonnel items such as travel or supplies. At the state level transfers between programs or units that are within a given department typically require central clearance. Transfers between departments, however, are far less common without legislative approval.[8]

In the case of an agency proposing to hire new staff, not only will the usual pre-audit procedure be used, but in addition, a central personnel office may have authority to review the request. This procedure, known as personnel complement control, is used in part to avoid increasing personnel commitments and corresponding increases in budget requirements. Without such control, an agency might hire a permanent employee near the end of the fiscal year, involving perhaps only $1,000 in expenditures with sufficient funds in the budget to cover this cost; but that person's salary for the following year could be $12,000, thereby increasing the agency's budget base (see Chapter 11).

The agency also will not be free to purchase nonpersonnel items from the private sector, because these items will be under the control of a purchasing department. Interdepartmental transfers are used whereby funds are transferred from the line agency to the general stores office, and in return the agency receives the supplies it has requested.[9] The General Services Administration performs this function for the national government.

Special permission may be required for acquiring some items, even though ample resources are included in an agency's budget. Items that

---

[7] This discussion is based upon previously unpublished data. The survey was conducted in conjunction with the Institute of Public Administration of The Pennsylvania State University and the Pennsylvania Budget Office.

[8] *Budgetary Processes in the States*, Table XIII.

[9] A. Wayne Corcoran, "Financial Management," in Aronson and Schwartz, eds., *Management Policies*, pp. 263–69.

often require such approval include air-conditioning units, carpeting, and photocopying machines to name just a few. Air-conditioning controls are used to avoid overloading building electrical systems and to avoid higher utility bills. Carpeting controls are intended to avoid increased housekeeping costs. Photocopying is controlled where a central duplicating office exists.

Bidding procedures are common in purchasing.[10] The purpose is to obtain quality products or services at the lowest possible price. Contracts are awarded through bidding for items of general use to all agencies; large quantities of office supplies are obtained through private bidding, with the supplies being placed in general stores and drawn out as needed by the operating agencies. Other items may be placed on bid only as needed, such as a request for bids on several new buses. Intergovernmental arrangements are sometimes used, such as cities joining with each other or with their state government in purchasing large numbers of police cars or truck tires. Purchasing operations are usually conducted by a purchasing unit in a city department of administration or a general services agency or department at the state and national levels. Common complaints by line agencies are that the items purchased may not be satisfactory—"the ink from the ballpoint pens smudges"—and that bidding procedures are too slow.

Controls may also be imposed in terms of management practices. The budget office or some other central staff unit may have responsibility for studying agency procedures and for recommending or prescribing new procedures. These organization-and-management studies can recommend changes in the department's structure such as realignments of bureaus and their responsibilities. An agency having been allowed to establish a new program is likely to be supervised closely in implementing the program. Considerable conflict may arise between the agency and the central staff, perhaps the budget office, as to how implementation should proceed.[11]

Even the seemingly trivial item of preparing a new form may constitute a major problem for the agency. In some jurisdictions, all forms that are to be used by agencies for other than internal purposes must be

---

[10] James T. Carter and Ronald Welf, "Purchasing Practices in Counties," in *The County Year Book, 1975* (Washington: National Association of Counties, 1975), pp. 74–98; David Neuman and Paul M. Carren, "State and Local Government Purchasing," *Management Controls*, 22 (1975): 78–89; *State and Local Government Purchasing* (Lexington, Ky.: Council of State Governments, 1975).

[11] For a review of the literature on the implementation process, see Donald S. Van Meter and Carl E. Van Horn, "The Policy Implementation Process: A Conceptual Framework,'" *Administration and Society*, 6 (1975): 445–88.

approved by the central budget office or some other central staff unit. A state department of education, for example, would be free to prepare a form for its own staff to complete for reporting contacts made with local school districts; however, a form to be mailed to school districts for reporting average daily attendance might have to be screened by the budget office. Forms control, however, is not trivial. This control is used to avoid possible political embarrassments, such as an agency requesting information that might be considered an invasion of privacy. Forms control also can be used to avoid situations in which two departments request basically the same information from the same source.

Still another set of controls would be periodic reporting to the budget office. This may be on a weekly, monthly, or quarterly basis depending upon the extensiveness of the information to be supplied. Agencies may be required to report not only the status of their expenditures but also the status of programs. Reports on work load may be required, such as the number of clients seen to date; such work load reports can be compared with what the agency projected earlier for the entire year.

As the fiscal year approaches its end, agencies will attempt to zero-out their budgets; an agency having unexpended funds at the end of the fiscal year may be considered a prime candidate for cuts in the upcoming budget. Also, unexpended or unencumbered funds often lapse at the end of the budget year. From the agency's perspective, it is a now-or-never situation on spending the available money. Another factor is that an agency may have delayed some expenditures, saving a portion of its budget for contingencies. This results in a spurt in expenditures, where perhaps equipment is purchased that is not really needed. An alternative is to allow the surplus funds to be transferred to the agency's new budget without requiring a reappropriation. A handful of states allow this.[12]

Just as variations among governments are extensive in budget preparation and approval, variations are great in budget execution. The controls that have been discussed may or may not be applied in any given jurisdiction. Some controls may be applied with more or less rigor; some may be applied with more rigor to one agency and less to another. A large state government may delegate some of these controls to departmental secretaries and their budget offices, with some departmental budget offices exercising extensive control and others not. The controls from year-to-year may be relaxed or more vigorously enforced. For example, in some years

---

[12] *Budgetary Processes in the States,* Table XV.

approval of transfers between object classes may be almost automatic but not in other years.

Day-to-day activities of budget execution require data to be collected and analyzed. As will be seen in the following sections, accounting and information systems are important in supporting the execution phase.

GOVERNMENTAL ACCOUNTING

Accounting can be defined as a means of recording financial transactions, particularly revenues or receipts on the one hand and expenditures or disbursements on the other.[13] Accounting is one but not the exclusive ingredient in accountability. In this section, we discuss the types of funds used in governmental accounting, the structure of the accounts, and the timing of when transactions are recorded.

Perhaps the most important feature that distinguishes governmental accounting from private accounting is government's use of a fund-accounting structure. Governments account for their financial resources in separate funds that are typically earmarked for designated purposes, whereas private enterprise does not. The use of separate funds means that separate accounts must be maintained to record receipts and expenditures as part of the overall concern for accountability. By accounting for each fund, the government is able to show that receipts were properly recorded and expenditures were used for authorized purposes.

There are eight major types of funds, with the most important one usually being 1) the *general fund*.[14] This fund is used to account for revenues available for the general operations of the government. At the local level, property tax receipts would be entered and would be available for public safety, recreation, streets, and so forth.

---

[13] For more detailed discussions of governmental accounting, see Ernest Enke, "Municipal Accounting," in Aronson and Schwartz, eds., *Management Policies*, pp. 283–302; Leon E. Hay and R. M. Mikesell, *Governmental Accounting*, 5th ed. (Homewood, Ill.: Irwin, 1974); Harry D. Kerrigan, *Fund Accounting* (New York: McGraw-Hill, 1969); Eric L. Kohler and Howard W. Wright, *Accounting in the Federal Government* (Englewood Cliffs, N.J.: Prentice-Hall, 1956); Edward S. Lynn and Robert L. Freeman, *Fund Accounting Theory and Practice* (Englewood Cliffs, N.J.: Prentice-Hall, 1975); Moak and Hillhouse, *Concepts and Practices in Local Government Finance*, pp. 329–57; Irving L. Tenner and Edward S. Lynn, *Municipal and Governmental Accounting*, 4th ed. (Englewood Cliffs, N.J.: Prentice-Hall, 1960).

[14] National Committee on Governmental Accounting, *Governmental Accounting, Auditing, and Financial Reporting* (Chicago: Municipal Finance Officers Association, 1968).

The other seven types are special funds, which by definition have more limited uses than the general fund. 2) *Special revenue funds* account for resources from special sources and are earmarked for special purposes. State tax receipts on gasoline are typically accounted for in a special revenue fund, with expenditures being limited to transportation and especially roads and highways. 3) *Debt service funds* are used to account for the accumulation of interest and principal on long-term debt. 4) *Capital project funds* are used to account for receipts and expenditures related to projects such as construction of a new park or city hall. If the project involves a bond issue, accounting for the retirement of the bonds is carried out through a debt service fund, while accounting for the construction is handled through the capital project fund. 5) *Enterprise funds* are used for business-like operations, particularly those supported by user charges such as parking garages and toll bridges. 6) *Trust and agency funds* include funds established to account for donations or resources held on behalf of others. An employee pension fund is an important example of a trust fund. 7) *Intragovernmental service funds* are used to account for transactions within the government, such as general stores, central duplicating offices, and data processing. 8) *Special assessment funds* account for particular improvements in services for specific beneficiaries. The proceeds of a per foot charge for sidewalk replacement in front of one's home would be accounted for in a special fund of this type.

In addition to accounting by fund, the accounting system records other aspects of transactions, particularly expenditures; these aspects include the appropriation, the organizational unit involved, and the object of the expenditure. When the legislative body appropriates, it is authorizing an expenditure out of one or more of the various funds of the government. At the state and federal levels, several appropriations bills for a given budget year may be made against one fund, most notably the general fund. There may be separate education and police appropriations bills passed by the state legislature and applied to the general fund. The accounting system, then, must track transactions by appropriation to maintain accountability to the legislative body. In addition, the accounting system will classify transactions by organizational units, because these are the ones ultimately responsible for resource consumption. In some instances, organizational unit accounting is mandatory, because the appropriation approved by the legislature will have specified funds to be assigned to organizations. Most large governments will account not only at the departmental level but also at the bureau, office, or division level, even though the appropriation bill may only specify the departments and not subunits.

Expenditures also are accounted for in terms of the objects acquired—the objects of expenditure. Broad groupings of objects are called major objects and their subdivisions are called minor objects. Table 11 shows the

TABLE 11
Federal Object of Expenditure Classification

Code	Title
11.1	Permanent positions
11.3	Positions other than permanent
11.5	Other personnel compensation
11.7	Military personnel
11.8	Special personal services payments
	Personnel benefits
12.1	Civilian
12.2	Military
13.0	Benefits for former personnel
21.0	Travel and transportation of persons
22.0	Transportation of things
	Rent, communications, and utilities
23.1	Standard level user charges
23.2	Other rent, communications, and utilities
24.0	Printing and reproduction
25.0	Other services
26.0	Supplies and materials
31.0	Equipment
32.0	Lands and structures
33.0	Investments and loans
41.0	Grants, subsidies, and contributions
42.0	Insurance claims and indemnities
43.0	Interest and dividends
44.0	Refunds
91.0	Unvouchered (confidential)
92.0	Undistributed
93.0	Administrative and nonadministrative expenses (revolving and trust funds)
94.0	Change in selected resources
95.0	Quarters and subsistence charges

Source: Office of Management and Budget, "Preparation and Submission of Budget Estimates," Circular A-11 (July 19, 1976), Section 34.2.

object classifications for the federal government. The "11" series in the table is for direct personnel expenditures, the "12" series for employee benefits, and the "13" series for retired personnel. Together these can be treated as the "10" series covering personnel costs. Similar classifications are used by state and local governments. Series commonly used in addition to personnel include travel, supplies, equipment, and utility and other service costs.

Accounting systems can become unwieldy if the minor classifications are greatly expanded. A general series classification might be for materials and supplies but this can be carved into every conceivable item that is used in government. While it is possible to assign special account numbers to paperclips, pencils, carbon paper, rubber bands, and the like, the data produced probably would be of little benefit to anyone.

Object classifications are frequently used for control purposes to limit the amount of money that may be spent in a given object class. Control can be exercised by designating specific minor objects. While there may be little interest in defining paperclips as an exclusive minor object, travel may be treated in considerable detail. For executives and legislators who are concerned that employees might travel at government expense for nongovernmental purposes, detailed breakouts of travel in the object classification may be encouraged. Travel can be classified for a state government as within or outside the state, by the purpose of travel (meet with federal officials or attend a conference), and by the type of expense (lodging, meals, and transportation).

Because accounting systems must produce information for various purposes, numerical codes are established to simplify the processing of transactions. Not only will there be a code number for the major and minor objects of expenditures involved but also for the fund, appropriation, department and bureau, and year. Each transaction, then, is posted to a subsidiary ledger, for example, the operating expense ledger. Summary information on expenditures is then posted in the general ledger.

Accounting systems facilitate the conduct of post-audits. Financial post-audits focus upon whether transactions were recorded in conformance with prescribed standards and whether funds were expended within limits set forth by appropriations. Therefore, the post-audit examines both the accounting system itself as well as the actual transactions. These activities are carried out at the federal level by the General Accounting Office, which is headed by the Comptroller General. At the state level, the auditor or comptroller is responsible.[15] Local governments frequently use private accounting firms for their post-audits.

Turning to the matter of timing, accounting systems are distinguishable in terms of when transactions are recorded. The oldest system is cash accounting. On the receipt side, transactions are recorded at the time funds are received from various sources. On the expenditure side, disbursements are recorded either when checks are issued or when checks are paid (cleared through the banking system).[16] Accounts on a cash basis thus show the immediate cash position and the need for any assumption of debt to cover cash requirements. This form of accounting serves the control function of budgeting and may be useful in dealing with cash flow problems noted above.

A second type of system is encumbrance accounting. Rather than first recording expenditures when disbursements are made, appropriations are reduced when purchase orders are written or contracts are entered into. An encumbrance system helps ensure that a governmental unit will not overspend its appropriations.

A third type of system is accrual accounting. Revenues are recorded when the government earns the income, or in other words, when the taxpayer incurs a tax liability. Expenditures are recorded when the government incurs a liability to pay for goods or services, regardless of when payment for those goods or services might actually be made.

Cost accounting, the fourth type of system, shifts from reporting the status of appropriation balances to the actual costs of providing goods and services.[17] A fundamental element in the definition of cost is that of resources used regardless of when acquired. For example, gasoline purchased for a state highway department could be accounted for when the

---

[15] For a state-by-state presentation on state auditors, see relevant sections of the current *Book of the States* (Lexington, Ky.: Council of State Governments). Also see Mortimer A. Dittenhofer, "Progress in State Auditing," *State Government*, 46 (1973): 125–31.

[16] Note that there may be several definitions of cash. From the viewpoint of an agency, a cash expenditure is a charge against an appropriation as soon as a check is issued. From the treasury standpoint, a cash requirement is not felt until checks are cleared through the banking system. On the receipt side the cash basis has meant the time when funds are deposited to the government's bank accounts. At the federal level, the concept has been changed to the time when the Treasury is notified of the collection by the agency first receiving the money.

[17] Karney A. Brasfield, "The Role of Accounting in Cost Budgeting," *The Federal Accountant*, 4 (1954): 25.

order is made (encumbrance), when the goods are received (accrual method), when the vendor is paid (cash method), or when the gasoline is consumed (cost method).

The concepts of inventory and depreciation are entailed in the use of cost accounting. If an agency builds up its inventory in a given year, the expenditures for that inventory are not considered part of the costs of providing services in that year; only as items in the inventory are used will they be regarded as costs. Similarly, it is possible to isolate capital goods and depreciate them over their useful lives. If a police department acquires several new patrol cars in one year, costs are expressed each year for the value being consumed in the production of police services through the use of automobiles. This approach provides a relatively accurate picture of what resources are being consumed but may distort the cash flow picture. From a cash-flow standpoint, it is of little immediate interest to know that police cars will be of use for three years and more important to know that the full bill for the cars must be paid the first year.

Cost accounting can be useful for program budgeting in that it can identify the costs of producing impacts, outputs, and activities. For example, cost accounting would show the resources being used for a program element of municipal street lighting. With the addition of more specified account codes, the cost of work activities such as repairing and replacing lights could be recorded. Further subdivisions could focus on the type of light (incandescent, sodium vapor, etc.), the section of the city in which the light is located, and even the time of day when the work was conducted. The number of possible measures around which costs could be assembled is infinite, but obviously there is some point of diminishing returns where the data collected would be of little use. What that point is, however, is not obvious.[18]

It should be understood that these four approaches to accounting are not substitutes for each other. From the standpoint of a treasury department, a cash basis of recording receipts and expenditures is necessary because the department has the legal responsibility to receive revenue and issue checks to cover expenditures. This responsibility includes determining whether there are sufficient funds to cover checks to be issued. An

---

[18] An example of an extremely detailed accounting system is being developed in a Philadelphia suburb. Parking meter activities identified in the accounting system include meter collections in lots, meter collections on streets, benchwork meter repairs, meter maintenance, meter replacements, meter post repairs and replacements, and even vandalism.

encumbrance basis is important to ensure that appropriations are not overspent. An accrual basis is important for management purposes in that it shows the current status of assets and liabilities. Accrued expenditures are also recommended as a more accurate reflection of annual activity and the impact of governmental expenditures on the private sector than cash or encumbrance accounting.[19] Cost accounting is valuable in identifying the resources consumed as distinguished from resources acquired and placed in inventory.

Governments use each of these approaches and often a blend, but a standard complaint has been that too much emphasis rests on cash accounting. Largely because cash accounting is the least complicated to use, most small- to medium-size municipalities probably have little more than a cash system. The 1956 amendments to the Budget and Accounting Procedures Act of 1950 required the adoption of accrual methods in all federal agencies as soon as feasible. Yet eleven years later the President's Commission on Budget Concepts emphasized that major agencies (including Defense) had still not developed accrual systems.[20] The Commission, recognizing the inherent difficulties of installing accrual accounting, recommended that it not go into effect until the fiscal 1971 budget rather than the 1969 target for most other changes. Even this later date was not met, and today accrual accounting is used mainly for business-type agencies and not others.[21] The same problems abound at the state level.

Variations in the types of accounting practices are widespread among governments and within larger governments. State departments of urban affairs have tended to encourage local governments to adopt "model" systems as has the National Council on Governmental Accounting (NCGA).[22] A standard accounting system for local governments would

[19] President's Commission on Budget Concepts, *Report* (Washington: U.S. Government Printing Office, 1967), p. 37.

[20] President's Commission on Budget Concepts, *Report*, pp. 36–46.

[21] OMB Circular A-11, "Preparation and Submission of Budget Estimates," July 16, 1976, Section 37.3.

[22] Harlan E. Boyles and Randall P. Martin, "A Statewide Accounting System for Local Government," *Governmental Finance*, 3 (February, 1974): 13–15; Robert J. Freeman, "Governmental Accounting Research and Standards-Setting: The Role of the NCGA," *Governmental Finance*, 5 (May, 1976): 6–13; James M. Patton, "Standardization and Utility of Municipal Accounting and Reporting Practices: A Survey," *Governmental Finance*, 5 (May, 1976): 15–20; Robert W. Peterson, State Auditor, and Bureau of Governmental Affairs, University of North Dakota, *Accounting System for North Dakota Townships* (Grand Forks: Bureau of Governmental Affairs,

allow greater exchange of information among these governments. State governments and the federal government do not have standardized government-wide accounting systems. Each agency may have one or more systems. At the federal level, there are approximately 160 civilian agency systems and 125 systems in the Department of Defense.[23] The Comptroller General is responsible for first approving the principles and standards of each system and then the system design, with the agencies being responsible for operating the systems.[24]

The complexity of the flow of funds into, within, and out of government is immense, and for that and other reasons governments have sought new methods that facilitate information handling. In the next section, we consider the flow of both financial and program information.

MULTIPURPOSE INFORMATION SYSTEMS

Contemporary approaches to budgeting, as has been seen, require considerable amounts of information for decision making. Accounting systems, having been limited largely to resource information and especially revenues and expenditures, provide only a portion of the needed information. The information from accounting systems is essential for control, management, and planning and for budget preparation, approval, execution, and audit. Nevertheless, program information about impacts, outputs, and activities is equally important and needs to be juxtaposed with financial information. Information systems, then, constitute an effort to bring about greater coordination of organizational units in the collection, storage, manipulation, and retrieval of data.[25] The term management information systems (MIS) is most commonly used to describe the effort, in which "manage-

University of North Dakota, 1976); John B. Welsh, *Manual of Accounting and Related Financial Procedures for Pennsylvania Townships and Boroughs* (Harrisburg: Commonwealth of Pennsylvania, 1969).

[23] For the current status of these systems, see most recent issue of Comptroller General, *Annual Report* (Washington: U.S. Government Printing Office).

[24] Accounting and other financial matters are coordinated through the Joint Financial Management Improvement Program (JFMIP), consisting of the Comptroller General, Secretary of the Treasury, the Director of the OMB, the Administrator of General Services, and the Chairman of the Civil Service Commission. See *Financial Management Functions in the Federal Government* (Washington: U.S. Government Printing Office, 1974).

[25] For more detailed information on state and local information systems, see reports issued by the National Association for State Information Systems (NASIS) and the Urban and Regional Information Systems Association (URISA).

ment" refers to planning, administration, and control functions and "system" suggests a categorizing or ordering of information processing. In this section, we first review the problems involved in designing an MIS and then consider how these systems can be used in program budgeting.

Management Information Systems Several questions must be answered in the design of a management information system. These include: 1) What information is needed? 2) Who needs it? 3) Who should and should not have access to it? 4) Who will collect it? 5) To what extent will it be kept current? and 6) How will it be stored? Perhaps the most important question is the first: What information is needed? Each public agency already collects much information, virtually all of which will be argued to be useful to the internal operations of the agency. In all probability, much of the data collected are of limited use. Data are often collected and reports produced through habit, though there is seldom any call for these materials. In recent years there has been growing alarm over the amount of information collected. In part as a response to this situation, the U.S. Commission on Federal Paperwork was created in the 1970s. Also the Privacy Act of 1974 allows federal agencies to collect only that information which is "necessary and relevant."[26]

While much of the data that are collected are of little use, some needed information is not generated, especially output and impact data. Impact data collection is expensive because by definition it involves reaching sources external to the agency. For example, output or work load information on the number of grants made by a federal agency to local governments is readily counted, while the impacts of those grants are not.[27] Impact measurement would require some means of monitoring local-level changes which stemmed from the grants that were made (see Chapter 6).

Related to the problem of what information is needed is that of who needs it. An agency needs much more data about itself than the budget office needs about the agency; indeed, more and more data from the agency is likely to produce "noise" in the system and not information. Similarly, a personnel department needs much information on agency personnel while the budget office needs some but not nearly as much.

---

[26] Senator Richard S. Schweiker (R, Pa.) has proposed legislation affecting education that would require each federal agency to justify information it proposed to collect and among other things compute the cost to states and school districts of supplying the information to Washington.

[27] Robert V. Graham, "Toward a More Effective Audit of Federal Grant-in-Aid Programs at the State Level," *State Government*, 46 (1973): 119–24.

Some users need data simply to have it and not to study it. Congress, state legislatures, and city councils often demand detailed financial data that will not be analyzed. Legislative bodies sometimes suspect the executive of hiding something important unless forced to produce detailed object of expenditure data. The fact that legislators could look at any particular detail helps keep the executive honest.

Access to information is another consideration in the design of an MIS. In recent years, much controversy has centered around the accessing of data of one agency by another. A program analysis unit in a state budget office may encounter difficulty in accessing welfare department records on clients, with the agency protesting that these are confidential records. The Privacy Act mentioned above is intended to protect individuals about whom files are maintained by federal agencies; but perhaps in conflict with that legislation is the Freedom of Information Act of 1966 and amended in 1974 which opens many records to public inspection.[28] A 1974 congressional study found that the federal government alone had 858 data banks, and of 765 of these for which information was available, there were at least 1.2 billion records on individuals in a nation of less than 230 million people.[29]

If agreement can be reached that a given set of data are needed, the next step is to determine who will collect the data. Double and triple reporting is common, because various agencies collect similar or identical data. Within the governmental system, local governments carry much of the burden of duplication in data collection. Both state transportation and community affairs departments might ask municipalities for reports on

---

[28] Mary Hulett, "Privacy and the Freedom of Information Act," *Administrative Law Review*, 27 (1975): 275–94; Albert Mindlin, "Confidentiality and Local Information Systems," *Public Administration Review*, 28 (1968): 509–18; Robert L. Saloschin, "The Freedom of Information Act: A Governmental Perspective," *Public Administration Review*, 35 (1975): 10–14; Secretary's Advisory Committee on Automated Personal Data Systems, U.S. Department of Health Education and Welfare, *Records, Computers and the Rights of Citizens* (Washington: U.S. Government Printing Office, 1973); C. Wayne Stallings, "Local Information Policy: Confidentiality and Public Access," *Public Administration Review*, 34 (1974): 197–204; Alan F. Westin, "Civil Liberties Issues in Public Databanks," in Alan F. Westin, ed., *Information Technology in a Democracy* (Cambridge, Mass.: Harvard University Press, 1971), pp. 301–10.

[29] U.S. Senate Committee on the Judiciary, Subcommittee on Constitutional Rights, *Federal Data Banks and Constitutional Rights*, Vol. 1, 93rd Cong., 2nd sess. (Washington: U.S. Government Printing Office, 1974), pp. xxxviii–xxxix. Also see this entire 6-volume set.

road expenditures, as possibly might HUD, the Department of Transportation, and the Census Bureau on the federal level. As noted earlier, central budget offices sometimes exercise forms control to avoid such duplication, but this can be a rather hit-or-miss process. For that reason an information system is used to attempt a more thorough review of who should collect what. A case can be made for having a central unit responsible for collecting information of general applicability to several departments, while line agencies collect more specialized information. For example, demographic and economic forecasts are relevant to the programs of many different departments. For each department to attempt to collect the same information would be inefficient and could produce anomolous situations in which agencies were projecting future program requirements on the basis of differing anticipated futures. An education department might be expecting a rapid population growth, while a housing department might be anticipating a stabilization of population.

Timeliness is another criterion. Some data need to be maintained on a daily basis. An accounting department needs daily reports on the status of funds, cash balances, and the like, whereas some agencies may need only weekly or monthly reports about their budgets. A central budget office does not need daily reports from agencies on program performance such as outputs and impacts. Some information may need to be available only upon request with a lag time of perhaps a week or more before the requested information is provided.

Inextricably associated with the problem of structuring an MIS is the method of data storage. With the advent of computers, more collection, storage, and manipulation of data were made possible. New minicomputers are reducing prices so that more units can afford electronic data processing (EDP). A 1974 study showed that 86 percent of all federal data banks are computerized.[30] The new computer technology offers the benefit of handling and access of data but also threatens proliferation of data banks with little or no linkage among them. Of course, computers are not the only location of data. Paper records in filing cabinets abound along with newer processes such as microfilm and microfiche.

Some extremes can be described as how not to organize an information system. One extreme is a giant data bank housing all information in the government and the other is total decentralization with each agency

---

[30] Senate Committee on the Judiciary, *Federal Data Banks and Constitutional Rights.*

maintaining its own files. Sometimes a set of directories or look-up tables is proposed as an information system; users are expected to refer to the directories to determine what agency has the needed information. Directories of this type, while providing some help, tend to be unwieldy and easily become outdated. Also directories cannot promptly produce information. Although all-encompassing data banks can be equally unwieldy, some centralization of electronic data processing operations can result in savings.[31]

Seemingly the most viable approach to an information system design is to develop modules or subsystems that can be linked with each other. The use of information is viewed as a system within which subsystems provide information for different purposes and users. This can be conceptualized as a series of broadly defined program modules such as human services and protection of persons and property, with each further divided into smaller modules. These modules or subsystems can be considered vertical in contrast with finance and personnel modules which are horizontal and extend across program areas and agencies.[32] Subsystems can be devised within a financial module. Wichita Falls, Texas, for example, has Purchasing Order Processing (POPS), a subsystem within its financial module. The city, along with several others, was supported by the Urban Information Systems Inter-Agency Committee (USAC), a group of federal agencies.[33]

---

[31] Charles L. Guest, "Central EDP Pays Off for Mississippi," *Government Data Systems*, 3 (July/August, 1974): 14–15.

[32] The vertical/horizontal approach is taken in Carl F. Davis, Jr., ed., *A Municipal Information and Decision System: Fiscal Subsystem, Personnel Subsystem, Property Subsystem* (Los Angeles: School of Public Administration, University of Southern California, 1968). Also see F. S. Pardee, *The Financial Portion of a Management Information System* (Santa Monica, Cal.: RAND, 1961) and *PIMISS: A Plan for the Implementation of the Management Subsystem of the Commonwealth [of Pennsylvania] Management Information Center* (Washington: Planning Research Corporation, 1969).

[33] Christopher Burpo, "POPS Eases Municipal Procurement," *Government Data Systems*, 3 (July/August, 1974): 17+. Also see W. K. James "Computerized General Ledger and Budgetary Accounting Systems," *Governmental Finance*, 5 (May, 1976): 27–32; Anthony G. Kerr, "The Principles of a Financial Information System for Municipalities," *Governmental Finance*, 2 (May, 1973): 7–11+; Kenneth L. Kraemer, "The Evolution of Information Systems for Urban Administration," *Public Administration Review*, 29 (1969): 389–402; Kenneth L. Kraemer, et al., *Integrated Municipal Information Systems: The Use of the Computer in Local Government* (New York: Praeger, 1974); Kenneth L. Kraemer, "USAC: An Evolving Governmental Mechanism for Urban Information Systems Development," *Public Administration Review*, 31 (1971): 543–51; Robert E. Quinn, "The Impacts of a Computerized Information System on the Integration and Coordination of Human Services," *Public Administration Review*, 36 (1976): 166–74.

The transformation from conceptualization to operations, however, has not been resolved adequately. The modular approach is attractive in concept but difficult to implement. The problem is linking the modules to each other, and in the real world it is not just a matter of literally plugging one module into another. Although a financial module may be suitable for capturing financial transactions, the problem remains of linking that data with program information that presumably would be stored in a vertical module. In other words, there might be no easy linkage about what a city department of recreation spends with what it produces. Toronto and the Province of Ontario have developed the Provincial-Municipal Simulator (PROMUS) which consists of a Community Model System containing program-type information and a Financial Policy Planning System which consists of four budget-related modules, but the two main modules are only linked manually.[34] A more narrowly focused package is the Financial and Accounting Management Information System (FAMIS) developed by Peat, Marwick, and Mitchell, which handles only financial data with no linkage to program information.[35] The USAC project, costing millions of dollars and now defunct, clearly documents the remaining difficulties in designing and installing information systems.[36]

For most complex governmental jurisdictions, the requirements of a comprehensive information system imply the usage of automated data processing equipment.[37] Automation of existing information, however,

---

[34] Donald F. Blumberg, "PROMUS—An Urban Management System " *Governmental Finance*, 3 (May, 1974): 8–14.

[35] E. Reece Harrill, "An Information System for Local Government," *Management Controls*, 19 (1972): 129–40; and E. R. Harrill, T. E. Richards, and J. M. Wallman, "FAMIS—A Financial Accounting and Management Information System for Local Government," *Management Controls*, 21 (1974): 85–94.

[36] See Charlotte, North Carolina report which is extremely negative about the accomplishments there under USAC. City of Charlotte, *The Charlotte IMIS Project Completion Report* (Washington: National Technical Information Service, U.S. Department of Commerce, 1975).

[37] For a brief discussion of the development of information technology and data processing and its impact on management, see Thomas L. Whisler, *Information Technology and Organizational Change* (Belmont, Cal.: Wadsworth, 1970). Discussions of information systems in two state governments are found in Robert J. Mowitz, *Design and Implementation of Pennsylvania's Planning, Programming, Budgeting System* (Harrisburg: Commonwealth of Pennsylvania, 1970), pp. 31–38 and Management Sciences Group, Executive Office of the Governor, *State of Michigan Management Information System (SOMMIS) Master Plan* (Lansing: State of Michigan, 1971): pp. 15–18 and 33–49. Also see Richard A. Bassler and Norman L. Enger, eds., *Computer Systems and Public Administrators* (Alexandria, Va.: College Readings, 1976); Edward F. R. Hearle, ed., "A Symposium: Computers in Public Adminis-

does not a management information system make. Most large governmental jurisdictions possess some computer systems' capability. A recent survey found that, in about 30 states, agencies prepare their budget requests with the aid of computers and the state budget is prepared in part by computer.[38] For the most part, however, computer systems, both hardware and software support, have been introduced haphazardly at agency levels with no overall direction. Governments that have begun development of an integrated information system have usually discovered that there is little compatability among agencies' systems. A major task, then, involves inventorying existing system capabilities and developing comparability among the systems.

Until recently it was often assumed that small governments would not be able to afford electronic data processing and that noncomputerized information systems needed to be devised. The advent of minicomputers and the increasing use of time sharing, where two or more jurisdictions use the same facility, have brought computer support within the reach of all but the smallest governments.[39] Housekeeping chores, such as record keeping for payrolls, are usually the first to be automated.[40] Also, frequently used files, such as police department records, are becoming increasingly automated. Some states are developing model budget systems for local government that can be operated with or without computer support. Smaller jurisdictions, however, may be committing some of the same mistakes that larger ones did earlier; they may be taking a haphazard approach to information processing that will take years to untangle.

Just as a financial reporting system requires an independent audit to assess both the adequacy of the system and the credibility of the data, a

---

tration," *Public Administration Review*, 28 (1968): 487–518; U.S. Congress, Joint Committee on Congressional Operations, *Modern Information Technology in the State Legislatures*, 92nd Cong., 2nd sess. (Washington: U.S. Government Printing Office, 1972).

[38] Discussion is based upon previously unpublished data from the survey conducted by the National Association of State Budget Officers noted above.

[39] See Frank Bigley, "Electronic Data Processing in Small Municipalities," *Governmental Finance*, 3 (May, 1974): 20–24 and Lennox L. Moak and Kathryn K. Gordon, *Budgeting for Smaller Governmental Units* (Chicago: Municipal Finance Officers Association, 1965).

[40] At least one observer has concluded that most municipal systems are for housekeeping and few are "real" information systems; see testimony of O. E. Dial in U.S. House of Representatives, Committee on Government Operations, *Federal Information Systems and Plans*, Part I, 93rd Cong., 1st sess. (Washington: U.S. Government Printing Office, 1973), p. 71.

comprehensive information system should be subject to audit. The phrase "garbage in–garbage out" can be applied to those systems that do not provide for an auditing process. No information system can be any better than the data within it.

Information Systems and Program Budgeting[41]   Underlying program budgeting is the assumption that while information will continue to be assembled by organizational units, information will also be required by program. Programs in program budgeting are often fictional in that they constitute portions of several organizations, yet on a day-to-day basis government operates by organizations and not programs. Assembling program and resource data is difficult in that the vehicles used for collection of data–departments, bureaus, and offices–do not necessarily parallel programs.

If the functions performed by a government were constant over time, one possible solution would be a once-and-for-all reorganization of agencies to coincide with program structure. However, other criteria are relevant to the choice of organization structure. Geographic considerations may lead to one configuration; organization according to clientele might suggest a very different division of functions among agencies. Further, because functions change, sometimes radically and rapidly, such a solution is clearly not feasible.

Similarity of work may be a more important criterion in structuring an organization. A municipal public works department, for instance, may be part of a community development program regarding its streets activities, part of a health program involving water works and sewerage, and part of a public safety program involving fire alarm boxes and police call boxes. All of these activities entail mechanical-type work and frequently require the use of trucks and other heavy equipment. For organizational purposes, therefore, a public works department may be an efficient method of providing services and should not necessarily be carved up so that police and fire departments maintain their call boxes, a health department runs sewers and water, and a community development department builds and repairs streets.

Because a grand scheme for agency reorganization offers no panacea, some other arrangement for providing the needed data must be developed.

---

[41] Several of the ideas in this section were suggested by Robert J. Mowitz, Director of the Institute of Public Administration, The Pennsylvania State University.

One approach is to force the program structure to conform with the organizational structure. This has the weakness of assuming that each department and bureau has a coherent and relatively homogeneous set of objectives, when such is not the case as evidenced in the example of a public works department. Another approach is to use an estimation process in which total expenditures of organizational units—bureaus, agencies, departments—are allocated among the various components of the program structure. The total of program element expenditures would equal total government expenditures. Here the only linkage with the accounting system would be the verification of the sum of elements as equaling total expenditures. This approach has been adopted in several jurisdictions that utilize some form of program budgeting.

An estimation procedure of this type suffers from one major deficiency—lack of credibility. Regardless of who does the estimating, the results are held suspect, especially because the procedure is done on a lump-sum basis; for example, 60 percent of costs are assigned to one element and 40 percent to another. One method is for a central budget office, either the departmental office or chief executive's office, to make the estimations by translating regular budget request submissions into a program format. Another approach is for the agency to do the estimating. No matter who does the calculations, all parties involved realize that such methods are only approximations of program totals; little confidence can be expressed in such totals. Because of the lack of credibility, agencies, departments, and the chief executive and his staff will tend to ignore or to place little value on program estimates in the decision-making process.

The lack of credibility in program estimates may be particularly pronounced in the legislature. Appropriations are based upon organizational units, and accounting and auditing systems are established to verify compliance with these appropriations. Such a verification procedure is nonexistent for budget information based upon program estimates, thereby giving the legislative body little reason to analyze and base decisions upon such information. The legislature may conclude that the information is actually misinformation and should be ignored.

Something more structured than estimating is essential to have a program budgeting system supported by believable information; some linkage with the financial accounting system is needed. The translation of financial data from organization to program structure presents no accounting problem, either when the program and organizational structure are identical or when each organizational unit supports only one program element. This is indicated in Figure 9 by the solid arrows, where office "a"

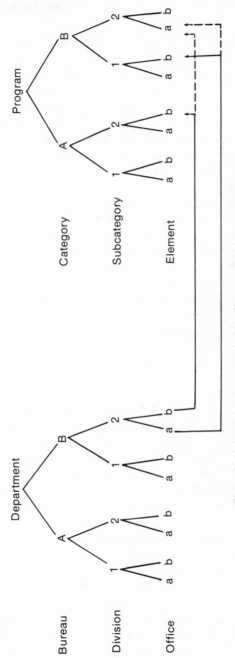

Figure 9. Linkages between organizational structure and program structure.

233

supports program element "b" in one subcategory and office "b" supports program element "b" in a different subcategory.

The problem becomes more complicated when a given organizational unit supports more than one program element. An example might be a city planning office that supports elements for economic development planning, transportation planning, and recreation planning; during the course of a year, all staff members of the planning unit will have participated in each of these types of planning. A further complication is when portions of two organizational units support one program element. An example of this type is a state welfare department that is organized into regional offices, with each carrying out all the functions of the welfare department and, therefore, contributing to numerous elements such as child day care services, child protection services, income maintenance, and family counseling. The dotted arrows in Figure 9 illustrate these two problems.

In response to somewhat comparable problems in the private sector, the accounting profession has developed the concepts of responsibility centers and cost centers. These concepts are being applied increasingly to the public sector. A responsibility center is "any organizational unit that is headed by a responsible manager," and a cost center is used for "accumulating items of cost that have common characteristics."[42] The sum of cost centers within a responsibility center yields an organizational budget, and the sum of cost centers within a program element yields an element budget.

The cost center may be an organizational unit but more frequently is part of a unit. Where a given office and program element are identical, the responsibility and cost centers are identical. When an office supports two program elements, however, two cost centers are identified. The use of these cost centers within a responsibility center is easiest when persons and/or equipment can be isolated as contributing to only one center. A given office might have no formal structure in terms of suborganizational units, but it may be possible to identify one group of workers as constituting one cost center and another group constituting the other cost center.

---

[42] Robert N. Anthony and James S. Reece, *Management Accounting: Text and Cases*, 5th ed. (Homewood, Ill.: Irwin, 1975), pp. 673 and 454. Also see Anthony and Herzlinger, *Management Control in Nonprofit Organizations*, pp. 17 and 81–82; Robert N. Anthony and Glenn A. Welsch, *Fundamentals of Management Accounting* (Homewood, Ill.: Irwin, 1974), pp. 65–66 and 78–81; Francis E. McGilvery, "Program and Responsibility Cost Accounting," *Public Administration Review*, 28 (1968): 148–54.

The problem is greater when all employees in the office contribute to both centers.

There is no maxim that governs the solution to this problem. One method is to code each transaction according to program element as well as to continue the use of existing codes, such as organizational unit, appropriation, and object of expenditure. This method yields knotty issues: if an agency wishes to purchase a typewriter that will be used to serve many program elements, must the single purchase of a typewriter be treated as several different transactions because data need to be collected by program element? This can produce a highly unwieldy accounting system that boggles the minds of clerks responsible for ordering equipment.

At this point some form of estimating is almost inevitable. Costs that are clearly identifiable as contributing to one and only one element can be assigned to that element, and other costs can be translated periodically into program elements. Using the welfare agency example, costs of the regional offices would be allocated to program elements only monthly, while costs by organization unit would continue to be recorded on a daily basis.

A method for increasing the validity of the translation into cost centers and elements using the estimation process is better record keeping on the work conducted by employees. Agencies may require daily time sheets to be completed by their employees; in a police department this would permit isolating the effort devoted to traffic and crime control. A less cumbersome approach is to have a weekly report completed by a supervisor, such as a police squad leader or a foreman of a road crew.

Still, many problems remain in developing suitable accounting systems to provide program cost information. Protocols for allocating costs can be developed to provide some uniformity across agencies in the assignment of costs to program elements. Commercial accounting practices for distributing costs are sufficiently well established as to suggest that the problems are not insoluble. Perhaps the private experience may be applicable to many governmental programs, and the public sector also has experience to contribute. Hospitals, for example, have considerable experience in accounting techniques for arriving at end-product or patient-care costs.[43]

The ability of organizations to cope with these problems will vary. Those governmental jurisdictions that already have well developed cost

---

[43] McGilvery, "Program and Responsibility Cost Accounting," p. 151.

accounting systems should normally have the least difficulty linking their financial reporting systems to program structures. Government organizations not using cost accounting techniques are likely to find the problems less familiar.

The discussion here has concentrated largely upon financial data, but program information is also an essential ingredient. As was seen in the preceding discussion of management information systems, program information abounds in numerous locales throughout any government; data can be found in agency computers, filing cabinets, microfilm files, and desk drawers. As long as activity, output, and impact data remain dispersed throughout the bureaucracy, they can be of little value in program budgeting. However, the preceding discussion also indicated that a giant governmentwide data file is probably impractical in most cases.

The problem of linking program data with financial data in a program structure format is partially a function of how data are collected and used. Financial accounting systems record transactions daily, and these data are compiled into weekly, monthly, and other summary reports. Because financial constraints are real and unavoidable, information needs to be kept as current as possible. Program information, on the other hand, may not be kept as current. For example, police officers may submit daily activity reports that are stored in files and only periodically compiled on paper or entered into a computer; other police data, such as information pertaining to automobile thefts, will be computer inputted immediately and possibly entered into a statewide computer network. This lack of uniformity in the currency of program information is not necessarily a problem. Because program readjustments are unlikely to occur each day, program information may be updated suitably only monthly, quarterly, or semi-annually. These data can be fed into a central budget file—computerized or paper file—and thereby be linked with financial data. This approach avoids the problem of attempting to link together various agency computer systems with a central system, a process that would involve extensive computer programming and probably the acquisition of additional computer hardware.[44]

Once accounting for program results and costs has been established, the issue arises as to whether the appropriations structure should be changed to correspond to programs rather than organizations. As noted

---

[44] Because this is a book on budgeting, we leave for others to consider the solution to the more general problem of information processing within a department and government.

above, it is unlikely that legislatures would be willing to alter their methods of appropriating to fit program budgets based on estimates that are divorced from credible accounting data. With program accounting, however, it is at least feasible to appropriate in terms of programs rather than organizations. Legislatures could, of course, continue to obtain agency data as well as data arranged by program.

Such a change has far-reaching implications for the political process. It would in most cases be difficult for members of the legislature to determine clear lines of authority for program expenditures because these would frequently cut across agency lines. It would also be difficult to examine agency witnesses testifying in budget hearings because the extent of any one witness's responsibility for specific appropriation amounts would be unclear. As argued previously (Chapter 8), one method members of the legislature use to decide on complex program issues is to probe agency officials who are responsible for expenditures on narrow administrative details. The lack of clear lines of organizational authority for program expenditures is probably the biggest barrier to altering appropriations structure to correspond to programs.

SUMMARY

Execution is the conversion of plans embodied in the budget into day-to-day operations. At stake are factors such as devising means of observing legislative intent as prescribed in appropriations, managing the flow of cash, purchasing materials and services, and ultimately providing the services that have been authorized. The execution phase is not routine but instead involves numerous decisions about what and how services will be provided. Line agencies commonly strive for relative independence in the execution of their programs but find themselves constrained by numerous financial procedures.

Governmental accounting is characterized by procedures intended to guarantee agency conformance with legal requirements. One of the most important distinguishing features of governmental accounting is the use of numerous special funds in addition to the general fund. Separate accounts are maintained within each fund, with transactions being recorded by appropriation, organizational unit, object of expenditure, and so forth. These transactions necessarily deal with the inputs to government and consequently foster emphasis upon the control function, thus keeping agencies honest.

Cash, encumbrance, accrual, and cost accounting serve different purposes. Cash accounting is the oldest type and meets the need for treasury control on cash operations. Encumbrance accounting ensures that appropriations will not be overspent. Accrual accounting is a more recent innovation in governmental accounting and is intended to show a more accurate picture of what the government has done in the way of financial transactions even if checks have not yet been issued to cover those actions. Questions about cash, encumbrance, and accrual accounting are basically questions about timing, about when financial transactions should be counted. Cost accounting also involves timing questions, but goes beyond that. Costs are measured at the time when the resources are actually consumed by government, but costs can also be measured in terms of the output-oriented activities of the organizational unit.

With the increasing use of both program and resource information in the budgetary process and more generally in government, systematic approaches to the management of information are emerging. Management information systems are being designed to avoid needless gaps in information and duplication of information gathering that results when agencies are allowed to collect whatever information they deem appropriate. Problems abound on the design of these systems, such as what information should be collected and how the various components of the system will be linked with each other. Recent developments in computer technology have increased the capabilities of data processing and have brought these capabilities within the reach of all but the smallest of jurisdictions. Yet, computer hardware and software by themselves offer no panacea for developing an information system.

Program budgeting has posed new problems for information systems, especially in the area of financial information. Program structures cut across agency lines, while accounting systems traditionally stop at agency lines. In order to link accounting-produced financial data to program results, adjustments in accounting procedures become essential. Government agencies already having cost accounting systems will have less difficulty with this linkage problem than other agencies.

10

CAPITAL BUDGETING AND DEBT MANAGEMENT

Not all resources for which expenditures are made in a given budget year are consumed. Some resources are acquired for future as well as current use. The expenditures associated with the construction of a new school will produce benefits once the school is in operation and for many years in the future. This is capital formation. Because these current expenditures that result in capital formation differ importantly from expenditures that are consumed in the current year, the argument can be made that they should be treated differently in the budgetary process. In the first section of this chapter, we consider the approaches to the concept of capital expenditures and the relationships between capital and operating budgets.

Because future benefits can be derived from current expenditures, the argument can also be made that some current expenditures need not be financed by current revenues. Because future generations will benefit from these expenditures, they should also help finance them. This is one rationale for government borrowing, which means going into debt. Borrowing is also an instrument of national economic policy, spending more than revenues in a given year to stimulate the economy (discussed in Chapter 13). The second section of this chapter concentrates upon the size of governmental debt and the instruments used in funding state and local debt.

CAPITAL BUDGETING

In a narrow accounting sense, a capital expenditure involves fixed assets—tangible, physical items that will be of use for more than the current budget year.[1] The purchase of land, including not only the sale price but legal and other fees associated with the purchase, would be one form of capital expenditure. Similarly, the construction of a building or an addition to a building would produce a tangible or fixed asset. Other construction such as street resurfacing and sidewalk replacement can be considered capital projects. Machinery and equipment also are fixed assets.

Defining what is and is not a fixed asset can present problems, particularly in the area of machinery and equipment, and usually shortcuts are taken in setting cutoff limits. One approach to simplifying the problem is to set a dollar limit to separate operating and capital expenditures. For example, any item costing less than $500 might be considered operating and anything $500 or more is capital. In such a case, the purchase of a filing cabinet would be an operating expenditure, and the purchase of an automobile would be a capital expenditure. An alternative is to set a limit on the useful life of a piece of equipment or machinery—perhaps three years. Using this method, the acquisition of police cars might be treated as an operating expense, while desks, filing cabinets, and even pencil sharpeners would be regarded as capital investments. Books and periodicals, while neither equipment nor machinery, present a similar classification problem. When these items are purchased by a library, they can be expected to be of use for many years and can be treated as capital investments; on the other hand, a periodical purchased by a line agency may have a very short useful life-span and would be an operating expense.

Similar problems exist regarding building remodeling. The addition of a new wing to an office building is clearly a capital investment, but what of making modest alterations to the main entrance of the building? Should replacing the tiles on the lobby floor be considered a capital improvement? In most jurisdictions, the tiles would be treated as an operating expense. To avoid such problems, governments usually use combinations of dollar and time ceilings plus somewhat arbitrary lists of items to be treated as capital.

Most governments that separate capital from current expenditures probably undercount their investments. Pencil sharpeners and staple machines are not worth counting as capital, even though these items

---

[1] Leon E. Hay and R. M. Mikesell, *Governmental Accounting,* 5th ed. (Homewood, Ill.: Irwin, 1974), pp. 329–59.

presumably will produce benefits in future years. Also, accounting systems often are not geared to capture total capital costs. As was seen in the preceding chapter, object classes will often identify such items as land, buildings, equipment, and the like. These accounts, however, frequently only capture the direct costs for tangible items. The accounts are unlikely to capture related costs, especially personnel costs. For example, the price of a truck will be recorded as capital but not the cost of staff time involved in purchasing the truck. The purchase of equipment for road resurfacing may be treated as a capital investment, but the resurfacing material will be counted as supplies, and the staff time used in resurfacing will be counted under an object class for personnel.

A broader approach to the fixed-asset definition of capital is any expenditure that will produce future benefits.[2] All federal, state, and local expenditures for education could be considered capital investments under this definition; society can be expected to benefit in the future because of the investments in education made today. The same can be said for mental health programs, police programs for juveniles, and family counseling programs. All forms of research projects—criminal recidivism, drug abuse, highway safety, and the like—could be treated as capital. This broad conceptualization is so difficult to bound that almost any governmental expenditure might be considered a capital investment. As a result, the fixed-asset approach is the one that is typically employed.

A distinction needs to be made between a capital budget statement and a capital budgeting process.[3] A capital budgeting statement refers to a section of the budget document or a supporting capital document intended to segregate capital costs from operating costs. The statement is mainly for information purposes. Each year the federal government provides such a statement (see Table 12). Investments reported include physical assets such as public works; additions to state, local, and private assets; and developmental outlays covering improved health and education services. Taken together, these constitute about 15 percent of federal outlays.

In contrast, a capital budgeting process refers to separate decision making on capital items. The federal government, for example, does not have a separate capital budgeting process, but Congress can make decisions

[2] A. John Vogt, "Capital Planning and Budgeting for Local Government," *Popular Government* (University of North Carolina, Chapel Hill), 41 (Fall, 1975): 12–13.

[3] Lennox L. Moak and Albert M. Hillhouse, *Concepts and Practices in Local Government Finance* (Chicago: Municipal Finance Officers Association, 1970), pp. 95–118.

TABLE 12
Federal Civil Investments, 1973–1977 (Percent of Total Budget Outlays)

Investment-type outlays	1973 actual	1974 actual	1975 actual	1976 estimate	TQ[a] estimate	1977 estimate
Additions to federal assets						
Loans	0.2	0.7	1.3	1.5	1.4	0.8
Other financial investments	0.1	0.2	0.2	0.3	0.3	0.2
Public works—sites and direct construction	1.3	1.3	1.3	1.3	1.4	1.4
Major commodity inventories	−0.2	−0.1	0.1	0.1	–	–
Major equipment	0.1	0.1	0.1	0.1	0.1	0.1
Other physical assets—acquisition and improvement	0.3	0.2	0.2	0.3	0.3	0.3
Subtotal, additions to federal assets	1.8	2.3	3.1	3.4	3.6	2.7
Additions to state, local, and private assets						
State and local assets	3.0	3.0	2.7	3.0	3.2	3.4
Private assets	0.4	0.3	0.3	0.3	0.2	0.2
Subtotal, additions to state, local and private assets	3.4	3.3	3.1	3.3	3.4	3.7

Developmental outlays						
Education, training, and health	6.3	6.0	6.3	6.8	6.3	5.8
Research and development	2.9	3.0	2.7	2.7	2.7	2.8
Engineering and natural resource surveys	0.1	0.1	0.1	0.1	0.1	0.1
Subtotal, developmental outlays	9.2	9.0	9.1	9.6	9.0	8.7
Total investment-type outlays	14.4	14.6	15.2	16.2	16.0	15.1

[a]Transition quarter to new fiscal year beginning October 1.

Source: Office of Management and Budget, *Budget of the U.S. Government, 1977: Special Analyses* (Washington: U.S. Government Printing Office, 1976), p. 66.

on capital items by prescribing amounts for equipment and land through the normal appropriations process.[4] Similarly, many state legislatures appropriate by object classes, including classes for equipment, land, and other capital items. Besides these capital items included in an object classification, the legislative body may act on a separate capital budget, especially when items in that budget are to be financed through bonding. In other words, capital items are likely to be found in both the operating and capital budgets.

As would be expected, jurisdictions vary greatly in the amount of detail presented in their budgets on capital expenditures. For example, the capital outlay section of the Michigan 1975–76 budget included items ranging from $500 for a concrete ramp on a building to a $5.7 million lump sum for a women's correctional facility.[5] The 1975–76 Fort Worth budget showed a detailed breakout for replacement and new items, including such things as $50 to replace "two straight oak chairs" and $390 for "three executive chairs" in the fire department.[6]

Whether a capital budgeting statement or process is used, either may provide important information to decision makers and the general public. Capital budgets and statements indicate the extent to which investments are being made with current expenditures. From a political perspective, governmental officials can show the citizenry that much of government spending has gone for the acquisition of useful items and not solely to such unpopular items as bureaucrats' salaries.

Capital budgeting and related debt can be advantageous for state and local governments. States and especially local governments provide many of the public service facilities in use today. These facilities include schools, roads, parks, and sewer and water systems, to name only the more obvious. Because all of these facilities are expensive and have long-term uses, going into debt for their construction may be appropriate; future beneficiaries of these facilities will help pay the costs by paying taxes to retire debt. Also, given that capital projects are expensive, they should be treated carefully, that is, decided upon in a separate budget process.

---

[4] Richard A. Musgrave, "Should We Have a Capital Budget?" *Review of Economics and Statistics,* 45 (1963): 134–37; Maynard S. Comiez, *A Capital Budget Statement for the U.S. Government* (Washington: Brookings, 1966).

[5] *Executive Budget* (Lansing: State of Michigan, 1975), pp. AA-9–AA-44.

[6] *1975–76 Annual Budget and Program Objectives* (Forth Worth, Tex.: City of Fort Worth, 1975), p. 508.

On the negative side, capital budgeting can encourage political logroll-ing, in which various political interests agree to help each other. A capital budget can be a political grab bag, a fund in which every interest can find a project. A state capital budget may provide highway projects in every county, even though real need is concentrated in a small number of counties. In providing everyone with something, some important needs will not be met while less pressing needs are. Also, the exclusion of capital costs from the operating budget may give the impression that capital investments are costless. This is especially true if the capital fund is financed by borrowing. Then any new project seems "free" in that costs will not appear for a year or more.

Separate capital and operating decision processes can lead to lack of coordination between the two. The purchase of a new, more sophisticated piece of equipment through a separate capital budgeting system may result in unanticipated increases in annual equipment maintenance costs in the operating budget. A state highway may be built out of the capital budget without funds being provided in the operating budget for maintenance, snow removal, and traffic patrol. Not only can such lack of coordination occur, but the end result will be a permanent impact on the operating budget, forcing additional expenditures on highway maintenance each year and periodic resurfacing. Further, because so much public attention is focused on the general operating budget, the amount included in a sepa-rate capital budget may be less visible, thus understating the cost of government.

A recent survey has shown increasing integration of capital and operat-ing budget decisions at the state level. In 1970, executive decision making tended to separate the two items in seventeen states, but in 1975 the number had dropped to eight. In twenty states, executive budget offices said they considered capital and operating expenditures together in terms of the programs being served. The remaining states integrated capital and operating decisions to a lesser extent. Sixteen state legislatures were said to be still treating capital and operating decisions independently and fifteen considering them together; the other legislatures were between these two extremes.[7]

---

[7] Discussion based upon previously unpublished data from survey of state budget offices conducted by the National Association of State Budget Officers with the Pennsylvania Budget Office and the Institute of Public Administration of The Pennsylvania State University.

Whether or not a separate budget process is used for capital items, a strong case can be made for capital facilities planning. Major facilities, once built, largely will be limited to the uses for which they were designed; inadequately conceived facilities can result in inadequate services, major financial burdens, or the need for expensive alterations. Excess capacity built into a community sewer system cannot be converted into other uses. Too little acquisition of land for parks in a rapidly growing suburban area may later result in a shortage of recreational opportunities.

The need or demand for a type of facility must be forecast in combination with alternative facilities and possible fee structures. A contemplated toll bridge may have no nearby competitors and so the assumption can be made that the bridge will attract all would-be travelers between the two points that will be connected. On the other hand, a high-fee structure may deter some use. Obviously, a $10 per day admission fee to a community swimming pool is likely to attract only the most affluent. Here a good understanding of the elasticity of demand is essential. Demand may be quite elastic; any increase in cost to customers will reduce demand. Municipal public transit is one of the best examples, where increased fares have encouraged commuters to use their automobiles. If the anticipated capital expenditure is expected to be self-supporting, some projection must be made of the number of users at various fee levels. The size of the facility, then, will vary accordingly, with a smaller facility being needed as the projected number of users declines.

Total construction costs need to be considered along with operating costs. Construction costs can include land acquisition, land development and the actual construction of a facility. Using the swimming pool example, not only will costs include the land and the pool but may also include parking facilities. Projections need to be made for equipment costs and their anticipated replacements, general repair and maintenance costs, and the cost of staffing the pool.[8]

The capital project plan, then, requires a multi-year perspective in terms of both operating and maintenance costs and the demand for services. The City of Philadelphia has used this approach (Table 13). The city's capital program not only shows investment costs by project but also estimated changes in operating costs; a six-year funding schedule for each

[8] J. Richard Aronson and Eli Schwartz, "Capital Budgeting," in J. Richard Aronson and Eli Schwartz, eds., *Management Policies in Local Government Finance* (Chicago: Municipal Finance Officers Association, 1975), pp. 303–27.

TABLE 13
Selected Capital Expenditures for Philadelphia Police Department, 1976–1981
(in Thousands of Dollars)

Judiciary and law enforcement

Police facilities Projects	Estimated change in annual operating cost	Total estimated cost	Cost thru 1975 capital budget	Cost scheduled 6-year period	Six-year funding schedule 1976	1977	1978	1979	1980	1981	Cost to complete beyond 1981
Parking at stations	M 2 / d 190	1,767	ca 392 / 392	cn 750 / ca 125 / 875	cn 125 / ca 125 / 250	cn 125	cn 125	cn 125	cn 125	cn 125	cn 500
Central air conditioning at stations	M 30 / d 197	1,834	ca 290 / 290	cn 750 / ca 150 / 900	ca 150	cn 150	cn 150	cn 150	cn 150	cn 150	cn 644
Police training academy—indoor pistol range	M 2 / d 57	530		ct 530	ct 530						
Police training academy improvements and additional classrooms	M 7 / d 79	734		ct 734	ct 734						
Tow squad headquarters improvements—25th and South Sts.	M 3 / d 65	609	ca 220 / 220	cn 189 / ca 200 / 389	cn 189 / ca 200 / 389						
Dog kennels—police training academy	M 51 / d 27	250		cn 125 / ca 125 / 250		cn 125 / ca 125 / 250					

M, annual operating costs; d, annual debt service; z, industrial development fund; f, federal; s, state; t, township; p, private; a, assessments; gr, city grant revenue; xn, self-sustaining new loans; xa, self-sustaining prefinanced loans; xt, self-sustaining carried over loans; cn, tax-supported new loans; ca, tax-supported prefinanced loans; ct, tax-supported carried over loans; cr, tax-supported operating revenues.

Source: *1976–1981 Capital Program* (Philadelphia: City of Philadelphia and School District of Philadelphia, 1975), p. 150.

project is provided, including the method of financing the project. The multi-year funding schedule is important in ensuring that means will be available in subsequent years to meet debt obligations, the subject of the next section.

DEBT MANAGEMENT

Although capital facilities constitute a major reason why governments borrow, there are other reasons as well. In this section, we review trends in public debt, the instruments used in borrowing, the processes of borrowing, and debt administration.[9]

As of 1974, the combined debt of all governments was $692.9 billion.[10] Per capita debt, as can be seen from Figure 10, has risen for all levels of government since 1950. In 1974, all governments together owed $3,270 for each person, with the federal government alone accounting for $2,294 of the total or for 70 percent of all public debt.

Data and graphs such as these sometimes seem to suggest that public debt is out of control. However, public debt may not be as large as one might conclude judging from the heated debates that recur on this issue. In comparison with the private debt, the public debt has diminished steadily since World War II. In 1950, 49 percent of the net public and private debt was governmental, but the comparable figure for 1974 was 23 percent. Whereas earlier, public debt accounted for half of all debt, now it accounts for less than a quarter.[11]

Another way of putting public debt into perspective is to compare it with the gross national product (GNP). Figure 11 shows a steady decline since 1950 in total public debt as a percent of GNP. Federal, state, and local debt in 1974 was equal to 50 percent of the GNP, compared with

---

[9] Among the most valuable sources on this topic are Lennox L. Moak, *Administration of Local Government Debt* (Chicago: Municipal Finance Officers Association, 1970); Moak and Hillhouse, *Concepts and Practices in Local Government Finance,* pp. 245–327; Roland I. Robinson, "Debt Management," in Aronson and Schwartz, eds., *Management Policies in Local Government Finance,* pp. 229–47; Alan W. Steiss, *Local Government Finance: Capital Facilities Planning and Debt Administration* (Lexington, Mass.: Lexington Books, 1975). These sources have been used extensively in this section. Also see Advisory Commission on Intergovernmental Relations, *Understanding the Market for State and Local Debt* (Washington: U.S. Government Printing Office, 1976).

[10] See Chapter 13 for a discussion of GNP.

[11] Bureau of the Census, *Statistical Abstract of the United States, 1975* (Washington: U.S. Government Printing Office, 1975), p. 473.

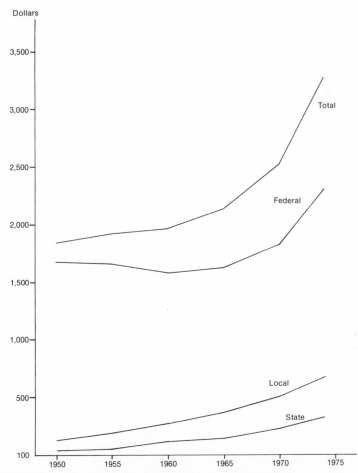

Figure 10. Per capita debt by level of government, 1950–1974. Sources: Bureau of the Census, *Statistical Abstract of the United States, 1975* (Washington: U.S. Government Printing Office, 1975), pp. 5 and 250; Bureau of the Census, *Governmental Finances in 1973–74* (Washington: U.S. Government Printing Office, November 1975), pp. 10 and 28.

almost 100 percent in 1950. This dramatic decline indicates that the economy has been growing faster than public debt. Moreover, the decline can be attributed largely to federal debt. Federal debt increased about 90 percent between 1950 and 1974, which seems large until compared with the growth in state and local government debts. In this same time period,

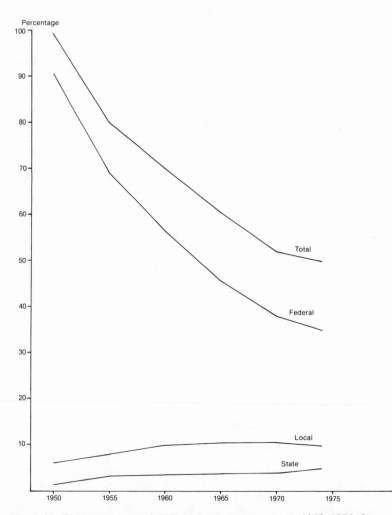

Figure 11. Debt as percent of GNP by level of government, 1950–1974. Sources: Bureau of the Census, *Statistical Abstract of the United States, 1975* (Washington: U.S. Government Printing Office, 1975), pp. 250 and 381; Bureau of the Census, *Governmental Finances in 1973–74* (Washington: U.S. Government Printing Office, November 1975), pp. 10 and 28.

state debt increased 1,200 percent and local debt 700 percent. As a reflection of this growth in state and local debt, federal debt as a percent of all public debt has dropped from about 90 percent to 70 percent. State debt has increased from 2 percent in 1950 to about 10 percent today. Local debt has risen from 7 percent to 20 percent of all public debt.

Also, the interest paid on debt remains comparatively small. In 1948, close to 10 percent of all public expenditures went for interest paid on debt. That figure declined to 2 percent in the 1960s but rose to about 7 percent in the mid-1970s. Debt as a percent of total expenditures is more than 7 percent for the federal government, about 2 percent for states, and 4 percent for local governments.[12]

Generally, wealthier states will have more debt than poor states. In New York State, state and local governments combined have a per capita debt of about $2,000, compared with only about $500 in Arkansas. At the same time great variations exist regardless of wealth. California, with a per capita personal income about equal to New York's, has a per capita debt about half of New York's.[13]

Indebtedness is not distributed evenly among the various types of local governments. Municipalities account for the largest share of local debt— more than 40 percent. School districts account for about 20 percent, but when the school portion of municipal debt is combined with school district debt, the total for schools is 26 percent of local debt. Special districts account for another 20 percent, followed by counties, and then townships.[14]

It should be noted that these figures on debt do not reflect the full scope of debt. As will be seen in the following chapter, pension programs for public workers constitute a form of debt and often are not adequately funded. Debt also has an intergovernmental aspect. The financial solvency of one government can have severe repercussions on others. The best example in recent times, of course, is New York City's near collapse, its impact on New York State's finances, and ultimately its rescue by the federal government.

The record on defaults on indebtedness has been good since the depression of the 1930s. In that decade about 4,800 state and local units

[12] Bureau of the Census, *Historical Statistics on Governmental Finances and Employment* (Washington: U.S. Government Printing Office, 1974), pp. 49–50; Bureau of the Census, *Governmental Finances in 1973–74* (Washington: U.S. Government Printing Office, November, 1975), p. 5.

[13] Bureau of the Census, *Statistical Abstract,* pp. 263 and 388.

[14] Bureau of the Census, *Governmental Finances,* pp. 28 and 30.

defaulted on their debt obligations. While that number may seem large, it was out of a total of 150,000 governments. Most of the defaults involved small jurisdictions; less than 50 had populations of more than 25,000.[15] Since that time, the number of defaults has been low. Only nineteen bankruptcy cases were filed between 1955 and 1974 under the Municipal Bankruptcy Act originally passed in 1934.[16] Between 1945 and 1970, there were defaults of $450 million, equal to less than half of 1 percent of all municipal debt outstanding in 1970. Three-quarters of the defaulted money was accounted for by three projects—West Virginia Turnpike, Calumet Skyway Toll Bridge, and Chesapeake Bay Bridge and Tunnel.[17] Not only have there been few defaults, and they involved relatively small sums of money, one also should understand that defaults rarely mean bond holders lose all of their investments. Defaults result in repayment plans to investors over a longer period of time than was originally required by the bonds.

In an attempt to avoid defaults, state constitutions and statutes set limits on state and local government borrowing, but often these debt limits are circumvented. Until the late 1960s, for example, Pennsylvania's constitution had a debt limit of $1 million for a state with a multi-billion dollar budget. Pennsylvania like other states created a special authority, primarily responsible for capital facilities construction, to issue bonds that the courts held not subject to the constitutionally imposed debt ceiling. Similar use of authorities is common at the local level. Another practice intended to limit governmental borrowing is to require voter approval of proposed bond issues; because bond referenda are often defeated, governments may not incur as much debt as might otherwise be the case. In an

---

[15] George W. Mitchell, "Statement before the Committee on Banking, Housing and Urban Affairs," *Federal Reserve Bulletin,* 61 (1975): 728–30.

[16] U.S. House of Representatives, Committee on the Judiciary, Subcommittee on Civil and Constitutional Rights, *Hearings: Bankruptcy Act Revision,* 94th Cong., 1st sess. (Washington: U.S. Government Printing Office, 1975), p. 36. The law was declared unconstitutional by the Supreme Court in 1936, reinacted in 1937, approved by the Court in 1938, and amended in 1940 and 1946. In response to the New York City crises, the law was amended in 1976, simplifying the procedure by which a jurisdiction may file for bankruptcy. Also see George H. Hempel, "An Evaluation of Municipal 'Bankruptcy' Laws and Procedures," *Journal of Finance,* 28 (1973): 1339–51; Advisory Commission on Intergovernmental Relations, *City Financial Emergencies: The Intergovernmental Dimension* (Washington: U.S. Government Printing Office, 1973), pp. 9–30.

[17] Mitchell, "Statement." Also see George H. Hempel, *The Postwar Quality of State and Local Debt* (New York: National Bureau of Economic Research, 1971).

obvious response to the New York City crisis, for example, voters in November 1975 rejected 93 percent of all state and local bond proposals.[18]

There is no one best way to determine the appropriate ceiling for general obligation debt at the local level, but several criteria have been suggested. Debt as a percent of assessed property value is the most common standard, with 10 percent frequently being considered a maximum; many states impose this type of ceiling on municipalities. Debt as a percent of market value is also used. Per capita debt is still another possible standard, along with debt as a percent of personal income. Debt payments—principal and interest—as a percent of total expenditures is sometimes used.[19]

At the federal level, much of the controversy over debt has swirled around the issue of whether the rising debt ultimately will result in economic collapse; the government has been compared with a family that overcommits itself through borrowing. Most economists have long rejected this comparison. The case hinges upon the concept of internal and external debt. When a family borrows it accepts an external debt; it is borrowing resources that must be paid back to the lender at a later date. Federal borrowing, on the other hand, is internal; borrowing occurs within the country. In the family case, borrowing increases present resources at the expense of future resources because it must forgo future consumption in order to repay the debt. Government borrowing, on the other hand, does not alter the total resources available in the country. Thus, "we owe the debt to ourselves," and no future generation has been harmed because only current resources and products are consumed.

At the same time, some words of caution are advisable. Deficit spending results in the sale of interest-bearing bonds that must be financed with tax dollars. Some would argue that increased taxes necessary to finance the debt result in disincentives to produce and thereby penalize future generations. A loss in output today can mean that future generations will inherit a less developed economy than would have been possible otherwise.

Moreover, in some respects deficit spending may penalize future taxpayers vis-à-vis bond holders. In other words, public debts can redistribute income in favor of bond holders. As Otto Eckstein has noted, when wars produce public debt, bond buyers relinquish their claim on consumption

---

[18] *The New York Times*, November 6, 1975.
[19] Roland I. Robinson, "Debt Management," pp. 233–34.

during wartime, but later, through the sale of their bonds, they will be able to make claims on the economy. In this way, it may be possible to shift economic burdens to future generations.[20]

The federal debt controversy as well as state and local debt debates reflect the differing purposes for which debt is incurred. Federal debt, as will be seen in Chapter 13, is one of the most important instruments of national economic policy; the use of federal securities is discussed in that chapter. At the state and local levels, borrowing is not used for economic policy but for other purposes, in part reflected by the length of the term for repayment.

Short-term borrowing, usually for one year or less, is sometimes used to handle cash flow problems discussed in the preceding chapter. Borrowing occurs in anticipation of revenues, and once the revenues are received, the loan is repaid. Unanticipated emergencies such as severe winter storms or summer floods force governments to borrow on a short-term basis. Short-term borrowing is also used to accelerate work on capital projects. Many months may pass before a jurisdiction sells long-term bonds, and in the interim short-term borrowing may be used to provide funds in order to get a project underway. The instrument used for this form of short-term borrowing is called a bond anticipation note (BAN).

Short-term borrowing does need to be limited to avoid situations such as occurred in New York City in the mid-1970s. Borrowing had been used to the point where large notes were falling due every few months, and the City was forced to seek further short-term borrowing to refinance debts for which there was no revenue. New York City found itself in a situation similar to that of the family that overextended itself through the use of credit cards.[21]

Long-term borrowing, on the other hand, is used for long-term projects or problems. A general rule at the state and local levels is that such borrowing should not be used to meet current operating expenses. There-

---

[20] Otto Eckstein, *Public Finance,* 3rd ed. (Englewood Cliffs, N.J.: Prentice-Hall, 1973). Also see James M. Buchanan and Richard E. Wagner, *Public Debt in a Democratic Society* (New York: American Enterprise, 1967); James M. Ferguson, ed., *Public Debt and Future Generations* (Chapel Hill: University of North Carolina Press, 1964); Tilford C. Gaines, *Techniques of Treasury Debt Management* (New York: Free Press of Glencoe, 1962); William Hamovitch, ed., *The Federal Deficit: Fiscal Imprudence or Policy Weapon?* (Boston: Heath, 1965); David J. Ott and Attiat F. Ott, *Federal Budget Policy,* rev. ed. (Washington: Brookings, 1969), pp. 108–24.

[21] See Wyndham Robertson, "Going Broke the New York Way," *Fortune,* 92 (August, 1975): 144–49+.

fore, long-term bonds are usually used for major capital facilities projects or other capital investments such as the acquisition of fire trucks. Another use is to refinance short-term obligations resulting from major emergencies. Jurisdictions that defaulted in the 1930s typically refinanced their debts on a long-term basis. Today, more than 90 percent of both state and local debt is long term.

The most common form of long-term financing is the full-faith-and-credit or general obligation bond. By issuing such bonds the jurisdiction pledges to use its full revenue-generating powers to guarantee that bond holders will be repaid according to a designated schedule. Given the pledge of the government, these bonds are presumed to have the least risk and therefore they sell at a relatively low interest rate. The interest rate is critical in large bond issues, where a difference of 0.1 percent in the rate can affect total interest payments by hundreds of thousands or millions of dollars. One problem with these bonds, however, is that a state or local jurisdiction is limited in the sources from which it may draw revenue. Provisions in state constitutions and statutes may set limits on income, sales, and property tax rates. Therefore, the jurisdiction could have insufficient tax sources to meet the bond repayment schedule.

Special tax and revenue bonds are two other types of long-term financing. The special tax bond commits the revenue from a tax for repayment of bonds. An example is tax proceeds on gasoline used to repay highway bonds. Revenue bonds have the guarantee of revenue generated from the facility constructed from bond proceeds. Revenue bonds might be issued for the construction of a municipal parking garage, with parking fees being used to retire the debt. Revenue bonds are defended primarily on the grounds that persons deriving benefit from a project pay for it; in the case of the parking garage, only users of the garage pay, not the general taxpayer. From an intergovernmental perspective, the revenue bond device forces nonresidents who wish to use the parking garage to pay their "fair share" for the garage. Because both the special tax and revenue bonds make limited commitments on repayment, these bonds carry more risk and sell at higher interest rates than general obligation bonds.

Housing authority bonds are another form of long-term borrowing. Local housing authorities and state housing agencies may issue bonds for the construction of public housing. Repayment is provided from housing rentals and federal contributions, with the federal government guaranteeing repayment on the bonds.

One of the newest forms of long-term debt is the moral obligation bond. These bonds involve the greatest risk because there is little financial guarantee. The jurisdiction simply expresses a moral commitment to repay the loan. The various crises involving state and local debt in the mid-1970s made investors wary of such unsecured bonds so that these will be used far less frequently, if at all.

The differences between general obligation bonds, revenue bonds, and the others should not be overemphasized. These differences are primarily legal, but for governments the real world is the bond market. The jurisdiction that defaults on any bond is surely to have difficulty finding investors for all of its bonds. Consequently, if a capital facilities project is not generating sufficient income to meet revenue bond commitments, the jurisdiction will take action to cover the repayment schedule.

All of these bonds that have been discussed have tax-exempt status, which until recently has made them attractive to investors; however, in recent years state and local governments have encountered problems in selling their bonds, leading to a proposed new form, the taxable bond option (TBO). On the surface, taxable bonds would hardly seem to be a method of attracting investors, but the proposal calls for a federal interest subsidy on these state and local bonds. In this way, the total interest paid would be higher than tax-exempt bonds and therefore presumably more attractive to investors.[22]

In addition to these general types of bonds, different modes of repayment are used. One distinction is between callable and noncallable bonds. Callable bonds allow jurisdictions to pay the obligation in part or in full before the maturity date; investors who wish to commit funds for a specified time period without the possibility of having to make decisions about reinvesting at an earlier date will prefer noncallable bonds. Another distinction is between coupon and registered bonds. Coupon bonds have attached coupons indicating maturity date and the amount of payment, and whoever presents the mature coupons receives payment. Registered bonds, on the other hand, require that the owner register with the government issuing the bonds. The advantage of the coupon bond is that it is easily transferred from one owner to another, while the registered bond

---

[22] TBO legislation has been introduced by Senator Edward M. Kennedy (D, Mass.) and Congressman Henry S. Reuss (D, Wis.). For a general discussion of the proposal, see Ted Becker, "The Taxable Bond Option," *Public Management,* 58 (April, 1976): 2–4.

offers protection to investors in the event the bond is stolen, destroyed, or lost.

Still another distinction is between serial and term bonds. Term bonds in any given bond issue mature on a single date. To meet the future repayment date, jurisdictions establish sinking funds to which they deposit monies in order to have sufficient revenue available to repay the loan. Serial bonds, in contrast, mature in installments, usually yearly. In recent years serial bonds have largely replaced term bonds in part because of statutory prohibitions against term bonds. Investors holding term bonds obviously must be concerned with whether a jurisdiction is annually setting aside sufficient funds to be able to repay its debt.

To enable investors to make judgments on which bonds to purchase, two major corporations rate large bond issues. Moody's Investors Service and Standard and Poor's Corporation use similar rating scales from triple A for the best secured bonds to C for the worst. The rating may determine whether a jurisdiction will be able to sell its bonds. Jurisdictions that enjoy favorable ratings will pay lower interest rates and despite the lower rates are more likely to attract investors than jurisdictions with less favorably rated bonds.

Credit ratings seem to be associated with budgetary practices. A recent survey of 88 cities compared credit ratings with the control, management, and planning aspects of their budget systems. High credit ratings were most common in cities that had program budgeting systems, i.e., that had program classifications and program effectiveness measures in their budgets, that used cost benefit studies, and that had multi-year program and expenditure forecasts.[23] Another method of obtaining favorable ratings is to have bond repayments insured. The Municipal Bond Insurance Association, a consortium of private insurance companies, insures bond issues, thereby reducing risk and raising credit ratings.[24]

The interest rate associated with bonds is determined by either a public sale or negotiations. The public sale approach involves sealed bids submitted by would-be buyers. Public sales in theory guarantee the lowest possible interest rates, but for many jurisdictions there will be few interested investors in a public sale, thereby possibly eliminating the competi-

---

[23] Lewis Friedman with Gregory Morton, "City Budgets," *Municipal Performance Report,* 1 (August, 1974): 29–33.

[24] Carroll J. Fry, "Private Insurance for Municipal Bonds," *Public Management,* 58 (April, 1976): 12–14.

tive aspect.[25] Negotiated sales are conducted between investment banks and the issuing government. Large investment syndicates often negotiate bond issues, acquire the bonds, and then offer them for resale to individual investors.

All of the steps involved in issuing bonds cost money. In addition to principal and interest payments, a government will need to pay for financial advice and legal services. If a bond referendum is required, that too will cost money and time. The bonds, bond notices, and a bond prospectus will have to be prepared. Court fees are also involved.

Ultimately, numerous decisions must be made in deciding on a debt strategy. Before considering what types of bonds to issue, a jurisdiction will need to consider whether some proposed projects may be postponed until sufficient revenues are available to cover costs; preferences for pay-as-you-go systems to indebtedness are common. Total debt repayment schedules need to be considered, not just the repayment of a contemplated debt. In other words, outstanding debt in combination with a contemplated bond issue could prove excessively burdensome. The size of the issue and the denomination of the bonds would need to be judged in terms of need for revenues and the current status of the bond market. A common problem in recent years with large capital projects requiring years of construction has been failure to predict the impact of inflation on future year construction costs; the consequence is that bond proceeds often have been insufficient to cover construction costs. On the other hand, smaller bond issues may be more acceptable in the bond market.

Finally, once bonds are issued, careful debt administration is essential. Cash proceeds are managed so that required cash is available while the remainder is invested in U.S. Treasury notes and bills and in bank time deposits. Of course, procedures must be established to meet anticipated payments on the principal and interest. As was explained in the previous chapter, a debt service fund usually will be created for each bond issue. A record of bond holders will be maintained for registered bonds. Each year a combined debt statement will be prepared, often required by state law.

In coming years, the procedures used in creating debt and administering it are surely to be more prescribed. Defaults at the local level and threatened defaults at the state level have aroused the concern of citizens,

---

[25] See George G. Kaufman, "Improving Competitive Bidding Procedures for Municipal Bonds," *Governmental Finance,* 3 (August, 1974): 22–27.

government officials, individual investors, and financial institutions. Some states have inadequately supervised their own debt and that of their local governments, which increases the prospect of greater federal involvement. An increased role for Washington also can be expected because of its superior financial powers. However, even the federal government may not be immune from debt problems, and so more deliberate debt policy and management can be expected to be applied to the federal government.

SUMMARY

A capital expenditure can be defined from an accounting aspect as a fixed asset or more generally as an expense that produces future benefits. The latter could include many health, education, and welfare services. The more narrowly defined fixed assets approach includes land, buildings, other construction, equipment, and machinery.

The federal government provides a capital budget statement but does not use capital budgeting; state and local governments often have capital budgets. A capital budgeting system is particularly advantageous when facilities are to be built with borrowed funds, but a major disadvantage is that operating and capital expenditures may be largely uncoordinated. Regardless of whether a capital budget system is used, thorough project planning is needed.

While public debt is large and increasing, total public debt since 1950 has decreased in comparison with private debt and in proportion with the gross national product. Debt payments by governments remain relatively small portions of total expenditures, and defaults on debt obligations have been few. Still there is reason for concern that governments not overindulge in borrowing. What constitutes overindulging is yet to be determined, aside from the obvious point of default being overindulgence.

The size of the federal debt has been a major topic of debate for decades, but most economists agree that it is largely an internal debt that will not cause severe economic repercussions at some future date. However, crises at the state and local levels have caused some to have second thoughts about the increasing federal debt.

The instruments of debt can be divided into short- and long-term obligations. Short-term notes are due in a year or less. Long-term bonds include general obligation, special tax, revenue, housing authority, and moral obligation bonds. Bonds may be distinguished as to whether they are callable, coupon or registered, and serial or term. Credit ratings are important in terms of whether a government will be able to find purchasers for its bonds and the interest rate that will be required.

Greater controls on debt practices can be expected for all levels of government, with an increasing role being played by the federal government. New York City's financial crisis in the mid-1970s will serve as a catalyst for more stringent debt policies and management practices.

GOVERNMENT PERSONNEL

Government budgeting and personnel seldom have been treated jointly and in detail. This is indeed surprising, considering that personnel costs are commonly the largest single expense in operating budgets. In his classic work on government budgeting, A. E. Buck wrote, "Personnel is the most important single factor in government both from the operating and the fiscal point of view."[1] Yet, despite the importance of personnel to budgeting, rarely has there been any attempt to integrate the two. Budget literature has been almost silent on government personnel policies and procedures, and personnel literature has been equally silent on budgeting.[2]

Government personnel is reviewed here in three main sections. The first section reviews the impact of personnel decisions and expenditures on the budget. The second section suggests some of the reasons why budgeting and personnel administration have been separate activities. The third section discusses budget staffs, including sizes and skill mixes, and then considers the more general matter of personnel behavior in budget systems that focus upon program results.

PERSONNEL IMPACTS ON THE BUDGET

Personnel expenditures are typically the largest portion of any government's operating budget and may well be the largest portion of total

---

[1] A. E. Buck, *Public Budgeting* (New York: Harper and Brothers, 1929), p. 539.

[2] The standard reference on personnel administration is O. Glenn Stahl, *Public Personnel Administration,* 6th ed. (New York: Harper and Row, 1971). For brief

expenditures, including capital and operating expenditures. In 1973–74 direct personal services for wages, salaries, overtime, and the like, cost governments on the average about one-third of all expenditures. When retirement expenditures are added to direct personal services, the percentage is raised to 35 percent. Local government spends the highest proportion (50 percent) and the federal government the lowest (26 percent). The federal figure would be considerably higher if transfer payments, especially Social Security, were subtracted from total expenditures.[3]

Public employment also has been important for welfare purposes. Many persons have found comfortable, relatively well-paying careers in government. The awarding of positions to the economically needy and to the politically faithful has been a common practice. Patronage appointments have been common at all levels of government.

Administrators have used personnel tactics to build empires. A large staff is often regarded as evidence of success for the administrator. Moreover, when staff is increased, the administrator can make claims on other resources, namely increases in budget items for supplies, equipment, desks and chairs, more space, and even a new building. We do not suggest that all administrators are would-be kings. Empire building results in part from the desire for self-aggrandizement but also because of sincere convictions that increases in personnel will increase the effectiveness of an agency.[4]

Given the magnitude of personnel expenditures, the use of employment for patronage purposes, and tendencies toward empire building on the part of agencies, it becomes obvious why budgeting decisions often have focused on personnel practices. Budgets of many years ago indicated the names of individuals and their earnings; Table 14 shows the 1938 monthly earnings of individual staff members in the Political Science Department at the University of Washington. These and other state employees may have been embarrassed by such information being publicly

---

articles on government personnel, see *Public Personnel Management,* published by the International Personnel Management Association.

[3] Percentages calculated from the Bureau of the Census, *Governmental Finances in 1973–74* (Washington: U.S. Government Printing Office, November, 1975), pp. 5 and 27. See *Recent Federal Personnel Cost Trends* (New York: Tax Foundation, 1974).

[4] For a discussion of the relationship between bureaucratic self-aggrandizement and the public interest see Anthony Downs, *Inside Bureaucracy* (Boston: Little, Brown, 1967); William A. Niskanen, Jr., *Bureaucracy and Representative Government* (Chicago: Aldine-Atherton, 1971); Gordon Tullock, *The Politics of Bureaucracy* (Washington: Public Affairs Press, 1965).

TABLE 14

Political Science Salaries and Wages, University of Washington, 1938–1941 (Monthly Rate in Dollars)

Occupation	Name of present employee	Present (May 1938)	Requested	No. months employed or on duty	Amount ($) requested from state appropriations
Professor	Martin, C. E.	510.00	536.00	20	10,642.00
Professor	Cole, K.	360.00	389.00	20	7,693.00
Professor	Levy, E.		{150.00	3	450.00
			{158.00	17	2,686.00
Professor	Mander, L. A.	350.00	389.00	20	7,663.00
Professor	Wilson, F. G.	380.00	399.00	20	7,923.00
Associate Professor	Spellacy, E.	330.00	357.00	20	7,059.00
Associate Professor	None		342.00	21	7,182.00
Assistant Professor	Von Brevern, N.	260.00	284.00	20	5,608.00
Instructor	Biesen, C.	180.00		3	540.00
Research assistant	Epstein, J.	150.00	185.00	24	4,440.00
Research fellow	Jonas, F.	75.00		18	1,350.00
Research fellow	None		75.00	18	1,350.00
University fellows	Various			18	5,850.00
Graduate and undergraduate assistants	Various			18	540.00
Secretary	Christensen, V.	100.00	105.00	24	2,460.00
Stenographer (half-time)	Clyde, E.	40.00	50.00	24	1,200.00
Secretary	Foster, D. G.	100.00	105.00	24	2,460.00
Total Political Science					77,096.00

Source: *Governor's Budget Compiled for the Twenty-Sixth Legislature, for Biennium 1939-42* (Olympia: State of Washington, 1939), part 2, pp. 496–97.

displayed, but the purpose was to guarantee that individuals were not receiving exorbitant salaries.

Today the practice of naming employees in the budget is far less common. Salaries of heads of agencies are often reported in budgets, but itemized earnings of each employee are not. Still, budgets usually at least report personnel expenditures by agency and may provide more detail. Table 15 displays one portion of the personnel data reported for New York State's vocational rehabilitation program. Proposed expenditures are shown not only for salaries but also for holiday, overtime, and inconvenience pay.

One item to note from the New York State table is that it reports the number of positions. Similar displays may be found in many other state budgets, local budgets, and the federal *Budget Appendix*. Sometimes personnel tables are only for information purposes, i.e., to provide the legislative body and the general public with information about the size or personnel complement of agencies. In other cases, these displays exist for decision purposes. An agency may not be permitted to hire a new staff member, even though funds are available in its budget, without first receiving authorization for a new position. Budget offices and personnel departments often exercise such control, and sometimes the legislatures are involved as in Alaska, Massachusetts, New Hampshire, and Oregon.[5] Exercising complement control is one method of limiting growth in the bureaucracy and the budget.

During tight financial periods, complement control is used to reduce anticipated expenditures. As a budget year approaches its end, a freeze on all hiring may be imposed, including filling of existing vacancies as well as authorizing new positions. Such a practice produces inequitable situations where some affected agencies are short-handed, yet the practice is useful in affecting total expenditures. In more severe budget times, the extreme measure of furloughing people is taken. For example, in 1976 the City University of New York system simply closed the last month of the year, and employees received no salary for that time. These types of personnel actions can have an immediate effect on the budget, whereas many other parts of the budget are less controllable.

Salaries and wages are only part of the picture, with fringe benefits and particularly pensions being the other.[6] Retirement plans for public em-

---

[5] *Budgetary Processes in the States: A Tabular Display* (Lexington, Ky.: Council of State Governments, 1975), Table XVIII.

[6] See Eric Anderson, "Fringe Benefits for Municipal Employees," *The Municipal Year Book, 1973* (Washington: International City Management Association, 1973),

TABLE 15

Selected Personal Services for Vocational Rehabilitation, New York State, 1976–1977

	Total all programs			Administration of the department			Central services		
	No.	Amount ($)	Change ($)	No.	Amount ($)	Change ($)	No.	Amount ($)	Change ($)
Full-time positions	2503	31,586,167		140	1,714,181		286	2,840,653	
NS, OS positions	263	4,187,416		11	384,000		52	268,351	
Annualization of 1975–76 increments		142,698	+142,698		9,488	+9,488		11,605	+11,605
Full annual salaries		10,921	+10,921						
New positions	18	189,000	+189,000						
Locational pay		78,000	+3,000						
Inconvenience pay		12,900	–200						
Overtime compensation		39,000	–8,000					13,000	
Holiday pay		1,600	+200						
Temporary service		2,043,490	+119,090		31,000	–3,000		63,000	–4,700
Positions abolished during 1975–76			–565,681			–81,086			
Positions recommended for abolishment			–1,144,073			–76,991			–48,771
Additional compensation for 1975–76			–642,999			–36,307			–68,300
Personal service savings		–2,388,192	–78,556		–94,669	–4,104		–178,609	+166
Total	2,784	35,903,000	–1,974,600	151	2,044,000	–192,000	338	3,018,000	–110,000

Source: *Executive Budget, 1976–77.* (Albany: State of New York, 1976), p. 171.

ployees produce basically uncontrollable expenditures. There are 10 federal pension programs, the largest being the Civil Service Retirement System. In addition to these, there are about 200 state-administered systems, many of which include local government employees, and there are more than 2,000 local systems. Virtually all full-time government employees are covered by one of these retirement plans.

The adequacy of the funding of these plans is questionable. Typically employees and the government make equal contributions (7 percent of salaries at the federal level). What has become increasingly apparent is that many—if not most—systems are actuarially unsound, that is they are not obtaining sufficient funds through contributions and investments to be able to meet the benefits to which employees will be entitled.[7] Cities faced with financial crises often defer contributing to the system and use available revenues to meet other operating needs. This results in depleting the assets of the funds, ultimately leading to a pay-as-you-go system in which current contributions are used to meet current benefit payments. Indiana and Massachusetts are in this position.

As liberalized retirement benefits are granted, the situation becomes worse. The federal system has provided pension increases when the Consumer Price Index rises. A worker retiring in 1970 who would have received 56 percent of his salary was receiving 80 percent by 1976. Governments are accumulating great debts that really do not appear on debt statements. One estimate for the federal government is that in 1980 contributions will be at less than $6 billion and benefits at nearly $15 billion.[8]

How this hidden debt is to be met has not been resolved. Congress in 1974 passed the Employee Retirement Income Security Act, which set new standards for the operation of private pension funds. That legislation also mandated a congressional study of public pension programs and may lead to regulatory legislation. The problem, however, is money, not regula-

---

pp. 202–13; Thomas P. Beakney, *Retirement Systems for Public Employees* (Homewood, Ill.: Irwin, 1972); *Fringe Benefits in State Government Employment* (Lexington, Ky.: Council of State Governments, 1975).

[7] Advisory Commission on Intergovernmental Relations, *City Financial Emergencies: The Intergovernmental Dimension* (Washington: U.S. Government Printing Office, 1973), pp. 64–66; Board of Actuaries of the Civil Service Retirement System, *Fifty-Second Annual Report,* 94th Cong., 1st sess. (Washington: U.S. Government Printing Office, 1975); *Employee Pension Systems in State and Local Government* (New York: Tax Foundation, 1976).

[8] John C. Perham, "The Mess in Public Pensions," *Dun's Review,* 107 (March, 1976): 48–50.

tion. Federal legislation presumably will not provide the funds necessary for making state and local retirement systems actuarially sound. Given tight budgets in states and many central cities, a requirement of full funding of retirement systems could lead to extraordinary tax increases or bankruptcy for these governments.

Related to the pension problem is the advent of collective bargaining in the public sector. While federal employees do not negotiate over salaries and wages, unions are extremely effective in lobbying for increases in pay and benefits and do participate in wage determination processes.[9] Also management may negotiate matters affecting the budget of an agency. Bargaining at the state and local levels has become widespread; 40 percent of state and 56 percent of local full-time employees are organized.[10]

Collective bargaining is a nightmare for budgeters. Given the proportion of expenditures committed to personnel, a wage settlement can have a massive impact on the budget. In a survey of 400 state and local labor agreements, the U.S. Bureau of Labor Statistics found that one-quarter were for 12 months or less.[11] This complicates budget planning, because each year salaries and wages might be opened to negotiation. The number of bargaining units and unions further complicates the situation. When all employees are in a few units, budget planning is difficult because most of the costs of personnel will be uncertain until settlements are reached. Having many bargaining units may resolve that problem but results in continuous negotiations with unions, a process for which the budget office must at least provide information on costs of possible settlements and often must assume a leadership role for management. In a 1974 survey conducted by the Census Bureau, 20 of the 38 states with collective bargaining had 10 or more bargaining units; 14 states had 20 or more. Local governments typically had fewer units.[12] In some jurisdictions, negotiation impasses are settled by arbitration awards. In those situations,

---

[9] U.S. Civil Service Commission, *Collective Bargaining in the Federal Sector* (Washington: U.S. Government Printing Office, 1975) and Murray B. Nesbitt, *Labor Relations in the Federal Government Service* (Washington: Bureau of National Affairs, 1976).

[10] Bureau of the Census, *Labor-Management Relations in State and Local Governments: 1974* (Washington: U.S. Government Printing Office, 1976). Also see "Managing Labor Relations," *Public Management,* 57 (February, 1975): 2–18.

[11] Richard R. Nelson, et al., *Characteristics of Agreements in State and Local Governments, January 1, 1974,* U.S. Department of Labor, Bureau of Labor Statistics Bulletin 1861 (Washington: U.S. Government Printing Office, 1975), p. 5.

[12] Bureau of the Census, *Labor-Management Relations in State and Local Governments,* p. 115.

the budget office must wait for a decision from an arbitration panel regarding the cost of personnel.

Productivity bargaining, a common practice in industry, is gaining increasing acceptance in the public sector. In the early years of public-sector collective bargaining, one of labor's main arguments was that salaries and wages in the public sector needed to be increased to match the private sector. Much of the needed "catching up" has been accomplished, and now unions are being pressed to show that salary and wage increases are warranted by productivity increases. Detroit, for example, negotiated an agreement with sanitation workers whereby both the city and the workers benefited as per ton costs for solid waste handling decreased. [13] Orange, California, negotiated a police productivity agreement that coupled pay increases with reductions in crime.[14] Productivity bargaining and more general efforts to increase productivity, however, remain sensitive topics.[15] Increased productivity offers the prospect of lower costs to government, but there is concern among labor that these efforts are intended to benefit government at the expense of its workers.

PERSONNEL ADMINISTRATION AND BUDGETING

Because decisions related to personnel have major effects upon budgeting, some linkage between the two is needed. However, just as constant tensions exist between budget offices and line agencies, so do tensions persist between the budget and personnel systems.

One cause may be the rise of professionalism within budgeting and personnel administration. As each of these operations has become increasingly complex and technical, budgeters and personnel administrators may

---

[13] *Employee Incentives to Improve State and Local Government Productivity* (Washington: National Commission on Productivity and Work Quality, 1975), pp. 82–86.

[14] Paul D. Staudohar, "An Experiment in Increasing Productivity of Police Service Employees," *Public Administration Review,* 35 (1975): 518–22.

[15] John M. Capozzola, "Productive Bargaining: Problems and Prospects," *National Civic Review,* 65 (1976): 176–86; Steve Carter, "Trends in Local Government Productivity," *The Municipal Year Book, 1975* (Washington: International City Management Association, 1975), pp. 180–84; *Improving Productivity in State and Local Government* (New York: Committee for Economic Development, 1976); Chester A. Newland, ed., "Productivity in Government," *Public Administration Review,* 32 (1972): 739–850; "Productivity Management," *Public Management,* 56 (June, 1974): 2–27; John P. Ross and Jesse Burkhead, *Productivity in the Local Government Sector* (Lexington, Mass.: Lexington Books, 1974); Wayne E. Thompson, "Labor-Management Focus: Improving Government Productivity," *National Civic Review,* 64 (1975): 335–38.

have tended to view others as simply unqualified to make important contributions. Professional budgeters, taking a somewhat narrow view of their field, may have concluded that personnel administrators had little relevant expertise to contribute to budgetary decision making. Professional personnel administrators may have come to a similar conclusion regarding budgeters vis-à-vis personnel practices. Professionalism can lead to a search to establish independent and isolated domains that are protected against would-be interference.

An even more fundamental problem is that budgeting and personnel administration stem from differing historical backgrounds. As has been seen in earlier chapters, budgeting has arisen to provide information to executive and legislative decision makers. Central budget offices are intended to aid the chief executive, an elected politician. Budgeting is frankly political. Personnel administration, on the other hand, is a product of a reform movement designed to minimize political concerns, to base personnel appointments on the basis of what one knows rather than whom one knows. Personnel administration is expected to be apolitical.

Not only are budgeting and personnel distinct in their historical roots, but these differences have resulted in differences in organizational structures. Since the passage of the Pendleton Act of 1883, which established a merit system of employment to replace patronage in the federal government, the personnel function at all levels of government has tended to be organizationally separate from control by political executives. Although some personnel activities such as position classification may be within a personnel bureau or department subject to control by the chief executive, the critical activity of examination usually has been assigned to independent civil service commissions. These commissions have also tended to circumscribe the selection process. The justification for this independence has been that it insulates personnel matters from the caprices of politics.[16]

In recent years some staunch advocates of merit systems have concluded that these independent commissions should be abandoned. The Municipal Manpower Commission in 1962 and the National Civil Service League in 1970 endorsed the idea. The League reported:

It is apparent that in many jurisdictions they [the commissions] have outlived their usefulness and their continuation is incompatible with

---

[16] For a discussion of personnel agencies in the federal government, see Michael Cohen, "The Personnel Policy-Making System " in Robert T. Golembiewski and Michael Cohen, eds., *People in Public Service: A Reader in Public Personnel Administration* (Itasca, Ill.: Peacock, 1970), pp. 123–37. Stahl, *Public Personnel Administration,* pp. 335–72.

sound administrative concepts. Such commissions are often much more concerned with keeping people out of the public service than in developing new techniques to attract persons into public employment. The roadblocks that these commissions have managed to erect have, in numerous instances, managed to frustrate thoroughly and to cut the effectiveness of some of our most competent and responsible administrators.[17]

Of course not all independent commissions are useless. At the federal level, the President has authority to appoint the Chairman of the Civil Service Commission (CSC), and the prevailing evidence is that the Commission has been an innovative rather than negative influence.

The mere elimination of independent commissions, however, would not eliminate the tensions that exist between personnel and budgeting. The paramount fear of personnel administrators probably is the erosion of the merit principle, a concern that may not be appreciated sufficiently by budgeters. Personnel practices tend to concentrate upon inputs as a means of reducing political considerations; if people are selected on the basis of their technical and not political qualifications and are placed in appropriate positions, it is assumed that effective services will result. Budget offices, which increasingly are focusing upon results, may not share with personnel offices the same enthusiasm for rigid examination and selection procedures. Line agencies may view with equal skepticism the efficacy of many personnel practices.

Tensions between budgeting and personnel administration persist on other subjects. Complement control, for example, is both a personnel and a financial practice. Which office should have a dominant role in this matter? Some personnel offices have attempted to undertake personnel planning activities by focusing upon projected personnel skills requirements for various programs.[18] This type of planning, however, is unlikely to be productive unless linked with a budget office that provides guidance on expected program changes. In day-to-day operations, budget offices may be assigned the role of overseeing the management of agencies from the perspective of the chief executive. This role is unlikely to be welcomed

---

[17] *A Model Public Personnel Administration Law* (Washington: National Civil Service League, 1970), p. 5. Also see Municipal Manpower Commission, *Governmental Manpower for Tomorrow's Cities* (New York: McGraw-Hill, 1962), pp. 106–8.

[18] For a discussion of personnel planning, see Robert D. Lee, Jr. and Ronald W. Johnson, *Public Budgeting Systems,* 1st ed. (Baltimore: University Park Press, 1973), pp. 280–89.

by agency heads and is likely to result in conflicts between the budget office and the personnel agency. Collective bargaining is still another area of potential conflict. Given the financial implications of collective bargaining, the budget office may play a dominant role at the expense of a personnel department. From the perspective of the personnel administrator, the budget office might be viewed as a threat in assuming all personnel responsibilities and, even worse, as bringing politics into an area that should be apolitical.

PERSONNEL IN BUDGETING

It takes people to operate budgeting systems, people at the central location of a budget office, in line agencies, and in the legislative body. While only some personnel are assigned full-time to budget matters, all personnel are inevitably involved with budgeting and budget decisions. In this section, we discuss the size and skill mix of budget staffs and then consider personnel behavior in budget processes that increasingly emphasize the need for program achievements.

At the federal level, both the executive and legislative branches have sizable staffs. The Office of Management and Budget (OMB) has a staff of about 700, and each department has personnel whose main function is budgeting. Congress has the Congressional Budget Office (CBO), staffs for standing committees, staffs for each Congressman and Senator, the General Accounting Office (GAO), the Library of Congress (including the Congressional Research Service), and the Office of Technology Assessment. Altogether the legislative branch has about 38,000 employees. Most of these people, of course, do not work on budgeting such as the Government Printing Office (8,500 employees) and the Architect of the Capital (2,000 employees), but many are assigned to work on budgeting and substantive matters with budgetary implications.[19]

Of growing concern is how the various congressional staff units should relate to each other on budgeting.[20] The 1974 legislation which reorganized congressional budgeting produced three new staff units—the CBO

---

[19] U.S. Civil Service Commission, Bureau of Manpower Information Systems, *Federal Civilian Manpower Statistics,* Monthly Release (Washington: U.S. Government Printing Office, May, 1976). Also see *The Legislative Branch: The Next Billion Dollar Bureaucracy* (New York: Tax Foundation, 1976).

[20] See selected issues of *Congressional Quarterly Weekly Report* (Washington: Congressional Quarterly).

and staffs for the House and Senate Budget Committees—while retaining the other financial committees and their staffs—House Ways and Means, Senate Finance, and House and Senate Appropriations. As of 1976 the CBO, headed by Alice M. Rivlin, had a staff of about 200, while the House Budget Committee had a staff in the sixties and the Senate in the seventies. Rivlin aroused controversy when in 1975 she unsuccessfully requested an increase in her staff to 259. A concern was that the CBO would dominate information handling at the expense of the House and Senate Budget Committees. Also, there was evidence of duplication of effort with all three groups producing similar reports such as status reports on appropriation and authorization legislation. The 1974 legislation also authorizes the CBO to provide staff support to individual members of Congress, but by 1976 an effort was underway to strip the CBO of this authority, given that Congressmen and Senators have access to staff from the other sources mentioned above.

The sizes of state budget staffs vary greatly. California, the District of Columbia, Hawaii, Missouri, New York, and South Carolina have more than 200 persons in their executive budget agencies, although a majority of the state agencies have less than 100 and many have less than 50. These figures, however, reflect the variations in the functions performed by budget agencies. When the budget function is separated out, staff sizes become more uniform from state to state. California and New York remain as big staff states (between 120 and 150), followed by Pennsylvania, New Jersey, and Puerto Rico (between 50 and 70). All of the other states have less than 50 staff members.[21] Considering that many of the states have multi-billion dollar budgets, the staffs are not particularly large.

Permanent professional fiscal staffs are to be found in all state legislatures, except Kentucky and Wyoming. In 38 states, the two chambers of the legislature share their staffs; in this group, the largest is California, with 50 professionals followed by Texas and Maryland (in the twenties). Most of the other joint states have less than 10 professionals. States with separate house and senate staffs include New York (more than 20 professionals in each chamber) and Michigan (about 15 in each chamber). The other states have 10 or fewer professional fiscal staff members in each chamber. Although these numbers may seem small, one should recognize that state legislative staffs are a relatively new phenomenon. As recently as

---

[21] *Budgetary Processes in the States,* Table V.

1965, only 30 state legislatures had permanent professional fiscal staffs.[22]

Comparable figures at the local level are not available, although it is sure that most municipalities, counties, school districts, and special districts have fewer than 10 persons assigned to budgeting, exclusive of accounting, purchasing, and payroll personnel. Also, the legislative bodies have little or no financial staffs. Most legislative staff support in a municipality comes from the city clerk's office.

The question of how many staff members are needed can only be answered in terms of the expectations for the budget units. Small staffs handling multi-million or multi-billion dollar budgets obviously can be expected to do little more than superficially review materials prepared by agencies and perhaps devote in depth effort to selected "hot" issues. A large staff, on the other hand, is likely to mean more involvement in agency activities—perhaps from the agency perspective, more meddling.

Budget offices vary as to the purposes that are pursued and the activities undertaken, both of which are linked with the skill mix of budget personnel. The budget office emphasizing the control function of holding agencies accountable for spending in accordance with appropriations may prefer persons with business skills and particularly accounting training. At the federal level and to a lesser extent at the state level, skills in public finance may be important for developing policies for economic growth. Still other skills may be sought by budget units engaged in program analysis.

In developing the staff of the Congressional Budget Office, these various approaches were in competition with each other. One issue that has been resolved is that the CBO will not conduct program analyses; this function is being left for other agencies, notably the General Accounting Office. Some participants in the struggle over naming the first Director preferred a neutral type agency, much like the GAO, whereas others preferred a policy-oriented staff. In the first years of experience, the CBO has attempted to blend these, focusing upon economic policy but frequently avoiding making policy recommendations. For example, its first economic report, *Inflation and Unemployment: A Report on the Economy,* issued in June 1975, projected future economic problems associated with increasing energy costs and inflation but did not make specific

---

[22] James H. Bowhay and Virginia D. Thrall, *State Legislative Appropriations Process* (Lexington, Ky.: Council of State Governments, 1975), pp. 25 and 67.

recommendations. Still, the CBO staff has been criticized as being too liberal and economics-oriented. Many of the original appointees to the CBO came from RAND, the Brookings Institution, and the Urban Institute.

Important changes have been taking place in both the level of education and the type of education found in state budget offices. According to a recent survey by the National Association of State Budget Officers, the percent of staff members with less than a baccalaureate degree has remained at 10 percent or less, but there has been a noticeable increase in advanced degrees. In 1970, the average state budget office had 18 percent of its staff with a master's degree or more; by 1975 the figure had risen to 35 percent. Larger state governments tend to have higher-educated budget staffs.

State budget offices have shifted away from persons with business educations and toward the social sciences and other disciplines. The average state budget office in 1970 had two-thirds of its staff with business backgrounds; in five years that figure declined to 47 percent. Conversely, the social sciences have increased from 22 percent in 1970 to 34 percent. These averages, however, do not reflect the great variety in budget offices. As of 1975 states such as Delaware, Iowa, Massachusetts, Oklahoma, and South Carolina had 90 percent or more of their staffs with business backgrounds, compared with Kansas and Kentucky with 90 percent or more in the social sciences. Most states have a more even distribution between the two broad types.

Whether the composition of the staff has any bearing upon the way a state budget system operates is not clear. Certainly, a staff cannot do something for which it is not trained. Only those trained in program analysis would be expected to be able to conduct analysis. On the other hand, it is possible that budget offices might recruit program analysts and not use their talents. The available evidence suggests that the use of effectiveness analysis in decision making is not significantly greater in social science-oriented budget units than in business-oriented units.[23]

With the increasing emphasis upon program results, regardless of whether a government claims to be developing or operating a program budgeting system, the concern is for finding staff members who have skills

---

[23] Robert D. Lee, Jr., and Raymond J. Staffeldt, "Educational Characteristics of State Budget Office Personnel," *Public Administration Review,* 36 (1976): 424–28.

previously not used in budget offices. The crux of the problem is that there is no easy means of defining a bag of tricks one needs to know. No one academic field has a monopoly on producing the "right" skills. Analytic talents can be found in public administration, economics, management science, business administration, law, as well as the disciplines of philosophy, political science, and other fields. Yet, this does not mean that all graduates of these programs would be suitable.

A possible conclusion is that because there is no one discipline that perfectly matches the needs of budget units, the specific form of educational training may be largely irrelevant. One former official in the OMB has been paraphrased as saying:

> If you bring in bright young people, trained in a discipline, and if they understand what the process is about, it does not take much training. It requires perhaps three months or so on the job—really a buildup time—to be fully effective. The issues are not all that complicated—you have lots of people who have the special knowledge. It is the analytical ability that may be missing.[24]

This view if taken literally might suggest that intelligence test scores are the best guides in selecting staffs.

It would seem that whatever specific approaches a budget office was taking, the focus of budget innovations today requires persons who can think in a systems framework about governmental programs: What kinds of resources are needed to produce the desired outputs and impacts of a program? Following that, other skills are needed such as economic analysis, statistics, and computer science. The budget office that first develops or recruits persons highly skilled in quantitative techniques may frustrate these staff members and make little progress in reorienting its approach to budgeting. Where there has been no history of collecting resource and program information, a government may have little need for analysts who perform best only with extensive data.

Aside from recruiting personnel with new talents, existing personnel can be upgraded through training programs. The efforts of the 1960s to install planning-programming-budgeting systems (PPB) involved extensive training programs. The U.S. Civil Service Commission trained many state and local government officials as well as federal officials. Many of the

---

[24] Jack Carlson as paraphrased in Selma J. Mushkin, ed., *University Training in PPB for State and Local Officials* (Washington: Urban Institute, 1970), p. 18.

governments in the State-Local Finances Project (5-5-5) had major training programs; California alone trained thousands of its employees.[25]

Today's emerging budget systems can be considered to need three types of training.[26] The first is a general type that focuses upon concepts. The scope of this general training can range from one-hour orientation sessions to extensive courses in decision and systems theory. For the lower-level employee, the short orientation is useful in helping him or her understand the underlying concepts of results-oriented budgeting. More extended training is useful for administrators and policy makers in understanding how they can use program information in decision making. A second type focuses upon specific techniques and is not for everyone. This type is for the doers of analysis, concentrating upon statistics, operations research, systems analysis, and computer science. The third type deals with management practices, not in the general sense of how to manage but geared specifically to the practices and procedures to be used in budgetary decision making in a given jurisdiction.

In retrospect, much of the training for PPB was a bust, and the same may be occurring regarding training for management by objectives (MBO). The reason in part is a failure to provide the third type of training, which in many cases could not be provided because governments often did not have a management approach to budget innovation. The method of management must change in order to benefit from general and analytic training. The state official who travels to Washington for general instruction on program budgeting, decision making, or MBO and returns to his state to find that no changes in procedures are really being instituted is likely to conclude the training wasted valuable time. Similarly, the person who is trained at governmental expense to learn various analytical tools but not given the opportunity to use them becomes a skeptic.

Training has a payoff when it changes the ways in which people think and behave. Without changing the practices of budgeting, newly trained persons have little opportunity to change their behavior and may see few incentives for changing their mode of thinking. In short, training needs to be reinforced by changes in the administration of budget systems. If budget offices claim they are moving toward program budgeting but

---

[25] *PPB Pilot Project Reports* (Washington: State-Local Finances Project, The George Washington University, 1969), pp. 13–14.

[26] For a more general discussion on approaches to training, see Robert J. Mowitz, "Training Model for State and Local Governmental Personnel," *Public Personnel Management,* 3 (1974): 451–53.

continue to make decisions exclusively on grounds unrelated to program results, training will fail.[27]

The issue is particularly important at the local level. Faced with tight budgets, local governments can afford little training and especially want training that will bring results. Given that most local staffs are small, these jurisdictions usually cannot afford to sponsor their own training programs nor develop their own, unique budget systems. One prospect is for the development of model budget systems that with modifications can be adapted to specific municipalities and other local governments. If these models are complemented with training programs, perhaps sponsored by a state department of local government affairs, several jurisdictions jointly might be able to reorient their budget systems. Training, of course, is no panacea, but this suggested approach may be able to produce results at relatively low cost.[28]

In addition to central budget personnel are the employees in agencies and departments. What new roles can they be expected to assume and how are they likely to respond to budget systems that focus upon program results? One allegation against proposed changes in budget systems has been that the changes will result in centralized decision making at the expense of creative thinking and action in operating departments. Theories dealing with the motivation of workers maintain that employees, who through participation can have greater control over their own activities, will be more satisfied with their work and more productive.[29]

A balance between centralization and decentralization is needed. Some centralization is essential, otherwise each department is a government unto itself. Although centralization may sound akin to Big Brotherism, one must recognize that government was not created to provide a democratic/ participatory experience for its employees but to provide services to its

---

[27] Robert D. Lee, Jr., and Arthur C. Eckerman, "PPBS and the Dual Role of the Personnel Function," *Public Personnel Review,* 32 (1971): 39–43; Robert J. Mowitz, *The Design and Implementation of Pennsylvania's Planning, Programming, Budgeting System* (Harrisburg: Commonwealth of Pennsylvania, 1970), pp. 10–12.

[28] The approach is under development by the Institute of Public Administration of The Pennsylvania State University. Also, the Division of Community Services in the North Carolina Department of Natural and Economic Resources has taken some steps in this direction.

[29] Chris Argyris, *Personality and Organization* (New York: Harper and Row, 1957); Chris Argyris, *The Impact of Budgets on People* (New York: Controllership Foundation, 1954); Amitai Etzioni, *Modern Organizations* (Englewood Cliffs, N.J.: Prentice-Hall, 1964); Frederick Herzberg, *Work and the Nature of Man* (Cleveland: World, 1966).

citizenry. A balance needs to be achieved between democracy within government and government's response to public needs. Chief executives have an obligation to lead and manage. On the general issue of what budget changes are needed in a jurisdiction, personnel throughout the bureaucracy may be consulted. But it would be absurd to have employees vote on the proposed changes.

Extensive participation is required in the implementation of budgetary changes. Regardless of the term used to describe new approaches to budgeting, they all tend to emphasize the linkage of program and resource information to ascertain the extent to which resources are being used efficiently to achieve desired effects. Such approaches necessarily mean that budgeters and accountants will not be the only personnel involved. In the case of program budgeting, the design of program structure, the development of measures to be used in gauging program results, the preparation of program alternatives, the conduct of analyses, and the forecasting of future needs involve all segments of government. In these areas, participation can be extensive, involving program administrators and their staffs, planners, and personnel administrators as well as budgeters and accountants.

Real changes in how governments make budgetary decisions have effects on employees, but what will be those effects?[30] An emphasis upon the results or effects of governmental programs is surely to be a foreign concept to many. No longer is keeping busy an adequate justification for one's employment. Moreover, program budgeting can encourage managers to manage, rather than being a centralizing force that strips managers of their powers. This too may be a foreign concept. Managers may be expected to assess the relationship between the resources they request and the results produced. Depending upon one's perspective, this can be viewed as a welcome opportunity or a threat.

Limits exist on the extent to which incentives can be used in bringing about change. The incentive of increasing or decreasing an agency's budget according to how well it has performed can be used only on a limited basis. A welfare agency that is considered to be unproductive hardly can be penalized by eliminating its budget and thereby denying income main-

---

[30] See Selwyn W. Becker and David Green, Jr., "Budgeting and Employee Behavior" in Robert T. Golembiewski and Jack Rabin, eds., *Public Budgeting and Finance,* 2nd ed. (Itasca, Ill.: Peacock, 1975), pp. 262–75; Andrew C. Stedry, "Budgets and Forming Levels of Aspiration," in Golemiewski and Rabin, eds., *Public Budgeting,* pp. 251–61.

tenance payments to the needy. A city recreation department may be considered to be highly productive, but available revenues and existing priorities may preclude increasing the recreation budget.

The ability to grant monetary rewards to groups of employees or individuals is also greatly circumscribed. The budget office typically cannot single out a unit as being productive and award its employees a salary increase greater than what other employees are receiving. MBO may factor expected results down to individual employees, but again there may be many constraints in giving more productive workers bonuses or special salary increases. Still, some experimentation in this approach of financial incentives is being conducted, whether as part of MBO, productivity improvement, collective bargaining, or under some other rubric.[31]

Negative incentives are also difficult to apply. Some merit systems may provide excessive job security to the point where only the totally incompetent can be forced from office. Public employers generally do not have the same flexibility in hiring, dismissing, and reassigning employees that private employers have.[32]

Ultimately, the main reward to persons must relate to how one views one's work in bettering society. Government has been fortunate in attracting persons who are concerned with the public good. Program budgeting can help the manager gauge how well his or her unit is using resources that yield desired results.

SUMMARY

The impacts of personnel costs on the budget are immense. Because labor costs are a large segment of every operating budget, personnel may be the first to be cut during financially tight periods. Government pension systems constitute a growing problem. Many retirement programs at all levels of government are not being adequately funded and may present severe problems in coming years. Collective bargaining, while helping employees, has greatly complicated budgetary planning at the state and local levels; unresolved negotiations at budget time mean that personnel costs are unknown.

---

[31] Lynn Bell, "Employee Incentives in Local Government," *Municipal Year Book, 1975,* pp. 200–14.

[32] The discussion of various incentives is based in part on John C. Aplin, Jr., and Peter P. Schoderbek, "How to Measure MBO," *Public Personnel Management,* 5 (1976): 88–95.

Despite the apparent linkages between the budget and personnel functions, the administration of these systems has often not been integrated.
Tensions persist between the two, in part the result of differing histories.
Budgeting is openly a political process, while personnel administration has
a penchant for the apolitical.

Executive and legislative staffs in recent years have expanded in size
and changed in terms of their capabilities. Congress has substantially
increased its budget staffs with the Congressional Budget Office and staffs
for the House and Senate Budget Committees. State budget offices have
shown a shift toward persons with social science backgrounds, whereas
business administration types previously tended to dominate. Many local
governments face the problem of needing more budget staff but not having
the resources to acquire it.

Training can be a useful method of upgrading personnel as long as the
training is linked with real changes in budgetary practices. Training programs that make promises of future changes but are not integrated with
ongoing efforts to modify budget practices may be largely empty exer-
cises.

Emerging budget systems that focus upon program impacts or results
should be expected to affect employees. Indeed, if there are no effects on
employees, then there probably has been no real change in the budget
process. Program budgeting systems offer chief executives an opportunity
to manage government, but this does not mean a total centralization of
decision making to the detriment of agencies and their managers. Managers
can be encouraged to manage with program budgeting.

12

INTER-
GOVERNMENTAL
RELATIONS

Throughout most of this book, budgetary decision making has been treated as if it were a discrete concern of some particular level of government—federal, state, or local. In most senses, that treatment is accurate in that budgetary decisions for one level of government are not formally made at other levels. Each level of government has discrete financial decision-making processes that determine matters of revenue and expenditure. In another sense, however, decisions about revenues and expenditures at different levels of government are interdependent. Budgetary decisions made at one level are partially dependent upon budgetary and non-budgetary decisions made at other levels. This chapter examines the financial interdependencies among the federal, state, and local governments.[1]

---

[1] For economists' treatment of intergovernmental fiscal relationships the reader is referred to George F. Break, *Intergovernmental Fiscal Relations in the United States* (Washington: Brookings, 1967); Jesse Burkhead and Jerry Miner, *Public Expenditure* (Chicago: Aldine, 1971); James M. Buchanan and Marilyn R. Flowers, *The Public Finances: An Introductory Textbook,* 4th ed. (Homewood, Ill.: Irwin, 1975); John F. Due and Ann F. Friedlaender, *Government Finance: Economics of the Public Sector,* 5th ed. (Homewood, Ill.: Irwin, 1973); Bernard P. Herber, *Modern Public Finance: The Study of Public Sector Economics,* 3rd ed. (Homewood, Ill.: Irwin, 1975). More general discussions of intergovernmental relations include Daniel J. Elazar, *The American Partnership* (Chicago: University of Chicago Press, 1962); Richard H. Leach, ed., "Intergovernmental Relations in America Today," *Annals,* 416 (November, 1974): 1–193; and William V. Holloway, *Intergovernmental Relations in the United States* (New York: MSS Information, 1972).

The chapter is divided into three sections. The first section examines some of the basic economic and political problems that stem from having three major levels of government providing various services and having differing financial capabilities. The second section considers the patterns of interaction among the different levels, and the third section considers alternatives for restructuring these patterns of financial interaction.

BASIC PROBLEMS

For convenience purposes, we have commonly referred throughout this book to the three levels of governments, but at this point, this simplification must be set aside. In this section, we consider the problems associated with the functioning of these governments as they pertain to the setting of policy, the raising of revenues, and the provision of services.

From a geographical perspective, governments are piled upon governments in the United States. In addition to the federal government and the 50 state governments, there are somewhat less than 80,000 local governments. The local "level" is not a level but rather consists of numerous governments that may serve the same or parts of the same geographical area. Most states have county governments and within their boundaries are municipalities and townships as general-purpose governments. Superimposed over these are numerous independent school districts and special districts such as irrigation and sewer districts.

These various local governments are not merely subunits of their respective state governments, nor are the states subunits of the national government. Each government has substantial authority to decide what services will be provided, how they will be provided, and how and in what amounts revenues will be raised. In other words, this is not a centralized system in which policies are set by the national government and their administration is delegated to the states which in turn delegate responsibilities to local governments.

The use of this myriad of governments can be defended in several ways. By having multiple governments, an omnipotent, despotic type of government may be avoided; because power is diffused, the rise of dictatorial government may be prevented. Another presumed advantage is that the diversity of governments allows for differing responses according to the divergent needs of citizens in different locales. Uniformity of service levels and tax rates may be inappropriate in a nation of more than 200 million people and a geographical area of 3.6 million square miles.

The existence of numerous units of government increases the probability that greater choice will be afforded individuals in their own preferences. People may locate in specific communities that offer desirable mixes of taxes and services; of course, it is not suggested that such economic calculations are the sole criteria upon which location decisions are based.[2] Nevertheless, individuals and families may change their locations, particularly within metropolitan areas, to take advantage of better services, such as education or lower taxes. Interstate movements are probably less associated with preferences about the level of governmental services, though once the decision to move to another state has been made, the choice of a particular local jurisdiction within an area may very well be determined by such preferences.

Another advantage of multiple governments is that economies of scale may be achieved; that is, functions may be performed by the sized unit that is most capable of performing them. Just as it may be advantageous from the standpoint of efficient resource utilization for private, profit-oriented organizations to grow to a large scale, it may also be more efficient to conduct some governmental activities on a large scale by one unit of government. The defense of the nation is more economical when conducted by the federal government than it would be if each state were assigned the responsibility of defending its own territory.

On the other hand, to perform all governmental functions at the central level might result in inefficient conduct of some activities. Lessened flexibility of operations and other diseconomies suggest the need for some functions to be performed by units of government smaller than the federal government. Probably many services can be provided most efficiently at the local level.[3] Capital-intensive production activities where the marginal costs decrease as size increases are most efficient on a large scale because of the heavy cost of capital equipment. Most governmental activities, defense being one of the major exceptions, are labor intensive, and the scale of operation is less important.

Of course, all of these governments are not free to do whatever they please. The U.S. Constitution provides for federal government powers (especially Article I, Section 8) and reserves all other powers to the states (10th Amendment). Local governments have fewer constitutional protec-

---

[2] Charles M. Tiebout, "A Pure Theory of Public Expenditures," *Journal of Political Economy*, 44 (1956): 416–24.

[3] Due and Friedlander, *Government Finance*, p. 487.

tions, because these governments have been created by their states. Within these legal parameters, a higher-level government may impose standards upon lower levels. The federal government has been able to expand its responsibilities through broad interpretations of the defense, interstate commerce, and general welfare clauses of the Constitution so that today, for example, it prescribes safety standards for hospitals, including those operated by state and local governments. Similarly, the states have expanded their responsibilities through what is called the police power—protecting the health, safety, morals, and general welfare of the citizenry. As a result, states require children to attend school and prescribe for local school districts what courses will be taught and who may be hired as teachers. The standards or policies imposed by one government on another may have major impacts on budgets.

The existence of thousands of governments results in coordination problems both geographically and functionally. Municipalities in a metropolitan area need some coordinative mechanisms. Road networks, for example, need to be planned in accordance with commuting patterns within a metropolitan area, and such plans should not be restricted to the geographical boundaries of each municipality. Also, the use of numerous local governments may thwart economies of scale, and therefore, increasing emphasis has been given to providing services on a larger areal basis.[4] Recreation and parks programs, for example, may be provided on a metropolitan basis instead of by each municipality.

Functional coordination also is a problem in that the three main levels of government share responsibilities within program fields or functions. Criminal justice, for instance, is a function of all three levels; some type of police, court, and prison system exists at the local, state, and federal levels. The independent pursuit of similar objectives by these governments can result in ineffective services and wasted resources. Therefore, increasing emphasis has been given to developing mechanisms for functional integration. While program specialists stress functional integration, however, policy generalists may stress areal integration. This conflict has been popularized by Deil S. Wright as picket fence federalism, with each picket being a function such as mental health or education and all three levels of government being part of each picket.[5]

---

[4] This issue is discussed in most urban textbooks. See John C. Bollens and Henry J. Schmandt, *The Metropolis: Its People, Politics and Economic Life,* 3rd ed. (New York: Harper and Row, 1975).

[5] Deil S. Wright, "Intergovernmental Relations: An Analytical Overview," in

The conflict between area and function is played within the context of the need for services and the corresponding need for revenues, with differences in capabilities existing within levels of government and among levels.[6] Vertical imbalance, or noncorrespondence, refers to the relative abilities of different levels of government to generate needed revenue. Although one level of government may have a comparative advantage in terms of efficiency in providing a particular service, it may not have the revenue capability to provide the service. Another level of government, on the other hand, may possess sufficient revenue capability but not be the most efficient unit to provide certain services. In the United States, it is typically the federal government that possesses the revenue capacity but not the comparative advantage in providing many governmental services, while states and local governments are in the position of having functional expenditure obligations that are greater than their ability to raise revenue.

This disparity is attributed largely to the different revenue sources used by governments. The federal government, relying upon personal and corporate income taxes, has a more elastic tax structure in which revenues increase with any increase in economic activity. State and local governments rely less upon income taxes and more upon sales, user, and property taxes, which are more slowly affected by changing economic conditions. However, while state and local revenue sources are relatively inelastic, the demand for services provided by these governments is quite elastic.

The problem of vertical imbalance, or noncorrespondence, is obviously not insoluble. Comparative efficiency in the provision of governmental services does not necessarily mean that revenue must be raised for services at the same level at which the services are provided. By definition, however, when financing and spending are carried out at different levels, intergovernmental transactions are essential.

Superior fiscal capacity can be used by one level of government to entice or persuade another to provide a given service. This is the case in the federal government persuading the states to build an interstate network of freeways. Had the federal government not been willing to pay 90 percent of the cost of the system, it is certain there would be far fewer freeways today. State governments also use their revenue capability to pressure local

Leach, ed., "Intergovernmental Relations in America Today," pp. 1–16. For an excellent discussion of the area and function problem, see James W. Fesler, "The Basic Theoretical Question: How to Relate Area and Function," in Leigh E. Grosenick, ed., *The Administration of New Federalism: Objectives and Issues* (Washington: American Society for Public Administration, 1973), pp. 4–10.

[6] The discussion is based in part on Herber, *Modern Public Finance*.

governments, perhaps funding social services programs to be operated by counties or funding special educational programs for the handicapped.

The other half of the problem concerns fiscal capacities of governments at the same level. From state to state there are clearly differences in income and wealth, which are the basic sources of governmental revenue. Differences in income and wealth lead to differences in tax burdens, or the level of public services, or most likely differences in both. U.S. per capita personal income in 1974 was $5,434, but Connecticut's was $6,471 or 119 percent of the national average, and Mississippi's was $3,764 or 69 percent of the national average. The Middle Atlantic states of New Jersey, New York, and Pennsylvania had a per capita income equal to 111 percent of the nation, compared with only 78 percent for the East South Central states of Alabama, Kentucky, Mississippi, and Tennessee.[7]

If the distribution of the demand for governmental services were similar to the distribution of income and wealth, then there would be no problem with differences in revenue capacity among the states. Citizens theoretically could choose states with the level of services most corresponding to their own preferences. Unfortunately, the need for many governmental services is greatest in those states where the fiscal capacity to meet those needs is least. The problem is even more acute with respect to different local jurisdictions within the same state. Central city governments within large metropolitan areas are faced with demands for services that increase at a faster rate than does the value of revenue sources.

Disparities in fiscal capacity among governments at the same level lead directly to another problem, that of external costs and benefits of governmental functions. The lower level of services provided in states with lower fiscal capacity affects not only those states but others with higher levels of service as well. People of low income moving from states with low services to states with high services create new burdens on the high-service states. This is especially evident in the migration of the 1930s from impoverished areas to the West Coast and in the more recent migration from the rural South to cities in the North and West. Proportionately, more people who move from the lower-income to the higher-income states receive welfare payments and generate greater demands on other public services than do those moving from states with similarly high levels of income and services.

In the above example, some of the costs of the failure to provide comparable levels of service across state lines are borne by those outside

---

[7] Bureau of the Census, *Statistical Abstract* (Washington: U.S. Government Printing Office, 1975), p. 388.

the low-service states. The problem has an opposite side too. The provision of services at the level where it is most economical to do so may also result in spillover of the benefits into larger areas. The most obvious example of this is education. Higher levels of education generally yield higher levels of income. Given the mobility of the population, the benefits produced by one local educational system may spread far beyond the local boundaries. If decisions about the quantity and quality of educational services are left entirely in the hands of local jurisdictions, however, those making the decisions would presumably consider not the external, or spillover, benefits, but only those benefits the community itself receives. Thus, the level of the activity might be too low from the perspective of regional or national interests.[8]

Intergovernmental competition within levels constitutes another problem. This competition usually is intended to attract business firms to move to a particular area. Firms locate for a variety of reasons, such as access to markets, labor supply, and other resources. Because businesses seek to minimize production costs, advantages lie with jurisdictions that have high services and low taxes for industry.[9]

Competition for businesses among political jurisdictions has important consequences, one being distortions in revenue and expenditure patterns. When special concessions are granted to firms, needed revenues must be obtained elsewhere or the level of services must be reduced. Devoting resources to special facilities such as industrial parks, that are frequently financed by long-term debt instruments, may affect a community's ability to finance other capital projects such as a civic center or public housing for lower-income families. Another effect of such competition is felt nationally. The allocation of business activities among geographic sectors of the economy may be shifted to areas where the activities might not be economical if the free market were unimpeded by interjurisdictional competition.

The final problem, overlapping taxes, is restricted to the revenue side. Basically, the problem is that the sum of all governmental tax sources is the nation as a whole, even though governments vary as to what portions of that whole are taxed. Therefore, no matter what particular forms of taxation are used by the different levels of government, the same people and firms will be affected. Tax overlapping also occurs when all levels of

---

[8] Due and Friedlaender, *Government Finance,* pp. 488–89.

[9] Whether businesses actually move for these reasons or not is irrelevant to the argument. As long as governments compete with taxes and services, the effects are the same.

government tax the same specific source, such as federal, state, and local taxes on income.

Overlapping, or multiple taxation, in some sense is unavoidable and not necessarily undesirable. It causes serious problems only when one jurisdiction in effect preempts another lower level's ability to raise sufficient revenue. This can occur if the state sales tax rate is so high that it discourages local jurisdictions from levying such a tax. Because it may be deliberate policy to prevent local jurisdictions from using that form of taxation, other sources of revenue need to be made available as substitutes. The same kind of problem is evidenced with regard to the federal use of personal and corporate income taxes vis-à-vis states and local governments. These jurisdictions, while often criticized for failing to raise sufficient revenue to meet needs, may be largely preempted from major reliance upon income taxes because of the federal government's preemption of this revenue source.

When all of these problems are considered together, the mess in intergovernmental relations is obvious, but the solution is less obvious. The failure of governments both among and within levels to coordinate their activities results in overlapping services, gaps in services, and wastes in the use of resources. Because there is no mechanism by which the nearly 80,000 governments in the nation are coordinated, inequitable results are inevitable, although, of course, what is equitable ultimately must be defined by each observer (see Chapter 2).

PATTERNS OF INTERACTION AMONG LEVELS OF GOVERNMENT

Too often discussions of intergovernmental finance concentrate exclusively on financial assistance and neglect the more important factor of direct expenditures. Federal expenditures are not made in a vacuum but, rather, have varying geographical impact. The same is true for state expenditures. The location of facilities becomes particularly important. Political considerations are crucial at the state level over the location of highways, state hospitals, and parks. At the federal level, military installations, the awarding of defense contracts to corporations, which of course are geographically based, and other civilian installations arouse much lobbying. Some activities have constraints on their location; a naval shipyard located in Nevada would be preposterous. However, aside from the requirement of having an outlet to the sea, a shipyard could be located in numerous places. Local and state governments work actively to obtain federal projects in their jurisdictions as one means of guaranteeing future economic prosperity.

Beyond the physical items are various loan and grant programs to individuals and corporations that greatly affect jurisdictions. At the federal level these include Social Security, Medicare, support to farmers, small-business loans, and Aid to Families with Dependent Children. States also make large welfare and other human services payments.

Available evidence suggests that federal spending favors some states over others, but there is no discernible pattern of federal expenditures benefiting some types of locales more than others. Federal outlays tend to favor states outside the Northeast. "There is some relationship between distance to Washington, D.C. and the level of per capita outlays . . . The farther from Washington, the higher the per capita outlays."[10] At the local level, however, the patterns are less obvious. Federal spending pro-grams tend to offset each other. A rural county may benefit from Agricul-ture and Interior Department projects, while an urban county benefits from HEW and HUD. This is not to say that all counties benefit equally but that there is no consistent pattern of which types of county areas are the major beneficiaries of federal outlays.[11]

In addition to the intergovernmental literature's common lack of emphasis upon direct expenditures as they affect state and local jurisdic-tions, the literature tends to overemphasize federal aid to state and local governments and underemphasize state aid to local government. In 1973–74, federal aid to states was $31.6 billion and to local government was $10.2 billion. State aid to local government was $44.5 billion, greater than all federal aid to state and local governments.[12] Of course, state aid probably would be much smaller were states not receiving substantial federal support. As was seen in Chapter 2 (Table 3), states receive nearly a

---

[10] Clyde E. Browning, *The Geography of Federal Outlays: An Introductory and Comparative Inquiry* (Chapel Hill: Department of Geography, University of North Carolina, 1973), p. 62.

[11] The main source of data for analysis on outlays is from the Federal Informa-tion Exchange (FIX) maintained by the U.S. Community Services Administration. In addition to Browning, *The Geography of Federal Outlays,* see Robert D. Lee, Jr., *The Differential Impacts of Total Federal Expenditures, General Revenue Sharing, and Community Development Grants Upon Local Jurisdictions In Pennsylvania* (Univer-sity Park: Institute of Public Administration, The Pennsylvania State University, 1976), pp. 11–51 and Thomas H. Kiefer, *Federal Spending in West Virginia* (Morgan-town: Bureau for Government Research, West Virginia University, 1976).

[12] Bureau of the Census, *Governmental Finances in 1973–74* (Washington: U.S. Government Printing Office, November, 1975), p. 20.

quarter of their revenue from the federal government. Local governments receive about a third of their revenues from state government and less than 10 percent from the federal government; as can be seen in Figure 12, each type of local government obtains half or more of its revenue from its own sources.

Differences in federal and state support exist among the types of local governments (Figure 12). As of 1973–74, about half of all federal aid to

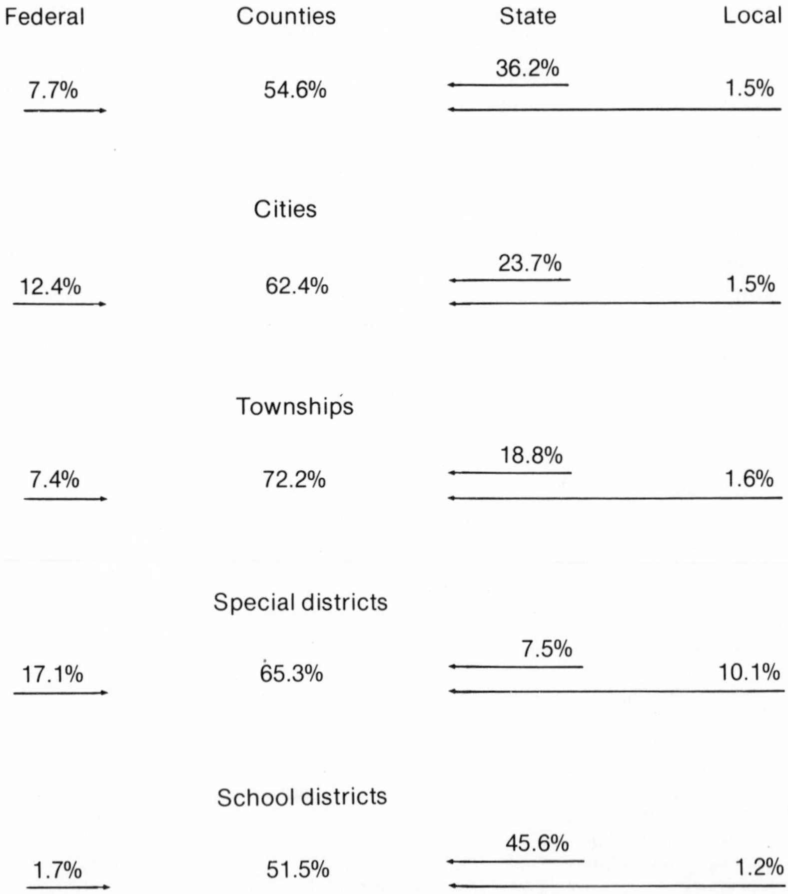

Federal	Counties	State	Local
		36.2%	
7.7%	54.6%		1.5%

Cities

| 12.4% | 62.4% | 23.7% | 1.5% |

Townships

| 7.4% | 72.2% | 18.8% | 1.6% |

Special districts

| 17.1% | 65.3% | 7.5% | 10.1% |

School districts

| 1.7% | 51.5% | 45.6% | 1.2% |

Figure 12. Intergovernmental sources of revenue for types of local governments, 1973–1974. Source: Bureau of the Census, *Governmental Finances in 1973–74* (Washington: U.S. Government Printing Office, November, 1975), p. 30.

local governments went to cities, but these monies constituted only 12 percent of city revenues. Special districts such as sewer and water districts are the type of local government most dependent upon federal aid—17 percent of their budgets. Nearly half of state aid went to school districts, with these monies accounting for about half of school district revenues. Most of the other state aid was divided evenly between counties and cities. State aid accounted for more than a third of county revenues but less than a quarter of city revenues. Federal aid to cities has received much attention, despite the fact it is equal to only half the amount states provide to cities.

These summary figures, of course, do not convey the great variety in state aid patterns. Some states provide much greater assistance to local governments than other states; some states may provide a given service and thereby make direct expenditures, whereas other states may fund local governments to provide a service. Unlike other states, Hawaii operates a statewide school system. New Hampshire provides only 14 percent of local government general revenues, compared with New Mexico at 51 percent. Comparable figures are California at 37 percent and Kansas at 24.[13]

Aid to elementary and secondary education, the largest portion of state aid to local government, rose sharply from 17 percent in 1930 to 40 percent in 1950. Since then the percentage has been more or less constant, but the dollar volume has increased greatly.[14] States use a formula for distributing these funds. The foundation plan, as it is called, is geared to guarantee a minimal amount of educational expenditures either on a per-pupil or per-classroom basis. Formulas typically are geared to real estate property assessments, with low assessment districts receiving more aid than high assessment districts. Additional formulas may be used for programs serving preschool, disadvantaged, and handicapped children.[15]

These formulas were attacked in the courts in the 1970s as being discriminatory, i.e., the foundation plans failed to equalize educational

[13] Bureau of the Census, *Governmental Finances in 1973–74*, pp. 31–32.

[14] Mary A. Golladay, *The Condition of Education: 1976 Edition* (Washington: U.S. Government Printing Office, 1976), p. 143.

[15] See Jesse Burkhead, *Public School Finance: Economics and Politics* (Syracuse, N.Y.: Syracuse University Press, 1964); Elchanan Cohn and Stephen D. Millman, *Economics of State Aid to Education* (Lexington, Mass.: Lexington Books, 1974): W. Norton Grubb and Stepan Michelson, *States and Schools: The Political Economy of Public School Finance* (Lexington, Mass.: Lexington Books, 1974); Roe L. Johns, et al., eds., *Status and Impact of Educational Finance Programs* (Gainesville, Fla.: National Educational Finance Project, 1971); and Eugene P. McLoone, *Profiles in School Support, 1969–70* (Washington: U.S. Government Printing Office, 1974).

opportunity among jurisdictions. While recognizing the great importance of education, the U.S. Supreme Court decided in a Texas case that the allocation of funds for education was a state responsibility and was not controlled by the Constitution.[16] Nevertheless, cases have been won in state courts, so that by 1973 there were ten states that had altered their educational financing schemes to minimize disparities in per-pupil expenditures among districts.[17]

Other state aid programs are comparatively small. Education is followed in size by welfare, general local government support, and highways. Welfare and highways are usually geared to some type of formula, the former often being a per-client reimbursement program. Virtually all states have some form of motor fuels tax-sharing formula in which local governments as well as the states benefit.[18]

Overall, state assistance has been more predictable than federal aid because of the extensive use of formulas. These facilitate budget planning at the local level, because jurisdictions from year to year have some knowledge of what state funds will be. The only major controversies have centered on the factors used in the formulas.

Turning to federal aid, it has been characterized by functional or categorical grants. Essentially the categorical grant is the provision of resources by one party, the federal government in this case, to others, states, and localities, with the condition that the recipients spend the money in a particular fashion and for a particular function. In the nineteenth century, federal conditional grants were principally in the form of land that was to be used for educational purposes. In this century, federal grants have been primarily in the form of money.

Federal grants have been aimed at inducing state and local governments to increase the level of services in specified areas. During the mid-1960s, almost 90 percent of all federal aid went to four basic functions—education, income security, health and hospitals, and highways. As can be seen in Table 16 there have been substantial shifts since 1967. General revenue sharing, enacted in late 1972, has climbed from almost nothing to over 10 percent of all federal aid. Education, transportation, and income security have decreased as a percent of total federal aid, while

---

[16] *San Antonio School District v. Rodriquez*, 411 US 1 (1973).

[17] Golladay, *The Condition of Education*, pp. 150–51.

[18] Federal Highway Administration, *Highway Statistics, 1974* (Washington: U.S. Government Printing Office, 1976).

TABLE 16
Percentage Function Distribution of Federal Grants-in-aid, 1952–1977

	Actual						Estimates	
	1952	1957	1962	1967	1972	1975	1976	1977
Natural resources, environment and energy	1	1	2	2	2	5	5	7
Agriculture	4	9	6	3	1	1	1	1
Commerce and transportation	18	24	36	27	15	12	14	15
Community and regional development	1	1	3	6	9	7	7	6
Education, training, employment, and social services	9	8	8	25	26	23	24	21
Health	8	4	5	10	17	18	17	17
Income security	57	49	38	25	26	19	19	19
Revenue sharing and general purpose fiscal assistance	2	3	2	2	1	14	12	12
Other	a	1	a	a	1	2	2	2
Total	100	100	100	100	100	100	100	100

a Less than 0.5 percent.

Source: Office of Management and Budget, *Special Analyses, Budget of the United States Government, 1977* (Washington: U.S. Government Printing Office, 1976), p. 261.

health has increased from 10 percent in 1967 to an estimated 17 percent in 1977.

Categorical grant programs have gone to areas where significant externalities exist. As was seen in the previous section, the incentives in some functional areas are for governmental units to provide less of a service than is warranted by national interests because the benefits fall outside the jurisdiction providing the service. Grant programs are used to offset these parochial interests. Matching provisions are usually required to ensure that grants will not merely result in a lessened tax effort by the recipients of the grants; without matching provisions, a $1 million federal grant could be offset by an equal reduction in local revenues supporting a program, thereby producing no increase in the level of services. Formulas for determining the amount of matching funds vary. The match may be a flat percentage or be on a graduated scale, depending upon the need in a given jurisdiction. Until the mid-1970s, approximately 10 percent of state and local revenues were used for grant matching, but this figure was expected to decline as a result of grant consolidation programs that require little or no matching.[19]

Federal aid to state and local governments is not of equal importance to all federal agencies. As can be seen from Table 17, HEW is by far the most important department, accounting for more than 40 percent of all federal grants. A different perspective, however, is gained when considering the portion of an agency's budget committed to grants. The Community Services Administration, the successor to the Office of Economic Opportunity, uses more than 90 percent of its budget for grants, followed by the Environmental Protection Agency at 80 percent, and HUD at 46 percent. Departments such as these are like philanthropic bankers and provide few direct services. HEW is comparatively low (20 percent) because much of its budget is committed to Social Security.

Just as total federal outlays are not uniform from state to state, so, too, are grants not uniform. In 1975, the national average was $233 per capita in federal grants to state and local governments. The region receiving the highest per capita grants ($283) was New York and New Jersey along with Puerto Rico and the Virgin Islands. The lowest ($195) was the group of Midwestern states of Illinois, Indiana, Michigan, Minnesota, and Ohio. Until recently, the Rocky Mountain states have received the highest

---

[19] Office of Management and Budget, *Special Analyses, Budget of the United States Government, 1977* (Washington: U.S. Government Printing Office, 1976), p. 260.

TABLE 17
Federal Agency Outlays and Grants to State and Local
Governments, 1975

Department or unit	Total Outlays	Grants	
		Outlays	Percent of total
Agriculture	9,722	2,936	30.2
Commerce	1,583	299	18.9
Defense (military)	85,020	74	0.1
Health, Education, and Welfare	112,411	22,010	19.6
Housing and Urban Development	7,488	3,439	45.9
Interior	2,139	557	26.0
Justice	2,067	722	34.9
Labor	17,649	4,012	22.7
Transportation	9,247	5,688	61.5
Treasury	41,177	6,423	15.6
Environmental Protection Agency	2,530	2,025	80.0
Community Services Administration	547	510	93.2
Veterans Administration	16,575	32	0.2
Other	16,446	996	6.1
Total	324,601	49,723	15.3

Sources: Office of Management and Budget, *The United States Budget in Brief, 1977* (Washington: U.S. Government Printing Office, 1976), pp. 64–65; and Office of Management and Budget, *Special Analyses, Budget of the United States Government, 1977* (Washington: U.S. Government Printing Office, 1976), p. 259.

grants per capita. These states with low population density received large highway grants and shared in revenues from lands owned by the federal government. The Rocky Mountain states, however, lost their lead as the interstate freeway construction program approached completion and as federal human services programs grew.[20]

These per capita grant figures must not be interpreted simply as what regions are winners and losers in the federal aid game. A state and its local governments might receive comparatively small amounts of grants but receive extensive economic support by direct federal expenditures, thereby making the state a winner. Another consideration is what the corporations and individuals in a state pay in taxes. The winner might turn loser when

[20] Office of Management and Budget, *Special Analyses*, pp. 262–63.

taxes paid were compared with federal dollars returned either as direct
expenditures or as grants. Assuming that the federal graduated income tax
has the effect of drawing proportionately greater resources from wealthy
states than less wealthy states, federal aid may amplify or dampen this
effect. Were the effect amplified, per capita federal aid to state and local
governments would increase as per capita personal income declined. This
pattern, however, is not evident, as can be seen in Figure 13. As income
increases, per capita federal grants neither consistently increase nor de-

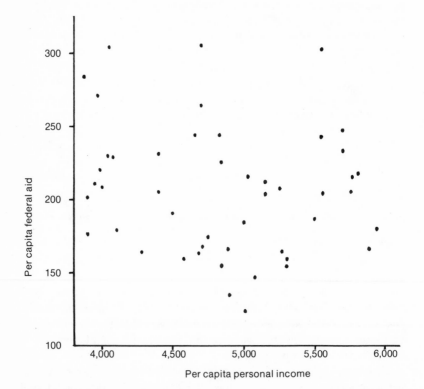

Figure 13. State personal income compared with federal aid to state and local
governments, 1973–1974. Each of the 49 points on the figure represents the
combined federal grants allocated to a state government and its local governments.
Alaska is not included—personal income of $5,933 and federal aid of $653. Sources:
Bureau of the Census, *Governmental Finances in 1973–74* (Washington: U.S. Government Printing Office, November, 1975), p. 47; Bureau of the Census, *State Government Finances in 1974* (Washington: U.S. Government Printing Office, August
1975), p. 59.

crease, suggesting that grant programs do not redistribute income in favor of either wealthy or poor states. The lack of a consistent pattern is explained by the numerous federal grant programs which tend to offset each other in benefiting particular types of states.

The magnitude of federal aid to localities has raised serious questions about the operation of the federal system. Many of these questions concern the proper role of the state government, the basic problem being the extent of state participation in local services funded by the federal government. In general, as legal creatures of the state, local governments cannot spend public funds, regardless of source, for purposes not authorized by the state government. This legal restriction is recognized in most federal legislation that authorizes grants and loans to local governments. Therefore, one of the main functions of states is to pass enabling legislation permitting local jurisdictions to participate in federal programs.

Federal programs for aiding localities can be provided directly to these communities or indirectly through the states. In the latter case, state officials are allowed some discretion in distributing federal funds, though federal regulations may require that a given amount "pass through" to localities and that some of this money be distributed according to set criteria such as population. When funds flow directly from the federal government to the local jurisdiction, the state may exercise some prior approval of local requests for aid or local plans for spending formula grants.

Federal programs that directly aid localities have been criticized as violating the principle that local jurisdictions, as created by the states, should be held answerable to the states. It is alleged, for example, that the poverty program was intentionally designed to bypass the states.[21] However, the argument that the states are powerless in federal-local aid programs is not fully persuasive. There are no legal barriers to states becoming involved, because states can exercise their "sovereign" powers over local jurisdictions.

Of almost equal concern has been the role of local public officials in federal aid programs to communities. In the War on Poverty, for example, the original legislation provided that federal funds to a community could be given to a private nonprofit agency, designated the Community Action Agency (CAA). Before 1967, 80 percent of all CAAs were private, mean-

---

[21] *Antipoverty Programs Under the Economic Opportunity Act* (New York: Tax Foundation, 1968), p. 58.

ing that municipalities could not directly control these programs. In response to demands of mayors and other local officials, the Green Amendment (Rep. Edith Green, D, Ore.) to the Economic Opportunity Act was passed, stipulating that local governments would have the option of either becoming the local CAA or designating the private organization. Supporters of the amendment saw it as a means of restoring power to local officials, but after passage of the legislation there was no major shift away from private agencies as originally expected.[22]

RESTRUCTURING PATTERNS
OF INTERGOVERNMENTAL RELATIONS

Numerous alternatives have been suggested for restructuring intergovernmental relations. Some deal with financial aid systems while others with the delivery of services. The latter range from cooperation among jurisdictions to the assumption of services now provided at lower levels by a higher jurisdiction.

Categorical grants, particularly those of the federal government, have been criticized for many years.[23] These grants, of which there were about 1,100 in 1976, often are focused narrowly in that jurisdictions can only spend monies for specified types of projects. Grants thus may skew local priorities. A jurisdiction possibly might apply for funds for one type of project, even though some other project, for which no funding was available, would provide greater benefits to the jurisdiction. Another criticism is that much time and energy are consumed in drafting grant proposals. Also, some communities do not obtain their "fair share" of federal dollars simply because of inadequate staff for proposal writing. Categorical grants make budget planning difficult, because proposals may be held pending for months. Frequently, there is no coordination among grants. For example, the City of Richmond, Virginia, in 1970 received $18.3 million in federal aid, but other federal programs in the area

---

[22] Joseph A. Kershaw, *Government Against Poverty* (Chicago: Markham, 1970), p. 164.

[23] See Daniel J. Elazar, "Fiscal Questions and Political Answers in Intergovernmental Finance," *Public Administration Review,* 32 (1972): 471–78; Thomas H. Kiefer, *The Political Impact of Federal Aid on State and Local Governments* (Morristown, N.J.: General Learning, 1974); General Accounting Office, *Fundamental Changes are Needed in Federal Assistance to State and Local Governments* (Washington: U.S. Government Printing Office, 1975).

received an additional $12.3 million, about which presumably the city government knew little.[24]

Although this is only a partial listing of the criticisms, one should also recognize some of the possible benefits of categorical grants. In the first place, needed dollars are provided. Also, the federal government has a responsibility to deal with national needs and is justified in channeling funds to meet those needs, not just the unique needs of individual localities. Categorical grants may encourage planning in that most proposals must show how the funds will be used and what the expected benefits will be. Given the extensive paperwork involved in proposal preparation, jurisdictions probably do not apply for anything and everything but rather only apply for funds to support projects that are needed. Another advantage is that the process of reviewing proposals allows for federal agencies to weed out many unsound projects.

In response to the criticisms of categorical grants, one proposal has been to simplify the application process and another has been to institute general revenue sharing. The Federal Assistance Review (FAR) program created in 1969, was responsible for developing easier and faster means by which governments applied for funds and federal agencies acted upon those requests; under FAR, for example, HUD supposedly was able to eliminate half of the paperwork involved and 40 percent of the processing steps.[25] In 1972 the Integrated Grant Administration program was created and was put into law in 1974 with the Joint Funding Simplification Act.[26] The latter instructs federal agencies to provide means by which local governments may apply to more than one agency for funding a given project and may integrate state and federal grants in support of the project. Under executive order, the Office of Management and Budget (OMB) is responsible for administering the program.

General revenue sharing (GRS), a dramatic alternative to categorical grants, was established by the State and Local Fiscal Assistance Act of

---

[24] Study Committee on Policy Management Assistance, *Strengthening Public Management in the Intergovernmental System* (Washington: U.S. Government Printing Office, 1975), pp. 11–12.

[25] Dwight A. Ink, "Federal Assistance Review (FAR) Program," *Public Management,* 54 (November, 1972): 19–21.

[26] General Accounting Office, *The Integrated Grant Administration Program: An Experiment in Joint Funding* (Washington: U.S. Government Printing Office, 1976). See OMB Circular A-111, "Jointly Funded Assistance to State and Local Governments and Nonprofit Organizations."

1972. Under this legislation, the federal government shares some of its revenue with states, counties, cities, and townships. The money can be used for a variety of purposes. To reduce uncertainties over how much revenue would be available from year to year, Congress appropriated $30.2 billion for a five-year period ending December 31, 1976 and in 1976 provided an additional $25.6 billion, extending the program through September 30, 1980.[27] Allocations are made by a series of complex formulas based upon population size, tax effort, personal income, and in some cases urban population and income tax collections. A ceiling i⸱ provided to limit how much any jurisdiction will receive as well as a floor to guarantee that most jurisdictions will receive something. A distinguishing feature of GRS is that jurisdictions receive funds without having to make application for these monies.

How jurisdictions have used general revenue sharing and what have been the effects is anyone's guess. The law provides for periodic reporting of GRS use in major categories such as public safety, environmental protection, public transportation, and the like. But the reports submitted to Washington, at least until 1977, have been worthless because jurisdictions can displace local dollars with federal dollars. A city can place $1 million of GRS into the police department budget, remove $1 million of

---

[27] The literature on general revenue sharing has become extensive. See for example, Advisory Commission on Intergovernmental Relations, *General Revenue Sharing: An ACIR Re-evaluation* (Washington: U.S. Government Printing Office, 1974); David A. Caputo, ed., "Symposium on General Revenue Sharing," *Public Administration Review*, 35 (1975): 130–57; David A. Caputo and Richard L. Cole, *Urban Politics and Decentralization: The Case of General Revenue Sharing* (Lexington, Mass.: Heath, 1974); Wolfgang W. Franz, "General Revenue Sharing: Impact on Local Decision Making," *National Civic Review*, 65 (1976); 20–24+; General Accounting Office, *Case Studies of Revenue Sharing in 26 Local Governments*, summary volume and 26 case studies (Washington: U.S. Government Printing Office, 1975); General Accounting Office, *Revenue Sharing and Local Government Modernization: A Conference Report* (Washington: U.S. Government Printing Office, 1975); *General Revenue Sharing Research Utilization Project,* several volumes (Washington: National Science Foundation, 1975); F. Thomas Juster, ed., *The Economic and Political Impact of General Revenue Sharing* (Washington: U.S. Government Printing Office, 1976); Robert D. Lee, Jr., *The Impact of General Revenue Sharing on Local Jurisdictions in Pennsylvania: Initial Findings* (University Park: Institute of Public Administration, The Pennsylvania State University, 1974); *Making Civil Rights Sense out of Revenue Sharing Dollars* (Washington: U.S. Commission on Civil Rights, 1975); Richard P. Nathan, et al., *Monitoring Revenue Sharing* (Washington: Brookings, 1975); Reese C. Wilson and E. Francis Bowditch, Jr., *General Revenue Sharing Data Study*, four volumes (Menlo Park, Cal.: Stanford Research Institute, 1974); Deil S. Wright, "Revenue Sharing and Structural Features of American Federalism," *Annals*, 419 (1975): 100–19.

local funds, and redistribute the latter among other programs. This is sometimes called the fungibility problem. The reports that have been submitted indicate that GRS has been committed largely to public safety, but in all probability many other programs have benefited. If a city faces a budget crisis, budget cuts may be more likely in recreation and library services than in police and fire services. These cuts may be avoided with revenue sharing, even though the report sent to Washington indicates that public safety has received most of the revenue sharing dollars.

GRS attempts to resolve some of the problems associated with categorical grant programs. Local priorities are presumed to be better served. Time and energy are not wasted in proposal writing. A jurisdiction can plan better in using these funds, rather than attempting to link together diverse small grants. Jurisdictions that need funds but do not have the staff capability to make application for categorical grants can now receive funds.

In contrast, there are many criticisms of GRS.[28] The formula may provide monies to jurisdictions not in need. The floor provision may prop up basically inefficient jurisdictions that might have been forced by economics into consolidating their services with other governments. The ceiling, on the other hand, denies needed funds to many jurisdictions, particularly central cities. The use of the personal income factor is inadequate in gauging the wealth of a community, because local jurisdictions obtain the largest portion of their revenue from sources other than the income tax. The provision that each state government receives one-third of the revenues coming into the state fails to take account of the great variations in the extent to which states provide services vis-à-vis their local jurisdictions. Too much money allegedly has been used for public safety and not enough for social services. Communities allegedly have been allowed to squander their GRS funds, whereas categorical grants require more planning. GRS has been criticized for not encouraging citizen participation in determining the use of funds, although the original legislation did not require that recipient governments consult with the citizenry. One of the most important criticisms is that revenue sharing has been used to discriminate against minorities.[29]

---

[28] For a more thorough summary of the issues, see Richard P. Nathan "General Revenue Sharing: A Glossary of Issues," *National Civic Review,* 65 (1976): 122–28.

[29] The original legislation prohibited discrimination on the basis of color, national origin, race, and sex, and the 1976 amendments added prohibitions against discriminating on the basis of age, handicaps, and religion. These provisions apply to all

A form of compromise between general revenue sharing and categorical grants is special revenue sharing or block grants. Under this system, a higher-level government shares part of its revenue with lower-level governments, but the use of funds is restricted to specified functions. State aid to education, using various formulas, is an example. State education funds come largely from general revenue. State aid for local roads is another form of special revenue sharing, with monies coming from earmarked taxes on motor fuels.

Block grants at the federal level have been proposed as a method of consolidating categorical grant programs. These categoricals are grouped together so that jurisdictions have greater flexibility within specified program areas. The application process is greatly reduced, because a jurisdiction applies for only one grant instead of several. The first such program in recent years was a grouping of diverse manpower programs under the Comprehensive Employment and Training Act (CETA) of 1973.[30]

A landmark in block grants is the Housing and Community Development Act of 1974.[31] The law mandates that 80 percent of the $8.4 billion available for the first three years is to be provided to metropolitan areas. As with general revenue sharing, community development (CD) funds are distributed by a complex set of formulas. The factors used are population, a double weighting of poverty, and housing overcrowding. A hold-harmless provision protects jurisdictions that would receive less under the law than they had been receiving. The law phases out programs for open space, public facility loans, water and sewer grants, urban renewal, model cities, and rehabilitation loans. The new funds may be used to continue these categorical projects and include such activities as clearing property, constructing public works, code enforcement in deteriorating areas, and relo-

---

activities of a recipient government unless it can provide evidence that a given activity is not being supported with revenue sharing funds. Procedures are specified for suspending payments for jurisdictions that violate these nondiscrimination provisions. Also, the amendments require public hearings on the proposed use of revenue sharing funds.

[30] Sar A. Levitan and Joyce K. Zickler, "Block Grants for Manpower Programs," *Public Administration Review,* 35 (1975): 191–95.

[31] See selected hearings and reports from U.S. House Committee on Banking, Currency and Housing and U.S. Senate Committee on Banking, Housing and Urban Affairs; Mary K. Nenno, "First Year Community Development Grant Experience: What Does it Mean?," *Journal of Housing,* 33 (1976): 171–76; Karen Kerns, "Community Development Block Grants: The First Year," *Nation's Cities,* 13 (July, 1975): 21–36.

cating persons from areas being redeveloped. Significantly, monies no longer are channeled directly to an urban renewal agency but to city hall; this is expected to bring greater coordination between the two. Unlike general revenue sharing, a city must apply for CD funds, and not only must an application be made but it must be reviewed through the complicated A-95 process discussed below.

Categorical grants, block grants, and general revenue sharing are not necessarily mutually exclusive alternatives. Each form has advantages and disadvantages. Currently, all three are in use and can be expected to continue. Debates will continue, centering largely on how much emphasis should be placed on each. Gerald Ford in his 1977 budget supported further grant consolidation and extension of the block grant approach to health care, elementary and secondary education, child nutrition, and community services.

An alternative to these forms of funding is to make various provisions in tax law at higher levels to assist governments at lower levels. By increasing the taxing powers of lower levels, the need for grants-in-aid may be reduced. For example, taxpayers may deduct most state and local taxes from gross income before computing federal tax liabilities. Included are state and local income taxes, general sales taxes, property taxes, and some other lesser taxes. For the federal government, allowing deduction of state and local taxes serves two purposes. First, it puts the federal income tax on a more uniform base across states by taking into consideration variations in the level of nonfederal taxation. The rationale is that state and local taxes provide for governmental services that are in the national interest and are compulsory for the citizen. Other individual taxpayer expenditures, while obviously necessary for life, are not normally compelled by government. Thus, a fairer basis on which to establish a national, progressive income tax is a base that excludes other governmentally forced expenditures.[32]

A second function performed by tax deductions is that of encouraging states and localities to meet their fiscal responsibilities by reducing somewhat the overall tax burden of individual citizens. State and local governments are thereby permitted to tax at a somewhat higher rate than they would be otherwise. This claimed benefit assumes that states and localities would not otherwise be able to tax at the higher rate because the burden would be too great on individual taxpayers.

---

[32] The discussion on tax credits is based largely on James A. Maxwell, *Tax Credits and Intergovernmental Fiscal Relations* (Washington: Brookings, 1962), pp. 97–106.

Tax deductibility, especially for property taxes, has been criticized by economists. The deduction of property taxes is a benefit felt largely by middle-income families. Lower-income families more often do not own homes, and higher-income families are not marginally much better off with the deduction. It is also argued that taxes on consumption items—motor fuel, liquor, cigarettes, and so forth—are not properly deductible items. These products should be regarded as ordinary consumption with the tax part of the price of consumption.

On the other side of the argument, tax deductions do provide some measure of latitude for state and local taxation. They reduce somewhat the differentials among states and among localities, and they mitigate some of the problems of tax overlapping. At least overlapping taxes may be held to a level that is not confiscatory. The strongest argument in favor of tax deductibility, however, is one of practicality. The principle is firmly entrenched, and any efforts at elimination of substantial areas of taxation from such provisions without compensating tax relief would be highly unlikely to succeed.

Tax credits potentially provide a much more substantial shift in revenue sources than do tax deductions. Tax credits allow individual taxpayers to apply taxes paid to one jurisdiction as credits against the tax liability to another jurisdiction. Given the relative fiscal capabilities of the federal, state, and local governments, tax credits are seen as a device to increase state and local revenues at the expense of federal revenues.

The federal government employs the tax credit device on only two taxes—estate or death taxes and unemployment insurance taxes. State death taxes paid can be credited up to a given percentage against the liability for federal estate taxes. Thus, in any state without a death or estate tax, the tax will be collected exclusively by the federal government. With a death tax, most of the revenues will go to the state with only a small increase in the taxpayer's total liability. The estate tax credit was adopted in 1924, partly in response to action by Florida to make a death tax unconstitutional in the state. The effect of Florida's action was to make the state a much more attractive place for wealthy persons to retire. Other states feared they would then have to follow suit in order to protect themselves. To prevent this negative form of tax competition, the estate tax credit in effect permitted states to retain their death taxes with little fear of loss of taxpayers to Florida, at least on the death tax score.

The federal unemployment insurance tax is somewhat more directive in its effects. A uniform federal tax on employer payrolls in all states is imposed. If a state has a satisfactory unemployment insurance law of its own—all states do—90 percent of the federal tax stays in the state. The remaining 10 percent can also be distributed among the states for administrative costs at the discretion of the federal government. This distribution of the remaining 10 percent is dependent upon state administrative procedures. The tax burden to the individual is the same wherever the tax revenues eventually go. Thus, it was clearly to the advantage of each state to pass unemployment insurance taxes and all did.

Tax credits of a more general nature are proposed as one possible solution to the revenue needs of states and localities. Depending upon how much credit is allowed, the taxpayer burden is not substantially increased by the adoption of or increase in a state or local tax. The basic effect is a redistribution of revenue from federal to lower levels. As was seen in the above two examples, tax credits have positive effects on intergovernmental tax competition. A tax credit on income taxes could encourage those states without income taxes to adopt them because the taxpayer would be less affected. However, if the tax credit is uniform regardless of income, it would benefit the wealthier states even more than the poorer ones. A graduated tax credit, where the maximum credit allowed decreases as the taxpayer's income increases, would solve that problem by having an equalizing effect because the credits would be concentrated at the lower end of the income bracket.

In addition to tax credits, there are several other intergovernmental devices that have been proposed and used. One concern has been that jurisdictions have inadequate information about grant programs. In response, the federal government publishes the *Catalog of Federal Domestic Assistance;* the catalog, which gives capsule descriptions of grant programs, is useful for the local government that is attempting to determine whether it might be able to secure federal funding for a project being contemplated. In the same vein, the Department of Agriculture has developed the Federal Assistance Program Retrieval System, a computerized system to provide information on the availability of funding.[33] Another information device is controlled by Treasury Circular 1082 or formerly OMB Circular A-98. TC 1082, issued to comply with the Intergovernmental Cooperation Act of 1968, provides a mechanism for federal agencies to report grants-in-aid to jurisdictions to their respective state government. The assumption is

---

[33] Spencer B. Child, "Now, A Way to Get at Those Grants and Loans," *Government Executive,* 8 (March, 1976): 26—30.

that the information provided will encourage better planning and coordination on the state level. Federal agencies, however, have had difficulty in complying with the circular. A study of California showed that it received reports on only two-thirds of the grants coming into the state and many of the reports did not supply all of the information that is required by the circular.[34] Another information type circular, A-85, requires federal agencies to consult with state and local governments in developing federal rules and regulations.

One of the most important budget circulars is A-95.[35] It is an outgrowth of the Intergovernmental Cooperation Act and requires a review and comment process on development type projects. The community development block grants must go through this process. The purpose is to provide greater coordination of projects and to reduce the extent of duplicating efforts within a given geographic area. A-95 provides for the establishment of three types of clearinghouses—state, area-wide or regional, and metropolitan. Metropolitan planning agencies or councils of governments are often designated as clearinghouses. The state budget office is sometimes designated as the state clearinghouse.

A-95 provides for several steps in review. A city planning to apply for a community development grant must notify the area-wide, metropolitan, and state clearinghouses of its intentions, describing the general program and other factors such as expected environmental impact. These clearinghouses may comment, perhaps objecting on the basis of environmental impact, duplication, or inappropriate use of land and energy. The next step is for the city to prepare a formal proposal, after which each clearinghouse has 30 days to review and comment. The proposal is distributed among interested parties; for example, a state budget office acting as a clearinghouse will distribute the proposal to the state departments or agencies for transportation, community affairs, and human relations. The city then modifies its proposal and sends it to the appropriate regional office of HUD. Assuming approval, the proposal is forwarded to Washington for final action.

The purpose behind A-95 can hardly be faulted, but the process employed is often criticized. The review and comment process offers the

---

[34] General Accounting Office, *States Need, But Are Not Getting Full Information on Federal Finance Assistance Received* (Washington: U.S. Government Printing Office, 1975), pp. 16–18.

[35] Advisory Commission on Intergovernmental Relations, *Regional Decision Making: New Strategies for Substate Districts,* Vol I (Washington: U.S. Government Printing Office, 1973), pp. 139–65.

potential for eliminating waste in the use of federal funds; a local jurisdiction is forced to consider its contemplated project in the context of a system larger than its own political boundaries. On the negative side, A-95 produces delays that frustrate mayors, their budget offices, and community development departments. For all of the time devoted to A-95, projects in many cases are implemented much as originally intended, over perhaps the objections of various clearinghouses.

In addition to the A-95 clearinghouses, there are numerous other types of coordinating agencies.[36] Units similar to the clearinghouse's have been established in accord with the National Health Planning Resources Development Act of 1974. Regional Health Systems Agencies and comparable state units review health project proposals. Also, state governments have developed standard regions and sought to coordinate the various programs of state departments through regional offices. The counterparts of these state offices at the federal level are the 10 Federal Regional Councils (FRC). These FRCs, consisting of representatives from federal domestic agencies, are intended to bring greater coordination among federal programs.[37] Councils of governments, consisting of local government representatives of a region, have been formed to provide forums for discussing regional problems and in some cases for delivering services. One experiment now underway is to link all three levels of government. The Pennsylvania Intergovernmental Council, perhaps the first of its type, consists of the chairman of the FRC, state legislative and executive representatives, and representatives from various local government associations such as the League of Cities.

Providing forums for discussion should be distinguished from action. Discussion and debates may produce no action, no coordination of services. On the other hand, these forums can serve as vehicles for lobbying efforts. Because much of the game of intergovernmental relations is to get some higher level of government to provide funding, it is possible that a united front can help win the game.[38] Available evidence suggests that the

---

[36] For example, see Victor A. Capoccia, "Chief Executive Review and Comment: A Preview of New Federalism in Rochester, New York," *Public Administration Review,* 34 (1974): 462–70.

[37] Martha Derthick with Gary Bombardier, *Between State and Nation: Regional Organizations of the United States* (Washington: Brookings, 1974), pp. 157–81.

[38] Some of the concerns here have been reduced to somewhat humorous "laws." "The level of government most appropriate to finance any given governmental program is a level other than that by whom one is presently employed." "The level of government most appropriate to deal with a given problem is that level by which one is presently employed." David J. Kennedy, "The Law of Appropriateness: An

OMB and its predecessor BOB (Bureau of the Budget) have been con-cerned that intergovernmental coordinating bodies not serve as lobbying agents, lobbying both with Congress and agencies. OMB has shown interest in re-establishing its own regional offices to act in part as a watchdog over federal agencies as they relate to state and local governments.[39]

Federal-state, interstate, and interlocal arrangements have also been developed for the provision of services as distinguished from forums for discussion. The Delaware River Basin Commission, established in 1961, was the first such organization to include federal as well as state represen-tation. One of the most successful interstate organizations is the New York Port Authority, established in 1921 by New York and New Jersey. Obtaining its funding through revenue bonds paid for by user fees, the Authority operates terminals, bridges, tunnels, and the World Trade Center.

At the local level, there are numerous types of cooperative arrange-ments. Some counties provide certain services such as water and sewage treatment on a contract basis for municipalities within their jurisdiction. This may be at the choice of the municipalities, as in the case of the Lakewood Plan whereby communities can contract with Los Angeles County for virtually all city services, or at the insistence of state govern-ments, which may require city-county cooperation for services such as police and fire protection. A survey of municipalities found that 61 percent had formal and informal agreements for providing services on an intergovernmental basis; such agreements are more common in larger cities and among cities in the West.[40] As some cities and their suburbs have grown into complex mazes of jurisdictions, there have been attempts at consolidation into metropolitan governments. Miami-Dade County, Florida; Nashville-Davidson County, Tennessee; and Indianapolis, Indiana are three examples.

With the increasing emphasis upon block grants and general revenue

---

Approach to a General Theory of Intergovernmental Relations," *Public Administra-tion Review,* 32 (1972): 135 and 138.

[39] See Derthick with Bombardier, *Between State and Nation;* Donald H. Haider, *When Governments Come to Washington: Governors, Mayors, and Intergovernmental Lobbying* (New York: Free Press, 1974); Gary Bombardier, "The Managerial Func-tion of OMB: Intergovernmental Relations as a Test Case," *Public Policy,* 23 (1975): 317–54.

[40] Joseph F. Zimmerman, "Meeting Service Needs Through Intergovernmental Agreements," *Muncipal Year Book, 1973* (Washington: International City Manage-ment Association, 1973), pp. 79–88.

sharing, greater attention has been focused upon the abilities of state and local governments to manage themselves. The granting of decision-making power over the use of federal funds—sometimes called "devolution"—has led to concerns for improving management capabilities at these levels. One proposal advocated in the original debate over GRS was that state and local governments would be required to submit plans to modernize and streamline their governmental structures in order to qualify for the funds.[41] More recently, the OMB-sponsored Study Committee on Policy Management Assistance recommended federal efforts to improve management practices at the state and local levels.[42]

A few words of skepticism are warranted here. Greater coordination of governmental programs, while a presumed virtue, is not necessarily going to provide answers to all governmental problems. The movement toward revenue sharing, both general and special, has been partially a result of federal categorical programs being ineffective or at least perceived as ineffective. One hope was that state and local officials, if freed from many of the strings of categorical aid, could produce desired results. Nevertheless, the prospects for finding the solutions for major problems in the immediate future are not good. Improving management capabilities may help, but one should not jump to any conclusion that Washington has superior management capabilities that if only transferred to the state and local levels will produce quick results. There is no readily available serum for curing the ills of intergovernmental relations and ineffective services.

A final suggestion for relieving both states and localities of some of their financial burdens involves shifting total responsibility for major functions to a higher level of government.[43] Most frequently advanced are proposals that education be taken over entirely by the states and welfare by the federal government. Such proposals provide an obvious form of financial relief, especially for local jurisdictions. Their principal weakness, however, is that they still do not face squarely the problem of interarea

---

[41] Henry S. Reuss, *Revenue-Sharing: Crutch or Catalyst for State and Local Governments?* (New York: Praeger, 1970).

[42] Study Committee on Policy Management Assistance, *Strengthening Public Management in the Intergovernmental System* and Ross Clayton, et al., eds., "Policy Management Assistance: A Developing Dialogue," *Public Administration Review* (1976): 693–818.

[43] See Advisory Commission on Intergovernmental Relations, *Pragmatic Federalism: The Reassignment of Functional Responsibility* (Washington: U.S. Government Printing Office, 1976).

fiscal differences and whether it should be national policy to eliminate those differences.

SUMMARY

Fundamental problems exist over how to structure intergovernmental relations. Functional integration results in picket-fence arrangements that may deter geographic integration. Fiscal capacities differ among and within levels of government, so that the government which perhaps should provide services often lacks the necessary funding capability. Failure to provide services results in externality problems, where one jurisdiction imposes burdens on other jurisdictions or benefits from the actions of other jurisdictions without sharing in the costs.

Both direct spending and grants-in-aid are important for intergovernmental relations. Decisions by federal and state agencies on the location and expansion of capital facilities affect the economic viability of local jurisdictions. Despite more extensive attention often being devoted to federal aid programs, state aid to local government is larger. Some states provide much of their local governments' revenue while others provide little, a point that should be stressed to avoid unjustified generalizations. Aid to education constitutes the largest portion of state aid, with monies typically allocated on a formula basis. Federal aid is concentrated in the areas of education, income security, health, transportation, and general revenue sharing.

Intergovernmental grants range from categoricals to block grants to general revenue sharing, all of which have advantages and disadvantages. Among the complaints against categorical grants are that they deter planning and coordination, skew local priorities, needlessly waste time in proposal preparation, and deny needed monies to many jurisdictions. On the positive side, the categoricals are said to force planning in the preparation of proposals and to allow for screening out inadequately conceived projects. GRS, on the other hand, is criticized as allowing governments to waste money, giving funds to many undeserving jurisdictions, providing funds for public safety when social services are needed, and allowing for continued discrimination against minorities. On the positive side, general revenue sharing supports local priorities and provides funds to jurisdictions that do not have staff available to apply for categorical grants. Block grants, a cross between categoricals and GRS, have the advantages and disadvantages of both. All three types can be expected to be used in the foreseeable future.

In addition to grant programs, numerous other devices are employed. These include tax credits, vehicles for furthering information about grants such as TC 1082, processes of review and comment like A-95, and coordinating bodies such as Federal Regional Councils and councils of governments. Also, mechanisms have developed for providing services on an intergovernmental basis such as with the New York Port Authority or the Lakewood Plan in California. Whatever the process or structure proposed for improving intergovernmental finance and relations, it should be understood that the existing problems defy solution and will persist.

13

GOVERNMENT AND THE ECONOMY

For good or for bad, government finance impinges greatly upon the economy. Government is large, and the sheer bulk of governmental expenditures alone necessarily affects the economy. In Chapter 2 we outlined the extent to which government is involved in the private sector, emphasizing that the distinction between private and public is often difficult to discern. Both the absolute size of expenditures and the dependence of some private industries upon government expenditures result in some form of an economic policy, even if such a policy is not explicit.

Today government, particularly the federal government, is legally responsible for setting explicit policies that will provide for a "healthy" economy. Adam Smith's laissez faire theory of the invisible hand has been largely discarded in favor of governmental intervention.[1] Smith contended that because a competitive market operates as if an invisible hand were controlling the economy, virtually no need exists for governmental involvement.

This chapter explores the problems associated with the contemporary approach of utilizing government to control the economy. First, the objectives of economic policy are discussed. Second, problems associated with forecasting future economic conditions are explained. Third, the roles of fiscal and monetary policy are reviewed. Fourth, some special effects of economic policy are considered.

---

[1] Adam Smith, *The Wealth of Nations* (New York: The Modern Library, 1937).

313

OBJECTIVES OF ECONOMIC POLICY

Economic policy can be distinguished from two other sets of policies—policies resulting in the provision of goods and services and policies affecting the distribution of income and wealth. Budget systems are devised for reaching decisions about what goods and services are to be provided to the citizenry; efforts to develop program budgeting systems particularly emphasize the need for more rational approaches to making decisions about services. Income policies are intended to alter the distribution of income from what otherwise would be the case were the private sector left uncontrolled; specific policies are directed toward increasing the incomes of the very old, the very poor, and the ill and disabled. Although economic policy to some extent focuses upon income distribution, the main concern is with the aggregate performance of the economy.[2]

The four basic objectives of economic policy are: 1) equilibrium in the international balance of payments, 2) full employment, 3) economic growth, and 4) price stability.[3] The first objective, the international balance of payments, refers to the value of goods and services, grants, and financial assets and liabilities flowing into and out of the United States. While international finance lies beyond the bounds of this book, it should be noted that the payments objective involves issues over international trade, the gold flow, American tourist and U.S. defense expenditures abroad, and foreign aid.

The other three objectives are particularly related to the domestic economy, though they have international implications as well. The first two, full employment and economic growth, are integrally related. Generally, as employment increases, so will production; a decline in employment will result in a decline in production. The main exception to this rule is that the introduction of new technologies can result in higher production, with either no increase in employment or possibly a decrease in employment.

The political system has a varying capacity to accept unemployment. A nationwide unemployment rate of 7 or 8 percent is clearly unacceptable by current standards and results in demands for governmental interven-

---

[2] Richard A. Musgrave and Peggy B. Musgrave, *Public Finance In Theory and Practice*, 2nd ed. (New York: McGraw-Hill, 1976), pp. 6–7.

[3] See *Fiscal and Monetary Policies for Steady Economic Growth* (New York: Committee for Economic Development, 1969), pp. 23–35, and Musgrave and Musgrave, *Public Finance*, pp. 517–610.

tion, but as the rate approaches 4 percent or less, acceptance increases. The extent to which society tolerates unemployment is partially dependent upon who is unemployed. Though there may be a tendency to accept high unemployment among low-skilled and minority-group workers, tolerance for unemployment may quickly dissipate when it reaches middle-income, white-collar workers. Also, the tolerance level may vary over time. When employment has been high for several months or years, any decline may be interpreted as evidence of a faltering economy. In such cases, 5 percent unemployment may be unacceptable. On the other hand, when unemployment has been high and then is reduced to 5 percent, this level may be viewed quite favorably and may even diminish demands for further governmental intervention to stimulate the economy. Full employment has been defined by the Council of Economic Advisers (CEA) as 4 percent unemployment or less. In the following discussion, high employment, full employment, or low employment refer to the same set of economic conditions.

Consensus is nonexistent as to what is the appropriate rate of growth, and there are even some questions about the appropriateness of economic growth as a policy objective. While probably most persons will agree that growth is preferable to economic stagnation or decline, there is increasing concern with the consequences of economic growth. According to Ezra J. Mishan, the costs of development include:

> the post-war "development" blight, the erosion of the countryside, the "uglification" of coastal towns, the pollution of the air and of rivers with chemical wastes, the accumulation of thick oils on our coastal waters, the sewage poisoning our beaches, the destruction of wild life by indiscriminate use of pesticides, the change-over from animal farming to animal factories, and, visible to all who have eyes to see, a rich heritage of natural beauty being wantonly and systematically destroyed—a heritage that cannot be restored in our lifetimes.[4]

Environmentalists have been successful in arousing concerns about the costs of industrial development, and some economists have raised questions about the long-term limits to growth.[5] Existing public policy does not seem to reflect these concerns by placing limits on growth. Rather,

---

[4] Erza J. Mishan, *The Costs of Economic Growth* (New York: Praeger, 1967), pp. 6–7.

[5] Robert Heilbronner, *An Inquiry Into the Human Prospect* (New York: Norton, 1974); Edward F. Renshaw, *The End of Progress: Adjusting to a No-Growth Economy* (North Scituate, Mass.: Duxbury, 1976).

present policies are designed to achieve growth while making some concessions to protecting and improving the environment. Some of the implications for public budgeting of possible no-growth economies are discussed
in the concluding chapter.

The American economy has experienced considerable fluctuation in
growth rates in the last few decades, ranging from a high of 16.1 percent in
1940–41 to minus 12.0 percent in 1945–46. During the 1960s, the range
was from 1.9 percent in 1960–61 to 6.5 percent in 1965–66; 1972–73
marked a high for the 1970s of 5.9 percent, which plunged the following
year to minus 2.2 percent.[6]

Price stability is the fourth objective, and as with the others, considerable debate prevails over the extent to which instability is tolerable,
assuming that absolute price stability is impossible to achieve. During the
Great Depression unemployment was the primary focus of attention, but
since that time prices have come to be of at least equal concern. Particularly, the problem has been one of avoiding or limiting inflation, a
condition in which the prices for goods and services increase without any
improvement in the quality of these products. Rising prices can damage
the nation's competitive position in the international economy and is
economically disastrous for individuals living on fixed incomes. Inflation
was the main economic problem throughout the latter half of the 1960s,
during the massive military campaign in Southeast Asia, and remained a
prominent concern in the 1970s. As the Committee for Economic Development has observed, an annual increase of only 3 percent would double
the price level in 23 years.

During the 1960s, an important shift occurred in the approach of
economic theory toward the pursuit of these objectives. Earlier, economic
policy was regarded as mainly corrective, responsible for leaning against
the prevailing winds of business cycles. A cycle is said to have four phases
of varying lengths: expansion, peak, contraction, and trough.[7] When the
economy was contracting or declining, government action was needed to
stimulate growth. During expansionary periods, safeguards would be taken
to avoid an overheated situation that would yield inflation.

The school of "new economics," led by former CEA chairmen Walter
W. Heller and Arthur M. Okun, as well as others, has advocated a more
positive approach to economic policy. The primary focus of this school is

---

[6] Bureau of the Census, *Statistical Abstract of the United States: 1975* (Washington: U.S. Government Printing Office, 1975), p. 382.

[7] For a thorough discussion of cycles, see the current edition of Paul A. Samuel-
son, *Economics: An Introductory Analysis* (New York: McGraw-Hill).

upon achieving the potential of the economy. Okun has written, "Today few research economists regard the business cycle as a particularly useful organizing framework for the overall analysis of current economic activity.[8] In Heller's terms, the new orientation is "propulsive": economic policy is used to propel the economy into achieving its potential growth.[9]

This growth policy brings into question the relationship between employment and price levels. Figure 14 provides some historical perspective by comparing unemployment with consumer prices from 1950 to 1975. This illustrates through the mid-1960s the traditional assumption that rising employment leads to price increases and declining employment leads to price decreases. For example, from 1950 to 1955 there was a steady drop in prices but a rise, with some fluctuation, in unemployment. More troubling, however, is the period since the mid-1960s, where rising unemployment was coupled with rising prices. The recession of the 1970s, the worst since World War II, did not result in falling prices. The new pattern suggests that full employment will produce price increases but less than full employment will not necessarily stabilize or reduce prices.

A major issue, then, is how much inflation will accompany a full employment economy. During the 1950s and 1960s, it was thought that a 3 percent inflation rate probably was necessary in order to reduce unemployment to 4 percent. More recently, analysis has indicated that the tradeoff point may be a 5 percent unemployment rate for 3 percent inflation.[10] The tradeoff between employment and prices was directly confronted in deliberations over the proposed Humphrey-Hawkins legislation. Originally introduced in Congress in 1975, the bill would guarantee work to every "able and willing" adult and would commit the government to a policy of 3 percent unemployment. The proposal was criticized on numerous grounds, including that it would produce intolerable rates of inflation; others objected to the provision for creating public jobs when private jobs were unavailable.[11]

---

[8] Arthur M. Okun, *The Political Economy of Prosperity* (New York: Norton, 1970), p. 33.

[9] Walter W. Heller, *New Dimensions of Political Economy* (New York: Norton, 1967), p. 62. The "new economics" discussed here should not be confused with the "Nixon new economics" of the early 1970s. The latter, as discussed later in this chapter, involved a series of wage and price controls that is not part of the "new economics."

[10] Arthur M. Okun and George L. Perry, eds., *Brookings Papers on Economic Activity 1:1971* (Washington: Brookings, 1971).

[11] The bill (HR 50 and S 50) was introduced by Senator Hubert H. Humphrey (D, Minn.) and Representative Augustus F. Hawkins (D, Cal.).

Figure 14. Percentage change in consumer price index and unemployment rate, 1950–1975. Source: *Economic Report of the President* (Washington: U.S. Government Printing Office, 1976), pp. 199 and 224.

PROBLEMS OF FORECASTING

If government is to achieve its economic policy objectives, sensitive and valid measures are needed to predict the direction of the economy. Advance warning of future events is essential in order to devise strategies to prevent undesired consequences. Because, as we will see, decision making for economic policy often is a slow process, early warning is needed in order to allow sufficient time for the political system to respond. To meet this need for data, several indexes or barometers have been developed; these can be classified roughly as lagging, coincident, and leading. Leading indicators presumably show in advance what the economy will do, whereas lagging indicators report what has already occurred. More than 50 of these are in use, and they are compiled by many different sources.[12]

Coincident indicators, those that report what the economy is doing now, are the ones that most commonly reach the public's attention; gross national product (GNP) is one of the most important. GNP, a measure of the goods and services produced by the nation, is the aggregate of personal consumption expenditures, gross private domestic investment, net exports of goods and services, and government purchases of goods and services. Because production can remain constant while prices rise or fall, GNP must be adjusted when comparisons are made across years. For instance, the unadjusted GNP for 1974 was $1,406.9 billion; in 1972 dollars, the figure translates to $1,210.7 billion.

Net national product (NNP) and national income (NI) are derivatives of GNP. NNP, derived by eliminating depreciation from gross investment, excludes those capital investments that are consumed in the production process. The main difference between NNP and national income is that the latter excludes indirect business taxes. These taxes, such as excise taxes on gasoline, are "hidden" in the prices of products sold. NI, unlike GNP, is based upon the costs of production or the earnings paid by businesses. These earnings are compensation of employees, proprietors' income, rental income of persons, corporate profits and inventory valuation adjustment, and net interest. Table 18 summarizes the relationships among GNP, NNP, and NI from 1950 through 1975.[13]

Price indices are also important measures that tend to be coincident with business trends. Wholesale prices are considered an earlier warning device than consumer prices. An increase in wholesale prices one month is likely to result in consumer price increases the following month. The wholesale index covers about 2,600 commodities in 17 product categories.

---

[12] For discussions of forecasting, see: Edward J. Chambers, *Economic Fluctuations and Forecasting* (Englewood Cliffs, N.J.: Prentice-Hall, 1961); John Maurice Clark, *Strategic Factors in Business Cycles* (New York: National Bureau of Economic Research, 1935); Bert G. Hickman, ed., *Econometric Models of Cyclical Behavior*, 2 vols. (New York: Columbia University Press, 1972).

[13] See Charles L. Schultze, *National Income Analysis*, 2nd ed. (Englewood Cliffs, N.J.: Prentice-Hall, 1967). For problems of the private sector attempting to forecast both the state of the economy and the effects of government policy, see Robert L. McLaughlin, "A New Five-Phase Economic Forecasting System " *Business Economics*, 10 (September, 1975): pp. 49–60.

TABLE 18
Relation of Gross National Product, Net National Product, and National Income, 1950–1975 (in Billions of Dollars)

	Item	1950	1955	1960	1965	1970	1975[a]
	Personal consumption expenditures	192.0	253.7	324.9	430.2	618.8	963.2
	Gross private domestic investment	53.8	68.4	76.4	112.0	140.8	183.3
	Net exports of goods and services	1.9	2.2	4.4	7.6	3.9	21.5
	Government purchases of goods and services	38.5	75.0	100.3	138.4	218.9	330.9
Equals:	*Gross national product*	286.2	399.3	506.0	688.1	982.4	1499.0
Less:	Capital consumption allowances	23.9	35.3	47.7	57.5	90.8	152.5
Equals:	*Net national product*	262.3	364.0	458.3	630.6	891.6	1346.4
Less:	Indirect business tax and nontax liability	23.4	32.2	45.4	62.6	94.0	137.2
	Business transfer payments	0.8	1.2	2.0	2.8	4.0	6.3
	Statistical discrepancy	2.0	2.5	-0.7	0.9	-2.1	-4.6
Plus:	Net subsidies of government enterprises	0.1	0.0	0.4	1.6	2.7	1.9
Equals:	*National income*	236.2	328.0	412.0	566.0	798.4	1209.5

[a]Preliminary.

Source: *Economic Report of the President* (Washington: U.S. Government Printing Office, 1976), pp. 171 and 183.

The consumer index is for goods and services paid by urban wage earners, clerical families, and single persons living alone; approximately 400 goods and services are covered.

Unemployment constitutes another key index. In simple terms, this is a percentage measure of the persons within the labor force who are not employed. For classification purposes, only persons 16 and older are considered part of the labor market. Serious problems of interpretation are associated with using the unemployment rate in that the sizes of both the employed and unemployed groups can vary from month to month as the size of the labor force fluctuates. As jobs become plentiful, persons previously not in the labor force may seek jobs; when jobs become scarce, these same people become discouraged, fail to seek jobs, and drop out of the labor market. Given that the total number of persons in the work force—employed and unemployed—varies from month to month, statistical aberrations are possible. For example, a decrease in the unemployment rate may not signal economic recovery, because the decrease can be the result of individuals dropping out of the labor market while the number employed remains constant or even declines.

One of the best indicators of business trends is the Industrial Production Index prepared by the Federal Reserve System. As its title suggests, the index covers industry—namely manufacturing, mining, and electric and gas utility output. Manufacturers of both durable and nondurable goods are included. (Durables are products such as machinery and transportation equipment; nondurables include textiles, paper products, chemicals, and rubber and plastic goods.) The durable portion of manufacturing is watched closely, particularly key industries such as steel. Steel sales reflect future intentions of manufacturing concerns. Falling sales may indicate lack of confidence in the economy and attempts on the part of firms to avoid stockpiling materials that will not be needed by a declining economy.

Though the above measures—GNP, price indices, unemployment, and industrial production—are useful measures of the economy, they state what is or what was rather than what will be, and these do not provide the lead time necessary for devising intervention strategies. The forecaster, as a result, turns to the leading indicators. The National Bureau of Economic Research (NBER), a nonprofit group, has identified more than 30 leading indicators, but only a few will be discussed here.

In the Bureau's view, the most important leading indicator is the average workweek of production workers in manufacturing. The argument is that the workweek indicates early changes in the economy sooner than the unemployment rate does. As the economy begins to decline, labor costs are curtailed, but this is done by contracting the workweek and by curtailing overtime rather than by laying off workers. Not until the decline is fully at hand are significant cuts made in the number of persons employed. By using this device, a firm is able to retain its staff in the short run and thereby maintain its capability to increase production if the decline is of short duration.[14]

Another sensitive employment measure is the average weekly initial claims for unemployment insurance. This indicator reflects whether the claims for insurance are increasing or decreasing from week to week. The indicator thereby senses the extent to which layoffs are increasing or decreasing.

Private, nonfarm housing starts constitute another leading indicator. A decline in the number of starts can signal future economic decline. Housing is thought to be sensitive in that it reflects the willingness of financial institutions and builders to invest dollars in an expensive commodity for which there is no buyer at the time construction begins.

Transactions on the nation's stock markets also are used as forecasting instruments. The New York Stock Exchange is the one most carefully watched. Dow-Jones surveys transactions on representative stocks of 30 industrial firms, 20 transportation, 15 utilities, and 65 general stocks. Two other important indices are those of the exchange itself and the Standard and Poor's Index, which NBER considers an important leading indicator.

It should be stressed that such stock quotations are highly volatile and that not all up-and-down swings have direct bearing upon the economy. For example, speculative actions by investors can boost stock prices beyond any "sensible" prices for stocks in terms of dividends being paid to investors. A major speech by the President or the release of new reports on consumer or wholesale prices can also cause major changes in the stock market. Despite these difficulties, Louis H. Bean has suggested that stock prices, and particularly industrial stocks, constitute the best leading indicator. The lead time provided is between 6 and 12 months. According to Bean, then, a downward trend in industrial stocks will be followed 6 to 12 months later by a slump in industry.[15]

---

[14] Stanley Bober, *The Economics of Cycles and Growth* (New York: Wiley, 1968), pp. 51–54.

[15] Louis H. Bean, *The Art of Forecasting* (New York: Random House, 1969), pp. 17–19.

A variety of combined indices exist for increasing the sensitivity of measuring economic changes and trends. The Bureau of Economic Analysis of the U.S. Commerce Department publishes a monthly series of indices.[16] These composites combine several individual indices, such as the composite of 12 leading indicators. Diffusion indices are another form of combined measures. A diffusion index measures the percentage of components of an index that are moving upward. In the case of the Dow-Jones averages, if industrials, transportation, and utilities increase in price but general stocks decrease, the diffusion index is 75 percent. This type of measure reflects the extent to which all components are moving in the same direction. Another example of a diffusion index is that prepared by Dun and Bradstreet for new orders in manufacturing industries.

Two other techniques for describing and forecasting the state of the economy are econometric models and attitudinal surveys. There are numerous econometric models utilizing combinations of the various economic indicators that have been described. Two of the best known models are the ones developed by the Brookings Institution in cooperation with the Social Science Research Council and the cooperative model of the Federal Reserve Board, the Massachusetts Institute of Technology, and the University of Pennsylvania.[17] Surveys of consumer intentions and anticipated business actions provide more information about the psychological components of the economy's behavior. A limitation of both formal models and attitudinal surveys, however, is that they are often more useful for long-term economic analyses than for short-term policy assessments.

Despite the variety of indicators and models available, forecasting remains a risky enterprise. Most forecasters failed to detect the mid-1970s recession and once the recession was real, most failed to anticipate its severity.[18] Part of the problem was that some indicators behaved contrary to normal expectations. For example, real GNP fell through 1974–75 and industrial production held up through most of 1974, while the expected pattern was for these two indicators to move together. The composite index of 12 leading indicators, which usually begins to decline six months before an economic downturn, continued to rise until mid-1974. Faced

---

[16] Bureau of Economic Analysis, *Business Conditions Digest* (Washington: U.S. Government Printing Office, issued monthly).

[17] See John F. Due and Ann F. Friedlaender, *Government Finance: Economics of the Public Sector*, 5th ed. (Homewood, Ill.: Irwin, 1973), pp. 588–96.

[18] "Why Economists Didn't Foresee the Recession," *Business Week* (July 14, 1975): pp. 104–6.

with conflicting trends, most forecasters chose more optimistic trends and considered the GNP decline to be a false trend. In retrospect, analysts did not realize the extent to which the continued rise in industrial production was resulting in overstocked inventories that later would lead to high unemployment rates.

Given the conflicting interpretations possible even with sound information, economic forecasters as well as political leaders interpret the data from their own perspectives. The technical problems involved are great, but inevitably forecasting becomes less a technical problem and more of a political one. The President and his staff may attempt to focus attention upon one indicator that shows signs of progress, for example, a decline in unemployment, while discounting less encouraging signs such as an increase in wholesale prices or downward trends in the stock market. The available data are subject to such a wide variety of interpretation that at times different spokesmen within the federal government may offer conflicting views about future economic prospects.

TOOLS AVAILABLE TO AFFECT THE ECONOMY

Governmental actions used to regulate the economy can be either discretionary or automatic. When discretionary action is taken, some policy making has occurred that results in decisions to intervene or not to intervene in the economy. The automatic or built-in features, on the other hand, require no action on the part of decision makers.[19]

The automatic stabilizers are countercyclical in that they tend to lean against prevailing trends, combating both expansionary and contractionary periods. To the extent that the stabilizers are effective in controlling undesired fluctuations in the economy, the need for discretionary governmental intervention is limited. Nongovernmental stabilizers include both corporate and personal savings. Recessions are resisted by individuals and corporations who utilize savings to maintain established levels of activities; conversely, expansionary trends are resisted. As income rises, greater proportions of income are placed in savings rather than being used for consumption.

In addition to these private stabilizers there are several automatic governmental activities that are countercyclical. The graduated income tax is one important example. During a contractionary period, income falls

---

[19] E. Cary Brown, "The Policy Acceptance in the United States of Reliance on Automatic Fiscal Stabilizers," *Journal of Finance*, 14 (1959): pp. 40–51, and Musgrave and Musgrave, *Public Finance*, pp. 557–59.

and so does the effective tax rate. As income declines, government takes a smaller percentage in taxes, and therefore individuals have larger shares of their gross incomes available for consumption. Unemployment compensation, welfare payments, and farm subsidies are other instances in which purchasing power is provided to individuals. The increased importance of these income supplements as countercyclical forces can be seen by contrasting the late 1950s recession with that of the mid-1970s. In the 1950s real per capita disposable income dropped by 2 percent when real per capita output dropped. However, disposable income did not fall in 1975 despite a decline in output.[20]

Economic observers generally concur that the automatic stabilizers, while useful, are insufficient tools for regulating the economy. It is at this point, then, that government is expected to utilize discretionary powers. The range of potential actions available to government is great. At one end of the spectrum are a host of activities that are variously labeled "jawboning," "moral suasion," or "voluntary controls." The intent of government officials is to persuade—directly or indirectly—business and labor leaders to act in the interest of the national economy. In recent decades, these tools have been used mainly as means of avoiding spiraling wages and prices, though these forms of persuasion can be used to combat recessions as well.

The concept of voluntary wage and price controls was cautiously endorsed in the 1958 *Economic Report of the President,* but the 1962 report is commonly cited as the turning point in formally recognizing this function. Beginning in January 1962, the Council of Economic Advisers issued specific percentage "guideposts" for wage and price increases. These guideposts were used during the Kennedy Administration to bring pressure upon negotiations between major labor unions and industry. The Kennedy Administration was also known for its use of direct pressure in 1962 to force the U.S. Steel Corporation to roll back announced price increases. The numeric guideposts, however, were abandoned in 1967. During the Johnson Administration, the President's famous "treatment" was used privately with labor and industry officials to persuade against wage and price increases. The early Nixon Administration used "inflation alerts" and some jawboning for the same purposes. President Gerald Ford's WIN (Whip Inflation Now) program was an attempt to enlist every citizen in a voluntary effort to fight inflation.

---

[20] *Economic Report of the President* (Washington: U.S. Government Printing Office, 1976), p. 81.

Efforts like these undoubtedly have some effect, but jawboning and inflation alerts cannot be expected to reverse major trends, particularly inflationary pressures. When inflation is an obvious reality, it is difficult to persuade unions not to seek higher wages. The same holds true for industry leaders vis-à-vis the pricing of goods.

As a consequence, growing interest in some form of direct wage and price controls has been evident. August 15, 1971, marked a turning point in economic policy. On that date President Richard Nixon made public a major package of changes intended to bolster a sagging economy and curtail inflation. One of the main features of that package was a 90-day freeze on prices, rents, wages, and salaries as authorized by the Economic Stabilization Act of 1970. Phase I, the first three months following the August announcement, also included a temporary surcharge on dutiable imports, postponement of a scheduled federal pay increase, a 5 percent reduction in federal employment, repeal of the 7 percent excise tax on automobiles, and a 10 percent tax credit for new investments in business.

Phase II, announced in October 1971, attempted to soften the rigid freeze, while providing sufficient mechanisms to stimulate the economy and restrict the rate of inflation. The administrative apparatus put into effect involved numerous commissions, boards, and committees, but four were assigned primary responsibility for this new departure in economic policy. At the top of the hierarchy was the Cost of Living Council (CLC); created during Phase I, it was given the duty of setting broad policy. The CLC was chaired by the Secretary of the Treasury and included as members the Director of the Office of Management and Budget; the Chairman of the Council of Economic Advisers; the Secretaries of Agriculture, Commerce, and Labor; the Special Assistant to the President for Consumer Affairs; and in an advisory capacity, the Chairman of the Board of Governors of the Federal Reserve System. Second, the seven-member Price Commission was created to supervise price increases. Third, the Pay Board was established to oversee wage increases; it consisted of five members each from labor, business, and the general public. Fourth, the Internal Revenue Service, through its Stabilization Office, was assigned the responsibility of interpreting policy in specific cases and enforcing wage and price guidelines throughout the country.[21]

The controls imposed in Phases I and II have been seen as a watershed in economic policy, placing the federal government in direct control of the

---

[21] See *Economic Report of the President* (Washington: U.S. Government Printing Office, 1972).

economy, as distinguished from the more indirect methods utilized in fiscal and monetary policy. As would be expected, the new approach had numerous problems. One of these was whether it was possible to regulate the economy without a sizable staff responsible for enforcement. The Nixon Administration relied heavily upon existing personnel in the Internal Revenue Service, thereby diverting staff time from normal responsibilities. The staff, however, was so small in comparison with the task that basically the program relied heavily upon voluntary compliance. Another problem was that of allowing for exceptions to guidelines on wage and price increases; such exceptions may be essential in the interest of fairness but can result in erosion of the guidelines. Another problem was whether business or labor was unfairly carrying the major burden of the controls. Moreover, the administrative machinery tended to separate inseparable issues: wage increases had to be negotiated through the Pay Board, but then industry had to apply to the Price Commission for price increases in order to cover larger payroll costs.

Rather than being phased out, the economic stabilization program disintegrated. Gradual decontrol of the economy was intended to be achieved by Phase III (January to June, 1973) and Phase IV (terminated April 1974). The CLC, Pay Board, and Price Commission were abolished by executive order in 1973 and 1974. Congress enacted legislation in 1974 that established the Council on Wage and Price Stability in the Executive Office of the President. The new council did not have authority to control wages and prices; its main function was to monitor them and to work with labor and management "to improve the structure of collective bargaining and the performance of those sectors in restraining prices" (PL 93-387). In the midst of the elimination of controls, the oil embargo by major foreign producers in October 1973 and the resulting energy crisis caused a rapid increase in fuel prices. At the same time, worldwide food shortages occurred, leading to major pressures on food prices. These inflationary problems were compounded by rising unemployment and the Watergate scandal which together left the economic stabilization program in disarray. Controls on fuel prices remained but were later eased. Struggles between the executive and legislative branches thwarted the development of a coherent set of policies on energy, prices, and employment. The Humphrey-Hawkins bill of 1975–76 emphasized employment, while opponents stressed the problem of inflation. Some participants stressed the need for developing domestic energy sources, while others were concerned with the possible resulting damage to the environment.

The ultimate impact of the economic stabilization program on the economy has yet to be determined. The short-term impact was rapid and positive; prices remained constant under Phase I and increased only slightly in Phase II. However, as both the Council of Economic Advisers and the Brookings Institution have observed, the subsequent rapid rise in price levels was clearly a partial consequence of worldwide events.[22] As a result, it is almost impossible to sort out what the economic stabilization program might have been able to accomplish had those events not occurred.

Fiscal Policy Beyond the built-in stabilizers, jawboning, and wage-price controls are the tools encompassed under fiscal and monetary policy, involving discretionary governmental regulation of the economy. Whereas built-in stabilizers are fundamentally passive, both fiscal and monetary policy are active in that they involve direct intervention into the economy.

John Maynard Keynes in his 1936 classic, *The General Theory of Employment, Interest, and Money*, was critical in reorienting economic thought toward recognition of the need for active governmental intervention.[23] The Depression of the 1930s had indicated that the economic "invisible hand" suggested by Adam Smith was not satisfactory in bringing the economy into equilibrium at full or high employment. Supply and demand could be balanced far below this level. Keynes concluded that traditional actions to combat depressions were unsatisfactory. Cuts in production in response to declining demand resulted in less purchasing power for consumers, which further reduced demand for goods and services. This still further-decreased demand resulted in further reductions in production levels. The emphasis, therefore, should be upon maintaining demand levels.

Keynes' position was fundamentally neoclassical in that his theory sought to preserve a "free" economy within bounds that avoided both depressions and inflation during expansionary periods. These bounds were

---

[22] Good concise accounts of the economic stabilization program and its impacts with contrasting views between the Administration and outside economists may be found in the 1974 and 1975 issues of the *Economic Report of the President* and in the Brookings Institution analyses of the fiscal 1975 and 1976 budgets. Barry M. Blechman, E. W. Gramlich, and R. W. Hartman, *Setting National Priorities: The 1975 (1976) Budget* (Washington: Brookings, 1974 and 1975).

[23] John Maynard Keynes, *The General Theory of Employment, Interest and Money* (New York: Harcourt, Brace, 1936). Also see Harlan L. McCracken, *Keynesian Economics in the Stream of Economic Thought* (Baton Rouge: Louisiana State University Press, 1961).

to be set through governmental intervention. Though Keynes' theory was conservative in the sense that it sought to preserve private enterprise, his ideas were slow to be accepted by governmental leaders.

Today, the President has a sizable staff of economic advisers at his disposal. The principal official one, the Council of Economic Advisers, was created by the Employment Act of 1946. It consists of three members appointed by the President with the advice and consent of the Senate. The Council, with a professional staff of over 25 in 1976, is responsible for analyzing the national economy and for making recommendations to the President. It is the primary agency involved in preparing the annual *Economic Report of the President.*[24]

Several other groups and individuals advise the President. The Office of Management and Budget (OMB) may play a major role in fiscal policy, depending upon the personal relationship the OMB Director has to the President. Staff members of the White House also may have important advisory roles on fiscal policy, as Arthur F. Burns did before he became Chairman of the Federal Reserve Board (the "Fed"). The Chairman of the Fed often plays a key advisory role. (The Board's functioning is considered more thoroughly in the next section.) In addition, solicited and unsolicited advice is provided to the President by private confidants and members of Congress, especially members of the major "money" committees and the Joint Economic Committee.

Taxes are among the most important tools available for fiscal policy. Aside from being necessary to fund governmental activities, taxation is generally used to affect economic conditions. According to the Keynesian prescription, when demand exceeds supply—too many dollars are chasing too few goods—demand should be contracted by lessening the dollars available for purchasing. This can be accomplished by increasing taxes. The reverse is applied under recessionary conditions; taxes are reduced in order to stimulate purchasing and production.

Governmental expenditures can produce similar effects. By increasing its expenditures during periods of economic decline, government can increase demand and increase purchasing power, which in turn will stimu-

---

[24] See Corrine Silverman, *The President's Economic Advisers* (Tuscaloosa: Interuniversity Case Program, University of Alabama Press, 1959); Hugh S. Norton, *The Role of the Economist in Government* (Berkeley, Cal.: McCutchan, 1969); Harold L. Wilensky, *Organizational Intelligence: Knowledge and Policy in Government and Industry* (New York: Basic Books, 1967), pp. 94–109; Lawrence C. Pierce, *The Politics of Fiscal Policy Formation* (Pacific Palisades, Cal.: Goodyear, 1971).

late a higher level of production. Cuts in expenditures that reduce demand can be used to slow down inflation during a period of high employment.

The effect of fiscal policy is based upon not only the taxes extracted from the economy and the expenditures put into it, but also upon a *multiplier*. This means that any transaction will generate several other transactions. For each expenditure of government paid to industry or an individual, part is taxed while the remainder is divided between consumption and investment. The private citizen or firm spends and in doing so places dollars in the hands of others, of which some will be taxed and the rest spent or invested. Therefore, an increase of $100 in governmental expenditures will be multiplied in its effect upon the economy. The same process works in reverse when expenditures are decreased.[25]

The difference between revenues and expenditures is what is referred to as a budget surplus or deficit. The popular notion is that the difference reflects the stimulative or restrictive effect of fiscal policy. By spending more than revenues, government is said to have an expansionary effect on the economy; budget surpluses, on the other hand, have a restrictive effect. By focusing upon this difference between expenditures and revenues, some misleading interpretations derived from looking only at taxing or spending can be avoided. For example, if government increases taxes in order to slow down the economy but then spends above the new revenue level, the result may be expansionary rather than contractionary as intended by the taxing policy.

The "new economics" maintains that budget deficits or surpluses alone do not reveal the actual fiscal policy in operation. That policy, so the argument goes, can only be understood in the context of the level at which the economy is performing compared with its potential level at full employment. The approach is to achieve a fiscal stance that promotes the economy toward attaining its full potential. This is known as gap closing—closing the gap between actual and potential.

To assess fiscal policy, the new economics begins with a calculation of the potential GNP under full employment and from that determines the revenues that would have resulted.[26] From these figures, economists derive the "full employment surplus"; that is, the extent to which

---

[25] David J. Ott and Attiat F. Ott, *Federal Budget Policy*, rev. ed. (Washington: Brookings, 1969), pp. 72–75.

[26] For an explanation of the way in which potential GNP is calculated, see Okun, *Political Economy of Prosperity*, pp. 132–45. Also see George Terborgh, *The New Economics* (New York: Machinery and Allied Products Institute, 1968).

revenues would exceed expenditures at full employment. The larger the surplus, the more difficult it is for the economy to achieve its potential. Increasing the full employment surplus, therefore, will put brakes on the economy, whereas decreasing the surplus will stimulate it.[27]

When the economy is operating at full employment, the resulting economic growth automatically will produce higher revenues. This rising level of funds, known as the "fiscal dividend," permits increased governmental expenditures without the addition of new taxes or higher tax rates. A "fiscal drag" occurs if the new receipts are not offset by either increased expenditures or tax reductions; the drag has the effect of siphoning funds from the economy.[28] Obviously, fiscal policy rejects the notion that budgets should be balanced annually. (For a discussion of government debt see Chapter 10).

The new economics rejects not only the idea of budgets balanced annually but also the concept of budgets balanced over the length of the business cycle. Earlier, a popular principle was that surpluses should be attained during growth periods to offset deficits incurred during contractionary periods. The current approach, as has been seen, is to concentrate upon moving the economy toward full employment, even if such a policy may require the accumulation of debt.[29]

Several problems of timing are associated with fiscal policy. The lack of complete information about the economy produces a perception lag. This is the period of time that elapses between an event—such as the beginning of an inflationary period—and its recognition. The perception lag contributes to a reaction lag. This is the time that is consumed between recognition and the decision(s) to act. Pluralistic or decentralized political systems may have associated with them rather substantial reaction lags. This was patently obvious in the case of President Lyndon Johnson's efforts to wage a war in Southeast Asia and avoid inflation in the war-time economy. In January 1967 Johnson proposed a surtax on income, but the proposed legislation was not submitted to Congress until August. The tax measure, though finally approved by the Congress, was not signed into law until July 1968.

---

[27] Heller, *New Dimensions of Political Economy*, pp. 64–69. Bernard P. Herber, *Modern Public Finance: The Study of Public Sector Economics*, 3rd ed. (Homewood, Ill.: Irwin, 1975), pp. 621–26.

[28] Joseph A. Pechman, *Federal Tax Policy*, rev. ed. (New York: Norton, 1971), pp. 14–18.

[29] Heller, *New Dimensions of Political Economy*, p. 39. Okun, *Political Economy of Prosperity*, p. 33.

One possible remedy for this type of situation would be to grant the President limited discretionary power to modify tax rates. Under such a system the reaction lag would be reduced. Some power of this type is already available to the executive. In instances of broadly worded legislation, the executive is empowered to interpret this legislation and in doing so assumes discretionary power. This was the case in January 1971, when President Richard Nixon "liberalized" business tax deductions for investments in equipment as a means of stimulating a sagging economy. Tax legislation simply provided that such deductions be reasonable, and the President determined what was reasonable.

A more important measure would be to allow the President to adjust personal and corporate income tax rates. President John F. Kennedy requested such power in 1962, but Congress did not accept the proposal. In President Lyndon B. Johnson's last budget message to the Congress (January 1969) he recommended similar legislation. Rates could be adjusted upward or downward by perhaps 5 or 10 percent, subject to congressional veto. A resolution passed by either house in opposition to the tax change would reject the presidential recommendation. This type of device might reduce the reaction lag while preserving constitutional protections in that taxing responsibilities would continue to reside ultimately in the Congress.[30]

Beyond the reaction lag is the implementation lag, the time required before action actually affects the economy. Tax measures clearly are felt within a short period of time. The introduction of a new tax does require time to establish the specific regulations and mechanisms for collection. Once the tax is established, however, comparatively little time is required to make adjustments for a larger or smaller tax rate.

In contrast, extended implementation lags are likely when expenditures are adjusted for fiscal policy purposes. In the short-term the apportionment process which allocates funds to agencies may have some marginal influence on spending patterns during the various quarters of the fiscal year (see Chapter 9). Potentially more influential tools are the use of rescissions and deferrals (see Chapter 8). Many expenditures, however, are basically uncontrollable in the immediate future due to previous commitments such as contracts for defense procurement and the guarantee of

---

[30] The three "lag" terms, with modification, are borrowed from Committee for Economic Development, *Fiscal and Monetary Policies*, pp. 20–22, and *Economic Report of the President* (1976), p. 20.

general revenue sharing funds to state and local governments. Were a cutback in expenditures preferred for fiscal policy purposes, only selected program areas would be available for possible reductions. The clientele supporting these programs, then, could mobilize against such selective reductions on the grounds that the action was discriminatory.

Capital construction on occasion has been suggested as one discretionary area where governmental expenditures could be used for fiscal policy purposes. In simplistic terms, blueprints for new facilities could be kept on file. Construction would be initiated during slack periods and curtailed during periods of high employment. To some extent, public construction has been used for this purpose, particularly by the federal government during the Depression. However, construction control has not been used as a conscious and continuous policy. In other words, there has been no coordinated policy over the years to provide for construction during periods of high unemployment and to curtail it during full employment.

Although this idea is appealing, it has many weaknesses. Some facilities may be in such great need that postponement of construction until a recession could retard the programs the facilities support. Further, considerable time is consumed between the decision to build and the actual start of construction; during that period, few dollars would be pumped into the economy. It could easily happen that by the time construction started, the economy would have been reversed and would be approaching full employment.

Beyond these problems of utilizing fiscal policy is the possibility that success may breed its own defeat. A concerted effort to halt inflation may be successful, but it may also produce increasing unemployment. Because unemployment is obviously unpopular and because elected officials prefer to be re-elected, they may seek to reverse their course by attempting to stimulate the economy. If fiscal policy measures did have immediate impacts upon the economy and if reaction lags were short, the ludicrous situation could arise in which government policies shifted daily between expansionary and contractionary measures.

Monetary Policy Monetary policy is the responsibility of the Federal Reserve System, a quasi-public institution. The system is headed by a Board of Governors consisting of seven members appointed by the Presidnet with the advice and consent of the Senate. The Chairman is designated by the President and traditionally has served long periods. When he retired in 1970, William McChesney Martin, Jr., had served as Chairman for almost 19 years. There are 12 Federal Reserve Banks and 24 branches throughout the country. The system also includes all national banks and those state banks and trust companies that have voluntarily joined. Thus, the system is public at the top and private at the bottom.[31]

Because the Fed serves as a bank for bankers it is able to control the supply of financial instruments—debts and equities that may be in the form of currency, bank deposits, bonds, loans, and the like. By expanding or contracting the supply of economic resources available to the private sector, the economy can be stimulated or slowed.

Of the three major monetary tools available to the Fed, the most important is open-market operations. These are conducted by the Open Market Committee, composed of the Board of Governors and five representatives from the Reserve Banks. Open-market operations affect the money supply by increasing or decreasing the funds available to banks for lending purposes through the purchase and sale of government bonds. These may range from short-term government bills (90 days) to long-term bonds. By purchasing government bonds, the Fed increases the reserves available to banks, thereby encouraging greater economic activity; by selling bonds, reserves are contracted. These bonds are not purchased by the average citizen but normally are purchased by large institutions such as insurance companies, major corporations, and commercial banks.

The second monetary tool is the discount rate. This is the interest rate charged to member banks for borrowing from the Fed. When the rate is increased, borrowing from the Fed is made more expensive and presumably will deter borrowing. A reduction in the rate encourages borrowing, and increased loans made by the Fed have the effect of increasing the money supply. Discounting, unlike open-market operations, is passive in that the Fed must wait for banks to come to it for loans.

The third tool, one that is seldom used, is that of changing reserve requirements. For every dollar in deposits, member banks are required to retain a specified percentage, with the remainder being available for loans. By increasing this percentage, the Fed is able to curtail immediately the amount of money available. Because this has such a powerful effect, the reserve requirement is changed only every few years whereas open-market operations are conducted daily.

To some extent monetary and fiscal policy can be treated as alterna-

---

[31] Michael D. Reagan, "The Political Structure of the Federal Reserve System," *American Political Science Review*, 60 (1961): 64–76.

tives, though more commonly they are considered to be companions. Kenneth Boulding has written:

> Thus, if inflation is fought by increased taxes, this operates mainly by reducing consumption. If it is fought by restricting credit, this operates mainly by reducing investment. If it is fought by "government economy" and restricting government expenditures, this operates mainly by reducing government absorption.[32]

However, as Boulding further notes, fiscal policy intended to combat inflation tends to reduce consumption and increase investments, while monetary policy limits investment through credit restriction. In this case, fiscal policy may be preferable in that it restricts inflation in the short-term but contributes to longer-term economic growth by stimulating investment.

Economists have debated long and heatedly over the relative merits of monetary and fiscal policy. The "new economists" advocate major reliance upon fiscal policy; fiscal policy is expected to be the active force, while monetary policy is accommodative.[33] In contrast, the monetary school, led by Milton Friedman of the University of Chicago, calls for greater reliance on the control of the money supply as a means of influencing the economy. The new economists counter that the correlation between money and economic activity is weak.[34]

One of the monetarists' most controversial proposals is that an automatic rule should replace discretionary monetary policy: the total supply of money would increase at an annual fixed rate somewhere between 3 and 5 percent. This recommendation, set forth by the Committee for Economic Development in 1947 and by Friedman in 1948, is predicated on the assumption that the relationships between money and economic activity are not known sufficiently well to allow for rational discretionary policy.[35] The rejoinder to the argument is that rigid rules are dangerous

---

[32] Kenneth E. Boulding, *Principles of Economic Policy* (Englewood Cliffs, N.J.: Prentice-Hall, 1958), p. 227.

[33] Okun, *Political Economy of Prosperity*, p. 53.

[34] For a summation of these conflicting views, see Milton Friedman and Walter W. Heller, *Monetary vs. Fiscal Policy* (New York: Norton, 1969). An interesting set of proposals for exclusive reliance on monetary controls, not only for regulating the economy but also for providing all revenues for all levels of government, is provided by Hugold Anderson, *Government Without Taxation* (New York: Exposition Press, 1965). Also see Barry N. Siegel *Aggregate Economics and Public Policy* (Homewood, Ill.: Irwin, 1974), pp. 315–31.

[35] *Taxes and the Budget: A Program for Prosperity in a Free Economy* (Washington: Committee for Economic Development, 1947); Milton Friedman, "A Monetary

and that flexibility or discretionary policy is needed, especially in influencing interest rates regarding balance of payments problems.[36]

The problem of achieving coordinated fiscal and monetary policies was particularly troublesome during the latter 1960s and the 1970s, when inflation and high unemployment existed simultaneously. These two conditions seem to indicate contradictory fiscal and monetary policies. Rising unemployment would indicate expansionary policies such as lower discount rates, higher governmental expenditures, and lower taxes; but continued inflationary pressures would indicate the reverse tactics.

The reasons for this conflicting pattern are not obvious, though it is apparent that psychological factors are important. When inflation becomes an expected way of life, then individuals and corporations base their actions upon that belief. Trying to protect themselves from anticipated inflation, workers press for higher wages, which in turn increase production costs. Management raises prices not only to offset higher labor costs but also to offset expected profit losses due to inflation. This process of spiraling wages and prices can occur, therefore, even though the economy may be slowing. Under such conditions, divergent recommendations regarding economic policy can be expected from economic observers. The dependence of the United States on imported fuels and world markets for food exports that was dramatically demonstrated in 1973–1974 further complicates the picture because fiscal and monetary policy must also account for external pressures.

Striking a balance between the use of fiscal and monetary policy is difficult because of structural features of the political system. One complication is that the President has little latitude over fiscal policy, because adjustments must be approved by the Congress. This may tend to encourage the chief executive to rely more heavily upon monetary policy, which is conducted by the Fed within broad parameters set by Congress. The quasi-autonomy of the Federal Reserve System, on the other hand,

---

and Fiscal Framework for Economic Stability," *American Economic Review*, 38 (1948): 254–64; Milton Friedman, *A Program for Monetary Stability* (New York: Fordham University Press, 1960), pp. 84–99; Milton Friedman and Anna Jacobson Schwartz, *Monetary Statistics of the United States: Estimates, Sources, Methods* (New York: National Bureau of Economic Research and Columbia University Press, 1970); Milton Friedman, *Dollars and Deficits: Inflation, Monetary Policy and the Balance of Payments* (Englewood Cliffs, N.J.: Prentice-Hall, 1968), pp. 153–94; Milton Friedman, *Capitalism and Freedom: Problems and Prospects* (Charlottesville: University Press of Virginia, 1975).

[36] Walter W. Heller, "Is Monetary Policy Being Oversold?," in Heller and Friedman, *Monetary vs. Fiscal Policy*, pp. 26–27.

means that the Fed will not always be willing to follow presidential advice. The Fed has been known to insist upon a quid pro quo; for instance, it might insist upon reductions in federal expenditures in exchange for any tightening of monetary policy. Moreover, the President may be powerless to prevent the Fed from acting. This was the case in 1965 when the Fed increased the discount rate, contrary to the wishes of President Johnson. Though the federal government has assumed responsibility for regulating the economy, the President has limited powers in carrying out that responsibility. Legislation has been introduced in Congress that would require Fed actions to be coordinated with the President and Congress.[37]

SPECIAL EFFECTS OF ECONOMIC POLICY

One set of problems not discussed to this point is that economic policy has specific effects as well as general effects upon the economy. Changing conditions in the economy do not affect everyone uniformly. This is one area in which Keynesian economic theory is weak, namely that it focuses upon aggregates and tends to ignore structural changes in the economy.[38]

As noted earlier, one of the key functions of government finance is the redistribution of income. Economic policy for stabilization purposes, whether passive or active, can also result in unintentional redistributive effects. Under inflationary conditions, when government is passive—takes no action to slow inflation—persons on fixed or relatively fixed incomes are penalized. This is especially true for retired persons living on pensions, but it is also true for nonunionized workers who did not have the bargaining power to command increases in wages from management. Concern over the differential effects of changing prices has led to growing interest in so-called "incomes policy," in which the federal government would be responsible for stabilizing the distribution of income between business and labor. Also related is the idea of a guaranteed income, perhaps provided through a negative income tax.

The incomes policy issue is particularly reflected in the choice of whether corporate or personal income taxes should be utilized in specific situations to influence the economy and especially what kinds of adjustments should be made in these taxes. An increase in either form of taxation can be expected to have an aggregate effect of slowing down the

---

[37] The proposal was part of the Humphrey-Hawkins bill.
[38] Burkhead, *Government Budgeting*, pp. 80–82.

economy, but increased corporate taxes may affect mainly investors, while personal income taxes will affect consumers.[39]

Several alternatives are available in changing personal income taxes. Adjustments can be made in the standard personal exemption and deductible items such as medical expenses and the interest paid on mortgages. Tax rates can also be changed. For 1976, a married couple with $500 taxable income paid 14 percent of that sum in federal income taxes, whereas another couple with income of $60,000 paid 44 percent. Changes in deductions and tax rates, however, greatly influence the distribution of income among groups within the society and therefore are not regarded as fiscal policy instruments. Uniform changes, such as the 10 percent surtax imposed in 1968 and the temporary tax rebate program introduced in 1975, are more typical fiscal policy devices.

On the corporate side, the federal government collects 52 percent of all earnings above $25,000. This tax influences the amount of resources available for reinvestment, an increase in the tax rate presumably reducing investments. Related to this are tax provisions for deductions for depreciation and investment. Liberalization of depreciation standards reduces taxes and encourages capital investments. The investment credit allows corporations to write off a given percentage of their investments against their taxes. This directly stimulates investments.

One issue that has been particularly important is the extent to which double taxation prevails and discourages economic growth. Corporate taxes are high, but after these taxes are paid, the tax system has not yet been satisfied. Dividends paid stockholders are also subject to taxes. To some extent, then, double taxation occurs. The argument can be made that the tax system discourages capital formation, first by taxing corporations that make profits and second by taxing dividends paid to investors.

While economic policy can have the specific effects mentioned, in other instances it cannot be expected to produce some desired consequences, especially in regard to structural features of the labor market. For example, workers with minimal or obsolete skills will always have difficulty finding employment, even under conditions of full employment. Similarly, economic policy cannot be expected to eliminate problems associated with an oversupply of skills, such as the overproduction of PhDs

---

[39] An extensive discussion of tax and expenditure incidence and consequences for policy decisions is in Musgrave and Musgrave, *Public Finance*, pp. 375–458.

that materialized in the late 1960s and early 1970s. Economic policy is also of limited assistance in coping with readjustments in the economy regarding defense and aerospace cutbacks. When military production is curtailed, chronic unemployment in some occupational fields is almost inevitable.

Additionally, there are several problems related to the federal nature of American government. Because economic policy is the exclusive domain of the federal government, state and local governments are left largely at the mercy of the national economy. These subnational governments do attempt to influence their economic bases, for example, by attempting to attract industry through low corporate taxes. Yet, states and localities are bound to be affected by major shifts in the national economy over which they have no control.

Given that state and local governments typically are more limited in their capacity to incur debts than is the federal government, accuracy in revenue estimating for these subnational governments is an important factor in budgeting. Taxes sensitive to economic conditions, such as sales and income taxes, present the greatest problems for revenue estimating; property taxes are less difficult, because assessments are not adjusted automatically in accordance with shifts in the economy. Estimates must be made of what level of economic activity will be achieved in order to determine the revenue yield. Overoptimistic assessments of economic conditions, of course, are feared most, because these can easily result in budget deficits.[40]

Expenditure patterns at the state and local levels can be counterproductive to federal economic policy during contractionary periods. Revenues generated from state and local taxes on sales, personal income, and corporate income necessarily decline during recessionary periods. Because these governments have greater limits on their ability to finance operations by incurring debts than the federal government, state and local governments will tend to reduce expenditures when revenues decline. This curtailment of public expenditures has the effect of reducing private purchasing power precisely at a time when it should be bolstered. Thus, state and local policy can exacerbate the economic decline.

---

[40] See Eugene P. McLoone, Gabrielle C. Lupo, and Selma J. Mushkin, *Long-Range Revenue Estimation* (Washington: State-Local Finances Project, The George Washington University, October, 1967).

SUMMARY

The field of governmental involvement in the economy is a vast one, and only some of the most important issues have been reviewed in this chapter. As has been seen, problems abound. One of the most critical problems is that of forecasting the direction in which the economy is moving. Issues then arise as to whether and when government should intervene. Some observers would argue for allowing the economy to pass through readjustment phases with no or minimal governmental action, while others would argue for intervention to push the economy toward achieving its potential. Even when there is agreement that intervention is warranted, it is likely that there will be substantial disagreement as to what form of action is needed. Should monetary policy, fiscal policy, or both be used? How much of each should be employed?

Finally, the political considerations are enormous. Though the federal government has officially assumed responsibility for regulating the economy, the means available for implementing this policy are greatly constrained. In most instances, the President is dependent upon Congress for adjusting fiscal policy, and he must rely heavily upon persuasion to move the Federal Reserve System. It is commonly believed that a depression such as that of the 1930s will never be allowed to occur, but the nation is far from having a decision system that can ensure a favorable international balance of payments, stable prices, high employment, and economic growth.

14

CHANGING
FUNCTIONS
OF BUDGETING

We concluded the first edition of *Public Budgeting Systems* with the observation that budgeting would never be entirely satisfactory to the needs of the present. Events of the years since that edition have emphasized the close connections between the basic structure of government and society and budgetary processes and reforms. While straight line projections of past and current trends into the future do not account for possibilities that alter the normal course of events, it is possible to anticipate general changes that are in the offing.

This chapter is an exploratory venture into the future, the preceding chapters having concentrated upon the rise of budgeting and its development to the present. Here we break from the specifics of preceding chapters—authorizations versus appropriations, callable versus noncallable bonds, and so forth—to explore more general trends. The first section examines the conditions for change in public budgeting. The second section focuses specifically on how changing conditions and critiques of the social order may affect public budgeting.

CONDITIONS FOR CHANGE

The basic stimulus for change is dissatisfaction. Dissatisfaction produces an interest in seeking new processes and new institutions that will depart

341

from existing patterns in finding solutions to problems.[1] According to this so-called "necessity" theory, institutional and procedural changes can be explained by reference to the problems that previous institutional and procedural arrangements were unable to solve.[2] The sources of dissatisfaction may be general problems that government has dealt with ineffectively—energy, inflation, unemployment—or they may be more fundamental criticisms of decision-making structures or of the basic social order. Both of these sources are reflected in the most common explanation for the development of executive budgeting and the establishment of formal budget procedures.[3] When government budget surpluses were replaced with deficits, necessitating a rise in taxes, and when corruption in government spending became flagrant, demands were made that something be done. The results were reforms at the local and state levels and the Budget and Accounting Act of 1921 at the federal level.

An alternative theory of change argues that innovation is likely to occur as a result of surplus resources, of slack that is not employed in short-term maintenance of organizational survival.[4] Some economists expected surpluses of revenue to occur at the federal level near the end of the 1960s and argued for their use in alleviating state and local financial difficulties.[5] The surpluses never materialized, and the massive deficits of the mid-1970s made it apparent that slack resources would be unlikely for the foreseeable future. The kinds of changes that are likely to occur, therefore, are most likely to be the result of dissatisfactions with the current state rather than innovative attempts to deal with surplus resources.

Today it is difficult to find any major cluster of people who are satisfied with existing conditions. Taxpayers, no matter what their political bent, commonly express displeasure and dismay with the rising cost of government and the parallel increase in taxes. For the average taxpayer, all of the income he or she earns between January and the spring in effect is

---

[1] See James G. March and Herbert A. Simon, *Organizations* (New York: Wiley, 1958).

[2] James Q. Wilson, "Necessity Versus the Devil," in Walter A. Hill and Douglas Egan, eds., *Readings in Organization Theory: A Behavioral Approach* (Boston: Allyn and Bacon, 1967), pp. 492–94.

[3] See, for example, Allen Schick, *Budget Innovation in the States* (Washington: Brookings, 1971), pp. 14–15.

[4] Wilson, "Necessity Versus the Devil."

[5] For example, Walter W. Heller's revenue sharing proposal. *New Dimensions of Political Economy* (New York: Norton, 1967).

absorbed by government. Politicians express the same disenchantment with the present. Legislation is enacted to end problems, yet they persist. The announcement of a major new program to solve some dire problem is received with much fanfare, but years later the problem seems as bad or worse than ever.[6] Indeed, politics threatens to become an empty process if it cannot produce intended beneficial effects. Complaints are heard from all points on the ideological spectrum.

The overriding complaint is that despite the expenditure of large sums of money, government has few accomplishments to cite. Different ideological positions may express different views of what are appropriate accomplishments, but there seems to be agreement that currently they are not being achieved. In part, this is the normal condition for collectivities such as government. Individual preferences vary widely; therefore, no large collective instution can represent adequately at any one time all individual preferences. Still, there are strong pressures for more effective methods of dealing with current problems.

The range of attitudes toward what government can and should do is perhaps so wide as to defy categorization. Nevertheless, categorization must be attempted if possible future states of public budgeting systems are to be assessed. One fundamental position is that government is impotent and incompetent to deal directly with social problems. In simpler times, that view might be labeled essentially conservative, but today left and right converge on that position. Another distinctive position regards government as an instrument for positive social action. According to this position, problems that have defied solution have not been met with the right amount and right combination of society's resources organized through government. New Deal liberalism and its contemporary versions characterize that view. Still another position argues that government, and society in general, focuses too much attention on "things" to be accomplished, on measurement of material success as the primary criterion for problem solving. This position holds that individual values are more important than the aggregate performance of the economy and society.

Each of these critiques of government and its role in society has implications for the future of budgeting. There is no particular set of budgetary techniques and procedures that is attached to each position described above. On some issues, adherents of each of the positions would

---

[6] Robert A. Levine, *Public Planning: Failure and Redirection* (New York: Basic Books, 1972), p. 3.

agree. For example, all agree that government operates without really knowing what kind of impact it is having on society at large and individuals in particular. The budgeting systems that attempt to focus attention on the ends to be accomplished rather than resources to be consumed are of some utility to all positions. Disagreement comes on the ends to be served and the specific governmental actions to accomplish these ends.

While budget reforms have often resulted from political upheaval, not every reform must be accompanied by upheaval.[7] Furthermore, not every political or social upheaval is accompanied by budget reform. Some current critiques of society and its political arrangements may produce substantial alterations in budgetary procedures, while others may have negligible effects. Budgeting and politics or budgeting and the social structure, while interrelated, are not isomorphic.

THE FUTURE OF PUBLIC BUDGETING

Current practices and the general trend of budgetary reforms in this century to introduce program information into the decision process are most compatible with the activist position characteristic of New Deal liberalism and some more contemporary systems perspectives. Program budgeting, management by objectives (MBO), reevaluation of programs from ground zero, or any comparable decision-making logic is predicated on the assumption that government should be held accountable for producing results. An action-oriented viewpoint would hold government responsible for accomplishing results in large areas of society. A more negative view of the competence of government, while desirous of restricting the area of activity, would also stress the necessity for assessing the results of governmental actions. The demand that government not just take action but do something that produces results will continue to encourage the use of program analysis and other devices that relate resources to program accomplishments. All critiques of government activities suggest that there will be further movement away from budgeting simply as an activity to finance the ongoing activities of well established bureaucracies.[8]

One likely effect will be a reduction in the perpetuation of half-truths

---

[7] Allen Schick, "Systems Politics and Systems Budgeting," *Public Administration Review*, 29 (1969): 149–50.

[8] Peter B. Natchez and Irvin C. Bupp, "Policy and Priority in the Budgetary Process," *American Political Science Review*, 67 (1973): 951–63.

or lies. The demand for results to prove the merit of expenditures and corresponding taxes will make even more difficult casual rhetoric that creating a program will solve a problem. Current hard questioning of governmental activity holds no doctrines sacred and therefore challenges the validity of each. Do social workers solve human problems? Does education help people escape the cycle of poverty? Does recreation reduce social tensions? Do government health programs reduce the level of disease? Do nuclear defense treaties reduce tensions and provide for adequate levels of self-defense? The experience has been that creating a program and spending public money are no sure guarantees that intended changes will occur. Having information about program results encourages the political system to recognize failures as well as successes.

The clamor for results will place a premium upon real budgetary reforms, as distinguished from many cosmetic changes that have been advertised as real. Such was the case with many planning-programming-budgeting (PPB) efforts:

> PPB's products have become its end-products. For so many practitioners, PPB is not some majestic scrutinizing of objectives and opportunities, but going through the motions of doing a program structure, writing a program memorandum, of filling in the columns of a program and financial plan.[9]

Going through the motions will no longer suffice. It will be demanded that the processing of forms have some bearing upon assessing the effects of governmental programs and some effect upon decisions relating to the continuation of programs and their funding.

This type of pressure will stimulate greater research and a greater share of tax monies being devoted to analyzing what government does or fails to accomplish. Though figures are not readily available, it seems certain that the private sector spends much more of its resources on research for product improvement and for new products than government spends for improving its services. This pattern is changing and even more of a premium will be placed on analytic talent in government.

These kinds of shifts would necessarily affect the relationships between and within the executive and legislative branches. This, however, does not mean that any strengthening of the executive must have a deleterious effect upon the legislature. Zero-sum conditions, in which a gain for the executive is matched by an equal loss for the legislative

---

[9] Schick, "Systems Politics," p. 149.

branch, do not prevail. Just as early budget reforms designed to strengthen the Bureau of the Budget were advocated as providing better means for Congress to exercise its will, other reforms can strengthen the position of the President and the Congress. Indeed, the 1974 congressional budget reforms, the growing use of oversight units in state legislatures, and proposals for sunset legislation suggest not a diminution of the legislature's role but an increase. Legislative bodies can be expected to place far greater emphasis upon program results within the budgetary process than has previously been the case.

This is not to say that all features of present budgetary practices will evaporate; such a prediction is unwarranted. W. F. Willoughby in 1927 foresaw the system established by the Budget and Accounting Act as leading to a diminution of congressional interest in government spending in home districts and an increasing concern for the national interest. [10] Decades later, that prediction has not come true. Many of the other aspects of congressional behavior (Chapter 8) are likely to persist. What is suggested here is that current legislative practices will be adjusted to accommodate a growing interest in budgeting for program results.

It should be understood, as has been indicated in previous chapters, that program budgeting as discussed here refers to the limited rationality model of decision making. In suggesting that program budgeting will gain in significance, the argument is not advanced that ideal rationality will emerge. The comprehensive review of alternatives and values explicit in the rationality model of decision making is recognized to be impossible.

Though the balance of power between the executive and legislative branches need not shift, reforms may alter the balance between the chief executive on the one hand and agencies and their clientele on the other. Program budgeting may well have a centralizing tendency through which departments and agencies are likely to lose their relative autonomy. The benefit will be a more direct form of responsibility for the executive, and the cost will be imposed upon those interests that previously had a direct say in the agencies' operations.

The demand for program results also can be expected to influence intergovernmental relations. Because so much of what government does is conducted by local government, the federal government and states need information from localities to determine what results are occurring. For

---

[10] W. F. Willoughby, *The National Budget System: With Suggestions for Its Improvement* (Baltimore: Johns Hopkins University Press, 1927), pp. 289–90.

instance, Washington and the state capitals need to know what the products are of local educational systems. This need will arise as long as aid programs exist. A sharing of information is important also from the standpoint that the three levels perform similar functions; for example, all three provide direct services in the law enforcement and health fields. The only way to avoid this exchange of information would be to eliminate the current intermingling of governments. Each level would be required to perform services exclusive of the others, and there would be no transfer of funds among levels. That alternative seems highly unlikely.

A coordinated set of information systems would be one step in the direction of integrating the levels of government (Chapter 9). Uniform collection and reporting of data would allow each level to gain knowledge of what other levels were doing. Under program budgeting, governments might adopt similar program structures in order to facilitate the exchange of data. Substantial movement in the direction of compatible information systems is currently evident. The process is taking place in substantive fields instead of on a governmentwide basis. Thus, educators are developing a consensus concerning what information should be collected, and the same applies to law enforcement, recreation, health, transportation, and other fields.

Not only is there likely to be greater demand for the exchange of information, but the demand for results is likely to stimulate interest in intergovernmental programs. If some of the social welfare programs of the 1960s proved anything, they probably proved that no one agency or government can effectively reverse major, undesirable, social conditions. Some effort in coordination has been attempted. The War on Poverty was partially based upon the value of a coordinated approach to solving the problems of the poor. Yet it would seem that, in many instances, private and public organizations may have shared in funds from the Economic Opportunity Act but programs were conducted as discrete affairs. The politics of the future are likely to place a growing emphasis upon coordinating governmental programs and, therefore, upon coordinating budgets.

Whether there will be structural realignment of governments is uncertain. Governments have only consolidated when compelled to do so. School districts reluctantly consolidated at the demand of states. Presumably, municipalities will demonstrate no greater interest in unification unless the problems of governing metropolitan areas become overwhelming. The drive to secure metropolitanwide government in the 1960s met with only a modicum of success, though the modest trend can be expected to continue. The reemergence of county government as an important local force may be possible. As municipalities' powers to govern and service themselves weaken, the county may be called upon to assume responsibilities. If that were to occur, municipalities might "wither away." One growing concern among those who promote local government consolidation is that revenue sharing and other assistance may avert financial crises for some local governments that should be allowed to disappear.[11] Consolidation, however, has its opponents who point to the efficiencies of a decentralized system that more closely matches governmental services with the varied demands of citizens.[12]

For the most part, the projected continuation of current trends reflected in the above paragraphs is primarily suggestive of the action-oriented, positive view of the role of government. This view is optimistic in the sense that government is seen as possessing the competence to solve major problems—if only the right amount of funds, coordinated properly among levels of government and tied to the right kinds of information, is applied to action programs. While other views of the role of government in solving social problems may agree with this positive view on the need to hold government accountable for results, they would nevertheless diverge from such a positivist stance.

Edward C. Banfield, for example, has suggested that there is little hope that government will be able to do much about the alleviation of urban problems, particularly those problems related to race and poverty:

> One of my main contentions is that we do not know and never can know what the real nature of the problem is, let alone what might "work" to alleviate or solve it.[13]

The urban problem is purported to be of such magnitude that it defies any conscious effort for resolution. Banfield's forecast is that many problems will be self-corrected as society progresses.

Another subscriber to the idea of governmental impotence and incompetence is Peter F. Drucker. With regard to welfare and farm programs, he

---

[11] See Richard P. Nathan, Allen D. Manvel, and Susannah E. Calkins, *Monitoring Revenue Sharing* (Washington: Brookings, 1975).

[12] Robert L. Bish and Vincent Ostrom, *Understanding Urban Government: Metropolitan Reform Reconsidered* (Washington: American Enterprise Institute, 1973).

[13] Edward C. Banfield, *The Unheavenly City Revisited* (Boston: Little, Brown, 1974), p. vii.

has concluded, "We certainly could not have done worse if we had done nothing at all."[14] More generally, he has written:

> But the greatest factor in the disenchantment with government is that government has not performed. The record over these last thirty or forty years has been dismal. Government has proved itself capable of doing only two things with great effectiveness. It can wage war. And it can inflate the currency. Other things it can promise but only rarely accomplish.[15]

The alleged reason for this failure is that government of necessity is characterized by red tape and forms. Without the cumbersome procedures required by the use of forms, dishonesty is likely to consume government. Therefore, "any government that is not a 'government of forms' degenerates rapidly into a mutual looting society."[16]

Drucker's prescription for change is separation of the functions of governing and doing.[17] Government is thought not to be suited to providing services directly but rather to governing or deciding what should be done. He has advocated a policy of "reprivatization" in which the responsibility for doing would be turned over to other institutions. Many of these would be private institutions, especially profit-oriented enterprises, but others would be quasi-public institutions such as the Communications Satellite Corporation (COMSAT).

The value of such an approach, according to Drucker, is that ineffective programs could be more easily halted than under present conditions. Established governmental bureaucracies, among other things, are committed to their own preservation, regardless of their merit. Private corporations are also committed to self-preservation, but the difference is that the market can eliminate nonproductive enterprises.

Others also have argued that major services now performed by government, even such functions as national defense,[18] actually could be provided more efficiently by private corporations licensed by the government. In addition, observers of the inability of public schools to reach ghetto

---

[14] Peter F. Drucker, *The Age of Discontinuity: Guidelines to Our Changing Society* (New York: Harper and Row, 1969), p. 227.

[15] Drucker, *Age of Discontinuity*, p. 217.

[16] Drucker, *Age of Discontinuity*, p. 230.

[17] Drucker, *Age of Discontinuity*, pp. 212–14.

[18] William A. Niskanen, *Bureaucracy and Representative Government* (Chicago: Aldine, 1971).

children and other deprived groups have advocated a competitive educational program through which citizens would be given the freedom to select their own private or public schools, and government would pay institutions on the basis of their enrollments.

Some have distinguished those functions more amenable to some form of private or competitive provision from those that would still require extensive governmental administration.[19] For those programs with extensive distributional or redistributional objectives, such as Social Security and income maintenance, centralized governmental provision has a comparative economic advantage over competitive, market-like operations. For others, however, including education and job training programs, the advantage may be with competition among service providers, whether those providers are public, private, or both. For example, a system of tax credits to private firms for providing job training may be more direct and may more readily produce employable skills than large, uniform public programs.[20]

Were some of these proposals adopted, contemporary budget systems would have to undergo substantial revision. In the first place, government would deal with a greater number of institutions. This would magnify exponentially the complexity of government operations. If government attempted to monitor each institution receiving public money, the current volume of paperwork deplored by Drucker would increase rather than decrease. One alternative would be to treat each organization as a black box; government would not look into the box to see by what means the job was done but would audit the organization to see that the promised results were produced at the agreed upon price.

Even without major alterations in the division of responsibilities between private and public organizations, there will likely be more arguments for organizational experimentation and more emphasis on developing flexible response patterns to environmental changes. The focus would be less on rationalistic conceptions of planning in terms of goal selection, program formulation, and program execution and more on organizational learning or adaptivity.[21] The "self-correcting" organization would be one with a variety of possible responses to environmental changes that are less

---

    [19] Levine, *Public Planning*, pp. 170–75.

    [20] Levine, *Public Planning*, pp. 170–75.

    [21] John Friedman, *Retracking America: A Theory of Transactive Planning* (Garden City, N.Y.: Anchor Press, 1973), pp. 4 and xix.

dependent on rigid hierarchies or fixed response patterns.[22] The discovery of solutions is an interactive process of trial and error; what is a satisfactory solution at one time becomes unsatisfactory at another time, and the problem must be "re-solved."[23]

The changes implied in those arguments are more psychological than systemic. One change component is a greater acceptance of the fact that many public policies fail or seem to fail. Rather than responding to failure by cutting off the funds, however, a greater willingness to fund experimentation—a greater willingness to risk trial and error—may be required. Although the tight financial position of both citizens and governments is not likely to encourage experimentation, less funding of full-blown but untried programs in favor of small-scale experiments may be possible.

While sharing some views of limited government with the essentially conservative position, an alternative critique diagnoses society's ailment as the fact that it is governed by a ruling elite. The power structure or the ruling class is said to make decisions for society. If only limited progress is made in dealing with problems such as poverty and discrimination, this is because those who rule oppose change. Changes that have occurred, while resulting from demands from "below" have been meted out on terms specified by the elite.[24]

A different conception of human nature is espoused by this radical view, especially in contrast with the conservative vantage point. While Drucker considers "government by forms" essential to protect society from its own evil nature, others have expressed a more positive view.[25] Humankind is not slothful and corrupt, but creative. Allowing greater human freedom will stimulate creative powers, while a society that imposes controls produces apathy, alienation, and stagnation.

Society is seen as becoming dehumanized, and one of the main causes

---

[22] Martin Landau, "On the Concept of a Self-Correcting Organization," *Public Administration Review*, 33 (1973): 533–42.

[23] Edgar S. Dunn, Jr., *Economic and Social Development: A Process of Social Learning* (Baltimore: Johns Hopkins Press, 1971), p. 241.

[24] C. Wright Mills, *The Power Elite* (New York: Oxford University Press, 1956); G. William Domhoff, *The Higher Circles: The Governing Class in America* (New York: Random House, 1970); G. William Domhoff, *Who Rules America?* (Englewood Cliffs, N.J.: Prentice-Hall, 1967); Edward S. Greenburg, *Serving the Few: Corporate Capitalism and the Bias of Government Policy* (New York: Wiley, 1974).

[25] Robert Theobald, "Policy Formation for New Goals," in Robert Theobald, ed., *Social Policies for America in the Seventies: Nine Divergent Views* (Garden City, N.Y.: Doubleday, 1968), pp. 164–66.

of this condition is the emergence of a technological society. Many commentators on American society, both radicals and the not-so-radical, have expressed concern about what will happen to the nation as it moves beyond the industrial age. As Zbigniew Brzezinski has written:

> What makes America unique in our time is that it is the first society to experience the future. It is becoming a "technetronic" society—a society that is shaped culturally, psychologically, socially and economically by the impact of technology and electronics, particularly computers and communications.[26]

Bertram M. Gross has called it a "post-industrial cybernetic service society."[27] Jacques Ellul has labeled it the "technological society."[28]

For radicals, technology can be a form of tyranny, with workers enslaved according to the dictates of technological processes.[29] New weaponry, no matter how dreadful, is considered essential. New industrial techniques, no matter how dehumanizing, are justified as necessary for making a profit. According to Herbert Marcuse,

> The people recognize themselves in their commodities; they find their soul in their automobiles, hi-fi set, split-level home, kitchen equipment. . . . Mass production and mass distribution claim the entire individual.[30]

What is required is a negation of technology for its own sake and a new consciousness.[31]

The radical prescription calls for the elimination of the existing power structure and its replacement by greater citizen involvement. Such a view raises anew the familiar questions of whether direct democracy is possible within a mass society. Until the relatively recent resurgence in the interest in citizen participation, the standard contention was that representative democracy rather than direct democracy was the best that could be expected. Citizens have little time for learning about government, and the

---

[26] Zbigniew Brzezinski, *The New York Times*, January 6, 1969.

[27] Bertram M. Gross, "Planning in an Era of Social Revolution," *Public Administration Review,* 31 (1971): 260.

[28] Jacques Ellul, *The Technological Society* (New York: Knopf, 1964).

[29] Theobald, "Policy Formation for New Goals," p. 159.

[30] Herbert Marcuse, "The New Forms of Control," in Maurice Zeitlin, ed., *American Society, Inc.: Studies of the Social Structure and Political Economy of the United States* (Chicago: Markham, 1970), pp. 379–80.

[31] Charles A. Reich, *The Greening of America: How the Youth Revolution Is Trying to Make American Livable* (New York: Random House, 1970).

best they can do is make yes–no choices on candidates, leaving policy decisions to their elected representatives. The increasing complexity of society is presumed to preclude the citizen from being capable of making knowledgeable decisions about governmental programs. Can the average citizen, for example, be expected to know how to judge the potential threats to safety that would have to be accepted in the decision to construct a nuclear power facility?

Radicals, particularly of the left, have expressed a greater faith in human nature:

> We regard men as infinitely precious and possessed of unfulfilled capacities for reason, freedom, and love. In affirming these principles we are aware of countering perhaps the dominant conceptions of man in the twentieth century: that he is a thing to be manipulated, and that he is inherently incapable of directing his own affairs.[32]

Proponents of greater participation on the part of the individual follow in part the socialist argument that workers should and must have the right to control their own labor and their fate. Adherents to this theme accept basic psychological theories that the worker who is able to govern his own actions is likely to be more creative and productive. When orders are dictated from above, the individual is thwarted in his own development and is forced into childlike or automaton-type behavior. The fear is that "a cult of efficiency within the bureaucratic climate will force man to identify his entire personality with his formal activities and the products of his labor."[33] This is the dehumanizing effect of technology.

Participation is also advocated as producing social as well as individual benefits. Community control is supported as essential for allowing the impoverished to break the cycle of poverty. People know their own needs and problems better than administrators and, if given sufficient resources, will be able to overcome their problems—without brokers.

The emerging demands for participatory democracy and community

---

[32] From the *Port Huron Statement* in Mitchell Cohen and Dennis Hale, eds., *The New Student Left: An Anthology*, rev. ed. (Boston: Beacon, 1967), p. 12. See also Jurgen Habermas, *Toward A Rational Society: Student Protest, Science and Politics* (Boston: Beacon, 1970) and *The Legitimation Crisis* (Boston: Beacon, 1975) (much of this book is written as a criticism of "systems thinking" and a leading German systems theorist N. Luhman); Charles Hampden-Turner, *Radical Man: The Process of Psycho-Social Development* (Cambridge, Mass.: Schenkman, 1970).

[33] Michael P. Smith, "Alienation and Bureaucracy: The Role of Participatory Administration," *Public Administration Review*, 31 (1971): 659; Gerald I. Susman, *Autonomy at Work: A Sociotechnical Analysis* (New York: Praeger, 1976).

control are strikingly in agreement with the pluralistic orientation to the study of politics.[34] There is an assumption made that if all important interests are part of the decision-making process, then good will result. There is an expressed faith in the process of political decision making as distinguished from the products of the process. This faith may be somewhat unwarranted, given what has emerged to date. As has been seen, having the power to decide does not always guarantee success. One may fight for and win the passage of legislation, only to find that the legislation does not eliminate the problem it was intended to resolve.

Moreover, citizen involvement in decision making is fundamentally related to decentralization. In order to achieve participation on a mass scale, political systems would have to be decentralized. This approach is somewhat in conflict with present tendencies to move toward the integration of all levels of government. Instead of unified policies, the radical position would encourage diversity. Revenue sharing might be used as a centralized means of raising funds, but the allocation of those resources would be made not at the federal, state, or even municipal level but at the neighborhood level. In some respects this is analogous to fixed-ceiling budgeting (Chapters 4 and 6) in which the overall distribution of resources is made above and decisions about how to spend the resources are made below. Any form of planning beyond the community level would be complicated by such a decentralized system.

The radicals' faith in human nature when coupled with their concern with technology has led to a set of ideas in conflict with current budgetary thinking. Cybernation is said to have produced an economy that can free people from work, because full employment is no longer essential for survival, growth, and abundance. The contradiction with current economic policy is obvious. Liberals have worked hard to persuade Presidents to adopt the new economics predicated on full employment, but the radical individualist point of view argues for freeing people from work and guaranteeing them "an adequate income as a matter of right."[35]

To the extent that techniques of analysis and program budgeting rely upon economic efficiency as the primary criterion for evaluating social

---

[34] For a critique of the pluralist's faith in process, see Schick, "Systems Politics and Systems Budgeting," pp. 137–51. Also see Thomas D. Lynch, ed., "Symposium on Involvement," *Public Administration Review*, 32 (1972): 189–223.

[35] The Ad Hoc Committee on the Triple Revolution, "Triple Revolution," in Priscilla Long, ed., *The New Left: A Collection of Essays* (Boston: Porter Sargent, 1969), pp. 339–54.

programs, they are inconsistent with the radical individualist point of view. Increasing individual participation may be inefficient from an economic point of view. Decentralization may produce somewhat less, rather than more, efficient decisions. In the post-industrial society, however, concern is less with increasing GNP and other standards of economic progress. [36] Thus, the loss in efficiency that may occur as a result of greater individual participation is regarded not as a loss but as a gain toward greater self-fulfillment.

The argument for decentralization is persuasive, but the need for a capability to respond to problems is equally persuasive and suggests more rather than less centralization. As has been seen throughout this work, budgeting consists of numerous subsystems which may not always be linked adequately with each other. The same is true for society as a whole. A small local government is not immune to regional, national, and international trends. That government may have to bargain collectively with a local of an international union. Economic trends will greatly affect the jurisdiction. Thus, while all subsystems—however they may be delineated— are linked with each other, there may be no set of mechanisms through which coherent macro policies may be derived. Further decentralization may exacerbate the situation, resulting in disintegration.

The continuing controversies over the triple-E problems of energy, the environment, and the economy are examples of how the political system has difficulty in coping with macro problems. Since the oil embargo of 1973–1974, the political system has haltingly dealt with each E but not all three as a whole. Perhaps the problems involved are beyond current knowledge and abilities, but the political system has provided little evidence of being capable of handling the problems. Probably the fact that there are so many governments in the U.S. has not simplified response to the problems; division of powers within government, especially the federal government, might also be viewed as a weakness. This critique, then, would suggest that greater centralization of decision making is essential in order to further the best interests of the entire society.

There are no guarantees that any of the above critiques of and prescriptions for society and their implications for budgeting systems will prevail. Certainly, the positivist view of governmental intervention to solve social problems with which current budgetary practices and reforms are most consistent has the edge, because it is the predominant theme of

---

[36] Alvin Toffler, *Future Shock* (New York: Bantam Books, 1971), pp. 452–57.

existing practice. The essentially conservative critique has made telling points, however, against an overly optimistic view of the ability of government to achieve solutions to all social problems. This is likely to result in greater experimentation in governmental encouragement of private-sector solutions to some social ills. The radical individual critique is harder to assess. Although rooted in what has been called the new left, it is not inconsistent with the basic conservative critique. The critique has already made an impact on poverty programs that require participation of the poor, although operationally the requirement has been subverted as much as it has been implemented. It is, however, safe to venture the guess that demands will increase, rather than decrease, for real individual participation in governmental decision making and consequently in budgeting.[37]

CLOSING COMMENT

Every book is a product of its time. Had this book been written a few years earlier or several years later, the preceding discussion would have been far different. For the moment, the crystal ball seems to indicate that disruption and confusion rather than tranquility are likely to characterize public budgeting systems in the coming years. Budgeting, only one aspect of society, cannot and should not be immune to changes that are in the making. The agenda for the future is not necessarily simply making successes out of previous budget reform failures. Many efforts have been made in changing public budgeting, and while none has fully succeeded, each has probably made some contribution to the current state-of-the-art. The art, however, has never really been satisfactory for the needs of the day, and the art of budgeting will be expected to change even more tomorrow.

---

[37] See Jeffrey Obler, "Technology and Politics," *Public Administration Review*, 31 (1971): 581, for a brief review of the pessimistic and optimistic views on the possibility of utilizing technology to solve societal problems.

BIBLIOGRAPHIC NOTE

This bibliographic note is intended to assist the reader in finding materials for further reading on public budgeting systems. Because the preceding chapters are extensively footnoted, we will not attempt to recapitulate the literature cited earlier. One useful approach for searching the literature is to begin with subject references in the index and read the sources found in the footnote references on the pages indicated. This note, then, is intended to aid in identifying general references relevant to public budgeting and also sources that have produced and can be expected to continue to produce literature on public budgeting.

Periodicals and government documents are two main sources that provide useful budgetary information. One of the most important indexes to periodicals is the *PAIS Bulletin* (Public Affairs Information Service). This index reports articles appearing in such generally useful journals as the *Public Administration Review* (American Society for Public Administration) and *The Public Interest* (National Affairs, Inc.). *The Accessions List,* published monthly by the Advisory Commission on Intergovernmental Relations, serves as a useful bibliography of current literature. Two excellent references that explain various types of documents and their sources are Laurence F. Schmeckebier and Roy B. Eastin's *Government Publications and Their Use,* 2nd rev. ed. (Washington: Brookings, 1969) and Joe Morehead's *Introduction to United States Public Documents* (Littleton, Col.: Libraries Unlimited, 1975). An annual index to many local, state, and federal documents is provided in *Bibliographic Guide to Governmental Publications—U.S.* (Boston: Hall). The following discussion indicates many of the pertinent periodicals and documents as well as currently available books and articles that pertain to various fields within budgeting.

Four of the "classics" in public budgeting, no longer subject to revision and updating, are William F. Willoughby, *The Problems of a National Budget* (New York: Appleton, 1918); A. E. Buck, *Public Budgeting* (New York: Harper and Brothers, 1929); Arthur Smithies, *The Budgetary Process in the United States* (New York: McGraw-Hill, 1955): and Jesse Burkhead, *Government Budgeting* (New York: Wiley, 1956). A good history of early budgeting is Vincent J. Browne's *The Control of the Public Budget* (Washington: Public Affairs Press, 1949). A useful perspective on the development of public budget systems can be found in Bertram M. Gross, "The New Systems Budgeting," *Public Administration Review,* 29 (1969): 113–37. For a general collection of readings, see Robert T. Golembiewski and Jack Rabin, eds., *Public Budgeting and Finance: Readings in Theory and Practice,* 2nd ed. (Itasca, Ill.: Peacock, 1975).

On the use of information in decision making, see Yehezkel Dror, *Public Policymaking Reexamined* (San Francisco: Chandler, 1968); Amitai Etzioni, "Mixed Scanning: A 'Third' Approach to Decision Making," *Public Administration Review,* 27 (1967): 385–92; David Braybrooke and Charles E. Lindblom, *A Strategy of Decision* (New York: Free Press, 1963); and Harold L. Wilensky, *Organizational Intelligence: Knowledge and Policy in Government and Industry* (New York: Basic Books, 1967). Also see the journal, *Decision Sciences* (American Institute for Decision Sciences).

On program budgeting and its antecedents, see Frederick C. Mosher, *Program Budgeting: Theory and Practice with Particular Reference to the U.S. Department of the Army* (Chicago: Public Administration Service, 1954); Roland N. McKean, *Efficiency in Government Through Systems Analysis, with Emphasis on Water Resource Development* (New York: Wiley, 1958); David Novick, ed., *Program Budgeting: Program Analysis and the Federal Budget* (Cambridge, Mass.: Harvard University Press, 1965) and 2nd ed. (New York: Holt, Rinehart and Winston, 1969); Charles J. Hitch and Roland N. McKean, *The Economics of Defense in the Nuclear Age* (Cambridge, Mass.: Harvard University Press, 1967); Charles L. Schultze, *The Politics and Economics of Public Spending* (Washington: Brookings, 1968); David Novick, ed., *Current Practice in Program Budgeting* (New York: Crane, Russak, 1973); and numerous books in the Praeger series, "Special Studies in U.S. Economic, Social, and Political Issues."

Several collections of readings on program budgeting are available. See Fremont J. Lyden and Ernest G. Miller, eds., *Planning-Programming-Budgeting: A Systems Approach to Management,* 2nd ed. (Chicago: Markham, 1972) and also see Harley H. Hinrichs and Graeme M. Taylor, eds., *Program Budgeting and Benefit-Cost Analysis* (Pacific Palisades, Cal.: Goodyear, 1969). A particularly useful collection of articles and testimony before Congress on program budgeting is in U.S. Congress, Joint Economic Committee, Subcommittee on Economy in Government, *The Analysis and Evaluation of Public Expenditures: The PPB System* 91st Cong., 1st sess. (Washington: U.S. Government Printing Office, 1969). Many of these articles can be found in Robert H. Haveman and Julius Margolis, eds., *Public Expenditures and Policy Analysis* (Chicago: Markham, 1970). Robert Dorfman, ed., *Measuring Benefits of Government Investments* (Washington: Brookings, 1965) provides examples of the application of analytic techniques to government services.

For extended discussions of analysis, see Elmer L. Struening and Marcia Guttentag, eds., *Handbook of Evaluation Research* (Beverly Hills, Cal.: Sage, 1975) and E. S. Quade, *Analysis for Public Decisions* (New York: American Elsevier, 1975). Journals specializing in this area include *Evaluation* (Minneapolis Medical Research Foundation in collaboration with National Institute of Mental Health), *Management Science* (Institute of Management Sciences), *Policy Analysis* (Graduate School of Public Policy, Berkeley, University of California Press), and *Policy Studies Journal* (Policy Studies Organization). Also, the U.S. General Accounting Office issues numerous, often nontechnical reports on programs. One of the best sources for identifying federally sponsored analyses in particular program areas is *Government Reports Announcements and Index,* published by the National Technical Information Service of the U.S. Commerce Department.

Standard works on budgeting as a political process include Richard F. Fenno, Jr., *The Power of the Purse: Appropriations Politics in Congress* (Boston: Little, Brown, 1966); Ira Sharkansky, *The Politics of Taxing and Spending* (Indianapolis: Bobbs-Merrill, 1969); and Aaron Wildavsky, *The Politics of the Budgetary Process,* 2nd ed. (Boston: Little, Brown, 1974). Also see Alan P. Balutis and Daron K. Butler, eds., *The Political Pursestrings: The Role of the Legislature in the Budgetary Process* (New York: Halstead, 1975) and Aaron Wildavsky, *Budgeting: A Comparative Theory of Budgetary Processes* (Boston: Little, Brown, 1975). Two of the best sources for current events in federal budgetary politics are the *C. Q. Weekly Report,* (Congressional Quarterly, Inc.) and the weekly *National Journal* (Government Research Corporation). Articles in the *American Political Science Review* (American Political Science Association) occasionally deal with budgetary politics.

The standard text in the field of accounting is Leon E. Hay and R. M. Mikesell, *Governmental Accounting,* 5th ed. (Homewood, Ill.: Irwin, 1974). Another useful work is Robert N. Anthony and Regina E. Herzlinger, *Management Control in Nonprofit Organizations* (Homewood, Ill.: Irwin, 1975). *The GAO Review* (U.S. General Accounting Office) and *The Government Accountants Journal* (Association of Government Accountants) contain numerous articles pertaining to accounting and auditing. Other technical works dealing with budgeting and accounting include David J. Ott and Attiat F. Ott, *Federal Budget Policy,* rev. ed. (Washington: Brookings, 1969); President's Commission on Budget Concepts, *Report* and *Staff Papers and Other Materials Reviewed* (Washington: U.S. Government Printing Office, 1967); and Wilfred E. Lewis, Jr., ed., *Budget Concepts for Economic Analysis* (Washington: Brookings, 1968).

There are no extensive discussions of government manpower vis-à-vis budgeting. For standard treatments of personnel practices, see O. Glenn Stahl, *Public Personnel Administration,* 6th ed. (New York: Harper and Row, 1971) and Felix A. Nigro and Lloyd G. Nigro, *The New Public Personnel Administration* (Itasca, Ill.: Peacock, 1976). Relevant journals include the *Civil Service Journal* (U.S. Civil Service Commission) and *Public Personnel Management* (International Personnel Management Association).

Economic treatment of public taxing and spending are found in Otto Eckstein, *Public Finance,* 3rd ed. (Englewood Cliffs, N.J.: Prentice-Hall, 1973) and Bernard P. Herber, *Modern Public Finance: The Study of Public Sector Economics,* 3rd ed. (Homewood, Ill.: Irwin, 1975). A more difficult book but one of the most worthwhile analyses of the purposes of public spending is Richard A. Musgrave, *The Theory of Public Finance* (New York: McGraw-Hill, 1959). Also see Richard A. Musgrave and Peggy B. Musgrave, *Public Finance in Theory and Practice* (New York: McGraw-Hill, 1973). Among the journals dealing with this subject area are the *American Economic Review* (American Economics Association) and *Public Finance Quarterly* (Sage).

Turning to the three main levels of government, materials abound on the federal government. The *Monthly Catalog of United States Govern-*

ment Publications (U.S. Government Printing Office) indexes most major federal government documents; individual federal agencies, however, publish some important materials that are not reported in this index. When searching for a given type of statistical information, refer to the *American Statistics Index* (Congressional Information Service); this index, although only covering federal documents, covers many materials containing state and local data. Several federal agencies, of course, produce particularly relevant materials. See Chapter 6 on the various federal budget documents prepared by the Office of Management and Budget and the Council of Economic Advisers. Among the most useful annual publications of the Bureau of the Census in the Commerce Department are the *Statistical Abstract, Governmental Finances,* and *Public Employment;* the census of governments conducted every five years provides extensive information on state and local governments. Congressional committees and the Congressional Budget Office are also important generators of budgetary documents. The Brookings Institution (Washington) publishes books on budgeting and annually publishes an analysis of the President's budget, *Setting National Priorities.* Other private organizations that frequently publish materials on the federal government include the American Enterprise Institute (Washington), the Committee on Economic Development (New York), the National Bureau of Economic Research (New York), and the Tax Foundation (New York); these organizations also publish materials on state and local governments.

Materials can be found on state governments in general and on individual states. S. Kenneth Howard's *Changing State Budgeting* (Lexington, Ky.: Council of State Governments, 1973) provides a general discussion of state budgetary processes. The most complete discussion of an operational program budgeting system at the state level is in Robert J. Mowitz, *The Design and Implementation of Pennsylvania's Planning, Programming, Budgeting System* (Harrisburg: Commonwealth of Pennsylvania, 1970). The Council of State Governments publishes numerous monographs related to budgeting as well as the periodical, *State Government,* and the general reference, *The Book of the States.* One of the best indexes to state documents is *State Publications Monthly Checklist,* prepared by the Library of Congress.

For textbook-type treatments of local government budgeting, see J. Richard Aronson and Eli Schwartz, eds., *Management Policies in Local Government Finance* (Chicago: Municipal Finance Officers Association, 1975) and Lennox L. Moak and Albert M. Hillhouse, *Concepts and*

Practices in Local Government Finance (Chicago: Municipal Finance Officers Association, 1975). The International City Management Association (ICMA) publishes the journal, *Public Management,* and the *Municipal Year Book.* The National Association of Counties in conjunction with ICMA publishes the *County Year Book. Governmental Finance* is a periodical that focuses on local government budgeting (Municipal Finance Officers Association). The National Municipal League's *National Civic Review* often includes budget-related articles and has a section in each issue devoted to "taxation and finance."

Happy reading.

INDEX